Neuromorphic Computing Systems for Industry 4.0

S. Dhanasekar
Department of ECE, Sri Eshwar College of Engineering, India

K. Martin Sagayam
Karunya Institute of Technology and Sciences, India

Surbhi Vijh
ASET, Amity University, Noida, India

Vipin Tyagi
Jaypee University of Engineering and Technology, India

Alex Norta
Tallinn University, Estonia

A volume in the Advances in
Systems Analysis, Software
Engineering, and High Performance
Computing (ASASEHPC) Book Series

Published in the United States of America by
    IGI Global
    Engineering Science Reference (an imprint of IGI Global)
    701 E. Chocolate Avenue
    Hershey PA, USA 17033
    Tel: 717-533-8845
    Fax: 717-533-8661
    E-mail: cust@igi-global.com
    Web site: http://www.igi-global.com

Library of Congress Cataloging-in-Publication Data

Names: Subramaniyam, Dhanasekar, 1983- editor. | Kulandairaj, Martin
    Sagayam, 1987- editor. | Vijh, Surbhi, 1993- editor. | Tyagi, Vipin,
    editor. | Norta, Alexander, 1972- editor.
Title: Neuromorphic computing systems for industry 4.0 / edited by:
    Dhanasekar Subramaniyam, Martin Sagayam Kulandairaj, Surbhi Vijh, Mayank
    Singh, Vipin Tyagi, Alexander Norta.
Description: Hershey PA : Engineering Science Reference, [2023] | Includes
    bibliographical references. | Summary: "The comprehensive and timely
    publication aims to be an essential reference source, on the available
    literature in the field of Neural computing-based Microchip Technology.
    This will provide further research opportunities in these dynamic
    fields. It is hoped that this handbook will provide the resources
    necessary for researchers, advanced level students, technology
    developers to adopt and implement the advances in technology and
    applications"-- Provided by publisher.
Identifiers: LCCN 2022056269 (print) | LCCN 2022056270 (ebook) | ISBN
    9781668465967 (hardcover) | ISBN 9781668465974 (paperback) | ISBN
    9781668465981 (ebook)
Subjects: LCSH: Neuromorphics. | Neural computers. | Artificial
    intelligence. | Industry 4.0.
Classification: LCC TA164.4 .N48 2023 (print) | LCC TA164.4 (ebook) | DDC
    006.3/2--dc23/eng/20230103
LC record available at https://lccn.loc.gov/2022056269
LC ebook record available at https://lccn.loc.gov/2022056270

This book is published in the IGI Global book series Advances in Systems Analysis, Software Engineering, and High Performance Computing (ASASEHPC) (ISSN: 2327-3453; eISSN: 2327-3461)

British Cataloguing in Publication Data
A Cataloguing in Publication record for this book is available from the British Library.
All work contributed to this book is new, previously-unpublished material.
The views expressed in this book are those of the authors, but not necessarily of the publisher.
For electronic access to this publication, please contact: eresources@igi-global.com.

Advances in Systems Analysis, Software Engineering, and High Performance Computing (ASASEHPC) Book Series

ISSN:2327-3453
EISSN:2327-3461

Editor-in-Chief: Vijayan Sugumaran, Oakland University, USA

MISSION

The theory and practice of computing applications and distributed systems has emerged as one of the key areas of research driving innovations in business, engineering, and science. The fields of software engineering, systems analysis, and high performance computing offer a wide range of applications and solutions in solving computational problems for any modern organization.

The **Advances in Systems Analysis, Software Engineering, and High Performance Computing (ASASEHPC) Book Series** brings together research in the areas of distributed computing, systems and software engineering, high performance computing, and service science. This collection of publications is useful for academics, researchers, and practitioners seeking the latest practices and knowledge in this field.

COVERAGE

- Virtual Data Systems
- Human-Computer Interaction
- Metadata and Semantic Web
- Network Management
- Distributed Cloud Computing
- Computer Networking
- Computer Graphics
- Storage Systems
- Engineering Environments
- Parallel Architectures

IGI Global is currently accepting manuscripts for publication within this series. To submit a proposal for a volume in this series, please contact our Acquisition Editors at Acquisitions@igi-global.com or visit: http://www.igi-global.com/publish/.

Titles in this Series

For a list of additional titles in this series, please visit:
http://www.igi-global.com/book-series/advances-systems-analysis-software-engineering/73689

Business Models and Strategies for Open Source Projects
Francisco José Monaco (Universidade de São Paulo, Brazil)
Business Science Reference • © 2023 • 300pp • H/C (ISBN: 9781668447857) • US $270.00

Principles, Policies, and Applications of Kotlin Programming
Duy Thanh Tran (University of Economics and Law, Ho Chi Minh City, Vietnam & Vietnam National University, Ho Chi Minh City, Vietnam) and Jun-Ho Huh (Korea Maritime and Ocean University, South Korea)
Engineering Science Reference • © 2023 • 457pp • H/C (ISBN: 9781668466872) • US $215.00

Concepts and Techniques of Graph Neural Networks
Vinod Kumar (Koneru Lakshmaiah Education Foundation (Deemed), India) and Dharmendra Singh Rajput (VIT University, India)
Engineering Science Reference • © 2023 • 247pp • H/C (ISBN: 9781668469033) • US $270.00

Cyber-Physical System Solutions for Smart Cities
Vanamoorthy Muthumanikandan (Vellore Institute of Technology, Chennai, India) Anbalagan Bhuvaneswari (Vellore Institute of Technology, Chennai, India) Balamurugan Easwaran (University of Africa, Toru-Orua, Nigeria) and T. Sudarson Rama Perumal (Rohini College of Engineering and Technology, India)
Engineering Science Reference • © 2023 • 300pp • H/C (ISBN: 9781668477564) • US $270.00

Adaptive Security and Cyber Assurance for Risk-Based Decision Making
Tyson T. Brooks (Syracuse University, USA)
Engineering Science Reference • © 2023 • 243pp • H/C (ISBN: 9781668477663) • US $225.00

For an entire list of titles in this series, please visit:
http://www.igi-global.com/book-series/advances-systems-analysis-software-engineering/73689

701 East Chocolate Avenue, Hershey, PA 17033, USA
Tel: 717-533-8845 x100 • Fax: 717-533-8661
E-Mail: cust@igi-global.com • www.igi-global.com

Editorial Advisory Board

Table of Contents

Chapter 12

Detailed Table of Contents

Chapter 1

    L. Jubair Ahmed, Akshaya College of Engineering and Technology,
        Coimbatore, India
    S. Dhanasekar, Sri Eshwar College of Engineering, Coimbatore, India
    K. Martin Sagayam, Karunya Institute of Tech. and Sciences,
        Coimbatore, India
    Surbhi Vijh, ASET, Amity University, Noida, India
    Vipin Tyagi, Jaypee University of Engineering & Technology, India
    Mayank Singh, JSS Academy of Technical Education, Noida, India
    Alex Norta, Tallinn University of Technology, Tallinn, Estonia

The process of using electronic circuits to replicate the neurobiological architectures seen in the nervous system is known as neuromorphic engineering, also referred to as neuromorphic computing. These technologies are essential for the future of computing, although most of the work in neuromorphic computing has been focused on hardware development. The execution speed, energy efficiency, accessibility and robustness against local failures are vital advantages of neuromorphic computing over conventional methods. Spiking neural networks are generated using neuromorphic computing. This chapter covers the basic ideas of neuromorphic engineering, neuromorphic computing, and its motivating factors and challenges. Deep learning models are frequently referred to as deep neural networks because deep learning techniques use neural network topologies. Deep learning techniques and their different architectures were also covered in this section. Furthermore, Emerging memory Devices for neuromorphic systems and neuromorphic circuits were illustrated.

Chapter 2

Neuromorphic computing is a rapidly emerging field that seeks to emulate the computational principles of the brain using novel materials and devices. While traditional computing architectures, such as the von Neumann architecture, have experienced exponential improvements in computational power due to the continuous shrinkage of transistor technology, the laws of physics will eventually limit the performance of these systems. Neuromorphic computing offers the potential to continue scaling technology by incorporating novel functional materials and devices into new computing architectures. In this chapter, the authors will explore the principles of neuromorphic computing and the key challenges that must be overcome in order to fully implement these systems. The authors will discuss the role of new nanostructured materials and devices in neuromorphic computing, and the importance of understanding charge and defects migration, fault tolerance, and manufacturability.

Chapter 3

A neuromorphic accelerator for a deep net having RRAM based processing elements has been implemented for emotion detection based on dialect. The proposed accelerator has been trained on the RAVDESS dataset in order to classify different emotion types. The RRAM based swish activation function has been employed to build the neuromorphic accelerator as it consumes less power (476μW), has lower operating voltage (1.23V), and has better performance and output characteristics. The proposed neuromorphic accelerator has been implemented using 1T-1RRAM Processing Elements on ST Microelectronics 28nm FD-SOI, also on Intel i3-8130U CPU and compared with NVIDIA GeForce GPU to highlight the advantages. The proposed accelerator achieves high-performance and consumes less power (1780μW) with on/off rate (13.81) and lower operating voltage (2V). The training accuracy for the FD-SOI implementation is 79.13% and has a learning rate of 0.01 and weight update interval of 1 epoch. This chapter also highlights the importance of the proposed neuromorphic accelerator from Industry 4.0 perspective.

Chapter 4

A unique strategy for optimum multi-objective optimization for VLSI implementation of artificial neural network (ANN) is proposed. This strategy is efficient in terms of area, power, and speed, and it has a good degree of accuracy and dynamic range. The goal of this research is to find the sweet spot where area, speed, and power may all be optimised in a very large-scale integration (VLSI) implementation of a neural network (NN). The design should also allow for the dynamic reconfiguration of weight, and it should be very precise. The authors also use a 65-nm CMOS fabrication method to produce the circuits, and these results show that the suggested integral stochastic design may reduce energy consumption by up to 21% compared to the binary radix implementation, without sacrificing accuracy.

Chapter 5

Skin disorders are one of the most common types of disorders that are primarily diagnosed visually with scientific screening observed through dermoscopic evaluation, histopathological evaluation, and a biopsy. Diagnostic accuracy has a strong relevance to physician skill. Painful effects of skin disease hamper the mental condition of a patient. The authors propose an approach to detect the skin diseases based upon image processing as well as machine learning techniques i.e., convolutional neural networks (CNN). CNN is a specific type of neural network model that allows us to extract higher depictions for the image content. It is a deep learning algorithm to perform generative and descriptive tasks. Machine learning generates two types of prediction-batches and real time.

Chapter 6

Ramesh A., Sri Eshwar College of Engineering, India
P. Sivakumar, PSG College of Technology, Coimbatore, India
E. Venugopal, Sri Eshwar College of Engineering, Coimbatore, India
Ahmed Elngar, Beni-Suef University, Egypt

Many robotic applications require autonomous decision making. The obstacles may be uncertain in nature. Because of the mobility, most robots might be battery operated. This chapter briefs the energy and performance analysis of robotic applications using artificial neural networks. This chapter is designed to understand the operation of robots from understanding sensor data (training), processing (testing) the data in an efficient manner, and respond (prediction) to the dynamic situation using self-learning and adaptability.

Chapter 7

Jagrat Shukla, Vellore Institute of Technology, India
Numburi Rishikha, Vellore Institute of Technology, India
Janhavi Chaturvedi, Vellore Institute of Technology, India
Sumathi Gokulanathan, Vellore Institute of Technology, India
Sriharipriya Krishnan Chandrasekaran, Vellore Institute of Technology, India
Konguvel Elango, Vellore Institute of Technology, India
Sathishkumar Selvaperumal, Asia Pacific University of Technology and Innovation, Malaysia

Machine learning has had an impact in the area of microchip design and was initially used in automation. This development could result in a tremendous change in the realm of hardware computation and AI's powerful analysis tools. Traffic is a pressing issue in densely populated cities. Governments worldwide are attempting to address this problem by introducing various forms of public transportation, including metro. However, these solutions require significant investment and implementation time. Despite the high cost and inherent flaws of the system, many people still prefer to use their personal vehicles rather than public transportation. To address this issue, the authors propose a bike-sharing solution in which all processes from membership registration to bike rental and return are automated. Bagging is an ensemble learning method that can be used for base models with a low bias and high variance. It uses randomization of the dataset to reduce the variance of the base models, while keeping the bias low.

    Nayan Keshri, Vellore Institute of Technology, India
    Swapnadeep Sarkar, Vellore Institute of Technology, India
    Yash Raj Singh, Vellore Institute of Technology, India
    Sumathi Gokulanathan, Vellore Institute of Technology, India
    Konguvel Elango, Vellore Institute of Technology, India
    Sivakumar Ponnusamy, Capital One, USA

The industrial world is facing swiftly changing challenges, including technical fluctuations, swings in global markets, and climate change. Digitalization and automation are the game changers to meet these challenges. Machine learning has made an impact on the area attributed to microchips, and it is initially used in automation. These practices will ultimately succeed the current VLSI design. A biometric authentication system is a form of biometric verification system that uses finger vein detection for biometric check framework. Consumer electronics development necessitates high security, high accuracy, and fast authentication speed. Since it presents the elements inside the human body, finger vein validation is a prominent technique in terms of security. Furthermore, it has a fair advantage over other personal authentication methods because to its contactless aspect. The main goal of the chapter is to provide a solution using machine learning for finger vein authentication and implementation using VLSI design.

    C. Udhaya Kumar, Bodhi Computing, India
    P. Saravanan, PSG College of Technology, Coimbatore, India
    N. Thiyagarajan, Sri Eshwar College of Engineering, Coimbatore, India
    Veena Raj, Universiti Brunei Darussalam, Brunei

Artificial Neural Networks (ANNs) are becoming increasingly important in the present technological era due to their ability to solve complex problems, adapt to new inputs, and improve decision-skills for different domains. The human brain serves as a model for Artificial Neural Networks (ANNs), a type of machine learning, as a reference for both structure and function. The existing work on ANNs supports tasks, such as regression, classification and pattern recognition separately. The discussion aims at resolving the above highlighted issues related to various ANN architectural implementations, considering the dynamic function exchange feature of FPGAs. With the aid of Zynq SOC, CNN and DNN architectures are designed in its Processing System, and the structure is accelerated using Programmable Logic. It also solves the issues due to trojans on design files, by introducing cryptography within the accelerator.

Chapter 10

Naveenkumar R., Karunya Institute of Technology and Sciences,
    Coimbatore, India
N.M. Sivamangai, Karunya Institute of Technology and Sciences, India
P. Malin Bruntha, Karunya Institute of technology and sciences,
    Coimbatore, India
V. Govindaraj, Dr.N.G.P. Institute of Technology, Coimbatore, India
Ahmed Elngar, Beni-Suef University, Egypt

The security aspects of neural networks (NN) have become a crucial and appropriate theme for basic research as a result of recent developments in neural networks and their use in deep learning techniques. In this research, the authors examine the security issues and potential solutions in computing hardware for deep neural networks (DNN). The latest hardware-based attacks against DNN are then described, with an emphasis on fault injection (FI), hardware Trojan (HT) insertion, and side-channel analysis (SCA). This chapter presents the various security issues in hardware-based attacks and security concerns in the hardware trojan (HT) and side-channel analysis are focused. Moreover, discussed the countermeasure for the hardware trojan and side channel attacks (SCA) is in neural networks.

Chapter 11

S. Ganeshkumar, Sri Eshwar College of Engineering, Coimbatore, India
J. Maniraj, KalaignarKarunanidhi Institute of Technology, Coimbatore,
    India
S. Gokul, Sri Eshwar College of Engineering, Coimbatore, India
Krishnaraj Ramaswamy, College of Engineering and Technology,
    Ethiopia

In recent years, there has been a trend towards more sophisticated robot control. This has been driven by advances in artificial intelligence (AI) and machine learning, which have enabled robots to become more autonomous and effective in completing tasks. One trend is towards using AI for robot control. This involves teaching robots how to carry out tasks by providing them with data and letting them learn from it. This approach can be used for tasks such as object recognition and navigation. Another trend is towards using machine learning for robot control. This involves using algorithms to learn from data and improve the performance of the robot. This approach can be used for tasks such as object recognition and navigation. A third trend is towards using more sophisticated sensors for robot control. This includes using sensors that can detect things such as temperature, humidity, and pressure.

Chapter 12

The biologically inspired spiking neural network can be said to mimic the most neural network models in existence that is evolved from artificial neural networks. This concept was derived from the nervous system and was able to generate electric impulses, commonly known as spikes or action impulses. Here the neural models try to replicate the biological neurons almost accurately and can be considered to be more powerful than its peers as it was able to integrate temporal information. As such they can said to have great potential in several complex applications like classification, mapping, and pattern recognition, etc. Out of the available spiking neuron models, Leaky-Integrate-and-Fire is very frequently applied. Spiking neural networks are gaining rapid importance in the last few years following the sharp incline in artificial intelligence field. In this modern era robots are incorporated in our daily life, and said to have the potential to increase economic growth and productivity.

Preface

With the significant advancement in technologies, it has been always a desire of the human race to focus towards a comfortable lifestyle. Apart from the lifestyle, technologies play a major role in conserving the natural resources which aid in a better environment for the human beings to live in this world. As artificial intelligence (AI) processing moves from the cloud to the edge of the network, battery powered and deeply embedded devices are challenged to perform AI functions like computer vision and voice recognition. Microchip Technology Inc. via its Silicon Storage Technology (SST) subsidiary, is addressing this challenge by significantly reducing power with its analog memory technology, the membrain neuromorphic memory solution. Based on its industry proven super Flash technology and optimized to perform vector matrix multiplication (VMM) for neural networks, Microchip's analog flash memory solution improves system architecture implementation of VMM through an analog in-memory compute approach, enhancing AI inference at the edge. The membrain solution is being adopted by today's companies looking to advance machine learning capacities in edge devices. Due to its ability to significantly reduce power, this analog in-memory compute solution is ideal for any AI application.

Chapter 1: The process of using electronic circuits to replicate the neuro-biological architectures seen in the nervous system is known as neuromorphic engineering, also referred to as neuromorphic computing. These technologies are essential for the future of computing, although most of the work in neuromorphic computing has been focused on hardware development. The execution speed, energy efficiency, accessibility and robustness against local failures are vital advantages of neuromorphic computing over conventional methods. Spiking neural networks are generated using neuromorphic computing. This chapter covers the basic ideas of neuromorphic engineering, neuromorphic computing, and its motivating factors and challenges. Deep learning models are frequently referred to as deep neural networks because deep learning techniques use neural network topologies. Deep learning techniques and their different architectures were also covered in this section. Furthermore, Emerging memory Devices for neuromorphic systems and neuromorphic circuits were illustrated.

Chapter 2: Modern computation based on the von Neumann architecture experienced exponential improvement in computational power due to continuous shrinkage of transistor technology. But as transistors reach atomic scale, computing performance will reach its limit given the laws of physics. To foster continued technology scaling, humanity is seeking to incorporate novel functional materials and devices into new computer architectures. One of the most promising developments is Neuromorphic computing. Neuromorphic computing is based on the principles of biological neural computation and emulation of neural systems is done using the implementation of neural elements in silicon. However, development of materials properties and devices are needed to overcome key research challenges in fully implementation of neuromorphic computer. New nanostructured materials that exhibit specific quantum properties with new device physics, understanding charge/defects migration, fault tolerance and manufacturability which are some of the key issues that needs to be investigated are discussed in this chapter.

Chapter 3: A neuromorphic accelerator for a deep net having Resistive Random-Access Memory based processing elements has been implemented for emotion detection based on dialect. The proposed accelerator has been trained on the Ryerson Audio-Visual Database of Emotional Speech and Song dataset in order to classify into different emotion types. The processing elements are designed as crossbar array grids with 1T-1RRAM devices at each row-column unit. The PFET/NFET transistors with constant length of 30nm and width of 80nm are used. The RRAM based swish activation function has been employed to build the neuromorphic accelerator as it consumes less power (476μW), has lower operating voltage (1.23V), has better performance and output characteristics. The proposed neuromorphic accelerator has been implemented using 1T-1RRAM Processing Elements on ST Microelectronics 28nm FD-SOI, also on Intel i3-8130U CPU and compared with NVIDIA GeForce GTX memory GPU System for determining the efficiency and performance of the accelerators. The proposed accelerator has been trained on 70% of the audio samples using stochastic gradient descent technique for achieving high-performance, to consume less power (1780μW). Also, has improved RRAM switching characteristics with on/off rate (13.81) and utilizes a lower operating voltage (2V) as compared to other memristor based accelerators discussed for various applications. The proposed accelerator has been designed to detect emotion categories such as angry, happy, sad, fearful, calm, neutral, disgusted and surprised. The training accuracy for the FD-SOI implementation is 79.13% whereas the GPU memory system has an accuracy of 77.02%. The proposed RRAM based neuromorphic accelerator for speech task has a learning rate of 0.01 with the weight update frequency (i.e., interval) of 1 epoch. This work also highlights the importance of the proposed neuromorphic accelerator from Industry 4.0 perspective.

Chapter 4: In this article, a unique strategy for optimum multi-objective optimization for VLSI implementation of Artificial Neural Network (ANN) is proposed. This strategy is efficient in terms of area, power, and speed, and it has a good degree of accuracy and dynamic range. The goal of this research is to find the sweet spot where area, speed, and power may all be optimized in a very large scale integration (VLSI) implementation of a neural network (NN). The design should also allow for the dynamic reconfiguration of weight, and it should be very precise. We also use a 65-nm CMOS fabrication method to produce the circuits, and our results show that the suggested integral stochastic design may reduce energy consumption by up to 21% compared to the binary radix implementation, without sacrificing accuracy.

Chapter 5: Skin disorders are one of the most common types of skin disorders that are primarily diagnosed visually with scientific screening observed through dermoscopic evaluation, histopathological evaluation, and a biopsy. Diagnostic accuracy has a strong relevance to physician skill. Painful effects of skin disease hamper the mental condition of patient. We propose approach to detect the skin diseases based upon the VLSI implementation on image processing as well as machine learning techniques i.e., Convolutional Neural Networks (CNN). CNN is a specific type of neural network model that allows us to extract higher depictions for the image content. It is a Deep learning algorithm to perform generative & descriptive tasks. Machine learning generates two types of prediction-batch and real time. This chapter aims to develop skin diseases diagnosis system with a combination of image scaling algorithm with web-based interface to produce a quality resized image with better performance, the system is built on a machine learning algorithm model to classify the infected images using confusion matrix and develop a web interface application to capture the images. Blurring reduction and edge enhancement was done with bilinear interpolation and spatial sharp filter, as well. The algorithms were implemented using MATLAB. Thus, by this method we could predict and detect skin diseases and provide the reference to the nearest practitioner.

Chapter 6: Many of the robotic applications require autonomous decision making. The obstacles may be uncertain in nature. Because of the mobility, most of the robots might be operated with battery power. This chapter briefs the energy and performance analysis of robotic applications using Artificial Neural Network (ANN). Existing Artificial Intelligence focuses on either computation performance improvement or energy consumption minimization. If performance is concentrated, then energy would be compromised and vice versa. Neuromorphic computing system have the ability to provide high performance and low power consumption to the robotic applications. In neuromorphic computing system, Neurons and synapses articulate the functionality for computation speed and power improvement. These systems also have adaptability, self-organization, real time operation, and information redundant capability. Most of these systems use edge cloud computing. This chapter is designed to understand the operation of robot from understanding sensor data (training), processing (testing) the data in an efficient manner, and respond (prediction) to the dynamic situation using self-learning and adaptability. Bio-inspired learning, robot manipulator operation, robot path planning, driverless cars, collaborative industrial robots, and energy consumption prediction are few of the examples can be considered for understanding the improvements using Artificial Neural Network.

Chapter 7: Machine learning has had an impact in the area of microchip design and was initially used in automation. These techniques will eventually replace current VLSI design concepts. Design creation has been automated by substituting time-consuming, traditional concepts developed by experts. This development could result in a tremendous change in the realm of hardware computation and AI's powerful analysis tools. Traffic is a pressing issue in densely populated cities. Governments worldwide are attempting to address this problem by introducing various forms of public transportation, including metro. However, these solutions require significant investment and implementation time. Despite the high cost and inherent flaws of the system, many people still prefer to use their personal vehicles rather than public transportation. To address this issue, we propose a bike-sharing solution in which all processes from membership registration to bike rental and return are automated. Bagging is an ensemble learning method that can be used for base models with a low bias and high variance. It uses randomization of the dataset to reduce the variance of the base models, while keeping the bias low. Bagging helps improve the performance and accuracy of machine learning algorithms and is used to deal with bias-variance trade-offs. This saves time and improves service availability, without the need for third-party vendors. Payments are made online, providing a trustworthy and efficient way to rent a bike.

Chapter 8: The industrial world is facing swiftly changing challenges, including technical fluctuations, swings in global markets and climate change. Digitalization and automation are the game changers to meet these challenges. Machine learning has made an impact on the area attributed to microchip and it is initially used in automation. These practices will ultimately succeed the current VLSI design. A biometric authentication system is a form of biometric verification system that uses finger vein detection for biometric check framework. Consumer electronics development necessitates high security, high accuracy, and fast authentication speed. Since it presents the elements inside the human body, finger vein validation is a prominent technique in terms of security. Furthermore, it has a fair advantage over other personal authentication methods because to its contactless aspect. The main goal of the paper is to provide a solution using machine learning for finger vein authentication and implementation using VLSI design. In addition, we perform a comparison analysis of the various algorithms in order to determine which algorithm can produce the most accurate results, maximum accuracy, and is most suited for the approach proposed. We also extract an image's GLCM features which portray a picture's surface by working out how frequently sets of pixels with given values and in a predetermined spatial relationship show up in a picture, framing a GLCM, and afterward gathering factual measures from this lattice.

Chapter 9: Artificial Neural Networks (ANNs) are becoming increasingly important in the present technological era due to their ability to solve complex problems, adapt to new inputs, and improve decision-skills for different domains. The human brain serves as a model for Artificial Neural Networks (ANNs), a type of machine learning, as a reference for both structure and function. The existing work on ANNs supports tasks, such as regression, classification and pattern recognition separately. The discussion aims at resolving the above highlighted issues related to various ANN architectural implementations, considering the dynamic function exchange feature of FPGAs. With the aid of Zynq SOC, CNN and DNN architectures are designed in its Processing System, and the structure is accelerated using Programmable Logic. It also solves the issues due to trojans on design files, by introducing cryptography within the accelerator.

Chapter 10: Deep Neural Networks (DNNs) are widely used in applications including computer vision, speech recognition, and machine translation, where DNN attacks are an increasing concern. Examining the effects of hardware Trojan assaults on DNNs is discussed this paper. One of the most difficult threat models in hardware security is the Trojan. Trojans are harmful alterations that adversaries place into the original integrated circuits (ICs), which, when activated, cause dysfunction. Because third-party intellectual property (IP) blocks are frequently found in current ICs, adversaries are able to carry out these assaults. Moreover security aspects of neural networks (NN) have become a crucial and appropriate theme for basic research as a result of recent developments in neural networks and their use in deep learning techniques. In this research, authors examine the security issues and potential solutions in the computing hardware for deep neural networks (DNN). The latest hardware-based attacks against DNN are then described, with an emphasis on fault injection (FI), hardware Trojan (HT) insertion, and side-channel analysis (SCA). In this paper presents the various security issues in hardware based attacks and security concern in the hardware trojan (HT) and side channel analysis are focused. More over discussed the counter measure for the hardware trojan and Side channel attacks (SCA) is in neural networks.

Chapter 11: In recent years, there has been a trend towards more sophisticated robot control. This has been driven by advances in artificial intelligence (AI) and machine learning, which have enabled robots to become more autonomous and effective in completing tasks. One trend is towards using AI for robot control. This involves teaching robots how to carry out tasks by providing them with data and letting them learn from it. This approach can be used for tasks such as object recognition and navigation. Another trend is towards using machine learning for robot control. This involves using algorithms to learn from data and improve the performance of the robot. This approach can be used for tasks such as object recognition and navigation. A third trend is towards using more sophisticated sensors for robot control. This includes using sensors that can detect things such as temperature, humidity and pressure. This information can be used to help the robot to navigate and carry out tasks more effectively. Overall, the trend is towards more sophisticated robot control. This is driven by advances in AI and machine learning, which are enabling robots to become more autonomous and effective in completing tasks. Robot controllers are responsible for the operation of robots, either individually or in groups. They provide the programming and execution of robotic tasks, and often interface with peripheral devices such as grippers, loaders, and vision systems. A spiking neural network is a type of artificial neural network that uses discrete time steps to simulate the firing of neurons. This type of neural network is often used to model the brain and nervous system. A spiking neural network-based robot controller is a type of artificial neural network that uses discrete time steps to simulate the firing of neurons in order to control a robot. A biologically inspired spiking neural network (SNN) is a type of artificial neural network that is inspired by the brain's structure and function. SNNs are composed of a network of neurons that fire action potentials (spikes) in response to input stimuli. The output of an SNN is a spike train, which is a sequence of action potentials that encodes information about the input. SNNs have several advantages over traditional artificial neural networks (ANNs). First, SNNs can process information in a more energy-efficient manner than ANNs. This is because SNNs only fire action potentials when they receive input, whereas ANNs are constantly active, even when they are not processing any input. Second, SNNs are more robust than ANNs to changes in the input signal. This is because SNNs can continue to function even when some of their neurons are damaged or removed. Finally, SNNs are more efficient than ANNs at implementing learning algorithms, such as those that are used for pattern recognition and classification. The article explores the trends in biologically inspired SNN for robot control.

Chapter 12: The biologically inspired Spiking Neural Network (SNN) mimic the most neural networks in existence. Here the neural models try to replicate the biological neurons almost accurately and can be more powerful than its peers as it was able to integrate temporal information. They have great potential in several applications like classification, mapping, and pattern recognition, etc. SNNs are gaining importance in the last few years following the sharp incline in Artificial Intelligence. In this modern era robots are incorporated in our daily life, and said to have the potential to increase the economic growth and productivity. The need for robots that fledge like humans and also perform better than humans is also increased.

SNNs can generate good control systems for autonomous robots because they have proven to be outstanding for biological animals. The evolution of SNNs as well as some significant research made by them for robotics is discussed in this chapter.

I am thankful to the authors and reviewers for their contributions towards this book. This edited book covers the fundamental concepts of Neuromorphic computing systems for Industry 4.0 and its application areas in detail which is one of the main advantages of this book. We hope it will be useful to a wide variety of readers and will provide useful information to professors, researchers and students.

Book Editors:

S. Dhanasekar
Department of ECE, Sri Eshwar College of Engineering, Coimbatore, India

K. Martin Sagayam
Department of ECE, Karunya Institute of Tech. and Sciences, Coimbatore, India

Surbhi Vijh
ASET, Amity University, Noida, India

Vipin Tyagi
Jaypee University of Engineering and Technology, Guna, India

Alex Norta
Tallinn University, Tallinn, Estonia

Chapter 1
Introduction to Neuromorphic Computing Systems

L. Jubair Ahmed
Akshaya College of Engineering and Technology, Coimbatore, India

S. Dhanasekar
ⓘ https://orcid.org/0000-0002-7660-2265
Sri Eshwar College of Engineering, Coimbatore, India

K. Martin Sagayam
Karunya Institute of Tech. and Sciences, Coimbatore, India

Surbhi Vijh
ASET, Amity University, Noida, India

Vipin Tyagi
Jaypee University of Engineering & Technology, India

Mayank Singh
JSS Academy of Technical Education, Noida, India

Alex Norta
Tallinn University of Technology, Tallinn, Estonia

ABSTRACT

The process of using electronic circuits to replicate the neurobiological architectures seen in the nervous system is known as neuromorphic engineering, also referred to as neuromorphic computing. These technologies are essential for the future of computing, although most of the work in neuromorphic computing has been focused on hardware development. The execution speed, energy efficiency, accessibility and robustness against local failures are vital advantages of neuromorphic computing over conventional methods. Spiking neural networks are generated using neuromorphic computing. This chapter covers the basic ideas of neuromorphic engineering, neuromorphic computing, and its motivating factors and challenges. Deep learning models are frequently referred to as deep neural networks because deep learning techniques use neural network topologies. Deep learning techniques and their different architectures were also covered in this section. Furthermore, Emerging memory Devices for neuromorphic systems and neuromorphic circuits were illustrated.

DOI: 10.4018/978-1-6684-6596-7.ch001

INTRODUCTION

In the field of artificial intelligence known as neuromorphic computing, in other words engineering, researchers create machines that mimic the functions of the human brain. It's more like creating devices that replicate human brain function. Development of parts that are similar like the human brain is required for computing neuro-morphic devices. In terms of construction, these devices might not resemble original shape of a brain; rather, they perform the functions of their biological counterparts. In conclusion, neuro-morphic computing includes establishing artificial brains. In the 1980s, Carver Mead introduced the concept of "neuromorphic computing." Mead, who seemed to be a Caltech professor, is well known as the "Father of VLSI.". The notion has also been referred to using many other terms, such as "brain-inspired computing," "brain-like computing," "brain-based computing," "biologic computing," "neuro computing," "neural network computing," "connectionist computing," and "cognitive computing." Originally, the term "neuromorphic" was used to describe a method of building analogue VLSI circuits that was motivated by the structure and physiology of the brain. Since then, the phrase has come to refer to any artificial system inspired by the brain, including digital systems.

Neuromorphic computing as a concept has been known for a while, but as a computational paradigm, it has only just started to be taken seriously. The ability to replicate brain-like systems with sufficient fidelity to be useful is made feasible in part by digital computers' growing capacity. It is also a result of our growing understanding of how the brain functions, which has prompted the creation of artificial neural networks that are adept at handling challenging tasks. There have been several failures in the historical past of neuromorphic computing. The connection machine, created in the 1980's by danny hillis, was the first significant effort. It has more than 65,000 processors and was known as the connection machine. It was not particularly successful in its attempt to simulate the brain. The Neurogrid, created by Kwabena Boahen in the 2000s, was the result of a significant effort (Ben Abdallah et.al,2022). A specially created hardware system called the Neurogrid was created to mimic the brain. It also did not have a good outcome. The SpiNNaker system, created by Steve Furber in the 2010's, is the most recent and effective attempt. SpiNNaker, the hardware platform, was designed specifically to mimic the brain. Although it is the most prosperous neuromorphic system to date, it is still in its growing stage. Neuromorphic computing's future is unclear. The creation of effective algorithms, the creation of reliable hardware, and the comprehension of how to apply these systems to address practical issues are just a few of the difficulties that need to be solved. Neuromorphic technologies, on the other hand, have the potential to transform computing.

The binary system is used by conventional and digital computers. It comprehends and gives responses in 0s, 1s, (or) yes/no. This sort of process is quite limited in the domain of advancing research. As a result, there is a highly rigorous framework for how problems in digital computers are solved. These methods are limited to binary language. Neuromorphic computers (Ben Abdallah et.al,2022), on the other hand, have a very open-ended problem-solving strategy and are very versatile. Making computers more similar to human brains is one method for getting around this barrier. According to the idea of "neuromorphic computing," computer chips are made using a kind of computation that is inspired by the functioning of the human nervous system. Compared to digital computers, neuromorphic computers use less energy. The neurons may learn as they complete tasks because of the way they are built. It is hoped that by creating a computer that functions like a brain, we would have the computational capacity necessary to mimic an object as complex as the brain.

NEUROMORPHIC ENGINEERING

A team of scholars has already initiated developing a computer that possesses some, or effectively more than all, of the critical elements that brains possess and which computers do not. Such approaches employ asynchronous communication, which requires less power, to simulate the brain's neurons and synapses shown in silicon (Figure 1) (Poon et.al, 2011). The system's speed is also increased because it doesn't need to be programmed. Thus, the area of electronics engineering has entered a new age marked by neuromorphic engineering. Analog and digital hardware solutions that replicate the operation of such biological neural networks in the human brain on silicon chips are together referred to as "neuromorphic engineering."

Figure 1. Biological and silicon neurons have much better power and space efficiencies than digital computers
(Poon et.al, 2011)

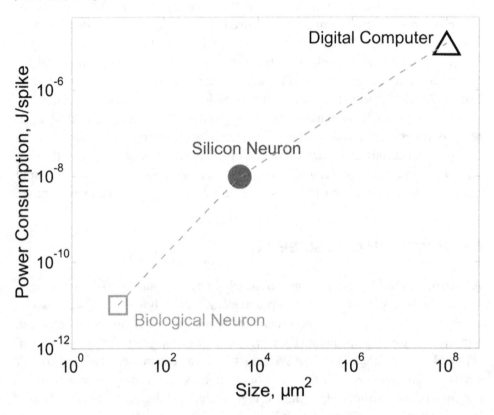

About to commence its 25th year as a field of engineering, neuromorphic engineering seems promising. During the first two decades, neuromorphic engineers concentrated on creating models of sensors such as silicon cochleas and retinas, as well as building blocks such as silicon neurons as well as synapses. Analog and mixed mode circuits were used to construct these sensors as well as neural networks in VLSI (Adarsh et.al, 2020). In the past ten years, computers and gadgets from many designers and even groups have been connected using the address event representation. This facility has proven crucial in the development of neuromorphic systems that integrate sensors, neural networks, and actuators. Future neuromorphic modelling efforts aim to maximize the biological realism and robustness of the neuronal analogues while also optimizing their integration density, computation, and power efficiencies (Ben Abdallah et.al,2022) (Adarsh et.al, 2020).

Neuromorphic Computing Motivating Factors and Challenges

The deployment of neural systems on silicon is known as "neuromorphic systems." Since the human brain can do a wide range of simple to complicated tasks with little energy consumption, even the most advanced computer clusters of today cannot compete with this capability. This is where the concept of basing the systems on computations in the mammalian brain came from. The brain performs 1016 complicated computations every second, using only a few watts of electricity. The efficiency of the human brain exceeds that of current digital technology by a factor of 1 billion and that of the most advanced digital technology by a factor of 10 million. Neuromorphic circuits are inspired by biology and employ simple physical processes as computational primitives, with information represented by relative values for analogue signals rather than true values of digital signals. Compared to equivalent digital systems, these analogue systems are 10,000 times more energy-efficient and utilize 100 times less silicon.

Spike representation is used by neuromorphic systems in communication, training, memory, as well as computation (Amirany et.al, 2022). Building energy-efficient as well as fault-tolerant systems that are suited for the upcoming generation of computing technologies can be accomplished using the event driven spike-based representation found in neuromorphic networks. Implants and prosthetics employ low power, high area efficient real-time neuromorphic circuits and systems that operate on analogue electronics principles. CMOS scaling greatly enhances the performance of digital circuits, but makes it more difficult to design complicated analogue circuits (Poon et.al, 2011). Therefore, the objective is to examine the reliability of implementing neuromorphic-hardware in current CMOS technology. It is currently hard to realise neuromorphic networks with biologically appropriate dimensions and power efficacy.

Human visual cortex has 5x105 neurons, while the neocortex of the human brain requires at least 2x1010 neurons. One of the foundational elements for better neuromorphic hardware is the development of integrated circuit manufacturing technologies. To replicate sophisticated brain activities, it remains challenging to create large-scale silicon neuron networks employing subthreshold CMOS circuits on VLSI devices (Ghasemzadeh et.al, 2020). One more issue in neuromorphic modelling includes achieving the size of the neural cortex as well as biological realism in circuitry implementations if the goal is to obtain the brilliance of biological complexity in an artificial system.

Need for Neuromorphic Computing

All facets of modern life now depend on computers, which are omnipresent across the world and are used for everything from process control, engineering, and research to entertainment and communications. Nowadays, data manipulation, transport, and processing consume between 5 and 15% of the world's energy. Researchers started looking at "neuromorphic" computing at the beginning of the 1990s. Analog computing systems modelled after the nervous system were thought to be a million times more energy efficient than those available at the time. Despite some remarkable achievements, traditional computational devices failed to perform some of the most fundamental functions that biological systems are capable of, such as voice and image recognition (Chandrakala et.al, 2017). As a result, incorporating inspiration from biology might result in fundamental advances in computational capabilities. Since then, CMOS technology has advanced at an extraordinary rate, leading to systems that use a lot less energy than originally thought. Over 5 billion transistors have been mass-produced in systems, and feature sizes are already getting close to 10 nm (Yang et.al, 2020). The transformation in parallel computing was made possible by these developments. Hundreds of millions of home computers and mobile phones now have multiple processors, and the biggest supercomputers have millions of CPUs. As a result, parallel computing is now a regular practice.

When traditional "non-learning" algorithms are unable to address issues with complicated and noisy datasets, "machine learning" software is utilized. Recently, by employing parallel processors, significant advancements in this field have been accomplished. These techniques have proven to be so successful that many major Internet and computer businesses now have "deep learning" research groups—the field of machine learning that develops tools based on deep (multilayer) neural networks (Ghasemzadeh et.al, 2020). In addition, computer science, mathematics, and statistics departments at the majority of top research institutions include machine learning groups. It was recently referred to as the "infrastructure for everything" since machine learning is a discipline that is expanding so quickly. Several teams have been working on deep neural network direct hardware implementations for many years. The models range from specialized, conventional processors that are tuned for machine learning "kernels" to systems that try to directly imitate an ensemble of "silicon" neurons, more commonly referred to as "neuromorphic computing.". Although the older methods can provide impressive results, such as 120 times less power consumption than that of a general-purpose processor, they do not essentially differ from current CPUs. Later neuromorphic systems were more in line with what scientists began experimenting with in the 1980s, when they created analogue CMOS-based systems inspired by biological neurons.

A biologically inspired chip ("TrueNorth") that incorporates one million spiking neurons as well as 256 million synapses on a device with 5.5 billion transistors has been one of the more recent achievements in neuromorphic computing (Poon et.al, 2011). It is obvious that progress on CMOS and computer hardware advancements in general will not be self-sustaining forever. According to well-supported projections based on reliable scientific and technical data, traditional methods of computation will run into a brick wall within the next ten years. In general, there are three main causes of this situation: (1) Basic (atomic) boundaries exist beyond which devices cannot be downsized, (2) local energy dissipation restricts device packing density; and (3) the growth in overall energy consumption and the lack of a foreseeable limit are becoming prohibitive. To attain the goal of creating computers that are more competent while using less power, novel strategies and concepts are required.

Spiking neural networks (SNN) are a technique used by neuromorphic systems, which are inspired by the brain and perform cognitive tasks (Lee et.al, 2020). These networks are composed of Silicon Neurons (SiN) as well as Silicon Synapses (SiS), which are in charge of transmitting electrical impulses or spikes via analog/digital VLSI circuits. Table 1.1 compares SNN with conventional ANNs to provide a deeper understanding of the SNN features. According to Table 1, SNN outperforms standard ANN methods in terms of ease of hardware implementation and huge parallelization, making it appealing in a variety of applications such as Various filtering methods for noise removal in biomedical images (Ahmed et.al, 2018) [(Jubairahmed et.al, 2017) artificial intelligence (AI), industrial robotics, the internet of things (IoT), biomedicine, and health (Ahmed et.al, 2018).

Table 1. Comparison traditional ANN and SNN. The SST term refers spatio- and spectro-temporal; FPGA is field programmable gate array; FPNA is field programmable neural array.

Properties	Traditional ANN	SNN
Biological Plausibility	Moderate: At network level and few types of artificial neurons	High: artificial neurons, synapses, and networks mimic biological; The data transmitted through spikes
Data representation	Scalars	Spike sequences
Dealing of SST data	Possible	Possible
Hardware	Standard Computers, FPGAs, microcontrollers; • Requires multiplier, adder blocks • The data transmission is in real numbers, requires databus • Difficult to implement asynchronous communication	Neuromorphic VLSI chips, FPGAs, FPNA, microcontrollers, standard computers; • No multiplication block • A single interconnect line to transmit data in spike events • Asynchronous communication is possible
Energy Consumption	High	Less
Parallelization of Computations	Moderate number of computations are possible	Massive parallel computations are possible (Emulating the human brain)
Synchronization	Synchronous with system clock	Asynchronous (spike-event driven)
No. of optimized parameters required	Less number of parameters (requires model parameters and hyper parameters)	Large number of parameters to optimize (addition to parameters in ANN, parameters associated with neural dynamics of neurons and synapse)
Gradient based optimization	Possible	Not Possible (discontinuous spike events)
Learning Algorithm	Back Propagation through time, Stochastic Gradient Descent	Hebbian learning, Spike-timing dependent plasticity (STDP) Triplet STDP, ReSuMe and SpikeProp

DEEP LEARNING

One of the newest areas in artificial intelligence is deep learning. Natural language processing, voice recognition, and computer vision are three areas where it is used to deal with neural networks. One of the byproducts of AI, known as machine learning, involves the computer extracting information from supervised experience (Bruntha et.al, 2022). With the use of a collection of training examples and manual error correction, a human operator assists the machine in learning. Large-scale neural networks used in deep learning enable a computer to learn and "think" alone without the need based on direct human involvement.

Choice of the Deep Net

Before selecting a deep net, it is important to understand whether the goal is to create a classifier or to look for patterns in the data. A set of unlabeled data is used to extract the pattern in unsupervised learning. For this, either an auto encoder or a restricted boltzmann machine (RBM) is utilized. The best algorithm that may be used for various supervised or otherwise unsupervised learning tasks is shown in the following Table 2.

Table 2. Choice of deep net

Different Labels	Various Algorithms
Image Recognition	DBN, Convolutional net
Text processing	Recursive neural tensor network, recurrent net
Object recognition	RNTN, Convolutional net
Speech recognition	Recurrent net
Time series analysis	Recurrent net
Classification	Multi-layered perceptrons, deep belief nets

Deep Learning Algorithms

1. Neural Network

Neural networks serve as the foundation of deep learning. The neurons, as well as the edges joining them together, make up the interconnected node system that makes up a neural network. The fundamental role of a neural network is to accept a collection of inputs, do more sophisticated computations, and then use the output to solve a problem. In many different applications, neural networks are employed. The neural network focuses mostly on classification. A group of items is classified using certain fundamental data features during the classification process. There are several classifiers available now, including neural networks, logistic regression, and support vector machines. A score is generated when a classifier or activation fires. When an item can fit into one of two categories, classification tasks are handled by neural networks(Ghasemzadeh et.al, 2020). The neural network has layers and is highly organised. The neural network generally consists of three layers. The input layer is the top layer, the output layer is the bottom layer, and the concealed layer is the layer in the centre as shown in Figure.2.

Figure 2. Architecture of neural network

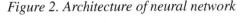

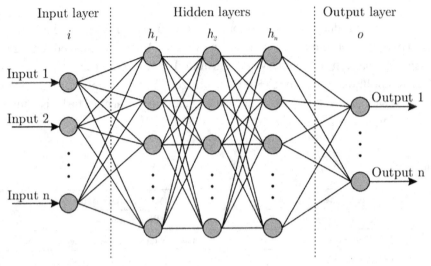

The first hidden layer receives a set of inputs, and the activation from that layer is sent to the next layer, and so on until the output layer is reached, where the classification results are decided by the scores at each node. This is repeated for each input set. Forward propagation, also known as "forward prop," is the term used to describe this sequence of actions that begins at the input layer and proceeds to the output layer. In order to address the shortcomings of an early classifier, the perceptron, the neural network was developed. By employing a layered system of perceptrons, prediction accuracy could also be improved. Multi-layer perceptron, or MLP (Ghasemzadeh et.al, 2020)..The classifier used by each node in the forward propagation is the same; therefore, if an input is entered multiple times, the same result will be produced. In the case of the hidden layer, the node of the hidden layer gets the same input, but the same value is not produced as the output. This is due to the fact that each piece of input is altered by special weights as well as biases. Each edge's weight and each node's bias are distinct from one another. As a result, the nodes fire in a distinct manner since each activation has a special combination. Training is the process of increasing a neural network's accuracy. The cost is calculated as the difference between the forward propagation output and the output that is known to be accurate as shown in equation (1).

Cost = Generated output-actual output equation   (1)

The cost should be kept as low as feasible. To achieve this, the net gradually changes the weights and bias values on until prediction and output are closely matched.

The neural network can estimate time correctly after successful training. When a single classifier can perform classification tasks reasonably well, the question of why develop and train a network of classifiers arises. The complexity of patterns is the answer to this question.

2.   Restricted Boltzmann Machine (RBM)

The model that was able to solve the vanishing gradient issue was RBM. The input is reorganised in order to detect patterns in the data. At the University of Toronto, Geoff Hinton introduced the RBM methodology (Ghasemzadeh et.al, 2020). He was also the first scientist to come up with the groundbreaking concept of deep net training. Geoff Hinton is frequently called the "father of deep learning" due to his innovative work. RBM is a thin, two-layer net. It interprets the input into a series of numerals that encode the input.

Figure 3. Structure of restricted Boltzmann machine

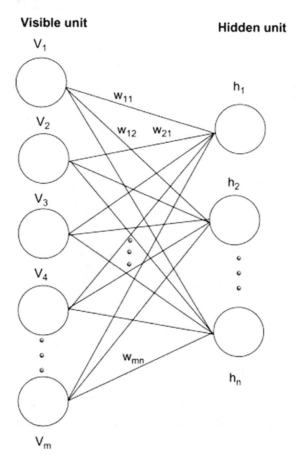

The following are the RBM steps:

1) The input is mixed with each individual weight as well as one bias in the forward pass, and the resulting output is transferred towards the hidden layer.
2) In the backward pass, each activation's individual weight and overall bias are merged, and the resulting information is transferred to the visible layer for reconstruction (as shown in Figure 4).
3) The original input and the reconstructed input are compared in the visible layer to assess the quality of the outcome. Steps 1) through 3) of the RBM are repeated with different biases and weights until the input as well as the reconstruction are as similar as is feasible. Step 3 employs KL divergence as shown in Figure 3.

Figure 4. Forward and backward pass

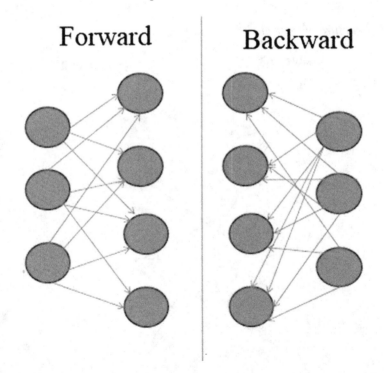

3. Deep Belief network

Deep belief networks, one of the alternatives to backpropagation, were suggested by Geoff Hinton (Bruntha et al., 2022) . A DBN is equivalent to a multi-layer perceptron in terms of network structure. But they are quite different when it comes to training. It may be thought of as a stack of RBMs, where the visible layer of the RBM "above" another one is the hidden layer of the one below.

The following is how a DBN is trained:

a)   First, RBM receives training to recreate its input as precisely as possible.

b)   Utilizing the outputs from the first RBM, the second RBM was trained using the hidden layer of its first RBM as the visible layer.

c)   This procedure is continued until the network's last layer has completed training.

Figure 5. Deep belief network

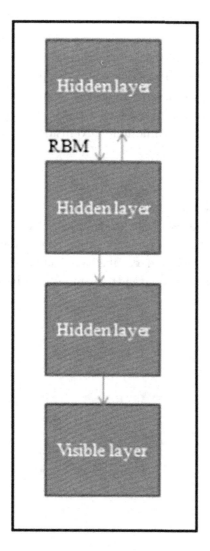

Although it is essential to remember that each RBM layer in a DBN learns the complete input. In the case of face recognition, the initial layers identify the edges in the picture, and later layers mould the facial characteristics using the results. A DBN works so effectively because RBMs stack and RBMs can discover intrinsic patterns in data. A small number of labelled samples are needed to introduce labels to patterns in order to name the patterns and characteristics. Because of the minor changes made to the weights and perceptions, the net's ability to recognize patterns and overall accuracy both marginally improve as shown in Figure 5. The training process is finished with the assistance of GPUs in a period of time that is significantly shorter than that of the CPUs.

4. Convolutional Nets

Yann Lecun introduced the idea of "convolutional neural networks," or CNN (Yang et.al, 2020). In recent years, CNN has entirely controlled the machine vision sector. CNN is the source of Facebook's face recognition algorithm. For picture classification, a well-known dataset (Yang et.al, 2020) including images from 1000 categories is employed. In 2012, a machine was able to categorize images into 1,000 different categories, marking a milestone n AI history.

5. Recurrent Nets

RNN became well-known thanks to the work of Juergen Schmidhuber, Sepp Hochreiter, and Alex Graves (Yang et.al, 2020).. The applications of recurrent networks span from voice recognition to autonomous automobiles. When the data is changing over time, RNN produces the best results. The output of one layer is combined with the subsequent input and transmitted back into that layer in a feedback loop as shown in Figure 6.

Figure 6. Architecture of recurrent neural nets

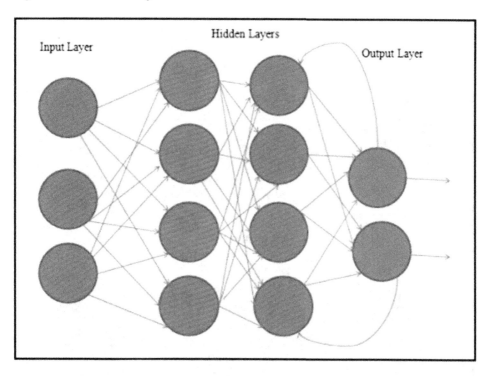

6.   Auto encoders

RBM is one of the most well-known applications of the auto encoder. In other words, it consists of the input layer, output layer, and hidden layer as shown in Figure 7. The auto encoders are unlabeled and very shallow. Encoding and decoding are basically the only two stages. The features are encoded using weights in the hidden layer, and the picture is decoded in the output layer. The auto encoder's feature extractor reconstructs the features after first encoding them. Using backpropagation and the loss metric, auto encoders are trained. The information that was lost during the network's attempt to reconstruct the input is measured by loss.

Figure 7. Architecture of auto encoder

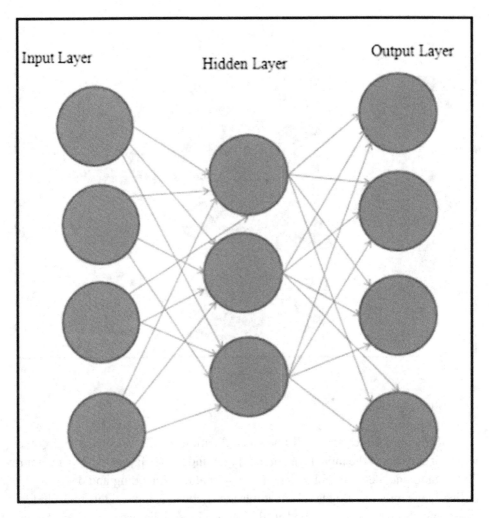

Deep Learning Algorithms Models

1. Recursive Neural Tensor Network

Richard Socher introduced the idea of RNTN in his Stanford Ph.D. thesis. Recursive neural tensor networks (RNTNs) are used to uncover the hierarchical structure of a piece of data. They were initially created for sentiment analysis, where the sentiment of a phrase depends not only on the individual words that make it up but also on the way that they are syntactically arranged (Jubair Ahmed et.al, 2022). The basic components of RNTN are the groups of parents (also known as the root) as well as the groups of children (known as the leaves). Both leaves are attached to the root, but the leaves are not connected to one another. A binary tree is made up of the components. A classifier is used by the root to fire after the groups of leaves have received data.

2.   Artificial Neural Networks

Training neural networks is essentially the act of determining the appropriate combination of synaptic weights to maximize the accuracy of the network. One of the major issues in the design of neuromorphic devices has been the incorporation of learning. Either on-chip or off-chip learning implementation is used in neuromorphic systems. The backpropagation learning rule is one of the common learning rules employed in training conventional ANNs. The synaptic weights of an ANN are modified throughout training by this learning algorithm depending on the mistake rate recorded during the first training phase. It may be used to train neural networks with feed-forward, recurrent, and convolutional topologies. The trained weights are then transferred to the neuromorphic chip and used to train ANN weights there. Backpropagation (BP) and its derivatives have been streamlined or made simpler for on-chip implementation in a number of neuromorphic system on-chip implementations (Yang et.al, 2020) (Jubair Ahmed et.al, 2022). Due to the rise of broadband wireless transmission networks, customer demands in high-speed wireless communication have risen significantly (Subramaniyam et.al, 2017) (Dhanasekar et.al, 2022)[14-15], (Dhanasekar et.al, 2022).Alternative supervised learning methods involve support vector machines as well as linear regression. This learning method is not frequently used; however, several unsupervised learning rules based on the self-organised maps (Ahmed et.al., 2022) [6, 35, 46] have been implemented on neuromorphic circuitry.

3.   Spiking Neural Networks

Artificial neural network models called "spiking neural networks" more closely resemble biological neural networks. SNNs incorporate several time scales into their computational model in addition to neuronal as well as synaptic states. Additionally, because SNN uses spike timings to encode information, very low transmission latency is also required (Yang et.al, 2020). The biologically inspired neuron model is shown in Figure.8 (a) Dendrites receive information from upstream neurons through synapses. The potential of the soma's membrane is integrated with incoming spikes. The neuron fires an outward spike to an axon unless the membrane potential exceeds the threshold. Through synapses, the axon transmits the spike to the downstream neurons. An illustration of a spiking neuron can be seen in Figure .8 (b)

Figure 8. (a) Biological neuron, (b) Spiking neuron

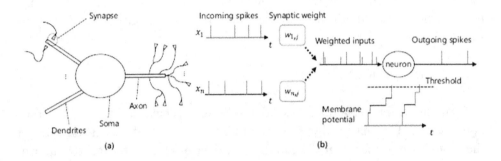

a.   Learning in Spiking Neural Networks

   The most common learning principle used in neuromorphic devices is spike timing-dependent plasticity (STDP). When a presynaptic spike comes before the postsynaptic neuron "Fire" and vice versa, the synaptic weight is raised, as shown in Figure. 9, and vice versa. This is how STDP works. Due to its supportive hardware resource, it is typically implemented on-chip as an unsupervised learning rule.

Figure 9. STDP architecture

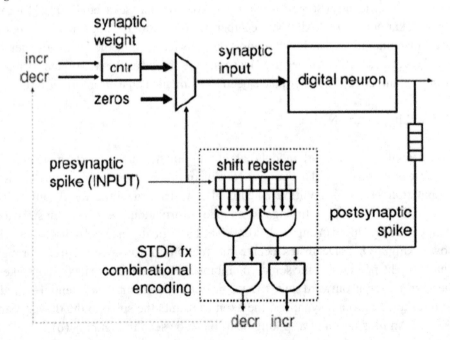

Spiking neuro-morphic system additionally implemented supervised learning principles in addition to the bulk of STDP (Yang et.al, 2020). However, spiking systems also use backpropagation. Furthermore, experts first train an ANN with BP, and then they transform it into an SNN by converting real-value inputs and activations to the typical firing rates of Poisson spikes. This technology may be used to achieve off-chip learning on spiking hardware.

EMERGING MEMORY DEVICES FOR NEUROMORPHIC SYSTEMS

The FLASH Memory

Flash memory was created and patented in the 1970s by Shunpei Yamazaki, (Dhanasekar et.al., 2022). Then he proposed a theory on the C-V hysteresis he saw in a device in 1966 after observing it. The idea of using a floating gate MOS structure to store data was initially suggested by Dr. Kahng. Because the floating gate was constructed of zirconium and the sides were visible from the air, Kahng's device was not regarded at the time as a revolutionary one. Figure 10 shows the construction developed by Yamakazis, which consists of a MOS transistor with a floating gate enclosed by a gate dielectric and entirely isolated from the environment. Such non-volatile technology was clearly the most affordable of them all, and it was also scalable, quick, and dependable. We now use FLASH-based external storage devices (such as pen drives, solid-state drives, micro SD cards, EEPROMs, M.2 NVME, etc.).Let's have a look at the fundamental construction of a FLASH transistor and attempt to figure out how it works.

Figure 10. An elementary structure of a floating gate MOSFET

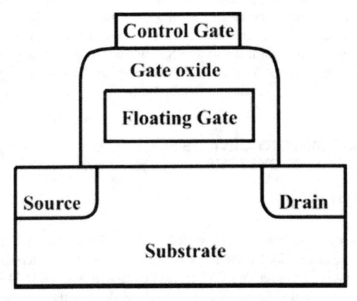

A normal MOSFET as well as a floating gate MOSFET may be differentiated from one another fairly quickly. The FLASH transistor differs from a traditional transistor by having an extra gate inside the dielectric. The NAND as well as NOR layouts are the two dominant layouts in the FLASH non-volatile field. They are applied in many fields due to their benefits and drawbacks. The NAND as well as NOR layouts are the two dominant layouts in the FLASH non-volatile field. They are applied in many fields due to their benefits and drawbacks.

Figure 11. (a); if you recall NAND = "NOT" series "AND"), whereas in NOR12 layout devices are in parallel connection (figure 11(b); NOR="NOT" series "OR")

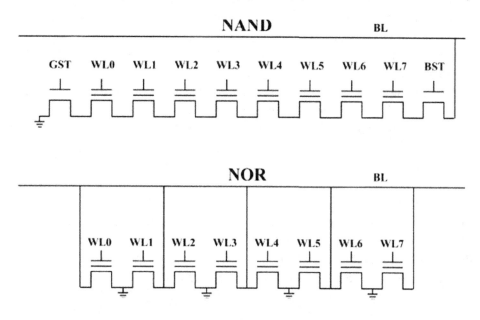

In a NAND configuration, the word lines are all linked in series with a single grounded connection only through ground select transistor. Instead, each and every device in the NOR structure has to be connected to the bit line and the ground. We must apply Vit to the specified word line of a NAND device in order to read data from that device, and we must turn on all other devices in order to read the high or low current. In addition, the GST and BST must continue to operate so that the user may access the block. In order to ensure that the current is only flowing through the appropriate device during reading and not unintentionally through any other cells of the block, the remaining bits for a NOR device must be in the off state (Dhanasekar et.al, 2022) . The floating gate will be drained out of the electrons in both of these architectures by passing a high voltage through the WLs.According to what we previously mentioned, FN tunnelling causes the electron to go from the FG to the control gate and turns all of the devices in a block to "1".The name was coined because both of these designs involve deleting the entire block in a "FLASH."

The Future

Normally, when scaling down on FLASH memory, there are short channel effects and difficulties in the manufacturing phase. When the gate dielectric and channel length are reduced, the device becomes more prone to failure prior to the direct tunneling effect (Hazra et.al, 2020). Most of the layout footprint is taken up by the metal interconnects for the substrate, control gate, source, and drain. Moore's law's deviance is proof enough that shrinking is one of the objectives that today's modern semiconductor industry is unable to achieve. Hence, the development of alternative techniques for long-term data storage has begun among scientists throughout the world. Among these, resistive RAM, phase change RAM, atomic switches, and magneto resistive RAM have all demonstrated significant potential. Let's go over each of these memory storage techniques individually.

1.   MRAM

The MRAM (Lee et.al, 2020) uses an electron's spin-transfer torque feature to store data. It is composed structurally of a thin conducting layer separating a ferromagnetic top electrode (TE) from a ferromagnetic bottom electrode (BE). While the TE is flexible and referred to as a "free state magnet," the BE typically consists of fixed ferromagnetic material or a "fixed state magnet" as shown in Figure 12.

Figure 12. Different resistive states of an MRAM depending upon the electron spins

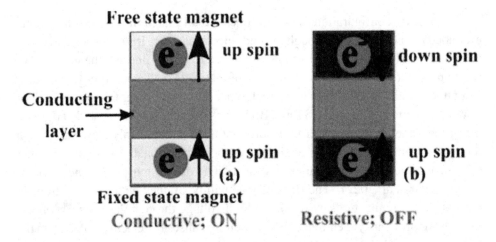

The circuit has a reduced resistance (state "1") and permits a high current to flow through it when both magnets are spinning in the same direction. The device exhibits a high resistive condition, which corresponds to state "0," when a significant current is forced through the free-state magnet to shift the direction of its electron spin.

2. PCRAM

A phase-changing material is placed between two electrodes in PCRAM15, which has a capacitor-like structure. The material can melt when exposed to a high-voltage pulse (or a high power laser pulse) due to joule heating. The material is quenched into an amorphous form during the cooling process, but a considerably slower cooling (by maintaining the crystalline temperature for a brief period of time) produces a crystalline phase. Similar to MRAM, PCRAM (Figure 13) retains information in various resistive states; the amorphous phase corresponds to a highly resistive state, while the crystalline/polycrystalline phase displays the conducting state.

Figure 13. A schematic diagram of a PRAM device with the heating element

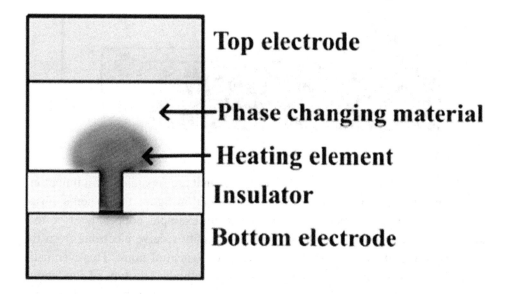

3. Atomic Switch

Atomic switches16 are two-terminal tunnel junctions (or three-terminal if an additional regulating gate is included) that also function as a resistive switch.

Figure 14. A single row-column pair of an atomic switch crossbar array; demonstrating the metallic filament formation in the tunneling gap

Under a strong electric field, two electrodes that are separated by a tunnelling gap frequently create a metallic bridge (as depicted in figure 14). When exposed to a positive bias, a low electronegative metal (for example, copper) tends to lose electrons and form a cation; these ions may readily receive electrons from the cathode (through direct tunnelling) and be reduced to neutral atoms. This eventually results in a metallic protrusion emerging from the cathode. This type of conducting filament (CF) formation and collapse (at negative bias) toggles the tunnelling gap's resistivity and can be used to represent two different states of logic (namely, "0" and "1"); as a result, it can be used as non-volatile memory.

4.   Resistive random access memory

Under voltage stress, several semiconductors and insulators (Dhanasekar et.al, 2022) can switch between resistive states. These insulators create the heart of a resistive ram. A resistive RAM device (Lee et.al, 2020) is composed structurally of two electrodes—the top and bottom electrodes—that are electrically isolated by the switching dielectric. By using varying voltage bias, it is simple to switch the device's resistive state between a high-resistive state (HRS) or off state and a low-resistive state (LRS) or on state. The figure 15 (a) shows a ReRAM device in action.

Figure 15. (a) A schematic illustration of a ReRAM structure at its HRS state, and (b) LRS state.

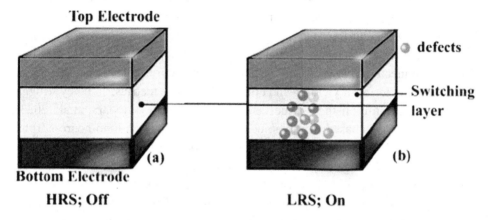

The ability to induce or produce electrically activated flaws in the layer depends on the electric field's strength. As seen in figure 15 (b), a sufficient number of these charged deficiencies can combine into a conducting filament or bridge (CF) between the electrodes. We will next discuss the causes and characteristics of these deficiencies as well as how they affect switching behavior. The effect is often reversed by applying voltage with the opposite polarity, which causes the CF to dissolve (or partially dissolve), re-isolating the top electrode (TE) as well as the bottom electrode (BE) electrically. The most exciting aspect of these occurrences is that once the state is altered, the dielectric keeps the state even when no field is present.

EMERGING TECHNOLOGIES FOR NEUROMORPHIC CIRCUITS

Due to the commercial CMOS process variability as well as temperature, the present subthreshold Silicon Neuron circuits, including transistors operating in a subthreshold region, are prone to mismatch. Subthreshold SoC circuits with minimal power are a solid option nowadays. In comparison to standard CMOS transistors, completely depleted silicon-on-insulator technology delivers a considerable reduction in threshold voltage fluctuation and device capacitance. It is suited for ultra-low-power subthreshold circuit applications. Neuromorphic analogue VLSI circuits have been implemented using this cutting-edge subthreshold CMOS technology. The ability to stack numerous linked bulk CMOS dies on top of one another has been made possible by recent developments in three-dimensional integrated circuit technology . This results in an enhanced effective VLSI footprint with significantly shorter interconnect wire lengths. The next generation for large-scale neuromorphic networks has new opportunities because to three-dimensional integrated circuit development.

Nanotechnologies like memristors, carbon nanotubes, nanowires, etc. are used in a new, emergent approach to large-scale neuromorphic modelling that goes beyond CMOS. Neuromorphic systems employ the memristor-based synaptic crossbar networks, which can simulate spike-timing-dependent synaptic plasticity with vast connections between CMOS-based silicon neurons. These devices are far less efficient in terms of yielding and other performance metrics, and they struggle with the same non-robustness issues as CMOS devices (Govindaraj et.al., 2023). A device like this is based on phenomenology rather than an iono-neuromorphic model of neural function. Therefore, it would not be suitable for neuromorphic systems that are biologically realistic and reliable. Carbon nanotube field effect transistors are a different product that is being investigated to replace MOSFETs. The top-gated CNFET structure is similar to the MOSFET structure used today, with the exception that the carbon nanotubes are arranged in parallel between both the source as well as drain in place of the channel. The gate oxide on the device's metal gate is made of a high-K dielectric substance. This technique assures further performance advantages as CMOS scaling matures over the next decades, delivering a greater potential quasi-ballistic-carrier velocity as well as mobility than MOSFETs.

In neuromorphic circuits, the specifically created, optically gated CNFET has been employed as a non-volatile synaptic device. These circuits have the capacity to change their conductances using programming pulses. If the whole brilliance of the brain should ever be represented on chip, neuromorphic modelling efforts must target not just the integration density and computing and/or power efficiency of the neural analogues but also their level of biological realism and resilience.

CHAPTER SUMMARY

An overview of neuromorphic computing, including emerging memory devices and emerging technologies used in neuromorphic circuits, was presented in this chapter. Although much of the effort in neuromorphic computing has focused on hardware development and emerging technologies will be critical for the growth of computing. Spiking neural networks are the most recent generation of artificial neural networks, spiking neural networks use biologically accurate models of neurons to perform the computation to close the gap between neuroscience and machine learning. Due to event-based operations and fewer operation computations, Spiking Neural

Networks can simulate biological neural networks with low energy consumption. Deep learning models are sometimes referred to as deep neural networks because most deep learning techniques use neural network topologies. Neural network designs that learn features directly from the data without the requirement for human feature extraction are used to train deep learning models on massive quantities of labelled data. Deep learning and the methods that support it are mostly used in this section. In this introductory section, we learned how deep learning transforms the job at a dynamic speed with a vision to produce intelligent software that can replicate it and work like a human brain. All of these algorithms are well known to aspiring deep learning engineers, and it is strongly recommended that beginners understand them before continuing their study of artificial intelligence.

REFERENCES

Adarsh, S., & Ramachandran, K. I. (2020). Neuro-fuzzy based fusion of LiDAR and ultrasonic sensors to minimize error in range estimation for the navigation of mobile robots. *Intelligent Decision Technologies*, *14*(2), 259–267. doi:10.3233/IDT-180109

Ahmed, L. J. (2018). Discrete Shearlet Transform Based Speckle Noise Removal in Ultrasound Images. *National Academy Science Letters*, *41*(2), 91–95. doi:10.100740009-018-0620-7

Ahmed, L. J. (2022). A Survey of IoT Based Pregnancy Woman Health Monitoring System. *2022 8th International Conference on Advanced Computing and Communication Systems (ICACCS)*. IEEE. 10.1109/ICACCS54159.2022.9785324

Amirany, A., Moaiyeri, M. H., & Jafari, K. (2022). Nonvolatile Associative Memory Design Based on Spintronic Synapses and CNTFET Neurons. *IEEE Transactions on Emerging Topics in Computing*, *10*(1), 428–437. doi:10.1109/TETC.2020.3026179

Arunkumar, N., Senathipathi, N., Dhanasekar, S., Malin Bruntha, P., & Priya, C. (2020). An ultra-low-power static random-access memory cell using tunneling field effect transistor. *International Journal of Engineering*, *33*(11), 2215–2221.

Ben Abdallah, A., & Dang, N. (2022). Introduction to Neuromorphic Computing Systems. Neuromorphic Computing Principles and Organization. doi:10.1007/978-3-030-92525-3_1

Bruntha, P. M., Dhanasekar, S., Ahmed, L. J., Khanna, D., Pandian, S. I. A., & Abraham, S. S. (2022). Investigation of Deep Features in Lung Nodule Classification. *2022 6th International Conference on Devices, Circuits and Systems (ICDCS)*. IEEE. 10.1109/ICDCS54290.2022.9780716

Bruntha, P. M., Dhanasekar, S., Hepsiba, D., Sagayam, K. M., Neebha, T. M., Pandey, D., & Pandey, B. K. (2022, September 5). *Application of switching median filter with L2 norm-based auto-tuning function for removing random valued impulse noise - Aerospace Systems*. Springer. https://link.springer.com/article/10.1007/s42401-022-00160-y

Chandrakala, S., & Rajeswari, N. (2017). Representation Learning Based Speech Assistive System for Persons With Dysarthria. *IEEE Transactions on Neural Systems and Rehabilitation Engineering, 25*(9), 1510–1517. doi:10.1109/TNSRE.2016.2638830 PMID:27992342

Dhanasekar, S., Bruntha, P. M., Ahmed, L. J., Valarmathi, G., Govindaraj, V., & Priya, C. (2022). An Area Efficient FFT Processor using Modified Compressor adder based Vedic Multiplier. *2022 6th International Conference on Devices, Circuits and Systems (ICDCS)*. IEEE. 10.1109/ICDCS54290.2022.9780676

Dhanasekar, S., Jothy Stella, T., Thenmozhi, A., & Divya Bharathi, N. (2022). Kamatchi Thiyagarajan, Pankaj Singh, Yanala Srinivasa Reddy, Ganganagunta Srinivas, Mani Jayakumar, and Samson Jerold Samuel Chelladurai. (2022). Study of Polymer Matrix Composites for Electronics Applications. *Journal of Nanomaterials, 2022*. doi:10.1155/2022/8605099

Dhanasekar, S., Ganesan, A. T., Rani, T. L., Vinjamuri, V. K., & Rao, M. N. (2022). Shankar., & Golie, W. M. (2022). A Comprehensive Study of Ceramic Matrix Composites for Space Applications. *Advances in Materials Science and Engineering*.

Dhanasekar, S., Abarna, V. K., Gayathri, V., Valarmathi, G., Madhumita, D., & Jeevitha, R. (2023). An Efficient Smart Agriculture System Based on The Internet of Things Using Aeroponics Method. 2023 9th International Conference on Advanced Computing and Communication Systems (ICACCS). https://doi.org/10.1109/icaccs57279.2023.10112884

Ghasemzadeh, P., Banerjee, S., Hempel, M., & Sharif, H. (2020). A New Framework for Automatic Modulation Classification using Deep Belief Networks. *2020 IEEE International Conference on Communications Workshops (ICC Workshops)*. IEEE. 10.1109/ICCWorkshops49005.2020.9145320

Govindaraj, V., Dhanasekar, S., Martinsagayam, K., Pandey, D., Pandey, B. K., & Nassa, V. K. (2023, January 9). *Low-power test pattern generator using modified LFSR - Aerospace Systems*. SpringerLink. https://link.springer.com/article/10.1007/s42401-022-00191-5

Hazra, P., & Jinesh, K. B. (2020). Vertical limits of resistive memory scaling: The detrimental influence of interface states. *Applied Physics Letters*, *116*(17), 173502. doi:10.1063/1.5139595

Jubairahmed, L., Satheeskumaran, S., & Venkatesan, C. (2017). Contourlet transform based adaptive nonlinear diffusion filtering for speckle noise removal in ultrasound images. *Cluster Computing*, *22*(S5), 11237–11246. doi:10.100710586-017-1370-x

Lee, S.-T., & Lee, J.-H. (2020). Neuromorphic Computing Using NAND Flash Memory Architecture With Pulse Width Modulation Scheme. *Frontiers in Neuroscience*, *14*, 571292. doi:10.3389/fnins.2020.571292 PMID:33071744

Poon, C.-S., & Zhou, K. (2011). Neuromorphic Silicon Neurons and Large-Scale Neural Networks: Challenges and Opportunities. *Frontiers in Neuroscience*, *5*. doi:10.3389/fnins.2011.00108 PMID:21991244

Subramaniyam, D., & Jayabalan, R. (2017). FPGA implementation of variable bit rate OFDM transceiver system for wireless applications. *2017 International Conference on Innovations in Electrical, Electronics, Instrumentation and Media Technology (ICEEIMT)*. IEEE. 10.1109/ICIEEIMT.2017.8116863

Subramaniyam, D., & Sagayam, M. (2019). An Improved Area Efficient 16-QAM Transceiver Design using Vedic Multiplier for Wireless Applications. *International Journal of Recent Technology and Engineering.*, *8*(3), 4419–4425. doi:10.35940/ijrte.C5535.098319

V, G., Chenguttuvan, E., & Subramaniyam, D. (2022). Design of Power and Area Efficient Carry Skip Adder and FIR filter Implementation. El-Cezeri Fen ve Mühendislik Dergisi. https://doi.org/ doi:10.31202/ecjse.1162711

Yang, J., Wang, R., Ren, Y., Mao, J., Wang, Z., Zhou, Y., & Han, S. (2020). Neuromorphic Engineering: Neuromorphic Engineering: From Biological to Spike-Based Hardware Nervous Systems (Adv. Mater. 52/2020). *Advanced Materials*, *32*(52), 2070392. Portico. https://doi.org/ doi:10.1002/adma.202070392

Chapter 2
Neuromorphic Computing:
Implementation and Open Issues

Shivakumar Hunagund

(iD) https://orcid.org/0000-0001-5201-5827

Intel Corporation, USA

ABSTRACT

Neuromorphic computing is a rapidly emerging field that seeks to emulate the computational principles of the brain using novel materials and devices. While traditional computing architectures, such as the von Neumann architecture, have experienced exponential improvements in computational power due to the continuous shrinkage of transistor technology, the laws of physics will eventually limit the performance of these systems. Neuromorphic computing offers the potential to continue scaling technology by incorporating novel functional materials and devices into new computing architectures. In this chapter, the authors will explore the principles of neuromorphic computing and the key challenges that must be overcome in order to fully implement these systems. The authors will discuss the role of new nanostructured materials and devices in neuromorphic computing, and the importance of understanding charge and defects migration, fault tolerance, and manufacturability.

INTRODUCTION

The field of computing has come a long way since the invention of the first electronic computers in the mid-20th century. Driven by the continuous shrinkage of transistor technology, modern computation based on the von Neumann architecture has experienced exponential improvement in computational power. However, as

DOI: 10.4018/978-1-6684-6596-7.ch002

transistors reach atomic scale, it is becoming increasingly clear that computing performance will eventually reach its limit given the laws of physics. In order to continue scaling technology and fostering progress in computing, it is necessary to explore alternative approaches and incorporate novel functional materials and devices into new computer architectures.

One of the most promising developments in this regard is neuromorphic computing, which is based on the principles of biological neural computation and involves the emulation of neural systems using silicon-based neural elements. Neuromorphic computing offers a number of benefits over traditional approaches, including the ability to process information in a more energy-efficient manner and the potential to perform tasks that are difficult or impossible for traditional computers, such as pattern recognition and machine learning.

Figure 1. Conventional, parallel, and neuromorphic computing lie in their underlying architectures, computational models, and applications
(*Intel, 2023*)

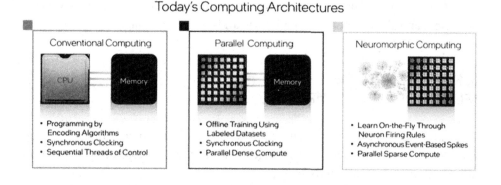

However, the full implementation of neuromorphic computing is not without its challenges. In order to fully realize the potential of this new computing paradigm, it is necessary to address a number of key research challenges. These challenges include the development of materials with specific quantum properties and new device physics that can be used to build neuromorphic systems, as well as understanding charge/defects migration, fault tolerance, and manufacturability in order to make neuromorphic systems more reliable and easier to produce at scale.

Another important aspect of neuromorphic computing is the use of new hardware architectures that are specifically designed to support this new computing paradigm. These architectures are designed to be much more flexible and adaptable than traditional architectures, making it possible to incorporate new technologies and materials as they become available. This is an important factor in the continued development of neuromorphic computing, as it will allow researchers to continue to explore new ideas and approaches as the field evolves.

In addition to these developments, there is also an increasing focus on the integration of neuromorphic computing with other emerging technologies, such as artificial intelligence and robotics. This integration is seen as an important step in the development of more advanced systems that can perform complex tasks with a high degree of accuracy and efficiency. There is also a growing interest in the potential applications of neuromorphic computing in the field of medicine, where it is being explored as a tool for diagnosing and treating diseases.

Throughout this chapter, we will delve into these and other open issues in the field of neuromorphic computing. We will discuss the current state of the art in addressing these challenges and explore the potential solutions that are being developed. Specifically, we will cover the development of materials properties and device physics, understanding charge/defects migration, fault tolerance, and manufacturability. We will also explore the use of spiking neural networks with hardware acceleration, which is an important area of research in neuromorphic computing. By exploring these topics, we hope to provide a comprehensive overview of the field and shed light on the path forward for neuromorphic computing.

CURRENT STATE OF THE ART IN NEUROMORPHIC COMPUTING

The field of neuromorphic computing has seen significant advancements in recent years, but there are still several challenges that must be addressed in order to fully realize its potential. One of the biggest challenges is the development of new materials and devices with specific quantum properties that can be used in neuromorphic systems. Another challenge is a deeper understanding of charge/defects migration, fault tolerance, and manufacturability in order to make neuromorphic systems more reliable and scalable.

Currently, the state of the art in neuromorphic computing is focused on developing new algorithms and architectures for neural networks. Researchers are exploring novel approaches to training these networks, such as unsupervised learning and reinforcement learning, which may lead to more effective and efficient models. Additionally, there is ongoing work to improve the efficiency and accuracy of neuromorphic hardware, such as by using novel materials and devices, such as memristors and spintronics.

There are also efforts underway to integrate neuromorphic computing with other technologies, such as edge computing and the Internet of Things (IoT). This integration could lead to new applications and use cases for neuromorphic computing, such as in smart homes and cities, where the low power consumption and real-time processing capabilities of neuromorphic systems could be leveraged.

Figure 2. Loihi 2, Intel's second-generation neuromorphic chip (left) and chip die (right) on a fingertip. Introduced in September 2021.
(Intel, 2022)

Another area of active research in the field of neuromorphic computing is the development of more advanced models of neural networks, such as deep neural networks (DNNs) and recurrent neural networks (RNNs). These models have the potential to achieve state-of-the-art performance on a range of tasks, such as image and speech recognition, and they could also be applied to new areas, such as drug discovery and financial forecasting.

The current state of the art in neuromorphic computing is characterized by ongoing efforts to address the key research challenges and to advance the technology in new and exciting ways. As the field continues to mature, it is likely that neuromorphic computing will become increasingly important and widely used in a range of applications, including artificial intelligence, robotics, and beyond.

RESEARCH AND DEVELOPMENT EFFORTS IN NEUROMORPHIC COMPUTING

Neuromorphic computing is an area of active research and development that is focused on several key areas, including:

Materials development is critical for neuromorphic computing, as it relies on the development of new materials that can mimic the behavior of biological neurons and synapses. To achieve this, exploration of new materials such as memristors and spintronics are underway. The potential for more efficient and scalable neuromorphic hardware that can process information in ways closer to biological systems is offered by these materials.

Understanding the **physics of neuromorphic devices** is essential to improving their performance and reliability. This involves the study of the behavior of these devices at the nanoscale and the development of new models and simulations to predict their behavior. Researchers are also investigating new materials and designs that can improve the efficiency and functionality of neuromorphic hardware.

Charge/defects migration within neuromorphic devices can significantly impact their performance. Strategies to mitigate this impact are being developed by studying the mechanisms behind charge and defect migration. This includes the design of new materials and devices that are less susceptible to these effects and the development of new control and calibration methods that can help maintain stable device operation.

To increase the reliability of neuromorphic systems, researchers are developing new techniques for **fault tolerance** such as redundancy and self-repair. This involves the development of new error correction codes and investigation of new designs and architectures that are inherently more fault-tolerant.

Manufacturability is essential for practical real-world applications of neuromorphic hardware. Researchers are exploring new manufacturing techniques and materials to make these systems more easily producible. This encompasses the design, fabrication, and testing processes required to create these complex architectures efficiently and reliably, that can enable large-scale production of neuromorphic hardware.

Spiking neural networks are a type of neuromorphic architecture that uses spikes or pulses of activity to communicate information between neurons. Researchers are developing hardware acceleration techniques such as field-programmable gate arrays (FPGAs) to improve the performance of these networks. This includes developing new algorithms and architectures that can be implemented on hardware and exploring new hardware designs that are optimized for spiking neural networks.

Overall, research and development efforts in neuromorphic computing are advancing the capabilities of these systems and improving their suitability for real-world applications. This research is supported by both industry and academia and is contributing to the continued growth and evolution of the field.

DEVELOPMENT OF MATERIALS PROPERTIES

The development of materials with specific properties is a key challenge in the field of neuromorphic computing. Traditional computing technologies rely on the use of materials such as silicon, which have excellent electrical conductivity and can be easily integrated into electronic devices. However, silicon is not well suited for the emulation of neural systems due to its relatively slow speed and low energy efficiency.

To overcome these limitations, researchers have explored a range of alternative materials that exhibit unique quantum properties and may be more suitable for use in neuromorphic systems. One such material is graphene, a two-dimensional form of carbon that exhibits excellent electrical conductivity and a high charge carrier mobility. Graphene has been shown to be a promising material for the development of neuromorphic devices due to its ability to mimic the properties of neural synapses and its potential for high-speed operation.

Other materials that have garnered attention in the field include transition metal dichalcogenides (TMDs), which are two-dimensional semiconducting materials with excellent electrical and optical properties. TMDs have been shown to exhibit a range of interesting physical phenomena, including valleytronics and spin-orbit coupling, which make them promising candidates for use in neuromorphic devices.

In addition to traditional materials, researchers have also explored the use of new nanostructured materials, such as nanowires and nanotubes, which exhibit unique electrical and optical properties that may be suitable for use in neuromorphic systems. For example, nanowires made of zinc oxide have been shown to exhibit a range of interesting electrical and optical properties, including piezoelectricity and piezotronics, which make them promising candidates for use in neuromorphic devices.

Figure 3. Key elements of neuromorphic computing: memristive materials, cellular memory and learning, and network requirements. Successful implementation of memristive devices in neuromorphic computing relies on reconstructing fundamental components (neurons and synapses) to meet their specific needs. Additionally, the development of adequate models at a cellular level is crucial for the transition to complex system architectures. (Ziegler, 2020).
Retrieved from Sci Rep website: https://doi.org/10.1038/s41598-020-68834-1)

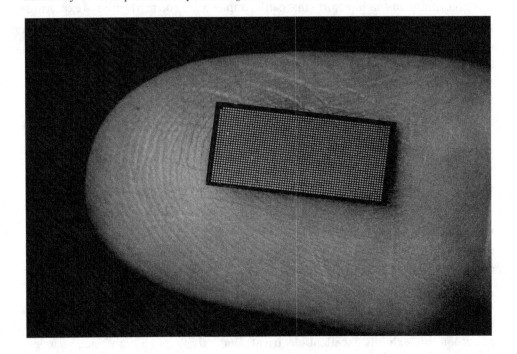

In recent years, researchers (Kim et al., 2020) have been exploring new materials for the Neuromorphic hardware systems that rely on neural networks, which can be divided into two types: deep neural networks (DNNs) and spiking neural networks (SNNs). DNNs require artificial synapses that have analog conductance modulation characteristics, while SNNs require artificial synapses that can emulate the spike-timing-dependent plasticity (STDP) used for unsupervised learning.

The key components of biological neural networks are synapses and neurons. In the human brain, synapses and neurons work together to perform memory and learning functions. Neurons are the basic information processing units, while synapses are the junctions between neurons where information is transmitted. To develop efficient neuromorphic devices that can emulate the functions of synapses and neurons, various types of artificial synapses and neurons have been evaluated.

Functions of Biological Synapses and Neurons

The human brain is composed of synapses and neurons, which together perform memory and learning functions. Neurons are the basic information processing units in a biological brain, consisting of a soma (i.e., cell body), dendrites, and axons. Dendrites receive information from the pre-synaptic neuron, while axons transmit information to the post-synaptic neuron.

Synapses, on the other hand, are the junctions between two neurons where information is transmitted. Synapses can be classified into two types: electrical and chemical synapses. Electrical synapses transmit information through direct electrical coupling between neurons, while chemical synapses transmit information through the release of neurotransmitters.

Artificial Synapses for DNNs and SNNs

A key component of these systems is the artificial synapse, which is responsible for mimicking the synaptic connections between neurons in the brain.

There are two main types of artificial synapses that have been developed: two-terminal devices and three-terminal devices. Two-terminal devices, such as memristors, ferroelectric tunnel junctions (FTJs), and phase change memories (PCMs), operate on the principle of resistance modulation due to ion migration, polarization switching of ferroelectric materials, and phase change of chalcogenide materials, respectively. These devices are attractive for their low power consumption, high endurance, and scalability, making them suitable for use in both deep neural networks (DNNs) and spiking neural networks (SNNs).

On the other hand, three-terminal devices, including electrochemical transistors, ferroelectric transistors, and charge-trapping transistors, can emulate the spike-timing-dependent plasticity (STDP) mechanism used for unsupervised learning in SNNs. The STDP mechanism is based on the idea that the timing of spikes between neurons can change the strength of their synaptic connection, and this is an important feature of biological neural networks.

Among the various types of two-terminal devices, memristors have gained significant attention due to their unique properties, such as non-volatility, scalability, and analog behavior. They are based on the idea of resistance modulation through the movement of ions within the device. Memristors have shown promising results in tasks such as image and speech recognition, and they are being explored for use in neuromorphic systems.

FTJs and PCMs, on the other hand, rely on the polarization switching of ferroelectric materials and the phase change of chalcogenide materials, respectively. FTJs have shown excellent endurance and scalability, making them suitable for use in large-scale neuromorphic systems. PCMs have also shown promise in terms of their scalability and speed, but their endurance is still a challenge.

Three-terminal devices, such as electrochemical transistors, ferroelectric transistors, and charge-trapping transistors, offer additional functionality over two-terminal devices. For example, electrochemical transistors are capable of spike-frequency modulation, which is important for encoding information in SNNs. Ferroelectric transistors can emulate the STDP mechanism and can also act as a synapse and a neuron in the same device. Charge-trapping transistors can also emulate the STDP mechanism and can be used for synaptic weight updates in SNNs.

Artificial synapses are an important component of neuromorphic computing systems, and various types of two-terminal and three-terminal devices have been developed to emulate their function. Memristors, FTJs, and PCMs are among the most promising two-terminal devices, while electrochemical transistors, ferroelectric transistors, and charge-trapping transistors offer additional functionality and are suitable for use in SNNs. As the field of neuromorphic computing continues to evolve, it is expected that new types of artificial synapses will be developed that can further improve the performance and efficiency of these systems.

Artificial Neurons

Artificial neurons can be developed using various types of memory devices such as memristors, PCMs, threshold switching devices, and ferroelectric transistors. Memristors and PCMs are known for their ability to exhibit spiking behavior similar to that of neurons, making them ideal for use in SNNs. Threshold switching devices and ferroelectric transistors, on the other hand, exhibit firing behavior similar to that of neurons, making them suitable for use in DNNs.

Memristors are two-terminal devices that have been extensively studied as artificial neurons due to their ability to modulate resistance based on ion migration. Memristors have shown to exhibit spiking behavior, making them ideal for use in SNNs. PCM, another two-terminal device, uses phase change of chalcogenide materials to store information. Similar to memristors, PCM has also shown to exhibit spiking behavior, making it a promising candidate for artificial neurons in SNNs.

Threshold switching devices, such as SiOx and TaOx devices, are three-terminal devices that can exhibit firing behavior similar to that of neurons (N Wang et al., 2019). These devices can achieve high conductance states at a specific voltage threshold, which can lead to firing behavior. Ferroelectric transistors, which are also three-terminal devices, can exhibit firing behavior by using ferroelectric materials to switch the polarization of the transistor channel (B. Y. Nguyen et al., 2020).

Challenges and Prospects

Despite the progress that has been made in developing neuromorphic devices and systems, there are still many challenges that must be addressed before these technologies can become widely adopted. In this section, we will discuss some of the key challenges that the field is currently facing and the prospects for the future of neuromorphic computing.

Hardware Design and Optimization

One major challenge in neuromorphic computing is the need for more efficient and effective hardware designs that can handle the complex computations required for these systems. The hardware design must be optimized to handle large-scale and parallel computation and be energy-efficient. Currently, neuromorphic hardware is not yet optimized to handle large-scale systems, and there is a need for better integration between hardware and software. Designing a hardware architecture that can efficiently emulate the spiking behavior of neurons is a complex task, but researchers are making progress. One approach is to use memristors, which are resistors with memory that can change their resistance based on the current flowing through them, to create artificial synapses that can learn from input data.

Figure 4. Loihi 2 chip arhitecture
(Intel, 2022)

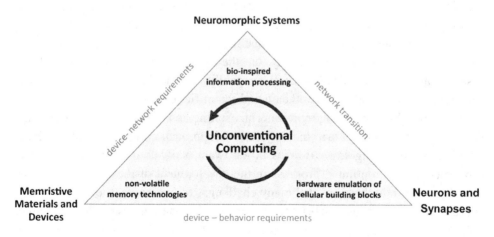

Sophisticated Algorithms

Another challenge in neuromorphic computing is the need for more sophisticated algorithms that can be used to train and optimize these systems. The complexity of neural networks requires advanced algorithms to efficiently process data and optimize the network. To improve performance, algorithms must be designed to take advantage of the hardware architecture to perform computations in parallel. This can be achieved using techniques such as backpropagation, which is a method for training neural networks by adjusting the weights of the network based on the error between the output and the target. The development of efficient algorithms for neuromorphic computing is an active area of research, and researchers are exploring novel techniques such as spike-based coding to improve performance.

Lack of Standardization

The lack of standardization in the field of neuromorphic computing is another significant challenge. This can make it difficult for researchers and developers to collaborate and share ideas. In order to overcome this challenge, there is a need for more open-source software tools and platforms that can be used to develop and test neuromorphic systems. By creating more accessible and standardized platforms, researchers can better collaborate and share ideas, leading to faster progress in the field.

Prospects for Neuromorphic Computing

Despite these challenges, the prospects for neuromorphic computing are promising. As the demand for more powerful and energy-efficient computing continues to grow, neuromorphic systems offer a compelling alternative to traditional computing architectures. By mimicking the way that the brain processes information, these systems have the potential to unlock new capabilities in fields ranging from robotics and autonomous vehicles to healthcare and scientific research.

Neuromorphic computing represents an exciting and rapidly evolving field that has the potential to transform the way that we approach computing and artificial intelligence. With ongoing advances in hardware, software, and algorithms, we can expect to see continued progress in the development of these systems in the years ahead. While there are still many challenges to overcome, the prospects for neuromorphic computing are bright, and it will be fascinating to see what the future holds for this exciting field.

Development of Materials

Finally, the development of materials with specific properties is a crucial aspect of the field of neuromorphic computing and is an active area of research. By developing materials that are more suitable for the emulation of neural systems, researchers hope to overcome key challenges and enable the full implementation of neuromorphic computing. One approach is to use organic materials to create devices that can mimic the functions of neurons and synapses. These devices can be integrated with existing semiconductor technology, leading to more energy-efficient and high-performance systems. Additionally, the use of novel materials such as 2D materials and ferroelectric materials is also being explored to exploit their unique properties for developing neuromorphic devices.

2D materials, such as graphene and transition metal dichalcogenides (TMDs), have emerged as promising candidates for neuromorphic devices due to their exceptional electronic, optical, and mechanical properties. For instance, graphene-based devices can offer high mobility, high mechanical flexibility, and excellent thermal conductivity, which can help in developing high-speed, low-power, and robust neuromorphic devices. Similarly, TMDs can offer high on/off ratios, bandgap tunability, and strong light-matter interaction, which can help in developing optoelectronic neuromorphic devices.

Ferroelectric materials, on the other hand, can offer fast switching speed, low energy consumption, and non-volatility, which can help in developing low-power, high-density, and high-speed neuromorphic devices. Ferroelectric materials such as $Pb(Zr,Ti)O_3$ (PZT) and $BiFeO_3$ (BFO) have been explored for developing ferroelectric memories, logic circuits, and transistors that can exhibit functionalities such as synaptic plasticity, spike-timing-dependent plasticity (STDP), and short-term memory.

Furthermore, the development of new materials and devices for neuromorphic computing is not limited to 2D materials and ferroelectric materials only. Other emerging materials and technologies, such as phase-change materials, magnetic materials, and spintronics, are also being explored for developing novel neuromorphic devices that can offer improved performance and functionality.

The field of neuromorphic computing is facing several challenges that need to be addressed to enable the full realization of its potential. However, with ongoing research and development in hardware, software, algorithms, and materials, the prospects for neuromorphic computing are promising. The development of novel materials with specific properties, such as 2D materials and ferroelectric materials, is a crucial aspect of this field and an active area of research. With the help of these materials, researchers can overcome key challenges and develop new neuromorphic devices that can offer improved performance and functionality for a wide range of applications.

DEVICE PHYSICS

The device physics of neuromorphic devices involves the study of fundamental phenomena, such as electronic transport, charge trapping, polarization switching, and ion migration. For instance, the ion migration and vacancy diffusion in memristors, the polarization switching in ferroelectric materials, and the phase change dynamics in chalcogenide materials are some of the fundamental physical processes that influence the behavior of neuromorphic devices. A deep understanding of these mechanisms helps in optimizing device performance, improving device reliability, and designing novel device architectures.

Another key aspect is the study of device characteristics, which include various electrical, optical, and thermal properties. These characteristics play a vital role in determining the behavior and performance of neuromorphic devices. For instance, the switching behavior of memristors, such as the voltage threshold and the speed of operation, is critical for their application in synaptic emulators. Similarly, the polarization switching behavior of ferroelectric materials in ferroelectric tunnel junctions (FTJs) and the phase change behavior of chalcogenide materials in phase change memories (PCMs) have a significant impact on their synaptic functionalities.

In addition to device physics at the microscopic scale, macroscopic factors such as device integration, circuit design, and system-level considerations also play a significant role in neuromorphic computing. Device scaling, interconnectivity, power consumption, and reliability are some of the challenges that need to be addressed to achieve practical neuromorphic computing systems. Researchers are developing new fabrication techniques, device architectures, and circuit designs to overcome these challenges and enable the integration of neuromorphic devices into large-scale neural networks.

Among the various types of devices investigated for neuromorphic computing, memristors have garnered significant attention due to their unique properties and potential for emulating the functions of biological synapses. In this section, we will delve into the technical aspects of memristor device physics, providing a fundamental understanding of their operation and behavior.

Memristors

Memristors are a type of passive electronic device that can change their resistance in response to applied voltage or current. The term "memristor" was coined by Leon

Chua in 1971, who predicted the existence of such a device based on fundamental circuit theory. However, it was only in 2008 that the first practical memristor device was demonstrated by researchers at Hewlett-Packard (HP) Labs.

Memristors have been of interest to researchers in various fields, including electronics, materials science, and computer science, due to their unique properties and potential applications in memory and computing devices. Memristors are often described as the fourth fundamental circuit element, alongside the resistor, capacitor, and inductor.

Memristor Operation Mechanisms

The operation of memristors is based on the movement of ions or defects in the device material, which can change the resistance of the device. There are several mechanisms that have been proposed to explain the behavior of memristors, including metal ion migration, oxygen vacancy diffusion, and filament formation.

One of the most widely studied types of memristors is the resistive switching memristor. These devices consist of two metal electrodes separated by a thin layer of insulating material, which can be a metal oxide, a polymer, or a semiconductor. When a voltage is applied to the device, a conductive filament can form in the insulating layer, which can change the resistance of the device.

Another type of memristor is the spintronic memristor, which operates based on the manipulation of electron spins. These devices use magnetic materials to control the spin of electrons, which can change the resistance of the device.

Memristor Device Structures

The device structure of memristors plays a critical role in their performance and behavior. Memristors can be fabricated in various device structures, each with unique advantages and limitations. Among the most commonly used device structures are metal-insulator-metal (MIM), metal-insulator-semiconductor (MIS), and metal-oxide-metal (MOM) configurations.

MIM memristors are perhaps the simplest and most straightforward device structure, consisting of a thin insulating layer sandwiched between two metal electrodes. MIM memristors typically exhibit non-linear current-voltage (I-V) characteristics, and they can be fabricated using relatively simple processes. However, MIM memristors have lower endurance and higher variability than other device structures, which limits their usefulness in some applications.

MIS memristors are similar to MIM memristors, but with the addition of a semiconducting material between the metal electrode and the insulator. The incorporation of a semiconducting material allows for transistor-like behavior and additional functionality, making MIS memristors more versatile than MIM memristors. However, MIS memristors are more challenging to fabricate, and they often exhibit higher variability than other device structures.

MOM memristors are perhaps the most complex device structure, consisting of an oxide layer sandwiched between two metal electrodes. The oxide layer can be composed of various materials, including titanium dioxide, tantalum oxide, and hafnium oxide. MOM memristors often exhibit highly non-linear I-V characteristics and complex device behavior due to the presence of the oxide layer. This complexity can be utilized for certain applications that require more complex dynamics, such as neuromorphic computing and non-volatile memory. However, the complexity of the device structure also makes MOM memristors more challenging to fabricate and control. The choice of memristor device structure is a crucial factor in determining the performance and behavior of the device. Each device structure has its unique advantages and limitations, and the selection of the appropriate device structure depends on the specific application requirements.

Materials and Interfaces in Memristors

The properties of memristors are strongly influenced by the materials and interfaces used in the device. The choice of materials can affect the device performance, such as the switching speed, endurance, and retention. The interfaces between the materials can also play a critical role in device behavior, such as the formation and dissolution of conductive filaments.

One of the most important aspects of memristor materials is the presence of defects, such as oxygen vacancies, metal ions, or grain boundaries. These defects can act as trapping sites for charge carriers and can influence the formation of conductive filaments. The presence of defects can also lead to variability in device performance, which can be both a challenge and an opportunity for device optimization.

Switching Mechanisms in Memristors

The switching behavior of memristors is a key aspect of their operation and performance. Memristors can exhibit various types of switching behavior, including unipolar, bipolar, and threshold switching, depending on the device structure, materials, and operating conditions. The switching behavior is controlled by the movement of mobile ions or defects within the device, which leads to changes in the resistance state. The dynamics of these ionic or defect migrations during the switching process are critical to the overall performance of the memristor as a neuromorphic device.

Unipolar switching refers to the change in resistance of a memristor in response to a single polarity of applied voltage, typically either positive or negative. This type of switching is usually observed in transition metal oxides (TMO) memristors, where the resistance change is due to the drift and redistribution of oxygen vacancies within the TMO layer. The oxygen vacancies can migrate under the influence of an applied electric field, leading to a change in the local conductivity and thus the overall resistance of the device.

Bipolar switching, on the other hand, involves the change in resistance of a memristor in response to both positive and negative polarities of applied voltage. This type of switching is often observed in organic and some inorganic memristors, where the resistance change is attributed to the migration of charged species or ions within the active layer of the device. The polarity-dependent migration of charged species can result in the formation or dissolution of conductive filaments, leading to the observed resistance change.

Threshold switching is a unique behavior exhibited by certain memristors where the resistance of the device abruptly switches from a high resistance state to a low resistance state at a specific threshold voltage. This behavior is often attributed to the formation or rupture of conductive filaments within the device, which can occur at a well-defined electric field or voltage threshold. Threshold switching memristors have been proposed for use in neuromorphic computing as they can mimic the spiking behavior of biological neurons, where an abrupt change in membrane potential triggers an action potential.

The understanding of the device physics of memristor switching is crucial for the design and optimization of memristor-based neuromorphic computing systems. It involves a detailed investigation of the materials, interfaces, and mechanisms that govern the switching behavior of memristors. Experimental techniques such as transmission electron microscopy (TEM), X-ray diffraction (XRD), and electrical characterization methods such as current-voltage (IV) measurements, pulse measurements, and impedance spectroscopy, are commonly used to study the device physics of memristors.

The underlying physics of memristor behavior involves the interplay of electronic, ionic, and electrochemical processes. The exact mechanism of memristor switching is still a topic of ongoing research, and different device designs and material systems exhibit different switching mechanisms. For example, in transition metal oxide (TMO) memristors, the migration of oxygen vacancies or metal cations can play a significant role in the resistance modulation, while in organic memristors, charge trapping and detrapping processes may dominate.

One of the key challenges in memristor physics is the non-linearity and variability of the device characteristics. Memristors exhibit highly nonlinear resistance-voltage (R-V) and current-voltage (I-V) characteristics, which can be strongly dependent on the device history, fabrication process, and operating conditions. This non-linearity and variability pose challenges in accurately modeling and predicting the behavior of memristors, and can also impact the reliability and reproducibility of device performance.

Furthermore, the electrochemical processes that take place within the memristor during the switching operation are crucial to understanding the device physics. These processes involve the migration of ions or defects within the active layer, the electrochemical reactions at the electrode-active layer interface, and the formation and dissolution of conductive filaments. The rates of these electrochemical processes, as well as the spatial distribution of ions or defects, can have a significant impact on the resistance modulation and switching dynamics of the memristor.

UNDERSTANDING CHARGE/DEFECTS MIGRATION

As briefly discussed in previous sections, the behavior of memristors is largely determined by the migration of charged defects within the device. Defects can include vacancies, interstitials, and impurities within the material. These defects can create a local region of higher or lower resistance within the device, which can be altered by the application of a voltage or current.

The migration of defects within the device is influenced by a number of factors, including the structure and composition of the device, as well as external stimuli such as temperature and electric fields. Understanding these factors is crucial for designing and optimizing memristor-based neuromorphic devices.

One of the key factors that influences defect migration is the structure of the device. Memristors can be fabricated in a variety of structures, including metal-insulator-metal (MIM), metal-insulator-semiconductor (MIS), and metal-oxide-metal (MOM) configurations. The choice of structure can have a significant impact on the behavior of the device, including its resistance, switching behavior, and stability. For example, MIS memristors can exhibit transistor-like behavior due to the integration of semiconducting materials, while MOM memristors often exhibit highly non-linear current-voltage characteristics due to the presence of an oxide layer.

The composition of the device is another important factor that can influence defect migration. Memristors can be fabricated using a variety of materials, including metal oxides, chalcogenides, and organic materials. Each material has its own unique properties and defects that can impact the behavior of the device. For example, metal oxide memristors often exhibit bipolar switching behavior due to the formation and dissolution of conductive filaments, while chalcogenide memristors can exhibit unipolar switching behavior due to the migration of charged defects.

External stimuli, such as temperature and electric fields, can also influence defect migration within the device. For example, high temperatures can cause defects to migrate more quickly, while the application of an electric field can cause the migration of defects in a specific direction. Understanding how external stimuli influence defect migration is important for optimizing the performance and stability of memristor-based neuromorphic devices.

Let's discuss the physics and mechanisms of charge and defect migration in neuromorphic devices, with a focus on oxide-based devices. We will also explore the methods used to control charge and defect migration in these devices.

Charge Migration in Neuromorphic Devices

Charge migration is the process by which electric charges move through a material due to the application of an external electric field. In neuromorphic devices, the migration of charges is used to encode and process information. The charge migration process can occur through various mechanisms, including drift, diffusion, and tunneling.

Drift is the dominant mechanism of charge migration in most neuromorphic devices. In this process, charges move in response to an electric field, with the speed of migration proportional to the strength of the field. The mobility of charges also depends on the properties of the material, such as its carrier concentration and crystal structure.

Diffusion, on the other hand, is a random process in which charges move due to thermal energy. This mechanism is less dominant in neuromorphic devices, but it can play a role in certain situations where there are gradients in carrier concentration or electric field.

Tunneling is a quantum mechanical process where electrons can pass through potential barriers without being affected by the electric field. This mechanism can occur in some types of neuromorphic devices that have thin barriers, such as memristors.

Defect Migration in Neuromorphic Devices

In addition to charge migration, defects can also play an important role in the behavior of neuromorphic devices. Defects are atomic-scale imperfections in a material that can affect its electronic properties. Examples of defects include vacancies, interstitials, and impurities.

Defect migration can occur due to a variety of mechanisms, including thermal activation, electric field effects, and diffusion. The migration of defects can affect the electrical conductivity of the material, leading to changes in its properties over time.

In some neuromorphic devices, the migration of defects is intentionally used to encode and process information. For example, in phase-change memory (PCM) devices, defects are deliberately created by heating and quenching the material to induce a reversible phase transition between the amorphous and crystalline states. The presence or absence of defects in the material can be used to represent binary information, and the migration of defects can be controlled by applying electric fields.

Charge and Defect Migration in Oxide-based Devices

Many neuromorphic devices are based on oxide materials, such as titanium dioxide (TiO_2) or hafnium oxide (HfO_2). These materials have unique properties that make them well-suited for neuromorphic applications, including high dielectric constants, high breakdown voltages, and the ability to form stable interfaces with other materials.

In oxide-based devices, charge and defect migration can be influenced by a variety of factors, including defects in the oxide layer, oxygen vacancies, and interface states between the oxide and other materials. These factors can affect the performance and reliability of the device, and understanding their behavior is essential for developing reliable and high-performance neuromorphic devices.

Controlling Charge and Defect Migration in Neuromorphic Devices

Controlling the migration of charges and defects is crucial for the reliable operation of neuromorphic devices. One approach to achieving this is through the use of materials engineering and device design.

For example, the choice of material can have a significant impact on the mobility of charges and defects. Materials with high carrier mobility, such as graphene or carbon nanotubes, can offer faster charge migration and reduced susceptibility to defect migration. Additionally, designing the device structure to minimize the effects of impurities and defects can improve the device performance.

Another approach is through the use of external stimuli, such as light or heat, to control the migration of charges and defects. This can be achieved through the use of optoelectronic materials or phase-change materials, which can exhibit reversible changes in their electronic properties under external stimuli.

Device design optimizations, such as the introduction of appropriate interfaces and engineered structures, can minimize charge and defect migration effects. Additionally, compensation techniques, including biasing and annealing, can counteract migration-induced variations, improving device performance and stability. Developing accurate models that capture the intricacies of charge and defect migration, as well as experimental characterization techniques for validation, will enable researchers to gain deeper insights into device behavior and further refine optimization strategies.

FAULT TOLERANCE

The reliability of neuromorphic devices, such as memristors and synaptic transistors remains a significant challenge due to inherent device variations and fabrication imperfections. This section focuses on the topic of fault tolerance in neuromorphic devices, aiming to explore the various fault models, detection methods, and mitigation strategies employed to ensure reliable operation. We will delve into the technical details and discuss the advancements made in this area.

Fault Models in Neuromorphic Devices

To effectively design fault-tolerant systems, it is crucial to understand the different fault models that can occur in neuromorphic devices. Faults can manifest in various forms, including stuck-at faults, resistive faults, variability faults, and aging-related faults. Stuck-at faults occur when a device element is stuck in either the high or low state, failing to switch between states as intended. These faults can be caused by material defects, fabrication errors, or aging effects. Resistive faults arise when the resistance values of the device deviate from their expected values, leading to inaccuracies in computations. Variability faults occur due to process variations during fabrication, causing inconsistencies in the behavior of individual devices. Aging-related faults arise over time as a result of device degradation, leading to performance deterioration.

Fault Detection Techniques

Fault detection is a critical step in ensuring the reliability of neuromorphic devices. Various techniques have been developed to detect faults and identify problematic elements in the device array. These techniques include voltage-based testing, current-based testing, and waveform analysis. Voltage-based testing involves applying specific input signals to the device array and measuring the resulting output voltages to detect any deviations from expected values. By comparing the measured voltages with predetermined thresholds, faulty elements can be identified. Current-based testing focuses on monitoring the current flow through the devices to identify faulty elements. Any significant deviations from the expected current levels indicate the presence of faults. Waveform analysis techniques analyze the shape and characteristics of the output waveforms to detect abnormalities and fault signatures. By comparing the measured waveforms with expected patterns, faults can be detected and isolated.

Fault Mitigation Strategies

Once faults are detected, appropriate mitigation strategies need to be implemented to ensure the continued operation of the neuromorphic device. Several fault mitigation techniques have been proposed, including redundancy-based approaches, error correction codes, adaptive learning algorithms, and reconfiguration techniques. Redundancy-based approaches involve incorporating additional device elements to compensate for faulty ones, ensuring fault tolerance through redundancy. By duplicating or triplicating the critical components of the device array, faults can be bypassed, and the overall system performance can be maintained. Error correction codes, such as parity check codes and Hamming codes, can be used to detect and correct errors in the computations. These codes add additional information to the transmitted data, allowing the receiver to identify and correct any errors that may have occurred during the computation process. Adaptive learning algorithms dynamically adjust the network's parameters to account for faulty elements and maintain accuracy. By continuously monitoring the device behavior and adapting the synaptic weights and connectivity patterns, the system can compensate for the impact of faults. Reconfiguration techniques involve rerouting computations or reallocating resources to bypass faulty elements and maintain system performance. By intelligently reconfiguring the network connections or redistributing the computation load, faulty elements can be isolated, and the overall system reliability can be improved.

Fault-Tolerant Neuromorphic Architectures

In addition to fault detection and mitigation techniques, the design of fault-tolerant neuromorphic architectures plays a crucial role in ensuring reliability. Several architectural enhancements have been proposed to achieve fault tolerance, including hierarchical architectures, adaptive routing, and self-healing mechanisms. Hierarchical architectures involve organizing the neuromorphic system into multiple layers, each responsible for specific functions. By compartmentalizing the system, faults can be isolated to specific layers or regions, minimizing their impact on the overall system performance. Adaptive routing techniques allow the system to dynamically reroute computations and data flow to avoid faulty elements. By monitoring the device behavior and continuously updating the routing paths, faults can be bypassed, and the system can adapt to changing fault conditions. Self-healing mechanisms involve incorporating self-repair capabilities within the neuromorphic device array. These mechanisms can identify faulty elements and automatically reconfigure the device to bypass the faults, ensuring uninterrupted operation.

To validate the effectiveness of fault-tolerant techniques in neuromorphic devices, numerous case studies and experimental evaluations have been conducted. These studies involve the implementation of fault detection and mitigation strategies in various neuromorphic architectures and the analysis of their impact on system reliability and performance. Experimental results demonstrate the successful detection and isolation of faulty elements using voltage-based, current-based, and waveform analysis techniques. The redundancy-based approaches showcase fault tolerance through the duplication and triplication of critical components, ensuring system robustness. Error correction codes exhibit their effectiveness in detecting and correcting errors, improving the overall accuracy of the computations. Adaptive learning algorithms adapt the system's parameters to account for faulty elements, maintaining accuracy and performance. Reconfiguration techniques demonstrate the ability to bypass faulty elements and dynamically adapt to fault conditions. The case studies and experimental results provide concrete evidence of the effectiveness of fault-tolerant techniques in improving the reliability of neuromorphic devices.

A review by M. Liu et al., on "Design of fault-tolerant neuromorphic computing systems," highlighted the current challenges and recent advances in designing fault-tolerant Resistive Random Access Memory (RRAM)-based neuromorphic computing systems (RCS). RRAM, a promising hardware implementation for neuromorphic computing, enables efficient vector-matrix multiplications and significantly improves energy efficiency. However, due to the immature fabrication process, RRAM-based computing systems are susceptible to defects, leading to a drop in accuracy. RRAM, offer solutions for computation-in-memory and multi-level storage, resulting in unprecedented energy efficiency.

However, RRAM-based architectures face reliability challenges due to device faults. The accuracy of practical RRAM circuits for deep learning is limited by device faults in RRAM cells, impacting the recognition accuracy of neuromorphic computing applications. RRAM, as a memristive device, exhibits unique characteristics, such as resistance state switching and multi-level resistance storage. These properties make RRAM compatible with CMOS fabrication processes and enable faster write speeds and lower power consumption compared to flash memory.

RRAM faults can be further classified as soft faults and hard faults. Soft faults arise due to variations associated with fabrication techniques and write/read operations, while hard faults result from resistance being stuck at fixed states, such as SA0 or SA1, which are caused by fabrication defects and endurance limitations.

Testing methods are essential for detecting and identifying faults, improving RRAM yield, and ensuring fault tolerance. The March C* test algorithm, designed for RRAM fault detection, achieves high fault coverage but requires a lengthy test time. On-line fault detection, which focuses on dynamic faults during read and write operations, plays a vital role in fault tolerance. Quick fault detection is essential in this context, and voltage comparison-based methods have been proposed to detect stuck-at faults in RRAM crossbars. These methods compare the actual output with reference outputs in a fault-free scenario. The on-line test solution, based on the voltage comparison technique, achieves high recall and precision rates, ensuring quick fault detection in dynamic scenarios.

Fault tolerance is a critical aspect of any computing system, and this is particularly true in the case of neuromorphic systems. Given the complex nature of neural systems and the large number of components that are typically involved in neuromorphic devices, the risk of failure is relatively high. As such, it is essential to design neuromorphic systems that are able to continue functioning even in the event of component failure or other types of errors.

MANUFACTURABILITY

The successful realization of neuromorphic systems relies heavily on the aspect of manufacturability. The manufacturability of neuromorphic computing encompasses the design, fabrication, and testing processes required to efficiently and reliably create these complex architectures.

Manufacturability in neuromorphic computing addresses the challenges associated with scaling up and mass-producing neuromorphic systems. It involves developing strategies and methodologies to ensure the seamless integration of thousands or even millions of neurons and synapses, while also considering factors such as process variations, scalability, testability, and yield enhancement.

Design Considerations for Manufacturability

Design for Manufacturability (DFM) is a key aspect of ensuring the successful fabrication and yield of neuromorphic systems. Design considerations for manufacturability involve robustness against process variations, scalability to accommodate large-scale integration, and testability to facilitate efficient testing and high yield. Techniques such as redundancy and adaptive calibration, and statistical analysis & modeling methods are employed to enhance design robustness against process variations. Moreover, modular design methodologies and standard interfaces enable scalability by allowing independent fabrication and integration of functional blocks.

Process variations are inherent in the fabrication of integrated circuits and can significantly impact the performance and functionality of neuromorphic systems.

These variations arise due to imperfections in manufacturing processes, material properties, and environmental factors. Designing for robustness against process variations is crucial to ensure consistent performance across different instances of the same design.

Process variations can be categorized into two main types: *systematic variations* and *random variations*. Systematic variations are predictable and repeatable, arising from known sources such as lithography limitations, device parameter fluctuations, and process non-uniformity. On the other hand, random variations are statistical in nature and stem from unpredictable factors like material impurities, temperature gradients, and equipment variations.

Systematic variations can lead to performance deviations across different instances of a design, while random variations introduce statistical uncertainties that affect yield and reliability. Designing for manufacturability in the face of these variations requires careful consideration of the potential sources and their impact on the system's functionality.

One effective approach to address process variations is through the use of **Redundancy** and **Adaptive calibration** techniques. Redundancy involves incorporating additional components such as neurons, synapses, or interconnects in the design. By providing extra resources, the system can adapt and compensate for performance deviations caused by process variations.

Redundancy can be implemented at various levels, including neuron redundancy, synapse redundancy, or even redundant subsystems. The redundant elements are selectively activated or calibrated during the system's operation to compensate for variations in their counterparts. Redundancy can also facilitate fault tolerance, allowing the system to continue functioning even in the presence of faulty components.

Adaptive calibration techniques continuously monitor the system's performance parameters and make necessary calibration adjustments in real-time to maintain accuracy and reliability. It involves measuring key performance metrics, such as synaptic weights, neuron thresholds, or interconnect delays, and dynamically adjusting their values based on the observed variations. Calibration algorithms and feedback mechanisms ensure that the system operates within the desired performance range despite the presence of process variations.

The calibration process can be performed during the system's initialization phase or dynamically during runtime. By adapting to variations, adaptive calibration techniques optimize the system's performance and compensate for deviations caused by process fluctuations.

Statistical analysis and modeling methods provide insights into the behavior and impact of process variations on the system's performance. These techniques leverage extensive data on process variations to identify patterns, correlations, and statistical distributions.

By analyzing the statistical variations, designers can develop models that capture the statistical behavior of different components, such as neurons, synapses, or interconnects. These models can then be used to guide the design process and optimize system performance. Statistical analysis can also guide the selection of appropriate redundancy levels and calibration strategies to account for process variations effectively.

Furthermore, statistical analysis enables the estimation of yield and performance metrics based on process variation data. This information is valuable for optimizing the design and making informed trade-offs between performance, power consumption, and yield.

Fabrication Challenges and Techniques

Fabrication challenges in neuromorphic computing arise from the complex architectures, mixed-signal nature, and incorporation of emerging devices. Mixed-signal integration techniques are employed to seamlessly integrate analog and digital circuits while minimizing noise and interference. The use of emerging devices like memristors and spintronics poses unique fabrication challenges due to their material properties and compatibility with traditional CMOS processes. Furthermore, 3D integration and advanced packaging techniques enable increased system density and efficient signal routing, enhancing overall manufacturability.

Neuromorphic systems typically consist of diverse components, including neurons, synapses, interconnects, and specialized circuits. Integrating these components poses challenges due to their heterogeneous nature and complex interdependencies. Different components in a neuromorphic system may require different fabrication technologies. Ensuring compatibility and seamless integration of various technologies, such as CMOS, memristors, or nanoscale devices, is critical. Techniques such as heterogeneous integration and system-on-chip (SoC) methodologies facilitate the integration of diverse components.

Efficient interconnect fabrication is crucial for enabling proper signal propagation and minimizing delays. Challenges arise in designing and fabricating interconnects with low resistance, high density, and minimal crosstalk. Choosing suitable materials for interconnect fabrication is essential to achieve low resistance, high conductivity, and reliable performance. Some common materials used in interconnect fabrication include:

Copper (Cu): Copper is a popular choice for interconnects due to its excellent electrical conductivity and low resistivity. It offers superior performance compared to traditional aluminum-based interconnects. Fabrication techniques such as physical vapor deposition (PVD) and chemical vapor deposition (CVD) are employed to deposit copper layers onto the substrate.

Low-K Dielectrics: Low-K dielectric materials with a low relative permittivity (K value) are used as insulating layers between interconnects to minimize capacitance and signal delays. Materials such as SiO2, SiCOH, and porous low-K dielectrics are commonly employed.

Barrier and Liner Layers: To prevent copper diffusion and improve adhesion between copper interconnects and dielectric materials, barrier and liner layers are used. Common barrier materials include tantalum (Ta), tantalum nitride (TaN), and titanium nitride (TiN), while liner layers are typically composed of materials like tantalum or tantalum nitride.,

To address the challenges associated with traditional interconnect fabrication, several advanced technologies have emerged in recent years. *3D interconnect technologies* enable vertical stacking of multiple layers, reducing interconnect lengths and improving signal propagation speed. Through-silicon vias (TSVs) and microbump technologies facilitate vertical integration, enhancing interconnect density and system performance.

Carbon nanotubes are promising candidates for interconnect fabrication due to their excellent electrical conductivity and high aspect ratio. CNTs offer lower resistance and higher current-carrying capacity compared to conventional materials. Techniques such as chemical vapor deposition (CVD) and transfer printing are used to fabricate CNT-based interconnects.

Photonic interconnects leverage light-based communication to achieve high-speed and low-latency data transfer. Silicon photonics, for example, integrates optical components with CMOS technology, enabling on-chip photonic interconnects. Photonic interconnects offer advantages such as high bandwidth, low power consumption, and immunity to electromagnetic interference.

3D Integration and Packaging

Stacking multiple layers of circuits and memory can significantly increase system density and reduce interconnect lengths. Through-silicon vias (TSVs), micro-bump bonding, and interposer technologies enable vertical integration and efficient signal routing. Packaging neuromorphic systems requires careful consideration of thermal management, electrical connections, and mechanical stability. Techniques such as flip-chip bonding, through-silicon vias (TSVs), and advanced packaging technologies ensure reliable integration and efficient heat dissipation.

Neuromorphic systems often generate significant heat due to the high-density integration of components and intense computational operations. Heat dissipation techniques, such as heat sinks, heat spreaders, and thermal interface materials, help efficiently transfer heat away from hotspots.

Flip-chip bonding offers high-density and high-speed electrical connections between the chip and the package substrate. It involves directly bonding the active side of the chip to the substrate, enabling shorter interconnect lengths and improved signal integrity. Through-Silicon Vias (TSVs) are vertical interconnects that penetrate the silicon substrate, enabling connections between different layers within the chip or between the chip and the package substrate. TSVs facilitate compact integration, reduced interconnect lengths, and improved electrical performance. Microbump technology involves creating small solder bumps on the chip or package substrate for electrical connections. It enables fine-pitch and high-density interconnections, allowing for efficient signal transmission.

By incorporating thermal management strategies, optimizing electrical connections, ensuring mechanical stability, and leveraging advanced packaging technologies, designers can achieve reliable, high-performance neuromorphic systems that meet the demands of complex cognitive computing applications.

SPIKING NEURAL NETWORKS WITH HARDWARE ACCELERATION

Spiking Neural Networks (SNNs) are a type of artificial neural network that is inspired by the way biological neurons function. SNNs operate by receiving inputs, which temporarily increase their membrane potential. However, this potential gradually decreases due to ion leakage. If multiple inputs are received in rapid succession, the membrane potential may reach a certain threshold voltage, causing the neuron to send an output spike to the neurons it is connected to.

There are various levels of complexity when it comes to modeling SNNs, ranging from the most biologically realistic to the most simplified. Examples of these models include the Hodgkin-Huxley model, which is a detailed model of a biological neuron that includes ion channels and other physiological processes, and the Leaky Integrate and Fire (LIF) model, which is a simpler model that captures the essential characteristics of a biological neuron. Other examples of SNN models include the Quadratic Integrate and Fire (QIF) model, the Adaptive Exponential Integrate and Fire (AdEx IF) model, the Izhikevich model, the FitzHugh-Nagumo model, and the Hindmarsh-Rose model.

Software simulators, such as NEST, Brian, NEURON, and Nengo, can be used to simulate the behavior of an SNN. However, these simulations can be slow, leading researchers to use high-performance parallel computing platforms to speed them up. For instance, the Bluebrain project uses an IBM BlueGene/Q supercomputer with 65,536 cores to simulate large-scale SNNs based on multi-compartment Hodgkin-Huxley models. The SpiNNaker system, on the other hand, is a custom multicore

ARM-based supercomputer that can be used for real-time and low-power simulation of simplified SNN models, such as LIF or Izhikevich. There are also GPU-based simulators, such as the CarlSim3 simulator, which can be used to achieve large-scale SNN simulation [3,6].

In order to make a simulation of an SNN run quickly and use less power, it is necessary to use hardware instead of software. Hardware implementation of SNNs can be more power-efficient than traditional Artificial Neural Networks (ANNs). There are various types of hardware platforms that can be used to develop hardware acceleration of SNN models, such as digital logic implementation with FPGA or ASIC, analog and mixed-signal circuit implementation, and emerging devices such as memristors.

Neuromorphic processors are special types of processors that are used to accelerate certain types of computations, such as image recognition and image segmentation. They often work as co-processors alongside the main processor (CPU) to assist with specific tasks. In contrast to other hardware accelerators, which are designed for a specific task, neuromorphic processors are more versatile because they can be configured to perform any task that can be done with neural networks. Examples of neuromorphic processors include the Qualcomm Zeroth co-processor and the Darwin Neural Processing Unit (NPU).

The Darwin NPU is a neuromorphic hardware co-processor based on the LIF SNN model, designed for embedded applications and with a high level of configurability. It has been prototyped on FPGA and fabricated as an ASIC. The NPU is composed of a network of digital neurons, each of which is connected to a configurable number of digital synapses. The neurons and synapses are implemented using digital logic, allowing for low power consumption and high speed. The NPU also includes a programmable interconnect, which allows for flexible routing of spikes between neurons. This enables the implementation of a wide range of SNN models and applications [6].

To demonstrate the capabilities of the Darwin NPU, the authors of the paper present two demonstration applications. The first application is a simple SNN model for image recognition, which is implemented on the NPU and compared to a software simulation on a CPU. The results show that the NPU is able to perform image recognition faster and with lower power consumption than the CPU.

The second demonstration application is a more complex SNN model for image segmentation, which is also implemented on the NPU and compared to a software simulation on a CPU. The results again show that the NPU is able to perform image segmentation faster and with lower power consumption than the CPU.

In conclusion, the Darwin NPU is a promising hardware accelerator for SNNs. It's hardware architecture is designed to efficiently implement the LIF SNN model, and it has been shown to perform image recognition and image segmentation faster and with lower power consumption than a CPU. The NPU's configurability and versatility make it a valuable tool for a wide range of SNN applications.

SNNs have the potential to revolutionize the field of artificial intelligence, as they offer several advantages over traditional ANNs. For example, SNNs can operate in an event-based manner, meaning they only send output spikes when necessary, rather than continuously outputting a signal. This makes them more energy-efficient and suitable for low-power applications. SNNs can also process temporal information, such as the timing of inputs, which is important for tasks such as speech recognition and natural language processing.

Despite these advantages, SNNs have not yet been widely adopted in industry, partly due to the lack of hardware acceleration. The Darwin NPU and other neuromorphic processors are helping to address this issue by providing a hardware platform for SNNs. As SNN hardware becomes more advanced and widely available, it is likely that we will see an increase in the use of SNNs in a variety of applications.

CONCLUSION

This chapter on Neuromorphic Computing has provided a comprehensive overview of various aspects related to the development, physics, defect migration, fault tolerance, manufacturability, and hardware acceleration of spiking neural networks. Each of these topics contributes to the overall understanding and advancement of neuromorphic computing systems.

Throughout this chapter, we have explored the multifaceted aspects of neuromorphic computing, from the fundamental understanding of materials properties to the practical considerations of manufacturability. The development of materials properties has been instrumental in creating novel materials with desired electrical and synaptic properties, enabling the realization of efficient and reliable neuromorphic devices. The understanding of device physics has deepened our knowledge of the underlying mechanisms and behaviors of these devices, facilitating their optimized design and operation.

One of the significant challenges in neuromorphic computing is charge/defects migration, which can impact device performance and longevity. By studying and mitigating these migration effects, researchers and engineers have made significant progress in enhancing device reliability and robustness. Additionally, fault tolerance techniques have been explored to ensure the resilience of neuromorphic systems in the presence of hardware failures, contributing to their overall reliability and long-term functionality.

The chapter also highlights the importance of manufacturability in neuromorphic computing. With the integration of various components and the fabrication of complex architectures, manufacturability considerations have become paramount. Techniques such as design for manufacturability and process optimization have emerged to address fabrication challenges and ensure high yield and quality in large-scale production.

Moreover, the integration of hardware acceleration for spiking neural networks has accelerated the performance and efficiency of neuromorphic systems. By leveraging specialized hardware architectures tailored to the computational requirements of spiking neural networks, researchers have achieved unprecedented capabilities in cognitive computing, enabling complex tasks such as pattern recognition, decision making, and learning.

The interplay between materials properties, device physics, charge/defects migration, fault tolerance, manufacturability, and hardware acceleration has shaped the development of neuromorphic systems. As we continue to push the boundaries of cognitive computing, these topics will remain at the forefront of research and innovation, driving the next generation of intelligent computing systems. With the collaborative efforts of scientists, engineers, and researchers across various disciplines, neuromorphic computing is poised to revolutionize the field of artificial intelligence and open up new frontiers in cognitive capabilities.

REFERENCES

Christensen, D. V., Dittmann, R., Linares-Barranco, B., Sebastian, A., Le Gallo, M., Redaelli, A., Slesazeck, S., Mikolajick, T., Spiga, S., Menzel, S., Valov, I., Milano, G., Ricciardi, C., Liang, S.-J., Miao, F., Lanza, M., Quill, T. J., Keene, S. T., Salleo, A., & Pryds, N. (2022). 2022 roadmap on neuromorphic computing and engineering. *Neuromorphic Computing and Engineering*, *2*(2), 022501. doi:10.1088/2634-4386/ac4a83

Chua, L. (1971). Memristor—The missing circuit element. *IEEE Transactions on Circuit Theory*, *18*(5), 507–519. doi:10.1109/TCT.1971.1083337

Davies, M., Srinivasa, N., Lin, T. H., Chinya, G., Cao, Y., Choday, S. H., & Plana, L. A. (2018). Loihi: A neuromorphic manycore processor with on-chip learning. *IEEE Micro*, *38*(1), 82–99. doi:10.1109/MM.2018.112130359

De, M. (2017). Darwin: A neuromorphic hardware co-processor based on spiking neural networks. *Journal of Systems Architecture, 77*, 43-51. doi:10.1016/j.sysarc.2017.01.003

Fuller, E. J., Gabaly, F. E., Léonard, F., Agarwal, S., Plimpton, S. J., Jacobs-Gedrim, R. B., & Talin, A. A. (2019). Li-ion transport and electrochemistry in nanoporous Li2O. *Science*, *365*(6453), 1015–1022.

Goi, E., Zhang, Q., Chen, X., Luan, H., & Gu, M. (2020). Perspective on photonic memristive neuromorphic computing. *PhotoniX*, *1*(1), 3. doi:10.118643074-020-0001-6

Hagleitner, C., Hierlemann, A., Lange, D., Kerness, N., Brand, O., Baltes, H., & de Rooij, N. F. (2001). Smart single-chip gas sensor microsystem. *Nature*, *414*(6861), 293–296. doi:10.1038/35104535 PMID:11713525

Harstad, S., Hunagund, S., Boekelheide, Z., Hussein, Z. A., El-Gendy, A. A., & Hadimani, R. L. (2018). Gd-Based Magnetic Nanoparticles for Biomedical Applications. In Magnetic Nanostructured Materials (pp. 137-155). Elsevier. doi:10.1016/B978-0-12-813904-2.00005-X

Hunagund, S. G., Harstad, S. M., El-Gendy, A. A., Gupta, S., Pecharsky, V. K., & Hadimani, R. L. (2018). Investigating phase transition temperatures of size separated gadolinium silicide magnetic nanoparticles. *AIP Advances*, *8*(5), 056428. doi:10.1063/1.5007686

Indiveri, G., Linares-Barranco, B., Hamilton, T. J., Schaik, A., Etienne-Cummings, R., Delbruck, T., Liu, S.-C., Dudek, P., Häfliger, P., Renaud, S., Schemmel, J., Cauwenberghs, G., Arthur, J., Hynna, K., Folowosele, F., Saighi, S., Serrano-Gotarredona, T., Wijekoon, J., Wang, Y., & Boahen, K. (2011). Neuromorphic silicon neuron circuits. *Frontiers in Neuroscience*, *5*, 73. doi:10.3389/fnins.2011.00073 PMID:21747754

Indiveri, G., Linares-Barranco, B., Hamilton, T. J., van Schaik, A., Etienne-Cummings, R., Delbruck, T., & Liu, S. C. (2011). Neuromorphic silicon neuron circuits. *Frontiers in Neuroscience*, *5*, 73. doi:10.3389/fnins.2011.00073 PMID:21747754

Jo, S. M. (2012). Nanoelectronic programmable synapses based on phase change materials for brain-inspired computing. *Nano Letters*, *12*(5), 2179–2186. doi:10.1021/nl201040y PMID:21668029

Kim, M. (2020). Emerging materials for neuromorphic devices and systems. *Iscience* *23*(12).

Kim, S., Kim, T. W., Lee, J., Choi, S., Choi, Y., Kim, S. J., & Hwang, S. (2019). Synaptic electronics towards neuromorphic computing. *Advanced Materials*, *31*(29), 1806133.

Kim, Y., Kim, K. H., Kim, S., Park, S., Park, S., Lee, H. G., & Hwang, S. (2018). Artificial optic-neural synapse for colored and color-mixed pattern recognition. *Nature Communications*, *9*(1), 5106. doi:10.103841467-018-07572-5 PMID:30504804

Kuzum, D. (2013). Synaptic Electronics: Materials Devices and Applications. *Nanotechnology*, *24*(382001). PMID:23999572

Kvatinsky, S., Satat, G., Wald, N., Friedman, E. G., Kolodny, A., & Weiser, U. C. (2014, October). Memristor-Based Material Implication (IMPLY) Logic: Design Principles and Methodologies. *IEEE Transactions on Very Large Scale Integration (VLSI) Systems*, *22*(10), 2054–2066. doi:10.1109/TVLSI.2013.2282132

Li, C. (2018). Recent progress of emerging synaptic devices for neuromorphic hardware. *Advanced Electronic Materials, 4*(10).

Liu, M., Xia, L., Wang, Y., & Chakrabarty, K. (2018). Design of fault-tolerant neuromorphic computing systems. *2018 IEEE 23rd European Test Symposium (ETS)*. IEEE. 10.1109/ETS.2018.8400693

Manju, M. R., Ajay, K. S., & Noel, M. D'Souza, Shivakumar Hunagund, R.L. Hadimani, V. (2018). Enhancement of ferromagnetic properties in composites of BaSnO3 and CoFe2O4, *Journal of Magnetism and Magnetic Materials, 452*.

Mayr, C. G., Andreou, A. G., & Rabaey, J. M. (2012). Design techniques and fault-tolerant approaches in neuromorphic engineering. *Proceedings of the IEEE*, *102*(5), 717–737.

Nguyen, B. Y., & Nguyen, T. D. (2020). Ferroelectric transistors for neurmorphic computing. *Journal of Applied Physics*, *128*(13).

Prezioso, M., Merrikh-Bayat, F., Hoskins, B. D., Adam, G. C., Likharev, K. K., & Strukov, D. B. (2015). Training and operation of an integrated neuromorphic network based on metal-oxide memristors. *Nature*, *521*(7550), 61–64. doi:10.1038/nature14441

Prodromakis, T. (2007). A scalable high performance neural prosthesis with integrated addressable CMOS nanoscale synaptic transistors. *Nanotechnology*, *18*(3).

Saw, A. K., Channagoudra, G., Hunagund, S., Hadimani, R. L., & Dayal, V. (2020). Study of transport, magnetic and magnetocaloric properties in Sr2+ substituted praseodymium manganite. *Materials Research Express*, *7*(1), 016105. doi:10.1088/2053-1591/ab636d

Schuller, I. (2019). *Neuromorphic Computing: From Materials to Systems Architecture Report of a Roundtable Conference*. US DoE | Office of Science

Shi, L. (2015). Development of a neuromorphic computing system. *2015 IEEE International Electron Devices Meeting (IEDM)*. IEEE. 10.1109/IEDM.2015.7409624

Strukov, D. B., Snider, G. S., Stewart, D. R., & Williams, R. S. (2008). The missing memristor found. *Nature, 453*(7191), 80–83. doi:10.1038/nature06932 PMID:18451858

Wang, N., Shu, L., & Jiang, L. (2019). Threshold Switching Memristive Devices for Neuromorphic Computing. *Advanced Intelligent Systems, 1*(5).

Wang, Z. (2017). Memristors for energy-efficient, neuromorphic computing. *Nature Materials, 16*(9), 101–110. doi:10.1038/nmat4756 PMID:27669052

Xia, Q., (2019). Memristor-CMOS hybrid integrated circuits for reconfigurable logic. *Advanced Materials 31*(4).

Yang, J. J., Strukov, D. B., & Stewart, D. R. (2013). Memristive devices for computing. *Nature Nanotechnology, 8*(1), 13–24. doi:10.1038/nnano.2012.240 PMID:23269430

Ziegler, M. (2020). Novel hardware and concepts for unconventional computing. *Scientific Reports, 10*(1), 11843. doi:10.103841598-020-68834-1 PMID:32678249

Chapter 3
An RRAM–Based Neuromorphic Accelerator for Speech–Based Emotion Recognition

Afroz Fatima
Birla Institute of Technology and Science Pilani, Goa, India

Abhijit Pethe
Birla Institute of Technology and Science Pilani, Goa, India

ABSTRACT

A neuromorphic accelerator for a deep net having RRAM based processing elements has been implemented for emotion detection based on dialect. The proposed accelerator has been trained on the RAVDESS dataset in order to classify different emotion types. The RRAM based swish activation function has been employed to build the neuromorphic accelerator as it consumes less power (476μW), has lower operating voltage (1.23V), and has better performance and output characteristics. The proposed neuromorphic accelerator has been implemented using 1T-1RRAM Processing Elements on ST Microelectronics 28nm FD-SOI, also on Intel i3-8130U CPU and compared with NVIDIA GeForce GPU to highlight the advantages. The proposed accelerator achieves high-performance and consumes less power (1780μW) with on/off rate (13.81) and lower operating voltage (2V). The training accuracy for the FD-SOI implementation is 79.13% and has a learning rate of 0.01 and weight update interval of 1 epoch. This chapter also highlights the importance of the proposed neuromorphic accelerator from Industry 4.0 perspective.

DOI: 10.4018/978-1-6684-6596-7.ch003

INTRODUCTION

Industry 4.0 or Fourth Industrial Revolution (4IR) is a popular term or phrase being used by academicians and industry professionals to highlight the conjunction of different technological advances like artificial intelligence, autonomous robots, gene editing etc. (Philbeck & Davis, 2018), (Chunguang et al., 2020), (Klaus, 2015). This conjunction has allowed realization of smart machines that are capable of handling wide spread societal and industrial problems with lesser human intervention. Several manufacturing technologies, process, applications going by few common phrases and names like Industrial Internet of Things (IIoT), cognitive computing, cyber-physical systems, cloud computing, edge/fog computing are being widely discussed in literature to define the advancements as part of Fourth Industrial Revolution (Armando et al., 2014), (Colombo et al., 2017). Though, to an extent the 4IR is being driven towards reality, but there still remain few social (Reluctance, Privacy), economic (Excessive Investments, Higher Costs), regulatory, legal along with few infrastructure and organizational issues (UK Gov Department for Business, 2019), (MinHwa, 2018), (Pedota & Piscitello, 2021), (Bresnahan et al., 2002). Apart from these, one more prominent challenge is that of 'Computing'. With huge amounts of data emanating through several sources, handling the computations responsible for generating adequate responses in a stipulated time/real-time has become a challenge. Neuromorphic Systems are being developed with novel-memory devices as candidates to handle such challenges (Mandal et al., 2014), (Geoffrey et al., 2017). This chapter proposes a novel neuromorphic accelerator for emotion recognition through speech and elaborately discusses its advantages and ability in addressing this challenge to some extent.

Emotion or neurophysiological behavior is a key aspect in judging a human personality. Interpreting the emotional psychology of human is naturally a complex motive to be fulfilled. The emotion can be expressed in a variety of ways such as expressions from face, spoken words, written phrases, physiological behavior etc. (Caridakis et al., 2007) (Kim et al., 2003). Understanding how a target emotion is observed or how the humans react to different life scenarios is an interesting and challenging topic for solving complex real-time problems (Manfredi & Gribaudo, 2008). This study can be applied in fields such as entertainment industry, education, health care, social platforms, stress monitoring and as a personal assistant to an individual (Poria et al., 2019). This study can also help resolve high-risk threats to a human's life while in emergency situations, blind personnel, an autistic child etc. (Lefter, 2011). Psychology/Emotion/Brain behavior are the topics very closely related. Given a scenario where a person is emotionally experiencing a particular feeling due to a bad day at work, their brain starts gathering all negative emotions until the situation is relaxed to a normal. Various abstractions through which the brain experiences change in emotion and projects different level of spikes establishing assortment of emotions are the critical points to be examined. Remarkable technological advancements have been achieved over time for evaluating human emotions accurately through certain automated techniques (John & John, 1998). Some popularly grown AI products as stated in (Kim et al., 2003) (Manfredi & Gribaudo, 2008) (John & John, 1998) (Robert et al., 2002) can predict the emotional state of a person in different ways. Also, the recent products and technology that can interpret the emotional intelligence of a human through speech include Apple's Emotient (DeMuth, 2016), MIT's Affectiva (Bosker, 2017), Eyeris's Emovu Driver Monitor System (Wayne, 2016) and nascent AI virtual assistants like Apple's Siri (William, 2019), Amazon's Alexa (Catherine, 2019), Google Assistant (Gemma, 2018) and Microsoft's Cortana (Gemma, 2018). These voice-based AI assistants are based on machine learning techniques such as convolutional neural networks (LeCun & Bengio, 1995), long short-term memory (Sepp & Jürgen, 1997) and deep learning (Goodfellow et al., 2016). Another interesting IoT based application is that of a hand sanitizer dispenser with temperature and level monitoring that gives out alerts in the form of human voice (Dhanasekar et al., 2022). Also, the statistical machine learning techniques such as Support Vector Machines (SVM) (Cortes & Vapnik, 1995), Bayesian Networks (Miyakoshi & Kato, 2011) have been widely employed for classifying emotions.

However, evaluating a true (or correct) emotion type involves multiple selection methods before the emotion can be detected. Certain factors that are necessary involve; selection of suitable machine learning algorithm (supervised/unsupervised) based on a target network so that the neural network learns to categorize the correct emotion type, the architecture to be created based on various levels of abstraction, annotated data vital for training a neural network and other desired design/ parametric considerations as detailed in section 3.

In this chapter, a popular deep learning approach called as Backpropagation (BP) algorithm has been considered for training the network and to derive the neurons as emotion classifier because this technique performs computations at much faster rate as compared to other learning techniques, it is an accurate method for calculating the error in a network, standard and efficient technique for image and speech recognition applications (Abdelwahab & Busso, 2015) (Ciota, 2005). Further, in (Ciota, 2005), described the possibilities of modern emotion recognition and its usefulness in verification systems while highlighting the choice of feature vectors as an important task. Fundamental frequency (speaking) and time-energy distribution vector were considered as important vectors for emotion recognition. The methods proposed by the author allows the comparison of features (Stored vectors of emotions recorded prior vs current speaker voice). Besides this, the author has also highlighted few possibilities for hardware realizations. Also, the authors discuss about categorizing the emotion into 8 different states. The speech-based emotion detection is the topic of interest in this chapter. Vocal based emotion identification has been an active area of research over the last two decades due to its real-life applications mainly in the areas of Human-Computer Interaction, as it is prevailing and efficient in determining the affective state of human (Schmitt et al., 2016).

Emotion recognition through speech has seen tremendous interest among researchers as it directly or indirectly has an influential role for the futuristic technologies like face-to-face interaction that are generally mediated by computers. Human-computer interaction is the main aim with which the majority of the international research community on speech-based technologies is being driven. This has further allowed to work on sub-challenges like automatic emotion recognition through continuous time acoustic low-level descriptors etc. End-to-End learning by way of machine learning where in the meaningful interpretations on the data is done by deploying Deep Neural Networks (DNN) and it is often seen as prominent ways of automatic emotion recognition. Much of the chapter moving further discusses the same, with a way of architecting such DNNs with help of Novel Memory Devices for automatic emotion recognition through speech-based data (Schmitt et al., 2016). However, classifying the emotions based on voice clips in machines/robots is increasingly challenging (Lee & Narayanan, 2005).

Developing algorithms for conversational interfaces may not be seen as a practical solution both in terms of quality and quantitative limitations. Data driven approaches, though in nascent stages are yet being seen as powerful tools when accompanied by real-time data from dialog systems of several call-centers (government or non-government) to classify the positive and negative emotional status of human beings. There has been a wide practice to judge user's state of emotion by way of spoken language information (lexical, acoustic etc.). Methods like k-nearest neighbors, Fisher linear discrimination methods, kernel regression, Bayes classification were all have been explored for emotion recognition from speech (Lee & Narayanan, 2005).

An extremely innovative and breakthrough hardware that caters to the Artificial Intelligence (AI) neuromorphic accelerator is indeed a requirement. Some of the predominant emotion based neuromorphic accelerators include; IBM's True north (Diehl, 2016) chip for power optimized and high-speed ML applications that garners NVM devices (RRAM and PCM) for its layout. The Fully Connected Neural Network (FCNN) of the IBM's chip is built upon the backpropagation training principle along with the Rectified Linear Unit (ReLU) for its implementation. This method considers word and sentiment pairs for training and analyzing the chip. Alternatively, the FCNN is also converted to a Spiking Neural Network (SNN) for fast bit-processing and is power efficient up to 50μW (Diehl, 2016). However, the performance of the FCNN architecture after converting it to SNN is at a toss when the weight discretization to be able to map to its original network is concerned. Also, while retraining and relearning the network, achieving the proper encoding and compatibility is extremely challenging in order to retain the original network's behavior.

Chen's group proposed DaDianNao (Chen et al., 2014) which is a multi-chip accelerator for Convolutional Neural Network (CNN) and Deep Neural Network (DNN) applications, considers a pipelined computational approach to understand the neuron classifications. However, this approach has major limitations in terms of memory bandwidth requirements for the synapses, besides increasing the energy cost up to 10x (Chen et al., 2014). (Esmaeilzadeh, 2012) has proposed to use an MLP accelerator to speed up (by approximating) certain functions within a program. With the tremendous emergence of AI, the emotion detection forms a basis for producing machines/robots that are capable of replicating human intelligence. The authors in (Esmaeilzadeh, 2012) have also successfully demonstrated the ability of neural accelerators to mimic diverse regions of approximal imperative code. While developing the hardware accelerator for the said application, the authors also saved significantly on energy (3x less energy) and increase in speed (2.3x) when the program level transformation considered different neural network topologies in contrast to a single topological execution and being tightly coupled with the main or host processor's pipeline. Additionally, the authors have also highlighted the quality loss to the tune of 9.6% in their work. The authors also claimed that Neural Processing units are a new class of accelerators that has the capacity of being trained for a potential application in the electronic domains of analog and digital. Emotion recognition also serves as a pathway at solving complex neuro AI based problems (Schmitt et al., 2016) (Diehl, 2016). Conventional analog/mixed-signal based neuromorphic accelerators have been widely introduced using planar Complimentary-Metal Oxide Semiconductor (CMOS) process (Musisi-Nkambwe et al., 2021).

Reducing memory fetches (reads and writes) for the required data and dependent computations has been a necessity while addressing the challenges of today's artificial intelligence-based applications. Architectures involving crossbar arrays designed with memristive devices to offer in memory computing have been developed to address few computational and memory related challenges but there still remains huge gap in research, in terms of variations that the circuitry and novel devices has to offer while designing the intended artificial intelligence-based analog-mixed signal architectures. Design challenges pertaining to off-chip communication through bus-networks and on-chip communication through network on-chip techniques also play a major role in attaining required performance metrics. The architects while designing neuromorphic accelerators using novel memory devices especially in the domain of analog or mixed signal, have to also take into consideration several circuit non-idealities, device variation, retention ability while maintaining required classification and training rates as per the algorithms considered. The design complexity further increases when pipelining of data through several crossbar nodes. Data processing/handling would become a major concern while aiming to achieve quality timing sign-off for the designed chips in such complex hierarchies (Musisi-Nkambwe et al., 2021).

In this chapter, the Fully-Depleted Silicon on Insulator (FD-SOI) technology-based neuromorphic accelerator has been simulated, as it consumes low power, requires lower operating voltage, is fast and has efficient performance over a network when employed with RRAM devices (ST Microelectronics, 2016) (ST Microelectronics, 2017). Market segment-based application benefits with 28nm FD-SOI technology include efficient RF and analog integration, ultra-low voltage operation that is essential need for Internet of Things (IoT) and wearable devices. As part of automotive, well managed leakage in high temperature environments and high reliability. Energy-efficient multicore networking infrastructure and optimized System on Chip integration to enable consumer and multimedia applications. The standard cell libraries of STMicroelectronics were used in this work to realize the said FD-SOI technology node and is augmented by specifically designed libraries for high performance and low-power applications. Also, the IO library of the STMicroelectronics 28nm FD-SOI offers dedicated functionalities that serve efficiently the analog Intellectual Property (IP) blocks along with multiple supply voltages and chip-layout configurations. Support for various industry standard IO protocols like USB, GPIO, I²C etc., is also provided. Technical advantages of using 28nm FD-SOI based technology also include body-biasing, good device electrostatics and wide operating voltage range. Another notable advantage of 28nm FD-SOI technology design used in this work include the immunity it has to offer against radiation. This technology offers high resilience to the radiation-based errors due to its ultra-thin body and buried oxide. The devices using this technology especially in sectors like automotive, space and medical offer parallel benefits of immunity against radiation errors besides intrinsic benefits of 28nm FD-SOI technology (ST Microelectronics, 2016) (ST Microelectronics, 2017).

Emerging potential memory candidates such as memristors has also been explored lately for the implementation of analog/mixed-signal based neuromorphic accelerators (Du et al., 2015) (Chang et al., 2019) (Xiao, 2020) (Sun et al., 2021). Especially authors in (Chang et al., 2019) have presented an innovative micro-architectural design of deep neural networks implemented through crossbar arrays of memories (analog). Interestingly, the authors have transferred the data in parallel fashion between arrays without the use of ADCs (Analog-to-Digital Converters). Further, to increase the efficiency of circuit the authors adopted few techniques that include source follower-based readout, transmit-by-duration, array segmentation etc. However, the design and analysis by the authors were carried out for full CMOS - 90nm technology node where in the simulations were extensively used to demonstrate both the deep neural network inference and training. Besides, the authors have also discussed elaborately the main challenges in designing analog based artificial intelligence systems.

(Sun et al., 2021), explored the effects of emotion inhibition and fatigue (mental) which are generally the self-regulation behaviours of the brain on the memory. The authors investigated this on the basis of emotion congruent memory. The authors implemented circuits for emotion activation function, variable learning rate and full-function memory besides forgetting and learning. The authors used memristors to achieve the said goal of design of neural network circuit of emotion congruent memory while verifying it using simulation-based results.

In this chapter, the Resistive Random-Access Memory (RRAM) (Chen & Yu, 2015) and Google brain's swish activation function (Ramachandran et al., 2017) has been used to implement and analyze the analog/mixed-signal based neuromorphic accelerator for audio-based emotion identification on 28nm FD-SOI. The chapter has been structured in the following way; section 2 discusses the proposed neural network architecture on which the training has been performed using a prominent speech dataset, section 3 elaborates the hardware implementation procedure of the 28nm RRAM based neuromorphic accelerator for identifying emotion types, section 4 presents the results of the architecture through a comparison from literature, section 5 concludes the chapter and section 6 presents future direction.

RELATED WORK

The novel RRAM based neuromorphic accelerator has been designed using 28nm process node for the target application of categorizing human emotion from speech. The speech accelerator works on the principle of deep learning technique called as Backpropagation. The training architecture has been designed using metal-oxide based RRAM devices having bipolar switching characteristics which has been calibrated with IMEC's TiN/Hf/HfO$_x$/TiN (Chen & Yu, 2015). The I-V characteristics of the RRAM device is modelled as per the eqn. (1) which explains the device switching behavior when a voltage or current is applied. Also, when the input voltage or current is applied to the RRAM device, the device switches its conductance state from High Resistance State (HRS) to Low Resistance State (LRS) and vice-versa which represents the respective set and reset process of the device. Therefore, this change of state is due to the movement of oxygen molecules in the insulator region (Hf/HfO$_x$) of the device when the voltage is applied to their top and bottom terminals.

I-V relationship of the RRAM model is given as (Chen & Yu, 2015),

$$I = Io \ exp\left(\frac{-g_x}{g0}\right) \sinh\left(\frac{V}{V0}\right) \tag{1}$$

where, 'g_x' is the gap distance between Top Electrode (TE) and Conductive Filament (CF) tip and 'I_0', 'g_0', 'V_0' are the fitting parameters.

The RRAM neuromorphic accelerator makes use of the forward-propagation and backward-propagation process for its implementation on 28nm FD-SOI technology. The analog circuit implementation of the forward-propagation method can be attained by propagating the data inputs in forward-mode (i.e., left to right) movement and the same is based on the eqn. (2). This implementation makes use of two crossbar array circuits and the activation functions in order to understand the forward-propagation principle and to map the neuron behavior. Further information about the design procedure can be seen in (Fatima & Pethe, 2021) (Fatima & Pethe, 2022a) (Fatima & Pethe, 2022b) using 180nm CMOS and 28nm FD-SOI technology.

Also, the RRAM neuromorphic accelerator implements the novel backpropagation training architecture with the help of the analog/mixed-signal RRAM based circuits. The RRAM based training architecture comprises of the novel RRAM based swish activation function and its derivative circuitry from eqn. (4), the error calculation and its derivative circuitry formulated from eqn. (5) to (7), the RRAM based weight update and sign control circuitry for the memory read/write upgrade implemented using RRAMs and transistor devices. The authors in (Fatima & Pethe, 2021) discusses the inference and training assumptions considered for the implementation.

In this chapter, a deep net of 20 input layer neurons, 22 hidden layer neurons and 8 output layer neurons are considered for the implementation of audio-based emotion accelerator. Crossbar array structures have been considered for accurate, fast multiply and accumulate operation of the row-column matrices called as the synapse matrix. The neuron-synapse have been represented using RRAM devices to form a better neural model as they have; better switching characteristics, utilize low power, have better data density than DRAM, perform faster than FLASH memory, and are reliable and resilient in nature (Chen & Yu, 2015).

Also, this chapter uses the novel design of RRAM based swish activation function implemented on 180nm and 28nm technology and has been discussed in (Fatima & Pethe, 2021) (Fatima & Pethe, 2022a) (Fatima & Pethe, 2022b) for improving the overall efficiency of a neural training architecture. The 20x22x8 neural network has been trained on the Ryerson Audio-Visual Database of Emotional Speech and Song (RAVDESS) dataset (Livingstone, 2018) for identifying eight different emotion states. The various neuron emotions classified are angry, happy, sad, fearful, calm, neutral, disgusted and surprised. The training performance has been evaluated using

Cadence, Matlab and Spyder IDE platforms. The neuromorphic accelerator has been discussed elaborately in section 3 and 4.

Highlights of the chapter:

- An RRAM based neuromorphic accelerator for vocal based emotion recognition has been designed, implemented and verified using simulations which is first of its kind using 28nm FD-SOI technology node.
- The proposed training architecture has been verified using RAVDESS dataset for characterizing different emotion states.
- The proposed FD-SOI based hardware accelerator shows better performance and characteristics as compared to the CPU based implementations.
- This chapter also showcases comparative analysis of the RRAM neuromorphic accelerator with the existing GPU based systems.

HARDWARE IMPLEMENTATION OF RRAM NEUROMORPHIC ACCELERATOR ON 28NM FD-SOI

Design and Implementation of 20x22x8 RRAM Neural Network Architecture

A deep net has been designed using 20 input layer neurons, 22 hidden layer neurons and 8 output layer neurons as depicted in Fig1. An analog/mixed-signal neuromorphic accelerator for the 20x22x8 neural network is designed using two Processing Elements (PEs) containing the RRAM devices as the neuron-synapse circuit elements, an error circuitry, a swish activation function circuitry and a memory read/write circuitry for its implementation as discussed in the following sub-sections.

The training steps of the proposed 20x22x8 accelerator are discussed through a flowchart shown in Fig2 comprising of two major steps – Forward Pass and Backward Pass – implemented using two 1T-1RRAM crossbars following a memory-update step. The Forward Pass block helps implement the inference process (*left-to-right*) and the Backward Pass block helps implement the backpropagation process (*right-to-left*) by utilising the sub-circuitry such as the derivative of the swish activation function, the error calculation, the derivatives of error at the hidden and output layers besides updating of memory, if the error attained is maximum at the output neurons. Presumably if the error obtained is minimum, then the model is certain to classify the correct category of emotion that has been trained on the model as discussed below.

The crossbar mainly comprises of the 1T-1RRAM structure to attain better performance characteristics, compact design, low power consumption etc. of the training architecture. Each crossbar array functions as a Processing Element (PE) of the RRAM based neuromorphic accelerator as shown in Fig3. Also in this implementation, the network comprises of a total of 616 synaptic weight connections which are driven by the crossbar array circuitry and allied with the individual neuron unit. Additionally, the network has been designed and computed using the stochastic gradient descent technique (Backpropagation circuit). RRAM based crossbar elements are rapid at evaluating the individual columnar currents for a given input voltage (x_i or V_i) with their RRAM conductance (w_i or G_{ij}) at each unit in the rail as described in eqn. (2) and (3).

Figure 1. Neural network having 20x22x8 neurons

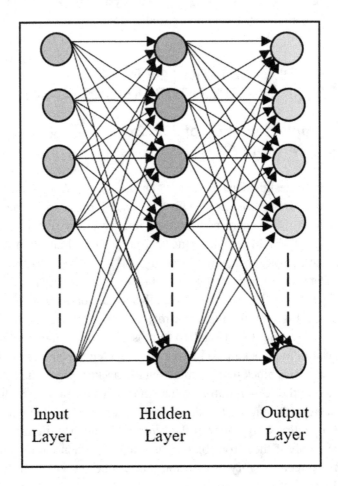

Input Layer   Hidden Layer   Output Layer

Figure 2. Flowchart of the Neuromorphic accelerator for a 20x22x8 model

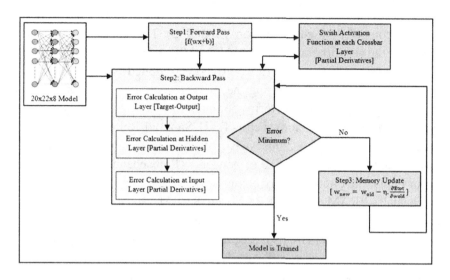

Figure 3. RRAM based neuromorphic accelerator for emotion detection

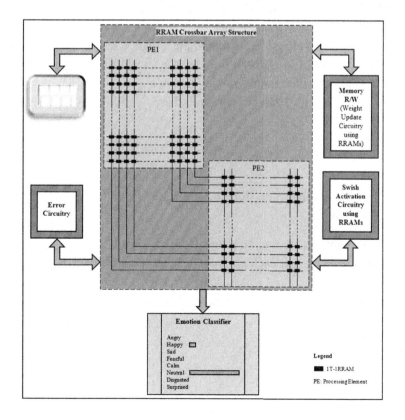

In order to analyze the performance of the proposed neuromorphic accelerator for the task of speech-based emotion recognition, initially the forward propagation operation is computed based on the eqn. (2) and (3). This operation combines the learning over the network through RRAM based PEs employed in the circuit. Also, the RRAM based swish activation function has been applied as a non-linear element and is shown in Fig4a for conferring the firing potential of a neuron. The swish activation function generally performs computations at a faster rate and is power efficient as compared to functions such as TanH, Sigmoid, ReLU, GeLU etc. (Fatima & Pethe, 2021). Importantly, this swish function is suitable for speech-based approaches and also for larger size of networks (Ramachandran et al., 2017). As shown in Fig4a, the circuit mainly comprises of transistors T_1 to T_{10} (N-Channel and P-Channel), RRAM devices ($RRAM_1$ and $RRAM_2$) and a multiplication circuit to produce the swish functionality implemented using ST Microelectronics 28nm FD-SOI technology. This circuit is operated by a DC voltage (V_{dd}) and the bias voltages ($\pm V_2$) at the transistors T_1 and T_2 are used to switch on/off the transistors from T_3 to T_{10}. Upon a high input voltage at the gates of the transistors T_3 and T_5, it allows the conduction of voltage through T_5 and no conduction through T_3 whereas, a low input voltage to T_3 and T_5 reverses the conduction behavior. As a result of the conduction, the devices $RRAM_1$ and $RRAM_2$ are turned on/off and changes their state from high-to-low and low-to-high i.e., a set/reset process for a fraction of time (milli-seconds or less) which is attained due to switching of oxygen molecules at the invoke of a typical voltage. Apparently, the signal x_1 and x are combined with the multiplication circuit in order to produce the swish functionality having non-monotonicity and one-sided boundedness at zero.

Output of a Neuron (N_o) can be represented as,

$$N_o = f\left(w_i x_i + bias\right) \qquad (2)$$

where; 'f' is the swish activation function given as $f\left(x\right) = \dfrac{x}{1+e^{-x}}$ (Ramachandran et al., 2017);

w_i are the weights and x_i are the inputs (for i=1 to n).

The output current (I_o) at each column in the grid can be expressed as,

$$I_o = \Sigma(Gij \times Vi) \qquad (3)$$

where; i and j = 1,2,3...n

The swish activation circuit is further used to perform derivative function as part of the backward propagation process which is a next step towards implementing the accelerator circuit. The swish derivative circuitry consists of blocks such as sigmoid circuit, sigmoid derivative circuit, multiplication and adder circuits combined together to compute the first order derivative of swish activation function designed and computed based on the eqn. (4) and shown in Fig4b. The sigmoid and its derivative circuits are simple transistor circuits implemented to behave as non-linear elements and are elaborated in (Fatima & Pethe, 2022a). Performing the swish derivative is one of the steps in the training of 20x22x8 architecture.

The first order derivative of swish activation function (f') is given as,

$$f'(x) = \frac{df(x)}{dx} = \sigma(x) + x.\sigma(x).(1 - \sigma(x)) \tag{4}$$

where; the sigmoid function is, $\sigma(x) = \dfrac{1}{1 + e^{-x}}$

Besides the above steps, the error function and their derivatives are also computed and implemented in order to perform rigorous training on the speech-based emotion architecture using 28nm process node. The purpose of this computation on error and its derivative circuitry is to minimize the network loss and also to enhance the learning performance and adaptation of the neural net. The error in the 20x22x8 network is typically computed from the eqn. (5) which helps in reducing the loss among the layer neurons. The analog circuit of the E_{Net} is depicted in Fig5a comprising of two difference amplifiers, two multipliers and an analog switch circuit to derive the error E_{Net} in the speech-based accelerator. It is also apparent to compute the first order derivative of the error function at both the hidden and output layer of the 20x22x8 neural network. This is performed using eqns. (6) and (7) and designed in Fig5b and Fig5c respectively. The Fig5b, shows the derivative of error at hidden layer neurons consisting of different block circuits such as Current to Voltage converter, difference amplifier, inverting amplifier, analog switch and multiplier. Each of these blocks serve the purpose of defining the $\dfrac{\partial E_h}{\partial w_{ij}}$ in the network. Likewise, the derivative of error at output layer neurons is also computed as shown in Fig5c containing certain block circuits such as inverting amplifier, difference amplifier, analog switch and multiplier in order to compute the $\dfrac{\partial E_o}{\partial w_{jk}}$ in the network. Here, the V_1, V_2 and V_3 are the threshold voltages in the respective circuits.

The error in the network is calculated as,

$$E_{Net} = \frac{1}{2} \sum_{i=1}^{n} \left(Target - Output \right)^2 \tag{5}$$

where; 'n' is the no. of neurons in the layer.
The error derivative at hidden layer,

$$\frac{\partial E_h}{\partial w_{ij}} = X'.\delta_h = X'.\left(e_h . \frac{\partial N_{oh}}{\partial w_{ij}} \right) \tag{6}$$

The error derivative at output layer,

$$\frac{\partial E_o}{\partial w_{jk}} = N_{oO}.\delta_O = N_{oO}.\left(e_O . \frac{\partial N_{oO}}{\partial w_{jk}} \right) \tag{7}$$

Figure 4. Circuitry for swish activation function using RRAMs

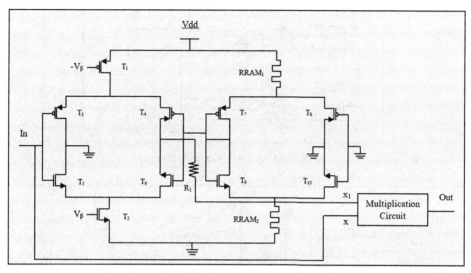

a.   Circuit for Swish Activation Function

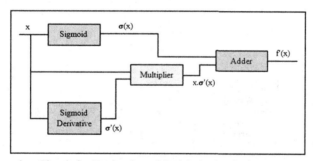

b.   Circuit for Derivative of Swish Activation Function

Figure 5. Circuitry for error and derivative of error in the 20x22x8 network

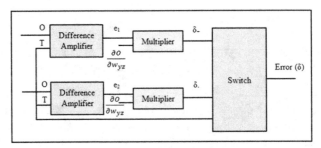

a. Circuit for Error Computation

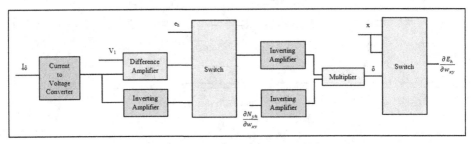

b. Circuit for Derivative of Error at Hidden Layer

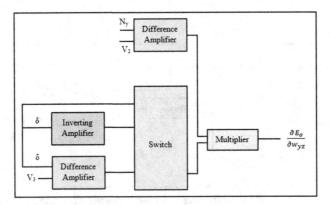

c. Circuit for Derivative of Error at Output Layer

Lastly, an RRAM based memory read/write circuitry is used to perform the read and write operation in the emotion based neuromorphic accelerator. This is done by adjusting the RRAM conductance in the PEs depending upon the error drop or mis classification ratio observed from a neuron as computed in the above steps. The memory update circuitry mainly consists of four op-amps, two RRAM devices and an analog switch designed from eqn. (8) and shown in Fig6a. The purpose of this circuitry is to update the memory (read/write) when the error in the 20x22x8 neural network is high. This circuitry continuously updates the conductance in the RRAM devices during the training process. Once the error in the network is minimal, the training of the network is stopped and the learning behavior is noted. The detailed implementation procedure and the operating parameters of the individual circuits of the neural network training architecture have been discussed in (Fatima & Pethe, 2021) (Fatima & Pethe, 2022a) (Fatima & Pethe, 2022b). The resource utilization of the RRAM based neuromorphic accelerator are also stated in Table1. The speech-based emotion accelerator has been implemented using STMicroelectronics 28nm FD-SOI technology having width of 80nm and length of 30nm for the NFET/PFET transistors. The RRAM based neuromorphic circuit is trained in order to compute the learned behavior of a network. The circuit is trained and the weights are updated in the RRAM devices over multiple epochs and to adapt the network for a given set of test data. The weights in the memory circuit are updated and it iterates until the loss is minimized, the process is terminated once the network learns to classify correctly.

$$[\ w_{new} = w_{old} - \cdot . \frac{\partial Etot}{\partial wold} \ ] \tag{8}$$

Additionally, the implementation uses a sign circuit to evaluate the sign ($\pm$) for the employed memory update circuit, as shown in Fig6b (Hasan & Taha, 2014). The RRAM weight sign circuit can be either combined with the crossbar array to control the weights in the synapse or used independently for storing the sign of the weight signal as on/off. When a positive voltage is applied to the V_c signal, the $RRAM_1$ device is on, and the voltage output signal of the switch is positive and vice-versa. If $RRAM_1$ = ON, the signal at V_c rises above the switching threshold, selecting a $+V_{out}$ signal. If $RRAM_1$ = OFF, the signal at V_c falls below the switching threshold, selecting a $-V_{out}$ signal. Here, $\pm V_{out}$ is the input voltage to the crossbar array. The overall device parameters are listed in Table 1.

Figure 6. Circuitry for memory read/write and sign control using RRAMs

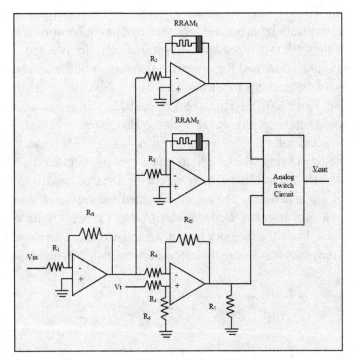

a. Memory Update Circuit

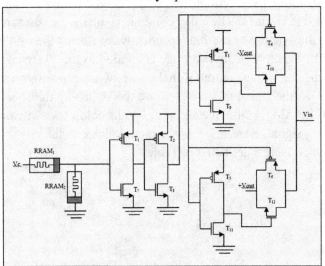

b. Memory Sign (±) Circuit

Table 1. Resource utilization of RRAM based neuromorphic accelerator

No. of RRAMs in Neuron Circuitry	12
No. of RRAMs in Synapse Circuitry	616
Total RRAMs	628
Operating Voltage	2V
Total RAVDESS Data Samples	4320
Total Male/Female Data Samples	2152
Training Data	70% (1506)
Validation Data	15% (323)
Testing Data	15% (323)

Emotion Recognition on 20x22x8 RRAM Neural Network Architecture

The RRAM neuromorphic accelerator discussed in the above section 3.1, has been trained on the Ryerson Audio-Visual Database of Emotional Speech and Song (RAVDESS) dataset for categorizing into various emotion types. The RAVDESS dataset is a large validated set of audio-visual speech and song in North American English. The dataset contains 4320 samples of male and female professional actor's audio speech and song that are distinguished for 8 emotion categories. The audio clips have various phoneme groups at a frequency of 48kHz describing different emotion types such as angry, happy, sad, fearful, calm, neutral, disgusted and surprised of 500 ms each. Two example cases from the dataset have a voice clip portraying the phrases *'kids are talking by the door'* and *'dogs are sitting by the door'* typically for a period of 500 ms each, as different phonemes of speech and song that can be categorized into the above 8 emotion categories of the male or female actors (Livingstone, 2018).

The 20x22x8 neuromorphic architecture has been trained separately for male and female speech data samples. Out of the male/female data of 2152 samples each, the network has been trained for 70% of the data samples, validated and tested each for 15% of the data samples. The step-by-step process discussed in section 3.1 is followed in order to train the input-output neurons of the neural network. Once the 20x22x8 architecture is designed, the speech-based emotion dataset is used to train the network rigorously for several epochs so that the network learns to classify the correct emotion type. Once the backpropagation method is completed, the error is determined for any loss over the network. If the evaluated error is high, the training process is repeated for certain cycles until the error dips from high meanwhile updating the memory circuitry. The RRAM conductance (weights) in the network is adjusted until the error is minimized and the training process is repeated for multiple epochs to attain better learning accuracy. The process is stopped once the output neurons are able to detect the correct emotion type as per the trained samples. In this application, the audio samples have been trained with an update frequency (i.e., interval) of 1 epoch in order to classify into 8 emotion types. The trained network is able to recognize the 8 emotions correctly as per the training phenomena considered. More details about the performance, characteristics, acceleration and classification rate of the neuromorphic accelerator have been specified in section 4.

RESULTS AND DISCUSSION

The RRAM based neuromorphic accelerator with 20 input neurons, 22 hidden layer neurons and 8 output neurons have been implemented on 28nm FD-SOI technology. As discussed in section 3, the neural network has been trained on 70% of the audio samples of the RAVDESS dataset. The Table 2, presents the performance of the proposed accelerator, the accuracy of the RRAM based neuromorphic accelerator is 79.31% when trained for 8.4ms. The memory read/write of the RRAM device were observed at an interval of 1 epoch for a learning rate (adaptation) of 0.01 for the network. Also, the RRAM device on/off switching at the Processing Elements (PEs) was observed at 13.81.

Different characteristics are observed for the training architecture such as the error and its derivative, the memory updates of the two RRAM based PEs (crossbars) and the RRAM switching behaviour are plotted in Fig7. As seen from Fig7a, the error characteristics presents the minimization of error when the speech-based emotion accelerator is trained for 8.4ms. Also, the error and the performance accuracy are closely related; the minimum the error in the network, the better the accuracy and learning of the network. Additionally, the characteristics of derivative of error at the hidden and output layer are also captured for the accelerator in Fig7b and Fig7c respectively. Also, the memory read/write behavior of the RRAM devices at the PE-1 and PE-2 of the accelerator are also plotted in Fig7d and Fig7e to understand different variations while updating the memory of the RRAMs in PE-1 and PE-2 over a time interval. Importantly, the RRAM device switching characteristics for one of the devices are also shown in Fig7f in order to analyze the device on and off behavior. For the neuromorphic accelerator, the HRS/LRS ratio of the RRAM device is at 13.81 which is driven from the device switching on and off for a time period of 20000 ps.

Moreover, the training statistics of the RRAM accelerator are also presented which shows the percentage of correct classification and mis-classification rate of the emotions such as angry, happy, sad, fearful, calm, neutral, disgusted and surprised for the total samples considered in each case and are plotted in the Fig8. Besides the training statistics, the acceleration time of the FD-SOI based implementation using two 1T-1RRAM based Processing Elements (PEs) and the CPU implementation using Intel i3-8130U CPU for the speech-based emotion accelerator on 20x22x8 network is also plotted in Fig9. This figure clearly indicates that the FD-SOI implementation of the neuromorphic accelerator is much faster as compared to the CPU based implementation.

Additionally, the RRAM Neuromorphic Accelerator for the 20x22x8 neural network has been evaluated on 28nm FD-SOI, Intel i3-8130U CPU and is compared with NVIDIA GeForce GTX memory GPU System (Mustaqeem et al., 2020) for speech-based emotion recognition as shown in Table3. As depicted in the table, the FD-SOI based DNN (Deep Neural Network) design takes only 8.4ms for the training on RAVDESS, whereas the GPU based system consumes 6250 seconds while also considering the pre-processing (K-mean clustering, Short Term Fourier Transform, Normalization etc.) with CNN (Convolutional Neural Network) and multi-layer BiLSTM (Bi-directional Long Short-Term Memory) model as stated by (Mustaqeem et al., 2020). Besides the above, training accuracy of the neuromorphic accelerator for the speech-based emotion recognition when trained on RAVDESS dataset is 79.31% for the FD-SOI based implementation and 73.53% for the Python implementation which is better as compared to the GPU memory system having an accuracy of 77.02%. The major improvements for the training accelerator are due to the underlying factors such as the RRAM devices, the choice of activation function, the compact architecture and the technology on which the accelerator is designed. The proposed neuromorphic accelerator consumes low power (1780µW), has fast performance, better design characteristics with the device RRAM Ron= 63.53kΩ, RRAM Roff= 4.6kΩ observed at one of the crossbar arrays. Besides the above, the RRAM based swish circuitry is power efficient by 84.13% (476µW) and is faster as compared to ReLU, tanh and sigmoid based implementations.

Table 2. Performance metrics of RRAM based neuromorphic accelerator

Training Accuracy	79.31%
Weight Update Frequency (i.e., interval)	1 epoch
Learning Rate	0.01
Mis-recognition Rate	20.7%
Gradient	0.176
Training Time	8.4ms
RRAM Switching (HRS/LRS) Ratio	13.81

Figure 7. RRAM neuromorphic accelerator characteristics for RAVDESS Emotion on 28nm FD-SOI

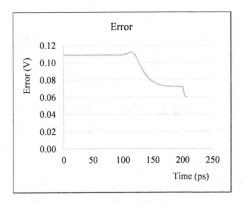

a. Error Characteristics

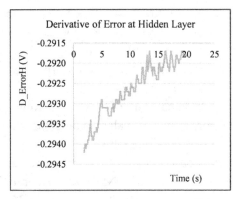

b. Derivative of Error at Hidden Layer

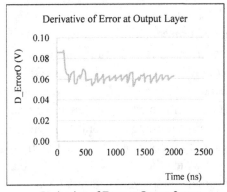

c. Derivative of Error at Output Layer

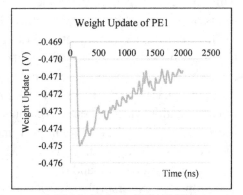

d. Weight Update of RRAM PE-1

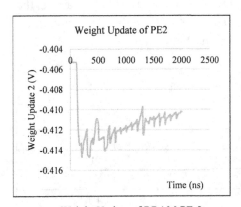

e. Weight Update of RRAM PE-2

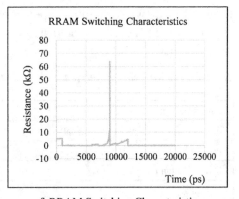

f. RRAM Switching Characteristics

Figure 8. Training statistics for the RRAM neuromorphic accelerator for emotion classification on 28nm FD-SOI

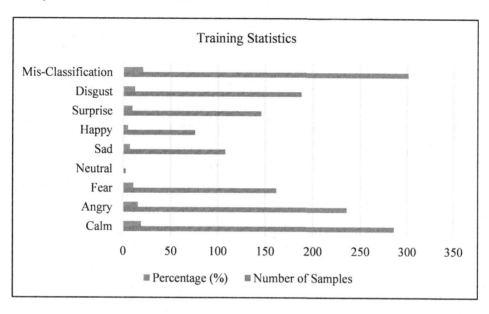

Figure 9. CPU vs RRAM neuromorphic accelerator on 28nm FD-SOI

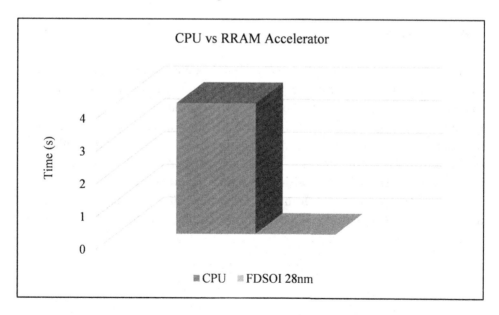

Table 3. Comparison of RRAM neuromorphic accelerator with a GPU based memory system

Parameters	RRAM Neuromorphic Accelerator (This work)	Multi-Layer BiLSTM (GPU-System) (Mustaqeem et al., 2020)	Python based execution – Spyder IDE (By authors of this work)
Deep Net Structure	20x22x8	Multi-Layer BiLSTM	20x22x8
Hardware Details	1T-1RRAM based Processing Elements (628 RRAMs) on 28nm FD-SOI	NVIDIA GeForce GTX 1070, 8 GB on-board memory GPU system	Intel i3-8130U CPU
Activation Function	Swish	Sigmoid/Tanh	Swish
Type of Algorithm	Stochastic Gradient based Backpropagation	ADAM	Stochastic Gradient based Backpropagation
Learning Rate	0.01	0.001	0.01
Target Application	Emotion from Speech	Emotion from Speech	Emotion from Speech
Dataset	RAVDESS	RAVDESS	RAVDESS
Epoch	60 iterations	-	57 iterations
Accuracy	79.31%	77.02%	73.53%
Time	8.4 milli-seconds (Time includes only DNN based processing)	6250 seconds (Time includes CNN model-based feature extraction and pre-processing)	4 seconds (Time includes only DNN based processing)

CONCLUSION

The hardware accelerator for identifying human emotions through audio data has been proposed for neuromorphic applications. By employing the potential memory candidate RRAM as the computation unit, the performance of the accelerator has been improved significantly. Also, with swish activation and the FDSOI technology, the training efficiency and acceleration has increased when compared with other memristor based neuromorphic accelerators and off-shelf CPU device, as discussed in results. However, the mis-classification rate of the proposed model is 20.7% for the trained samples which can further be reduced by running rigorous training for multiple epochs. This accelerator can further be employed to test different speech-based applications.

FUTURE WORK

The proposed neuromorphic accelerator can be applied to study different emotion categories that are not included in this work. Other improvisations based on the application-specific requirements can definitely be incorporated by adopting other memory candidates such as Phase Change Memory, Spin Transfer Torque Magneto Resistive Memory and other potential candidates that can co-relate the device characteristics and provide a guideline to the future neuromorphic approaches which can be utilized for commercial or research needs.

With the global Neuromorphic Computing market segment being valued at nearly 225 billion USD by 2027 (Research & Markets, 2022), both hardware and software-based design and developments targeted towards edge and cloud computing infrastructure is being carried out to ensure that the demand in application areas like Data Mining, Speech Recognition, Image Recognition, Autonomous Driving etc., is being met timely. Industry sectors like Aviation, Defense, Telecom, Medical are hugely broadening their research and development towards inclusion of Neuromorphic systems into their product chain with an aim to minimize the scope for human-based errors and other allied advantages the field has to offer in comparison to traditional technologies (Conrad et al., 2017). Though this chapter presents a neuromorphic based accelerator for the application of speech-based emotion recognition, the work can be easily extended to include many other applications from diverse fields and could be viewed with a potential of futuristic work involving key discussions in several areas constituting the fourth industrial revolution (4IR).

Though the forecasts often vary, the growth which is predicted in coming years for neuromorphic computing is indeed enormous in terms of advanced embedded systems. The major industry manufacturers are looking towards alternative technologies rather than mere advancements at node level. An interesting report by Sheer Analytics and Insights (Neuromorphic Computing Market, 2020), estimates the Neuromorphic Computing market to be valued around 780 million USD by 2028 growing at 50.3% CAGR (Compound Annual Growth Rate). The market is supposedly going to spread across the geographies like Middle East and Africa, besides Asia-Pacific, Europe and Latin America with much growth potential in North America. Some of the key but not limited, industrial players including Samsung Electronics Co Ltd., Hewlett Packard, IBM Corporation, Qualcomm Technologies Inc, Applied Brain Research Inc, AMD, Intel Corporation that are investing hugely into Neuromorphic Computing and allied technologies. At this point in time, though it is unlikely that Neuromorphic systems would replace the traditional Central Processing Units (CPUs), Graphics Processing Units (GPUs) etc., as much of the work is still regarded to be in its Research and Development stage. Hopefully, the near future commercialization and success of neuromorphic systems is surely going to emerge as an alternative for the traditional computing paradigm. Hence, the work in the direction of Neuromorphic Computing system design and development would surely help in realizing the needs of both society and industry in a larger way.

REFERENCES

Abdelwahab, M., & Busso, C. (2015). Supervised domain adaptation for emotion recognition from speech. *IEEE International Conference on Acoustics, Speech and Signal Processing (ICASSP)*, (pp. 5058-5062). IEEE. 10.1109/ICASSP.2015.7178934

Armando C. W., Stamatis K. & Thomas B. (2014). Towards the Next Generation of Industrial Cyber-Physical Systems. *Industrial Cloud-Based Cyber-Physical Systems*, 1–22.

Arunkumar. (2022). *A Survey on IoT-based Hand Hygiene Dispenser with Temperature and Level Monitoring Systems*. 8th International Conference on Advanced Computing and Communication Systems (ICACCS). Coimbatore, India. . doi:10.1109/ICACCS54159.2022.9785176

Bosker, B. (2017). *Affectiva's Emotion Recognition Tech: When Machines Know What You're Feeling*. The Huffington Post.

Bresnahan, T. F., Brynjolfsson, E., & Hitt, L. M. (2002). Information technology, workplace organisation, and the demand for skilled labour: Firm-level evidence. *The Quarterly Journal of Economics, 117*(1), 339–376. doi:10.1162/003355302753399526

Caridakis, G. (2007). Multimodal emotion recognition from expressive faces, body gestures and speech. In C. Boukis, A. Pnevmatikakis, & L. Polymenakos (Eds.), *Artificial Intelligence and Innovations 2007: from Theory to Applications. AIAI 2007. IFIP The International Federation for Information Processing* (Vol. 247). Springer. doi:10.1007/978-0-387-74161-1_41

Catherine, G. (2019). *Use New Alexa Emotions and Speaking Styles to Create a More Natural and Intuitive Voice Experience*. Alexa Skills Kit Blog. Amazon Developer. https://developer.amazon.com/en-US/blogs/alexa/alexa-skills-kit/2019/11/new-alexa-emotions-and-speaking-styles.

Chang H.Y. et al. (2019). AI hardware acceleration with analog memory: Microarchitectures for low energy at high speed. *IBM Journal of Research and Development, 63*(6), 1-14. . doi:10.1147/JRD.2019.2934050

Chen, P. Y., & Yu, S. (2015). Compact modeling of RRAM devices and its applications in 1T1R and 1S1R array design. *IEEE Transactions on Electron Devices, 62*(12), 4022–4028. doi:10.1109/TED.2015.2492421

Chunguang, B., Patrick, D., Guido, O., & Joseph, S. (2020). Industry 4.0 technologies assessment: A sustainability perspective. *International Journal of Production Economics, 229*, 107776. doi:10.1016/j.ijpe.2020.107776

Ciota, Z. (2005). Emotion Recognition on the Basis of Human Speech. *18th International Conference on Applied Electromagnetics and Communications,* (pp. 1-4). IEEE. 10.1109/ICECOM.2005.205015

Colombo, A. W., Karnouskos, S., Kaynak, O., Shi, Y., & Yin, S. (2017). Industrial Cyber physical Systems: A Backbone of the Fourth Industrial Revolution. *IEEE Industrial Electronics Magazine, 11*(1), 6–16. doi:10.1109/MIE.2017.2648857

Conrad, D. J., James, B. A., Nadine, E. M., Craig, M. V., Fredrick, H. R., Kristofor, D. C., Samuel, A. M., Timothy, J. D., Aleksandra, F., Matthew, J. M., John, H. N., & Steven, J. P. (2017). A historical survey of algorithms and hardware architectures for neural-inspired and neuromorphic computing applications. *Biologically Inspired Cognitive Architectures, 19*, 49-64. doi:10.1016/j.bica.2016.11.002

Cortes, C., & Vapnik, V. (1995). Support-vector networks. *Machine Learning, 20*(3), 273–297. doi:10.1007/BF00994018

DeMuth, C. Jr. (2016). *Apple Reads Your Mind*. M&A Daily. Seeking Alpha.

Diehl, P. U., Pedroni, B. U., Cassidy, A., Merolla, P., Neftci, E., & Zarrella, G. (2016). TrueHappiness: Neuromorphic emotion recognition on TrueNorth. *International Joint Conference on Neural Networks (IJCNN).* (pp. 4278-4285). IEEE. 10.1109/IJCNN.2016.7727758

Du, Z. (2015). Neuromorphic accelerators: A comparison between neuroscience and machine-learning approaches. *48th Annual IEEE/ACM International Symposium on Microarchitecture (MICRO).* (pp. 494-507). IEEE. 10.1145/2830772.2830789

Esmaeilzadeh, H., Sampson, A., Ceze, L., & Burger, D. (2012). Neural Acceleration for General-Purpose Approximate Programs. *International Symposium on Microarchitecture, 3*, 1–6. 10.1109/MICRO.2012.48

Fatima, A., & Pethe, A. (2021). NVM Device-Based Deep Inference Architecture Using Self-gated Activation Functions (Swish). In M. K. Bajpai, K. Kumar Singh, & G. Giakos (Eds.), *Ma-chine Vision and Augmented Intelligence—Theory and Applications. Lecture Notes in Electrical Engineering* (Vol. 796). Springer. doi:10.1007/978-981-16-5078-9_4

Fatima, A., & Pethe, A. (2022a). *Implementation of RRAM based Swish Activation Function and its Derivative on 28nm FD-SOI*. International Electrical Engineering Congress (iEECON). 10.1109/iEECON53204.2022.9741701

Fatima, A., & Pethe, A. (2022b). Periodic Analysis of Resistive Random Access Memory (RRAM)-Based Swish Activation Function. *SN Computer Science, 3*(3), 202. doi:10.100742979-022-01059-3

Gemma, G. L. (2018). Emotional answers from virtual assistants. *Emotional Seo.* https://emotionalseo.com/emotional-answers-from-virtual-assistants/

Geoffrey W. B., Robert M. S., Sebastian A., Kim S., Seyoung K., Sidler S., Virwani K., Masatoshi I., Pritish N., Alessandro F., Lucas L. S., Irem B., Manuel L. G., Moon K., Jiyoo W., Hwang H. & Leblebici Y. (2017). Neuromorphic computing using non-volatile memory. *Advances in Physics, 10,* 89-124. doi:10.1080/23746149.2016.1259585

Goodfellow, I., Bengio, Y., & Courville, A. (2016). *Deep Learning.* MIT Press.

Hasan, R., & Taha, T. (2014). Enabling back propagation training of memristor crossbar neuromorphic processors. *International Joint Conference on Neural Networks (IJCNN)* (pp. 21-28). IEEE. 10.1109/IJCNN.2014.6889893

John, S. B., & John, E. B. (1998). *Modeling emotion and personality in a computer user interface.* Microsoft Technology Licensing LLC. https://patents.google.com/patent/US6185534B1/en

Kim, K., Bang, S., & Kong, D. (2003). *System and method for recognizing user's emotional state using short-time monitoring of physiological signals.* Samsung Electronics Co. Ltd. https://patents.google.com/patent/US7547279B2/en

Klaus, S. (2015). The Fourth Industrial Revolution. *Foreign Affairs.* (https://www.foreignaffairs.com/world/fourth-industrial-revolution)

LeCun, Y., & Bengio, Y. (1995). Convolutional networks for images, speech, and time-series. In M. A. Arbib (Ed.), *The Handbook of Brain Theory and Neural Networks.* MIT Press.

Lee, C. M., & Narayanan, S. S. (2005). Toward detecting emotions in spoken dialogs. *IEEE Transactions on Speech and Audio Processing*, *13*(2), 293–303. doi:10.1109/TSA.2004.838534

Lefter, I., Rothkrantz, L., & Van-Leeuwen, D. (2011). Automatic stress detection in emergency (telephone) calls. *International Journal of Intelligent Defence Support Systems.*, *4*(2), 148–168. doi:10.1504/IJIDSS.2011.039547

Livingstone, S. R., & Russo, F. A. (2018). The Ryerson Audio-Visual Database of Emotional Speech and Song (RAVDESS): A dynamic, multimodal set of facial and vocal expressions in North American English. *PLoS One*, *13*(5), e0196391. doi:10.1371/journal.pone.0196391 PMID:29768426

Mandal, S., El-Amin, A., Alexander, K., Rajendran, B., & Jha, R. (2014). Novel synaptic memory device for neuromorphic computing. *Scientific Reports*, *4*(1), 5333. doi:10.1038rep05333 PMID:24939247

Manfredi, G., & Gribaudo, C. (2008). *Virtual assistant with real-time emotions.* Kallideas S.P.A. WO2008049834A2. https://patents.google.com/patent/WO2008049834A2/en

ST Microelectronics (2016). *28nm FD-SOI Technology Catalog.* ST Microelectronics.

ST Microelectronics (2017). *Efficiency At All Levels.* ST Microelectronics.

Lee, M., Yun, J., Pyka, A., Won, D., Kodama, F., Schiuma, G., Park, H., Jeon, J., Park, K., Jung, K., Yan, M., Lee, S., Zhao, X. (2018). How to Respond to the Fourth Industrial Revolution, or the Second Information Technology Revolution? Dynamic New Combinations between Technology, Market, and Society through Open Innovation. *Journal of Open Innovation: Technology, Market, and Complexity, 4* (3), 21. . doi:10.3390/joitmc4030021

Miyakoshi, Y., & Kato, S. (2011). Facial emotion detection considering partial occlusion of face using Bayesian network. *IEEE Symposium on Computers & Informatics*, (pp. 96-101). IEEE. 10.1109/ISCI.2011.5958891

Musisi-Nkambwe, M., Afshari, S., Barnaby, H., Kozicki, M., & Sanchez Esqueda, I. (2021). The Viability of Analog-based Accelerators for Neuromorphic Computing: A Survey. *Neuromorphic Computing and Engineering*, *1*(1), 012001. doi:10.1088/2634-4386/ac0242

Mustaqeem, M. Sajjad & Kwon S. (2020). Clustering-Based Speech Emotion Recognition by Incorporating Learned Features and Deep BiLSTM. In IEEE Access. (vol. 8. pp. 79861-79875). IEEE. doi:10.1109/ACCESS.2020.2990405

Neuromorphic Computing Market. (2020). *Industry analysis, size, share, growth, trends, and forecast, 2020-2028.* Sheer Analytics and Insights, Report Id: TECIT 127. https://www.sheeranalyticsandinsights.com/market-report-research/neuromorphic-computing-market-21

Temam, O., Luo, Lao., Chen, Y. (2014). DaDianNao: A Machine-Learning Supercomputer. *Proceedings of the 47th Annual IEEE/ACM International Symposium on Microarchitecture* (MICRO-47). (pp. 609–622). IEEE.

Pedota M. & Piscitello L. (2021). A new perspective on technology-driven creativity enhancement in the Fourth Industrial Revolution. *Creativity and Innovation Management.* Wiley. doi:10.1111/caim.12468

Philbeck, T., & Davis, N. (2018). The Fourth Industrial Revolution. *Journal of International Affairs, 72* (1), 17–22.

Poria, S., Majumder, N., Mihalcea, R., & Hovy, E. (2019). Emotion recognition in conversation: Research challenges, datasets, and recent advances. *IEEE Access : Practical Innovations, Open Solutions*, 7, 100943–100953. doi:10.1109/ACCESS.2019.2929050

Ramachandran, P., Zoph, B., & Le, Q. V. (2017). *Swish: A Self-Gated Activation Function.* Google Brain.

Research and Markets. (2022). The Worldwide Neuromorphic Computing Industry is Expected to Reach $225.5 Billion by 2027. *Globe News Wire.* https://www.globenewswire.com/en/news-release/2022/05/24/2449227/28124/en/The-Worldwide-Neuromorphic-Computing-Industry-is-Expected-to-Reach-225-5-Billion-by-2027.html

Robert, S. C., Jeff, F. M., Walter, R., Derek, S., & Richard, M. U. (2002). *Personal Virtual Assistant with Semantic Tagging.* Avaya Inc. https://patents.google.com/patent/US6466654B1/en?oq=US6466654B1

Schmitt, M., Fabien, R., & Björn, S. (2016). At the Border of Acoustics and Linguistics. *Bag-of-Audio-Words for the Recognition of Emotions in Speech*, 495-499, 495–499. doi:10.21437/Interspeech.2016-1124

Sepp, H., & Jürgen, S. (1997). Long Short-Term Memory. *Neural Computation*, 9(8), 1735–1780. doi:10.1162/neco.1997.9.8.1735 PMID:9377276

Sun, J., Han, J., Wang, Y., & Liu, P. (2021). Memristor-Based Neural Network Circuit of Emotion Congruent Memory With Mental Fatigue and Emotion Inhibition. *IEEE Transactions on Biomedical Circuits and Systems*, *15*(3), 606–616. doi:10.1109/TBCAS.2021.3090786 PMID:34156947

UK Gov Department for Business. (2019). *Regulation for the Fourth Industrial Revolution*. UK.gov. https://www.gov.uk/government/publications/regulation-for-the-fourth-industrial-revolution/regulation-for-the-fourth-industrial-revolution

Wayne, C. (2016). *Feeling sad, angry? Your future car will know*. CNET.

William, G. (2019). Future versions of Apple's Siri may interpret your emotions. *Apple Insider*. https://appleinsider.com/articles/19/11/14/future-versions-of-apples-siri-may-read-interpret-your-facial-expressions.

Xiao, T., Bennett, C., Ben, F., Sapan, A., & Matthew, M. (2020). Analog architectures for neural network acceleration based on non-volatile memory. *Applied Physics Reviews*, *7*(3), 031301. doi:10.1063/1.5143815

Chapter 4

VLSI Implementation of Neural Systems

Ashok Kumar Nagarajan
https://orcid.org/0000-0002-4034-484X
Mohan Babu University, India

Kavitha Thandapani
VelTech Rangarajan Dr. Sagunthala R&D Institute of Science and Technolog, India

Neelima K.
Mohan Babu University, India

Bharathi M.
Mohan Babu University, India

Dhamodharan Srinivasan
Sri Eshwar College of Engineering, India

SathishKumar Selvaperumal
Asia Pacific University of Technology and Innovation, Malaysia

ABSTRACT

A unique strategy for optimum multi-objective optimization for VLSI implementation of artificial neural network (ANN) is proposed. This strategy is efficient in terms of area, power, and speed, and it has a good degree of accuracy and dynamic range. The goal of this research is to find the sweet spot where area, speed, and power may all be optimised in a very large-scale integration (VLSI) implementation of a neural network (NN). The design should also allow for the dynamic reconfiguration of weight, and it should be very precise. The authors also use a 65-nm CMOS fabrication method to produce the circuits, and these results show that the suggested integral stochastic design may reduce energy consumption by up to 21% compared to the binary radix implementation, without sacrificing accuracy.

DOI: 10.4018/978-1-6684-6596-7.ch004

INTRODUCTION

Deep neural networks (DNNs), and deep belief networks (DBNs) in particular, have shown results that are considered to be state-of-the-art in a variety of computer vision and recognition applications has been used by the authors Dhanasekar S et al. The formation of a DBN may be accomplished by building a deep network by layering RBMs one atop the other, as seen in Figure 1 (Ashokkumar, 2019). RBMs that are employed in DBN undergo pretraining using gradient-based contrastive divergence algorithms, which is then followed by classification and fine-tuning with gradient descent and back propagation algorithms (Hinton, 2006). However, because to their high resource demand and significant power consumption, neural network implementations are now being investigated using application-specific integrated circuits (ASIC) and field-programmable gate arrays (FPGA). The development of the IoT provides a justification for bringing low-power machine learning algorithms to mobile devices.

Multiple RBM layers are used in the construction of a DBN, and at the very end, there is one more layer that is used for categorization. The core of the calculation is made up of hundreds of matrix–vector multiplications, which are then followed by nonlinear function evaluations at each layer. Current parallel or semi-parallel VLSI implementations of such a network have issues with having a large silicon area as well as having a high consumption of power. This is due to the fact that implementing multiplications in hardware is an expensive endeavour. There is also a large memory need due to the use of lookup tables (LUTs) to implement the nonlinearity function. In addition, a large amount of silicon real estate is required to support this network's hardware implementation. The reason for this is because the connections between layers produce a high level of routing congestion, which in turn causes a large silicon area. As a direct consequence of this, the efficient VLSI implementation of DBN remains an issue that has to be resolved.

Numerous applications for pattern recognition and signal processing may benefit from the implementation of neural networks in hardware thanks to the generalisation capabilities of these networks. Because the simulation of neural network models on sequential machines takes a significant amount of computation time, it is very challenging to study the behaviour of big neural networks and to determine whether or not they are capable of finding solutions to problems. The simultaneous activity of neurons in the nervous system is what allows it to tackle complex issues. The functions that are performed by these circuits will be executed simultaneously across several threads in real time (Sheu, 1995). These operations will be carried out in hardware. As a result, the neural network that they are a part of will be able to converge at a faster rate than its software-based competitors.

ARTIFICIAL INTELLIGENCE

In spite of the fact that a large number of other researchers primarily in the communities of biophysics and computational neuroscience have explored the application of dynamical principles to the design and implementation of information processing systems, this field of study is still regarded as being relatively niche in comparison to the statistical approach. These limitations are causing us to come to this realization. The point attractor, in contrast to the limit cycle, which has a dynamic memory that is only restricted in time, does not have any dynamical memory. Utilizing a chaotic attractor that was produced by a dynamical system that has second-order singularities is one approach that might be taken to address the issue of being too sensitive to noise (third-order ODE).

Having the computational power to achieve goals in the actual world is what we mean when we talk about intelligence. It is possible for a chaotic attractor to exist in a high dimensional space, yet this attractor is still a stable representation. In point of fact, intelligence is a biological term and is something that is gained via one's life experiences. Artificial intelligence is a term used to refer to the field of study that uses mathematics to describe intelligence (AI). The implementation of artificial intelligence involves the use of artificial neurons, and these artificial neurons are made up of a variety of analogue components. Figure 1 represented by the following equation: The use of a back propagation method for the purpose of data compression is discussed in the study that was offered as a step toward the implementation of neural network design. In addition to the multiplier and adder, the tan-sigmoid function is included inside the neuron that was chosen. Because the training method is executed in the analogue domain, the whole neural network is an analogue structure. [Case in point:] an is equal to f (P1W1+P2W2+P3W3+Bias), where is the weight of the neuron, is the input, and is the output of the neuron. The user chose whether or not to include the bias. A neuron in a network is its own straightforward processing unit, and as such, it carries an associated weight for each of the inputs that serve to bolster it and generates an output. The operation of a neuron consists of computing an output by adding all of the inputs together, and then passing on the result. In order to train the neural architecture, the back propagation method is used, and in addition, the network is a feed forward one. The developed neuron is adaptable for use in analogue as well as digital settings. The neural architecture that has been developed is not only capable of executing operations such as learning sine waves, amplifying signals, and multiplying frequencies, but it also has the potential to be used for analogue signal processing tasks.

The term "multi-objective optimization" refers to a strategy that entails either minimising or maximising a number of different objective functions while adhering to a predetermined list of constraints. Optimising the circuit for speed results in an increase in the amount of design overhead that occurs in the area, and vice versa. As seen in the following equation, optimising one parameter has an effect on the other. The goal of this study is to find a way to concurrently optimise many design parameters, such as area, speed, and power, in a VLSI implementation of an artificial feed neural network (NN). The design should also allow for the dynamic reconfiguration of weight, and it should be very precise.

Artificial neural networks, often known as ANNs, are essentially condensed versions of models of the human nervous system. The networks are made up of computing parts that have the capacity to react in some way to the stimuli that are input. ANN enables the development of effective processors for use in many domains, including, but not limited to, those of pattern recognition, signal and image processing, associative memory, classification, and adaptive control. It has a lot of useful traits, such as a strong performance and adaptable behaviour, among other things. Figure 1 presents a basic outline of an artificial neural network.

Figure 1. Basic diagram of an ANN

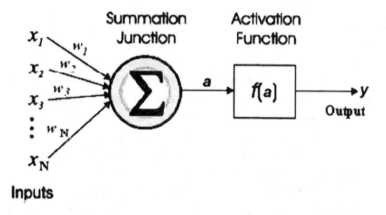

It is necessary to perform several training sessions on the given data in order for the network weights to be properly calibrated. As a result, the software implementation of ANN requires a significant amount of time to learn a specific example. However, training time may be reduced by a factor of many orders of magnitude if neural networks (NNs) were implemented in hardware. This is possible owing to the fact that such networks are able to operate in parallel and the quicker nature of the hardware. The development of VLSI design has made the process of physically realising hardware quite straightforward. Pulsed NN is another another form that researchers are looking at. Only a subset of the articles that were submitted was read through since we were limited on space.

NEUROMORPHIC CIRCUITS

The term "neuromorphic circuit" refers to a category of analog/digital electronic circuits built using complementary metal-oxide silicon (CMOS) standard very large-scale integration (VLSI) technology. According to the authors of Li (2011) and Li and Lilja (2014), the chips or systems made out of chips use these circuits, which explicitly implement biological-style processing. The logical structure of animal nervous systems served as a model for the development of neuromorphic circuits. These circuits operate in real time, are parallel and asynchronous, and react to input in the same manner. For them to function, the gate-to-source voltage differences of the transistors they use must be less than the threshold voltage. In this region, transistors exhibit thresholding, exponentiation, and amplification, all of which are useful for modelling neurons and brain systems (Natarajan, 2018).

Digital processing systems have been interfaced with traditional complementary metal oxide semiconductor (CMOS) sensors. This has allowed artificial sensory systems to be constructed and put into operation. However, the power consumption, size, and expense of these standard digital systems are often too high for meaningful real-time or robotic applications. The average performance statistics for conventional machine vision systems are well below their strong real-world capacity, with very few exceptions. In the case of traditional machine vision systems, this is particularly true.

The processing of pictures occurs directly at the focal plane level in neuromorphic vision systems since these systems are built on bespoke, unusual sensory components. These sensors often use circuits that are hardware analogues of the first stages of vision processing in biological systems. The authors of Rosselló (2010) and Nagarajan (2020) have showed in their previous work is that Neuromorphic circuits combine photoreceptors, memories, and computational nodes into a single silicon chip. These parts are assembled into regional circuits that perform spatial and temporal calculations on the analogue brightness signal in real time. Neuromorphic sensors, such as very-low-power-integrated-circuit (VLSI) silicon retina devices, may be effective even when they have a limited Nagarajan (2022) and Dhanasekar (2023) have discussed in their research, for instance, are able to function throughout an input range that spans several orders of magnitude. This is true even if the sensors are analogous to biological sensors. This amazing performance is made possible by a procedure that is not only straightforward but also densely parallel. Artificial sensory systems benefit greatly from the characteristics of neuromorphic VLSI circuits, such as their similarity to biological systems, high processing density, small size, and low power consumption.

Saliency-Based Models of Selective Attention

In the fields of computer science and neurology, researchers have developed a number of different computational models of selective attention. Some of these models are predicated on a theory known as "dynamic routing", in which salient areas are chosen by the dynamic alteration of network characteristics in response to top-down as well as bottom-up stimuli. The notion of "selective tuning" is pushed further by other models that are founded on similar premises. These models feature a pyramid-shaped structure for visual processing. This helps to ensure that the best possible results are obtained. Koch and Ullman were the ones who first proposed the saliency map. Such physiologically plausible and psycho-physical assessments, and have inspired a variety of software implementations that have found their way into machine vision and robotic operations. They have a natural affinity for being implemented in hardware, which is one of the reasons they particularly pique our interest.

Figure 2. Schematic of a model of selective attention based on salience

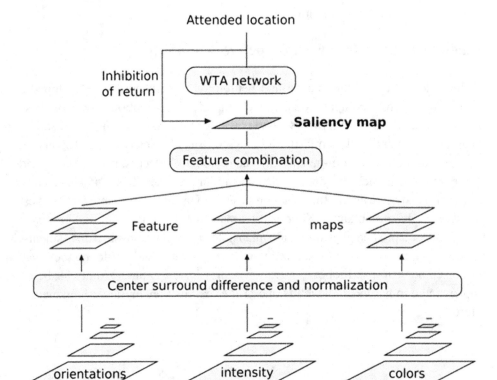

Figure 2 is a schematic that illustrates the primary processing phases of the sort of model being discussed. After processing the visual data, a collection of topographic feature maps is generated. After being normalised and integrated, all of the feature maps are then used to create a master saliency map. This map uses topographic codes to show where things are important in the whole visual scene. Then, spatial features vie with one another for attention by trying to shine out more than their neighbours. This most prominent venue is chosen to serve as the focal point of interest throughout a WTA tour. There are internal dynamics in the WTA circuit that cause changes in attention depends on a process called "inhibition of return." (IOR). This mechanism is a significant characteristic of many selective attention systems.

Methodology

ANN stands for artificial neural network and refers to the system that processes information using neurons G. E. Hinton(2006). The fundamental building block of artificial neural networks is called an artificial neuron. (1)a network with three parts: (1) a set of input nodes, indexed by, say, 1, 2,... N, that receive the pattern vector, x=(P1, P2,..., PN)T; (2) a set of synaptic connections denoted by w=(w1, w2,..., wI)T; and (3) an activation function a', Figure 3 provides an illustration of the primary components that make up an artificial neuron.

Figure 3. Simple neuron

$$a=\sum_{j=1}^{N} W_j P_j;$$

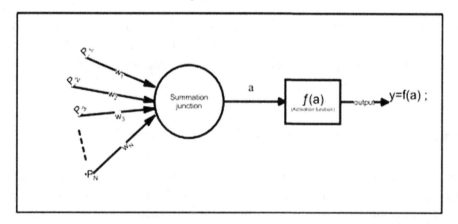

Often abbreviated to "multi-layer perceptron" or "MNN," this kind of feed-forward neural network has input layer, "hidden" layers of perceptrons, and a "uncovered" layer of output nodes. Output is the last layer. MLPs have been used effectively to solve a wide variety of complicated issues that arise in the real world and include non-linear decision limits. For the majority of these applications, three-layer MLPs have shown to be adequate, and a block diagram depiction of this structure may be seen in Figure 4.

Figure 4. Block diagram representation of three-layered MNN

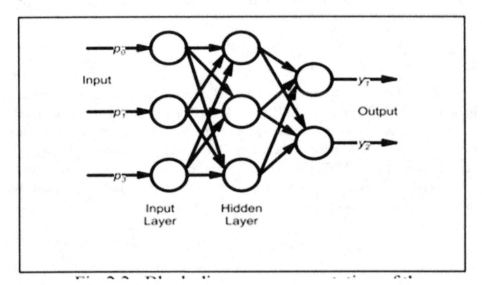

DIGITAL VLSI IMPLEMENTATION OF ANNS

The use of developed methods, and ease of communication are some of the benefits that come with the use of digital design. The digital application of ANN has seen great growth in spite of its drawbacks, which include the need for a big amount of Si space and a high amount of power, many different factors including small design, fast speed of operation, etc.

Different Threshold Functions

Aoyama G. E. Dahl (2012) conducted experiments with a variety of threshold functions using a back propagation (BP) technique (FPGA). Following the testing of the sigmoid function, sine function, and quadratic function, as well as the Bendy function, step function, and convex function, the following recommendations were developed. Extrapolation is a feature that the NN should have to make real-time learning easier. It is possible to speed up the process of learning BP by using a sine or quadratic function. The bendy function is going to be selected since it will be simpler to implement on FPGA.

Multipliers in ANN

The area-intensive multiplication process has to be addressed by the hardware implementation of ANN. There was an effort made to use a LUT-based technique for stochastic bit stream multiplication. The values of weights are denoted as powers of two, and the operations of shift and add have replaced multiplication. The process of scanning multiple bits is favourable to hardware but time-consuming. The LUT-based multiplier first calculates the logarithm, adds the results, and then calculates the inverse logarithm. However, the conversion time is somewhat lengthy. The parallel-array multiplier has a high throughput but requires a large amount of space. Carry-save adders and an extension known as Wallace tree multipliers are superior in both aspects of the comparison.

Multiplier-Free Design

In the digital implementation of ANN, multipliers take up the majority of the space in the hardware. Hikawa came up with the idea of a multiplier-less multilayer neural network (MNN) that has on-chip learning. A more space-efficient architecture may be achieved by changing the BP algorithm in pulse mode such that there is no multiply operation. In the forward route, the suggested MNN employs the utilisation of a tri-state function as the threshold.

Compact Design

There are just a few more strategies mentioned here that can guarantee small designs. It is possible to do multiplication in a serial fashion in order to save space on the Si chip; however, this results in an extremely poor processing speed. Utilizing stochastic logic allows for a reduction in the amount of space that is needed. However, stochastic bit stream production calls for a large number of random sources, which ultimately results in an increase in the required hardware. They stated that the compact multiplier only requires 70 configurable logic blocks (CLBs), in contrast to the approximately 400 CLBs that are required by a traditional multiplier. The design's computational speed has been enhanced, and the level of complexity in the routing has been decreased. In order to train the network, a modified version of the particle swarm optimization (PSO) technique is used.

Design Methodology

The strategy for the BNN application focused on optimising its performance in accuracy and its ability to save energy. For this reason, having an optimal typology and making use of APSoC are both essential components of the method that is shown in Figure 5.

Figure 5. The methodology behind the creation of our BNN, which includes the processes of training and deployment, is shown in a flow chart

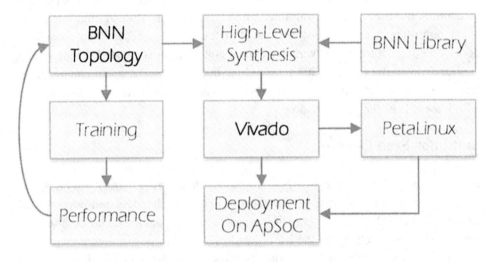

The first thing that has to be done is the design of the typology, since this is the most important component in determining the performance. The authors M. A. Arbib (2002) and P. Luo (2014) has explained in his research the network weight file and the BNN library are then compiled by the high-level synthesiser Vivado HLS 2019.1 into an intellectual property block. Finally, pre-processing and post-processing are also necessary for deployment, and all of these steps are taken care of by the processing system, as can be seen in Figure 6.

Figure 6. Programmable logic refers to programmable circuits, while the processing system consists of one or more non-customizable processing units

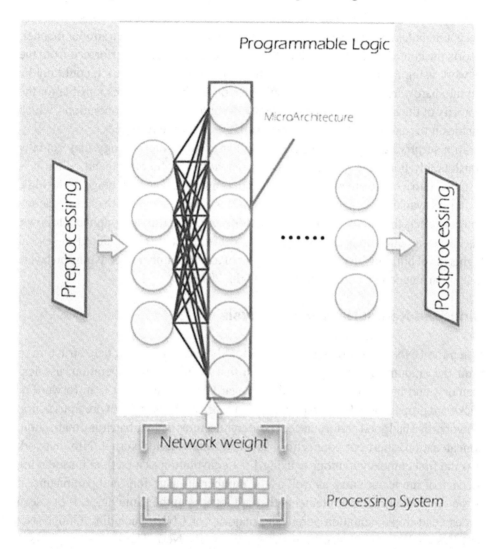

The application processes for BNN are divided into two distinct groups, each corresponding to a distinct set of characteristics. The processing system is in charge of processes that do not need a great amount of computations, such as pre-processing, post-processing, and sections of forward propagation. Examples of these kinds of procedures include. In addition to that, the processing system will start the accelerator by writing a weight file to the programmable logic. While the processing logic is responsible for handling the overwhelming bulk of normal forward propagation.

To get things started, the dataset has to be normalised as part of the pre-processing step. This is done in an effort to maximise both the accuracy and the convergence speed of the results. The processing system is in charge of the normalising procedure since it includes a significant number of float-point operations. In a similar manner, it sorts the confidence coefficient in the post-processing that is performed from the network using a recursive technique called rapid sort. This approach could not be put into hardware resources. As a result, programmable logic is responsible for the majority of the high-density and frequently occurring computing operations, which enables it to make effective use of the available hardware resources.

In a surprising turn of events, an irregular network morphology may actually considerably boost the performance of a network. On the other hand, when it is installed into a hardware platform, it squanders a significant percentage of the logic resources available. As a result, our technique takes into account both of these factors and constructs the micro-architecture that is described in the paragraph that follows. The micro-architecture was first suggested by Forrest et al., and it identifies several higher-level building blocks that are built up of a large number of convolution layers that are arranged in a certain fashion (Alaghi, 2013).

Binarized Neural Networks Analysis

When the BNN is resource-efficient, it should have a consistent data structure to limit the amount of data type conversion that occurs during operation, use less memory, and perform fewer operations, regardless of whether it is in forward or backward propagation. In this part, we will investigate the designs of previous neural networks that had good performance. These architectures include batch-normalization, concatenation, short-cut connection, and 1 x 1 convolution kernel. NIN network was the first company to propose using 1 x 1 convolution as a method for reducing the size of the feature map as well as the number of operations and parameters. It is the complete linking of elements that are located in the same place. It has seen widespread implementation across the majority of CNNs, including Google Net and Residual Neural Network, amongst others (ResNet). The inclusion of 1 x 1 convolution, on the other hand, will lead to a severe loss in performance in BNN topology. This is due to the fact that the quantization process will lose a significant amount of useful information.

In addition, concatenation is used in a variety of different topologies due to the effectiveness with which it boosts the overall performance of a network. The generalisation of the network is going to be improved by sparsifying, which will be done by parallelizing a large number of tiny convolution kernels. Using a neural network of the same size, this method provides a higher level of accuracy while also accelerating the rate at which it converges. In addition, the link that takes the shortcut is a wonderful technique to improve the generalisation capacity of the network. Its appearance solved the issue of the accuracy of the network deteriorating as the depth of the network increased, which allowed for a significant increase in the depth of the network. Because of the one-of-a-kind data structure used by the BNN, including new shortcuts into the topology might be challenging until a large number of addition operations using floating point or integer data are implemented. As a consequence of this, a shortcut is not the most effective strategy for enhancing generalisation when using completely BNNP (Nagarajan, 2020).

Batch-normalization, which is a technique for integrating scattered data and improving neural networks, is the last method that may be used. Batch normalisation has many effects, the most important of which are the prevention of internal covariate shifts during neural network propagation and the maintenance of data features inside the feature graph. On the other hand, Chen et al. (n.d.) suggest that its purpose is to smooth out the continuous optimization function. In order to complete the batch normalisation, the data types will need to be converted, and the floating-point arithmetic units will need to be operated on. Other divisors, such as the means of features, variances, and correction factors, are considered to be constant. As a result, the following constitutes the activation procedure of BNN during forwarding propagation:

Binarized Neural Networks Field-Programmable Gate Array Accelerator

The feature map buffer, an expansion block, a Finite State Machine (FSM) controller, and an XNOR-CNT matrix are the four components that make up the BNN FPGA accelerator core, which is shown as a hardware block diagram in Figure 7. This core is comprised of these four blocks. In this part, the design and optimization strategy for each individual hardware block are broken down in extensive depth.

Figure 7. The feature map buffer, an FSM controller, an expansion block, and an XNOR-CNT matrix are the four components that make up the BNN FPGA accelerator diagram

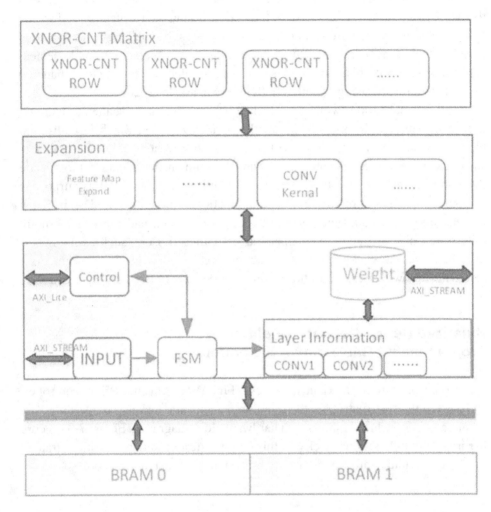

Finite State Machine Controller

The FSM controller is located in the heart of the whole acceleration core. It controls a total of three interfaces, one of which is an AXI4-Lite interface for acceleration core control, while the other two are AXI4-STREAM interfaces for feature map and weight transfer respectively. The AXI4-Lite interface is able to start, interrupt, and idle the acceleration core. Additionally, it can read the status of the acceleration core, which includes standby, operating, and completed. It enables the expansion of the feature map and the convolution core into a specific vector so that further operations may be performed. In addition to this, it organises the output in accordance with a certain data format while simultaneously storing the outcomes of the XNOR-CNT Matrix.

Expansion Block

The feature map as well as the convolution kernel are both transformed into binary vectors by the Expansion Block. Throughout the duration of this process, the convolution kernel will stay in place, and the local feature map vector will be iterated according to its position. One unit in this project represents the sliding step that makes up the 3x3 convolution kernel. As can be seen in Figure 8, when the convolution kernel realigns the initial section of the row, it needs inputs a total of three times in order to clear out the data from the row before it. Consequently, there is no need to provide additional bandwidth in order to send duplicate data at any point in the sliding filtering process.

Figure 8. The sliding filtering method is modelled from and imitated by the expansion block

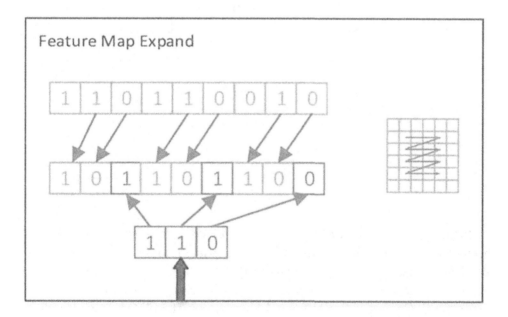

Input Buffer Memory

The motion detection is carried out using pixel blocks that are 4 by 4. Before any processing may occur, there must be accessible four rows of pixel data from the input picture. In order to accomplish this goal, the input buffer memory module is used to temporarily store (or buffer) all four rows of the incoming picture data. The dual memory architecture (Figure 9) is the one that is most suited to meet the needs of this form of real-time processing, which must be enabled. Memory (MEM1) and memory (MEM2) are both accessible at the same time. There are 24 bits across the breadth of each block in RAM (eight bits for each red, green, and blue colour channels). For the processing of colour video at a resolution of PAL, the full Input Buffer Memory Architecture requires a total of eight blocks of memory with a capacity of 36 KB each.

Figure 9. VLSI architecture for input buffer memory

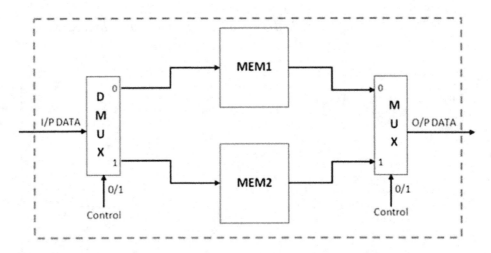

In this subsection of the paper, a clustering-based motion detection scheme has been proposed. The main objective of this architecture is to decrease the amount of Block RAM that is required for input memory, and it does so by using smart buffers. Figure 10 illustrates how the proposed design makes use of three First-in first-out registers (FIFOs) in addition to four 24-bit registers. The FIFOs have a length of 719 locations and a width of 24 bits. The width of the FIFOs is 24 bits. These three FIFOs were created on FPGA by using the Block RAMs for their architecture. Figure 8 illustrates the comprehensive design for the input buffer memory that makes use of Block RAMs.

Figure 10. Proposed buffer memory architecture

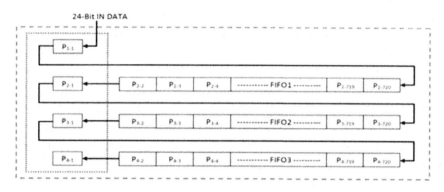

Figure 11. A comprehensive implementation of the architecture of the input buffer memory employing block RAMs and registers

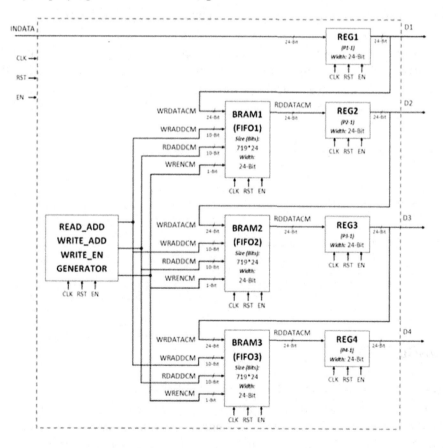

This design provides access to the four-pixel data that correspond to each of the four rows at the beginning of the fourth row. The functionality of the motion detector block is activated once every fourth row. The first-in, first-out procedure deletes all of the data that isn't essential for processing and only preserves the data from the four rows that are required for processing. When it comes to processing on a block-based basis, this approach is incredibly efficient. It is necessary to have an amount of FIFOs that is equivalent to the number of rows in the block minus one. The length of each FIFO is determined by subtracting one from the amount of pixels that make up one row. In comparison to the dual memory architecture for PAL size colour video processing, this new design is five 36-Kb Block RAMs more efficient, saving the user five.

Motion Computation Enable Unit

The motion computation enable (MCEN) signal is created and stored in REG1 based on the value of the row counter RW4C, which is reset after every fourth row and counts from 00 to 11, and the column counter CL4C, which resets after every fourth column and also counts from 00 to 11, respectively (Figure 12). The remaining building elements of the motion detection system are enabled with the help of this one-bit MCEN signal. Only if both RW4C and CL4C are "11," which implies that a 4 x 4-pixel block is accessible for processing, is it set to "1." This is because "11" indicates that a block of pixels may be processed.

Figure 12. Motion computation enable signal generation

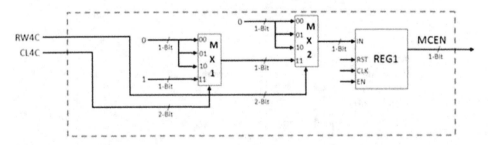

CONCLUSION

Researchers investigate several applications of ANNs, such as pattern recognition and processing, signal and image processing, associative memory, classification, adaptive control, and so on. It has been noticed that the software implementation of ANN requires a significant amount of time in order to learn a specific example owing to the nature of recurrent training. The implementation of NN in hardware, on the other hand, may speed up the training by many orders of magnitude, which is why VLSI implementation receives the attention it does. The purpose of this work is to provide a concise review of digital and pulsed neurohardware. Important topics, including the algorithm that was employed, the technique of compact design, and the method of high-speed operation, were covered in this article. The invention of additional benchmark circuits and the development of learning algorithms that are favourable to VLSI technology will be the focus of future research. The programmable platform provided by Xilinx Zynq-7000 is used in the creation of a fully working proof-of-concept system by the suggested BNN. The work presented here indicates that it is possible to create integrated BNN by making use of APSoC in FPGA. Even if the system operates well, there is always space for advancement in terms of throughput as well as energy efficiency. The challenging aspects of meeting the tight criteria for embedded BNN in terms of platform size, efficiency, and processing power continue to be present. The development of Artificial Intelligence (AI), although being a potentially useful technology, is now clouded by the absence of a complete body of ideas that can underpin essential design concepts. Is the future of artificial intelligence going to be deep neural networks or reinforcement learning? In addition, the development of new computer platforms is shrouded in mystery due to the fact that Moore's Law is gradually losing its validity and artificial intelligence is highly dependent on computing resources. It's possible that future AI applications on edge devices may run in the cloud or on local devices at a scale that's more manageable. In the not-too-distant future, there will likely be several computer platforms, each of which will provide its own unique set of advantages. When compared to the design that was developed and implemented for the original clustering-based motion detection technique, the memory-efficient new architecture requires roughly 41% less FPGA Block RAMs (on-chip memory) than the previous architecture. The whole system, including the camera interface, memory efficient motion detection architecture, and display interface, has been built on the Xilinx ML510 (Virtex-5 FX130T) FPGA Board. This includes both the camera interface and the display interface. The new memory-efficient system detects motion in real-world scenarios (both for the static backgrounds and the pseudo-stationary backgrounds) in real-time for standard PAL (720 576) size colour video, as was demonstrated on video sequences. This motion detection is robust and automatic, and it works for both the static backgrounds and the pseudo-stationary backgrounds. In a situation involving remote video surveillance, the system that has been constructed may be efficiently employed as a standalone system for the purpose of motion detection and filtering of frames of interest in order to reduce the amount of processing overhead and communication needs.

REFERENCES

Alaghi, A., Li, C., & Hayes, J. P. (2013). Stochastic circuits for real-time image-processing applications. In *Proc. 50th ACM/EDAC/IEEE Design Autom. Conf. (DAC)* (pp. 1–6). ACM.

Arbib, M. A. (Ed.). (2002). *The Handbook of Brain Theory and Neural Networks* (2nd ed.). MIT Press. doi:10.7551/mitpress/3413.001.0001

Bruntha, P., Malin, S. Dhanasekar, D. Hepsiba, K. Martin Sagayam, T. Neebha, M., Pandey, D., & Pandey, B. (2022). *Application of Switching Median Filter with L2 Norm-Based Auto-Tuning Function for Removing Random Valued Impulse Noise.* Aerospace Systems.

Dahl, G. E., Yu, D., Deng, L., & Acero, A. (2012, January). Context-dependent pretrained deep neural networks for large-vocabulary speech recognition. *IEEE Transactions on Audio, Speech, and Language Processing, 20*(1), 30–42. doi:10.1109/TASL.2011.2134090

Dhanasekar, S., & Govindaraj, V. (2023). *Low-power test pattern generator usingmodified LFSR.* Aerospace Systems.

Dhanasekar, S., Malin Bruntha, P., Jubair Ahmed, L., Valarmathi, G., Govindaraj, V., & Priya, C. (2022). *An Area Efficient FFT Processor using Modified Compressor adder based Vedic Multiplier.* In Proceedings of the 2022 6th International Conference on Devices, Circuits and Systems (ICDCS), Coimbatore, India. 10.1109/ICDCS54290.2022.9780676

Dhanasekar, S., Malin Bruntha, P., & Martin Sagayam, K. (2019). An Improved Area Efficient 16-QAM Transceiver Design using Vedic Multiplier for Wireless Applications. *International Journal of Recent Technology and Engineering, 8*(3), 4419–4425. doi:10.35940/ijrte.C5535.098319

Dickson, J. A., McLeod, R. D., & Card, H. C. (1993). "Stochastic arithmetic implementations of neural networks with in situ learning," in Proc. IEEE Int. Conf. *Neural Networks, 2*(Mar), 711–716.

Hinton, G. E., & Salakhutdinov, R. R. (2006). Reducing the dimensionality of data with neural networks. *Science, 313*(5786), 504–507. doi:10.1126cience.1127647 PMID:16873662

Ji, Y., Ran, F., Ma, C., & Lilja, D. J. (2015). A hardware implementation of a radial basis function neural network using stochastic logic. Proc. Design, Autom. Test Eur. Conf. Exhibit. (DATE), (pp. 880–883). IEEE. 10.7873/DATE.2015.0377

Kim, L.-W., Asaad, S., & Linsker, R. (2014). A fully pipelined FPGA architecture of a factored restricted Boltzmann machine artificial neural network. *ACM Trans. Reconfigurable Technol. Syst., 7*(1).

Kumar, A., Nagarajan, P., Selvaperumal, S., & Venkatramana, P. (2019). Design challenges for 3 dimensional network-on-chip (NoC). *International Conference on Sustainable Communication Networks and Application* (pp. 773-782). Springer, Cham.

Li, P., & Lilja, D. J. (2011). Using stochastic computing to implement digital image processing algorithms. Proc. IEEE 29th Int. Conf. Comput. Design, (pp. 154–161). IEEE. 10.1109/ICCD.2011.6081391

Li, P., Lilja, D. J., Qian, W., Bazargan, K., & Riedel, M. D. (2014, March). Computation on stochastic bit streams digital image processing case studies: IEEE Trans. Very Large Scale Integr. (VLSI). *Syst., 22*(3), 449–462.

Liu, Y., & Parhi, K. K. (2016, July). Architectures for recursive digital filters using stochastic computing. *IEEE Transactions on Signal Processing, 64*(14), 3705–3718. doi:10.1109/TSP.2016.2552513

Luo, P., Tian, Y., Wang, X., & Tang, X. (2014). Switchable deep network for pedestrian detection. Proc. IEEE Conf. CVPR, (pp. 899–906). IEEE. 10.1109/CVPR.2014.120

Nagarajan, P., Ashok Kumar, N., & Venkat Ramana, P. (2020). Design of implicit pulsed-dual edge triggering flip flop for low power and high speed clocking systems. *International Journal of Wavelets, Multresolution, and Information Processing, 18*(01), 1941009. doi:10.1142/S0219691319410091

Nagarajan, P., Ashokkumar, N., Arockia Dhanraj, J., Kumar T. & Sundari, M. (2022). Delay Flip Flop based Phase Frequency Detector for Power Efficient Phase Locked Loop Architecture. *2022 International Conference on Electronics and Renewable Systems (ICEARS),* (pp. 410-414). IEEE. doi:. doi:10.1109/ICEARS53579.2022.9752249

Nagarajan, N., Kumar, A., Dhanraj, J., & Kumar, T. (2022). Delay Flip Flop based Phase Frequency Detector for Power Efficient Phase Locked Loop Architecture. *International Conference on Electronics and Renewable Systems.* IEEE.

Natarajan, V., Ashokkumar, N., Pandian, N., & Savithri, V.G. (2018). Low Power Design Methodology. *Very-Large-Scale Integration.* IntechOpen.

Rosselló, J. L., Canals, V., & Morro, A. (2010). Hardware implementation of stochastic-based neural networks. *Proc. Int. Joint Conf. Neural Netw. (IJCNN)*, (pp. 1–4). Springer.

Sheu, B. J., & Choi, J. (1995). *Neural Information Processing and VLSI*. Kluwer Academic Publishers. doi:10.1007/978-1-4615-2247-8

Zeng, X., Ouyang, W., & Wang, X. (2013). Multi-stage contextual deep learning for pedestrian detection. Proc. IEEE Int. Conf. Comput. Vis. (ICCV), (pp. 121–128). IEEE. 10.1109/ICCV.2013.22

Chapter 5

Prediction of Skin Cancer Using Convolutional Neural Network (CNN)

Deepa Nivethika S.
Vellore Institute of Technology, Chennai, India

Dhamodharan Srinivasan
Sri Eshwar College of Engineering, India

SenthilPandian M.
Vellore Institute of Technology, Chennai, India

Prabhakaran Paulraj
St. Joseph University in Tanzania, Tanzania

N. Ashokkumar
 https://orcid.org/0000-0002-4034-484X
Mohan Babu University, India

Hariharan K.
Sri Sairam Engineering College, India

Maneesh Vijay V. I.
Sri Sairam Engineering College, India

Raghuram T.
Sri Sairam Engineering College, India

ABSTRACT

Skin disorders are one of the most common types of disorders that are primarily diagnosed visually with scientific screening observed through dermoscopic evaluation, histopathological evaluation, and a biopsy. Diagnostic accuracy has a strong relevance to physician skill. Painful effects of skin disease hamper the mental condition of a patient. The authors propose an approach to detect the skin diseases based upon image processing as well as machine learning techniques i.e., convolutional neural networks (CNN). CNN is a specific type of neural network model that allows us to extract higher depictions for the image content. It is a deep learning algorithm to perform generative and descriptive tasks. Machine learning generates two types of prediction-batches and real time.

DOI: 10.4018/978-1-6684-6596-7.ch005

INTRODUCTION

Any abnormalities on the skin, whether benign or malignant, are referred to as skin lesions. Cancer is present in malignant lesions. Cancer risk is reduced by early detection and treatment of precancerous skin lesions. According to WHO (World Health Organization) statistics, 132,000 cases of melanoma skin cancer and 2 to 3 million cases of non-melanoma skin cancer occur annually worldwide. A 10% reduction in ozone levels will lead to an increase in skin cancer cases of 3,00,000 non-melanoma and 4,500 melanoma. Although more prevalent, non-melanoma skin cancers like basal cell carcinomas as well as squamous cell carcinomas are less likely to spread and only partially cause disability or even death. Early detection and accurate or precise diagnosis of the skin cancer can aid in the recovery process, ensure proper medical care, and help prevent the worst side effects. Therefore, a system for early detection can help and raise public awareness purpose in identifying different types of skin cancer or other skin disorders like a benign tumour on the skin that look a lot like skin cancer is needed. The automatic classification of skin disorders can assist individuals in recognizing skin conditions as they develop and prompting immediate consultation with medical professionals to receive the necessary medical care. Medical professionals and other biomedical researchers can use a number of related studies are based on digital image processing for the detection along with classification of skin cancers as a means to diagnose skin conditions more precisely and quickly.

Visual inspection of dermoscopic images, in general, necessitates the expertise of a dermatology specialist. Skin lesion diagnosis is difficult, even for an expert physician. As a result, invasive biopsy of the affected lesion is required for doctors to make an accurate diagnosis. A dermoscopic imaging technique captures and visualises deep skin structures by using a non-polarized light source and also magnifying optics.

Without additional technical support, dermatologists have a 65%-80% accuracy rate in diagnosing melanoma. Andre Esteva et al. (2017) proposed method uses convolutional neural networks that classify skin lesions into benign or malignant eosin based on a novel regularized technique. A method for classification of melanoma skin cancer using convolutional neural network is proposed by Nachbar et al. (1994). The application uses the Convolutional Neural Network method and the LeNet 5 architecture for classification, and the percentage of accuracy achieved was 93% in training and 100% in testing. The variety of educational information used from 176 snapshots and 100 epochs.

On the exact diagnosis of the disease that helps aiding in decision-making clinically, early classification of the skin lesions can increase the likelihood of curing cancer before it spreads. Most skin disease images that are used for training are unbalanced and rare, making automatic skin cancer classification difficult to achieve. In addition, the cross-domain adaptability and robustness of the model are major obstacles. To address the above problems and obtain satisfactory results, many deep learning-based skin cancer classification methods have recently become popular (Estava, 2015). Reviews addressing the above borderline problems in relevance with skin cancer classification are even hard to come by. Therefore, in this article, we provide a comprehensive overview of the latest deep learning-based skin cancer classification algorithms. First, an overview of three different types of dermatological images is provided, and then a list of publicly available skin cancer datasets is provided. Subsequently, the successful uses of standard convolutional neural networks for skin cancer classification are reviewed. Highlights of this paper include a summary of several frontier issues such as data imbalance, data confinement, domain fitting, model robustness, and model efficiency and their corresponding solutions in the skin cancer classification task (Khan, 2018). In conclusion, by summarizing different deep learning-based approaches to address current problems in skin cancer classification, we can draw the general conclusion that the development of these methods is generally going in a structured, lightweight, and multimodal direction. Additionally, we have presented our results in figures and tables for reader-friendliness. Deep learning is becoming increasingly popular, but there are still many problems to be solved and opportunities to be pursued for the future (Kim, 2017; Manne, 2020).

Unlike the standard image recognition methods, where you do define the image features yourself, CNN extracts the raw pixel data of the image, in accordance it trains the model and then automatic extraction is being done for better classification. This approach has been developed for diagnosis of skin disease. It aids in the accurate diagnosis of the skin area that is afflicted, senior professional assistance, recommendations for nearby doctors, and advice on treatments and safety measures for a specific disease. This project aims to develop skin diseases diagnosis system with a web-based interface, the system is built on a machine learning algorithm model in order to classify the infected images using confusion matrix and develop a web interface application to capture the images. Thus, by this method we could predict and detect skin diseases and provide the reference to the nearest practitioner.

LITERATURE SURVEY

Skin Cancer ISIC Dataset

The International Skin Imaging Collaboration (ISIC) data set is used in this study. Squamous cell carcinoma and melanoma for skin cancer are included in the data set, while dermatofibroma and nevus pigmentosus are included for tumour conditions. Dermatofibroma: Skin's dermis layer can develop benign tumours called dermatofibromas when a variety of cell types proliferate too much. The skin growth that leads to dermatofibroma typically develops following a variety of minor skin traumas, such as insect bites or glass splinter wounds. The International Skin Imaging Collaboration (ISIC) data set is used in this study. Squamous cell carcinoma and melanoma for skin cancer are included in the data set, while dermatofibroma and nevus pigmentosus are included for tumour conditions.

Dermatofibroma Skin's dermis layer can develop benign tumours called dermatofibromas when a variety of cell types proliferate too much. The skin growth that leads to dermatofibroma typically develops following a variety of minor skin traumas, such as insect bites or glass splinter wounds. When exposed to pollutants, ultraviolet light, and harmful chemicals, nevus pigmentosus, which resembles birthmarks or moles, has the potential to turn into melanoma, a very deadly form of skin cancer. Nerve disorders like seizures, fainting, and vomiting are some other side effects of this disease for patients who experience complications.

Squamous cell carcinoma: The legs, arms, lips, ears, face, neck, and head are among the body parts that frequently encounter sunlight when developing squamous cell carcinoma. In comparison to other skin cancers, this disease is not particularly aggressive. If detected early enough, this disease tends to grow slowly and is easily treated with non-surgical therapy. Due to the delayed treatment, the benign tumour may continue to develop into cancer and spread to the bones, tissues, and even lymph nodes. Treatment for cancer is more challenging the more widely it has spread.

Melanoma: Skin cancer of the melanoma variety is extremely dangerous. This illness begins on human skin and can spread to other body organs. This condition is a form of skin cancer that develops from melanocyte cells, which are typically found in the skin and produce melanin. Melanoma is multicoloured and has an irregular shape. Melanoma-affected moles can itch and bleed, and they may be larger than typical moles.

However, the hardware integration of the neural network into VLSI system design hardware has just started its evolution in Google coral products range. It consists of a single computer that includes processor, RAM and AI, altogether. It helps in offloading Tensor flow algorithms from the main processor that helps to speed up the AI applications.

The application was built using the Python programming language and the Keras library as the Tensor Flow backend. This paper proposed the use of image processing techniques for the detection of melanoma skin cancer. The skin lesion image is taken as input and then by applying different image processing techniques, the proposed system checks the different melanoma parameters like asymmetry, border B. color, diameter (ABCD) etc. through texture, size and shape analysis for image segmentation and feature stages, and that Image is then classified as normal skin or melanoma cancer lesion.

Technological advancements play a lead role in every person's life. It eases the work of a person in all means that includes grooming, health care, etc. Electronic gadgets even though may benefit and hence one's life, the configuration of the gadgets being used vary from person to person. In case of skin cancer prediction with the available devices, the image resolution varies gadget to gadget depending upon the configuration used. So, this chapter proposes a method to enhance and scale up the melanoma targeted pixels. It is done by comparing with the nearby pixels and using efficient algorithms to fix the proper edges and to scale up the pixels. Some other alternate methods like antennas also used for this purpose. Stretchable antennas are placed over the skin to find out the cancerous tumors, either internally or externally.

PROPOSED METHODOLOGY: SYSTEM DESIGN

Image Scaling With VLSI

Figure 1. Image scale-up architecture

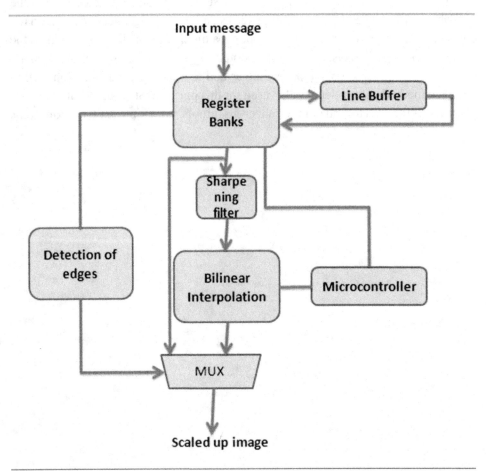

Figure 1 describes enhancing the pixels of the picture by scaling up the image. It consists of the register banks comprising 8 shift registers that fetches 8 nearest pixels of the targeted one. During the bilinear interpolation blurring occurs. To remove the blurring effects, the image is again sent to the spatial filter, which increases the center pixel with respect to the neighbours. The detection of edges is found out with edge detection and enhancement technique that helps to notice the sudden changes in pixel. The binary interpolation is a low complex and simplified interpolation technique in which the target pixel is chosen with the help of low complex image scaling interpolation algorithms. This linear interpolation is performed with specific directions. The microcontroller is basically used to control all the processes including shift registers, register banks, filters, enabling and disabling of interpolation algorithms, edge detection algorithms, finite state machines and other combinational circuits. This architecture suffices the need for a scaled-up picture of a melanoma/skin cancer.

Figure 2. Stage pipeline VLSI architecture for scaling up of skin cancer image

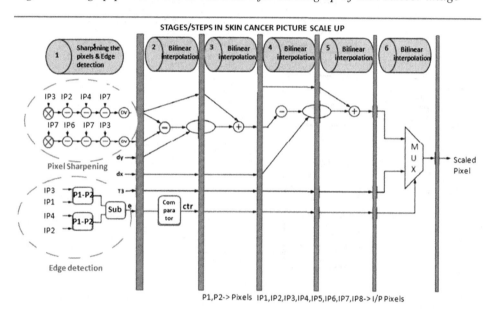

Scale up of the image occurs by 6 pipelining stages. The first stage is for edge detection, which includes sharpening of the pixels present in the image. It occurs in 2 levels. Level 1 is to sharpen the image with the help of multipliers, adders, and dividers. Level 2 is to detect the edges by subtracting the nearby edges with the help of recursion. Level 2 to Level 6 comprises bilinear interpolation, as stage 2 comprises of a comparator, comparison between the edges is done with the pre-fed value. Similarly, addition and subtraction of values are done in the following stages to get a scaled image with perfect edges. The final scaled image is then sent into the decision-making channel, where the input image is compared with the pre-fed melanoma images to provide a concise decision, as explained in Figure 2.

This section explains the methodology of the suggested system. The system design for the proposed model has been divided into two parts: Building the model and integrating it into a Web Application. Our Main moto is to sense and predict the disease.

Figure 3. Workflow

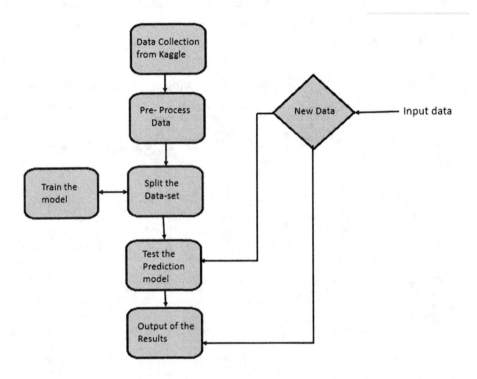

In Case of Workflow as shown in Figure 3, earlier detection of disease can be timely help and necessary measures could be taken to stop the spread of disease. Training the model was done as shown in Figure 3.

Figure 4. Train the model

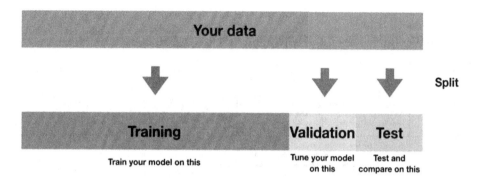

The presence of hair is the main problem in dermoscopic images, shown in Figure 4. If the skin lesion is covered by hair, the segmentation, pattern recognition, and classification task is difficult. Morphological filtering is the best technique for removing hair particles on skin lesions.

Imaging Dataset

Table 1. Different method for solving data imbalance and data limitation

Dataset	Highlight	Limitation	Performance
ISIC-2017	Seven GANs are coupled to produce seven images of skin diseases. By sharing the same parameters between the initial layers of GANs, they simultaneously increased the model's efficiency.	When the lesion area was blended with the skin's surface, the model struggled to distinguish it, and artefacts like human hair can interfere with the creation of new images.	Accuracy: 0.816 AUC: 0.88
ISIC-2018	Implied a GAN architecture tailored to the appearance of skin lesions. By adjusting the GAN network's generator and discriminator's progressive growth structures, it can simultaneously produce skin disease images with higher resolution and a wider range of skin conditions.	When compared to the original dataset, the content of the GAN-generated synthetic dataset was not diverse or complicated enough.	Accuracy: 0.952 Sensitivity: 0.832 Specificity: 0.743
ISIC-2018	CGANs were used to extract important data from all layers and create skin lesion images with a variety of textures and shapes while maintaining the training data's stability.	Data used for training were only a small amount.	. Accuracy: 0.941 Precision: 0.915 Recall: 0.799
ISIC	Archive investigated four different data augmentation techniques and a multi-layer augmentation technique for the classification of melanoma.	The data augmentation techniques examined in this has some limitations and hadn't been tested on a sizable number of datasets.	Accuracy: 0.829
HAM10000	To obtain domain-dependent noise vectors, they used a variational autoencoder network. Additionally, a student-like distribution was used to broaden the variety of the images, and an auxiliary classifier was employed to generate images of particular classes.	Medical images are very specific, so various image generation models could produce skin disease images that weren't in the same class.	Accuracy: 0.925
HAM10000	It introduced the Two-Timescale Update Rule to generate features with high fineness and combined the attentional mechanism with PGGAN to preserve global features of skin lesion images while improving the stability of GAN	Due to hardware limitations, this data propagation method was only tested with the resolution of 256,256 instead of the original resolution of 600,450 in the HAM10000 dataset.	AUC: 0.793
HAM10000	To address the issue of data imbalance, a class-weighted loss function and a focal loss were proposed. (Le DN, 2020)	The images in the training dataset have no artefact removal, which causes the model to be biased. Additionally, the computational complexity is quite high.	Accuracy: 0.93 Recall: 0.86
HAM10000	To address the imbalance issue with the dermatology dataset, a novel loss function was combined with balanced mini-batch logic of the data level.	There is still room for improvement in the classification accuracy for rare skin disorders with scant data.	Accuracy: 0.8997 Recall: 0.8613
HAM10000	Suggested a two-stage method for choosing the best augmentation method for mobile devices.	Given the uniqueness of lightweight CNN, additional data augmentation techniques and sources must be taken into account to address the overfitting issue.	Accuracy: 0.853
PAD-UFES	To address the issue of data imbalance, two evolutionary algorithms were developed and weighted loss function and oversampling were also used.	A bigger dataset was required to boost the performance even more.	Accuracy: 0.92 Recall: 0.94
PH2	a novel oversampling-based data augmentation method has been proposed (SMOTE).	Larger dataset experiments were also required because the proposed data augmentation method was not validated in the deep learning architectures.	Accuracy: 0.922 Sensitivity: 0.808 Specificity: 0.951

Figure 5. Sample images of HAM 10000

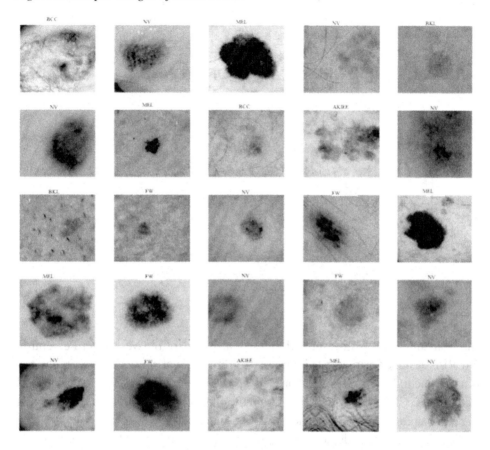

The HAM 10000 dataset is used in this research. There are 10015 dermoscopic pictures in the HAM10000 data set. These photographs were gathered from two separate locations: the Department of Dermatology at the Medical University of Vienna in Austria, and Cliff Rosendahl's skin cancer practise in Queensland, Australia. The collection includes images of skin lesions from seven distinct types of pigmented lesions from various populations. The pictures for the dataset were captured using polarised and non-polarized dermatoscopy instruments. Figure 5 shows some examples of pictures. The data collection includes sample instances of pigmented skin lesions that are useful in clinical practise, and most lesions encountered in clinical practise fit into one of the seven diagnostic categories described in the data set. Images of the same lesion captured at different magnifications or angles are also included in the collection. Images of the same lesion captured from different angles or magnifications are also included in the collection. Figure 6 depicts the architecture of the convolutional neural network. The dataset includes seven types of skin lesions: actinic keratoses, basal cell carcinoma, benign keratosis, dermatofibroma, melanocytic perivascular lesions, and melanoma.

CONVOLUTIONAL NEURAL NETWORK (CNN):

Figure 6. Architecture of CNN

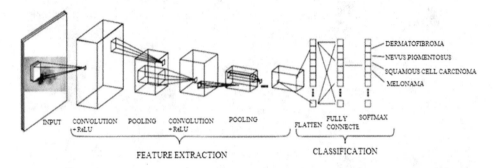

The Convolutional Neural Network (CNN), a version of the Multilayer Perceptron (MLP), is designed primarily to interpret two-dimensional input. CNN is categorized as a deep neural network since it has a deep network and is widely used to process picture data. CNN's design is comparable to that of other neural networks in that its neurons have weight, bias, and activation functions.

The CNN design is depicted in Figure 4, and it comprises of a fully connected layer with softmax activation as the classification layer, a convolution layer with ReLU activation as the feature extraction layer, and a pooling layer as the feature extraction layer.

Layer of Convolution: In the Convolution layer, the primary process that enables CNN is convolution. The convolution layer is the initial layer that processes the picture as an input system model. The picture will be convolved using a filter to extract features from the input image, also known as the feature map. Figure 7 depicts a depiction of the convolution process.

Figure 7. Illustration of the convolution process

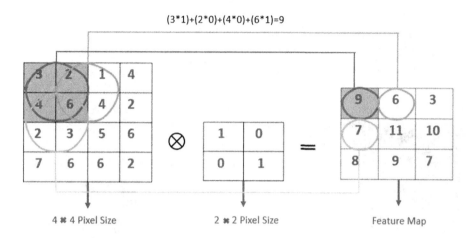

Activation Rel-U: Rectified Linear Units, or ReLUs, are activation layers in CNN that are used to speed up the training phase of neural networks, which has the benefit of minimising errors. When a pixel image has a value less than zero, Rel-U activation sets all of the pixels' values to zero.

$$f(x) = \begin{cases} x, x > 0 \\ 0, x \leq 0 \end{cases}$$

Rel-U Activation: There are several benefits to the pooling layer, which can gradually reduce the output volume on the Feature Map to control over-fitting. Polling layers are typically inserted after several convolution layers in the CNN method. Data is reduced using mean or max-pooling in the pooling layer. While the main pooling determines the average value, the max-pooling will choose the highest value. Figure 8 illustrates the pooling procedure using a four-by-four pixel input image.

Figure 8. Illustration of polling process

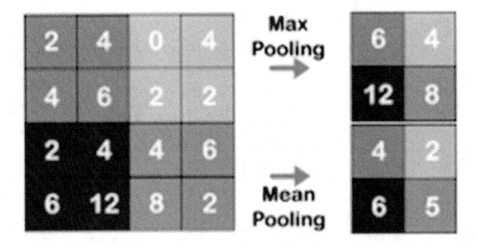

Layer Fully Connected: The final layer of the multilayer perceptron's architecture is known as the Fully Connected Layer. All the neurons from the preceding activation layer will be connected by this layer. This stage requires the flattening (or reduction to one dimension) of all input layer neurons. After that, the logistic regression algorithm can be modified to use softmax activation to classify more than two groups.

Hyperparameter: Hyperparameter has variable values that remain during the model training process that can affect the performance of the model railroad. An optimizer such as Stochastic Gradient Descent (SGD), Root Mean Square Propagation (RMSprop), Adaptive Moment Estimation (Adam) and Nesterov accelerated Adaptive Moment Estimation, is used as a hyperparameter in this study (Nadam). A repetitive optimization technique called stochastic gradient descent (SGD) aims to improve the model by using superior functions like differential or subdifferential equations. Each training sample is treated as a new parameter by SGD. Deep learning model design frequently makes use of Root Mean Square Propagation (RMSprop). This optimizer is a variation on the Root Propagation algorithm (Rprop). Rprop can't initially be applied to files containing a lot of data. Moving the average gradient at the model's time is the core of RMSprop. RMSprop and momentum are combined to create the Adam optimizer. The average gradient of weight is also used by this optimizer. Adam has the advantage over other optimizers in that it is quicker to compute, uses less memory, and can handle noisy problems with sparse gradients. Thus, Adam and NAG are combined to create Nadam (Nesterov-accelerated Adaptive Moment Estimation) (Nesterov accelerated gradient). In simple jargon, a convolutional neural network (CNN) is a sort of artificial neural network that analyses data using a perceptron, a machine learning unit method. CNNs can be used for image processing, natural language processing, and other cognitive tasks. Convolutional neural networks are sometimes known as convnets. The convolutional neural network, like other forms of artificial neural networks, comprises an input layer, an output layer, and several hidden layers. Figure 9 shows how some of these layers are convolutional and employ a mathematical model to transfer findings to subsequent levels. This CNN mimics part of the activity of the human visual brain.

Figure 9. Convent with corresponding layers

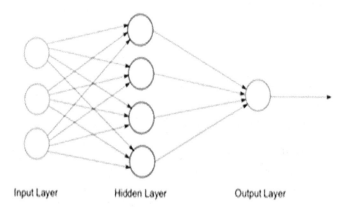

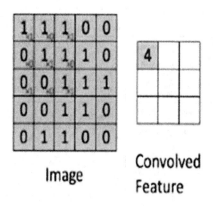

Table 2. Several methods for improving model efficiency: A comparative study

Data-Set	Highpoints	Boundaries	Performance Measures
Collected from various sources	To instantaneously transfer data between different models, a technique of knowledge distillation was proposed.	The proposed method has some other additional classification errors based on local objects and trades the local accuracy to achieve a higher global accuracy.	Accuracy: 0.75
Public -repositories	Proposed and successfully implemented a MobileNet-based classification technique in an Android application	More erudite sampling methods along with data pre- processing can be used to enhance the model's classification accuracy.	Accuracy: 0.944
HAM10000	Based on the ResNet architecture, an evaluation of the effectiveness of the attentional modules and the self-awareness modules in the section of skin cancer classification was presented.	Only a few attention mechanisms are being used for comparison.	Accuracy: 0.622 (attention) Accuracy: 0.737 (self-attention)
HAM10000	A weight pruning strategy introduced lightweight neural networks has been proposed to offset the loss of accuracy and improve the model performance and reliability in terms of skin cancer classification.	The proposed circumcision method was only validated using the skin disease dataset; More types of medical images are required to validate their effectiveness.	Accuracy: 0.975 AUC: 0.931 SH-11
HAM10000, PH2, Dermofit	MergePrune is a new pruning method that combines pruning and training in a single stage to reduce the computational cost of network retraining which is an advantage.	Additional domain data such as clinical images and patient metadata are required to evaluate this strategy.	Accuracy: 0.776 (avg.) Derm7pt, MSK, UDA
ISIC-2017	EfficientNet received a classification method which has been included in the attentional residual learning shortly known as (ARL) mechanism for the diagnosis of skin cancer.	The inter-pretability of the model must be further improved.	Accuracy: 0.873 AUC: 0.867
ISIC-2017	Skin cancer classification was tested using three dissimilar lightweight networks: MobileNet,NASNetMobile and MobileNetV2,	The number of the lightweight networks and the hyperparameters available for testing is limited.	Accuracy: 0.82 Precision: 0.812
ISIC-2017, PH2	To simultaneously segment and categorise skin lesions, an MT-Trans U Net network has been proposed.	Low-contrast skin disease images are difficult for the model to handle, and skin image trapping can affect segmentation performance.	Accuracy: 0.912
PH2, DermQuest	The development of a pruning framework to pick the most instructive colour channels to simplify complex architectures in skin lesion detection The complexity of several skin cancer categorization networks was also examined at the hardware level.	Simple networks respond well to the projected technique, but more complicated networks may not respond as effectively.	Accuracy: 0.9811 (PH2) Accuracy: 0.9892 (DermQuest)
SD-198, SD260	A curriculum-based knowledge distillation technique has been developed to differentiate herpes zoster from other skin conditions.	It necessitates manual hyperparameter adjustment based on various models and datasets.	Accuracy: 0.935
ISDerm, QuestDerm, NZDerm, "11K Hands"	It was suggested to classify four skin illnesses using the squeeze net-based expert system "i-Rash".	To increase the universality of the model, more clinical information and photos of skin conditions are required.	Accuracy: 0.972 Sensitivity: 0.944 Specificity: 0.981

DATA PRE-PROCESSING

The process of converting raw data into the format that the system needs is known as pre-processing. The information that is available could be inconsistent and/or have duplicate and empty fields. The duplicate photographs are eliminated from the dataset, and the remaining images are then divided into seven folders with names denoting the various categories of skin lesions. Along with being divided into training and testing datasets, the photos are also scaled. Data pre-processing ensures that the data set is uniform for utilisation. To diagnose the skin illness, the training data set is utilised to train the data model. After the model has been trained, the model is tested using test data to determine its correctness as depictrd in Figure 10.

Figure 10. Modeling of pre-processor along with complete workflow

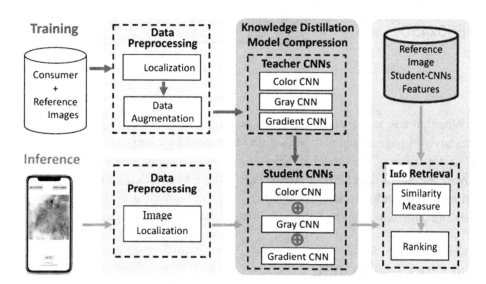

CONVERTING DATA TO IMAGE IMPROVEMENT

The procedure of augmentation is used to increase the quantity of photographs in the data set. The performance of the system is enhanced by adding more photographs to the dataset. There are a number of techniques accessible, including B. Flipping, random cropping, rotating, and colour shifting for enlarging the photos from which random cropping can be employed for enlarging, Figure 11.

Figure 11. Data augmentation process

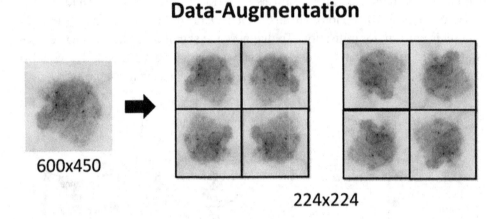

When photos are cropped randomly, just the portion needed by the algorithm is removed. Image augmentation is a step that must be taken in order to improve the performance of the model in order to create an accurate image classifier with a small amount of data (Goyal, 2020). This is done by enhancing the dataset using various augmentation techniques and increasing the number of images in each class to ensure consistency in the number of images used to train the model.

BUILDING THE MODEL

Using the training dataset, the model is developed. The process of training the model, also known as supervised learning, uses labelled images. The accuracy of the model is then assessed once the model has been evaluated using the testing data.

ANDROID STUDIO

In this task, we used Android Studio to put the model into practise. Based on IntelliJ IDEA, Android Studio is used as the official Integrated Development Environment (IDE) for the creation of Android apps.

IMPLEMENTATION

A machine learning model is constructed and developed using TensorFlow and Keras.

Some of the sample codes shown above for the skin care classification.

After the codes are executed in Android Studio, the model is trained for testing the inputs to a proper output.

Now on plotting the loss and accuracy graph, we get a positive result aSome of the example codes for the skin care categories are seen above.

The model is trained to test the inputs to produce the intended outcome after the programmes have been run in Android Studio.

After running a sample test of the model in Android Studio, we can now plot the loss and accuracy graph and get a favourable result. 12.a and 12.b, respectively.

Figure 12. a) Loss graph, b) recognition graph

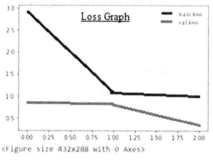
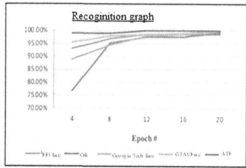

Figure 13 shows how readily machine learning can anticipate the given skin. Using the CNN model, the recognition rate of accuracy is 83%. Moving on to the first model, a forecast is made by an application.

DEPLOYMENT OF THE MODEL

Because the programme enables for the performance of a particular activity, Figure 10, we had employed it. An application is created for this architecture that allows users to obtain data from their own use, activity, and concerns. The goal of developing an application for our model is to make it simple to access, gather data, and anticipate events using machine learning.

Figure 13. Feature extraction and classification

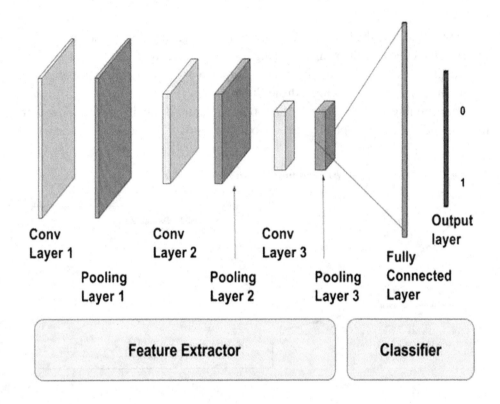

MOBILE APPLICATION

Figure 14 displays the outlook for the application.

Figure 14. Outlook of the mobile application

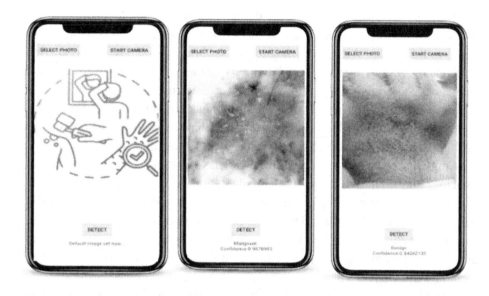

Patient's skin care classification and detecting the type of skin using data capture, and another module which gives the awareness on skin cancer and its treatments.

LIMITATIONS

This study has numerous limitations. The sample included 200 patients who presented to the oncology outpatient clinic. Firstly, this sample size of this study is relatively small and secondly, it was not randomly selected but dependent on patient availability. Therefore, the results presented here may not be fully generalized to the general population and there is a risk of sample bias.

CONCLUSION

As research and technology evolve, skin cancer classification's precision and effectiveness continue to rise. The accurate diagnosis of skin cancer used to frequently depend on the clarity of the image and the expertise of dermatological specialists, which is extremely subjective and has a high rate of misdiagnosis. Different CAD systems have been created to aid dermatologists in the diagnosis of skin cancer since the introduction of machine learning. By utilising handcrafted features, these CAD systems excelled at various tasks involving the classification of skin cancer. Due to deep learning's recent success in medical image analysis, multiple researchers have successfully used deep learning techniques to classify skin cancer from beginning to end. In the future, skin cancer diagnostics will be intrinsically tied to artificial intelligence. We provide a thorough summary of the most recent developments in skin cancer classification algorithms using deep learning in this article.

First, we went through three basic kinds of dermatological photos that are utilised for diagnosis and a few widely used datasets. After that, we'll talk about how common CNN-based categorization techniques are used. Following that, we go into a number of cutting-edge problems with the skin cancer classification challenge, such as data imbalance and limitation, cross-domain adaptation, model robustness and model efficiency, and pertinent deep learning-based techniques. We wrap up by providing a summary of the full review. The following details are critical: Unchecked cell growth in the skin is what leads to skin cancer. Skin exposed to the sun frequently harbours it. The three most typical kinds of skin cancer are melanoma, basal cell carcinoma (BCC), and squamous cell carcinoma (SCC).

The odds of successfully treating skin cancer are improved by early diagnosis (see Section 1 for more information). Clinical images, dermoscopic images, and histological images are the three most often utilised image types for diagnosing skin diseases. The most typical kind of image among them is one taken during a dermatoscopy. A growing number of datasets are being accessible to the public due to the increased demand for medical imaging resources in science. We give several well-liked datasets for the imaging of skin diseases and conduct research using these datasets. However, compared to databases for natural images, the variety and size of datasets for skin diseases are still quite small, which presents substantial difficulties for automated skin cancer diagnosis. When applying CNN-based skin cancer classification techniques, VGGNet, GoogleNet, ResNet, and their variants are the most often utilised deep learning models. Additionally, the use of ensemble learning has been suggested to reduce the error caused by a single model, and promising outcomes have been attained. Nevertheless, there are many different deep learning models. This work represents a better edge catching technique along with a low complex sharp filter. The hardware complexity was reduced with the help of bilinear interpolation equation. The edges of the targeted spot were reduced with the help of adaptive edge enhancing technique.

This deep learning approach can handle both generative and descriptive tasks. Machine learning makes it possible to make both batch and real-time predictions. Instead of starting with the raw pixel data from the image and heavily training the model, as is required by conventional image recognition techniques, CNN starts with the raw pixel data from the image and unintentionally extracts features for better organisation. To find skin problems, this method was developed. It helps senior experts create recommendations for neighbourhood doctors, assists in accurately identifying the skin's affected area, and provides treatments and precautions for specific ailments. The objective of this project is to develop a web-based interface for a system for diagnosing skin diseases. The solution is built on a machine learning model that classifies infected photos using a confusion matrix and a web application to interface with the images. Henceforth, this technique allows us to forecast and identify skin problems and recommend them to the closest doctor.

REFERENCES

Abayomi-Alli, O. O., Damasevicius, R., Misra, S., Maskeliunas, R., & Abayomi-Alli, A. (2021). Malignant Skin Melanoma Detection Using Image Augmentation by Oversampling in Nonlinear Lower-Dimensional Embedding Manifold. *Turkish Journal of Electrical Engineering and Computer Sciences*, *29*(SI-1), 2600–2614. doi:10.3906/elk-2101-133

Abdelhalim I.S.A., Mohamed, M.F., & Mahdy, Y.B. (2021). Data Augmentation for Skin Lesion Using Self-Attention Based Progressive Generative Adversarial Network. *Expert Syst With Appl*. doi:.2020.113922 doi:10.1016/j.eswa

Agarap, A. F. (2008). *Deep Learning using Rectified Linear Units (ReLU) 1*. Arxiv., https://arxiv.org/abs/1803.08375

Ahmad, B., Jun, S., Palade, V., You, Q., Mao, L., & Zhongjie, M. (2021). Improving Skin Cancer Classification Using Heavy-Tailed Student T-Distribution in Generative Adversarial Networks (Ted-Gan). *Diagnostics (Basel)*, *11*(11), 2147. doi:10.3390/diagnostics11112147 PMID:34829494

Ashokkumar, N., & Pappa, C. K. (2023). *Certain Investigation of Optimization Methods of Sensor Nodes in Biomedical Recording Systems*. 2023 9th International Conference on Advanced Computing and Communication Systems (ICACCS), Coimbatore, India. 10.1109/ICACCS57279.2023.10112688

Bisla, D., Choromanska, A., Berman, R. S., Stein, J. A., & Polsky, D. (2019). Towards Automated Melanoma Detection With Deep Learning. *Data Purification and Augmentation. Proc IEEE/CVF Conf Comput Vision Pattern Recognit Workshops*. 10.1109/CVPRW.2019.00330

Brinker, T. J., Hekler, A., Utikal, J. S., Grabe, N., Schadendorf, D., Klode, J., Berking, C., Steeb, T., Enk, A. H., & von Kalle, C. (2018). Skin Cancer Classification Using Convolutional Neural Networks: Systematic Review. *Journal of Medical Internet Research*, *20*(10), e11936. doi:10.2196/11936 PMID:30333097

Castro, P. B., Krohling, B., Pacheco, A. G., & Krohling, R. A. An App to Detect Melanoma Using Deep Learning: An Approach to Handle Imbalanced Data Based on Evolutionary Algorithms, in: *International Joint Conference on Neural Networks (IJCNN)*. Institute of Electrical and Electronics Engineers. 10.1109/IJCNN48605.2020.9207552

Chan, S., Reddy, V., Myers, B., Thibodeaux, Q., Brownstone, N., & Liao, W. (2020). Machine Learning in Dermatology: Current Applications, Opportunities, and Limitations. *Dermatology and Therapy*, *10*(3), 365–386. doi:10.100713555-020-00372-0 PMID:32253623

Deepa Nivethika, S., Sreeja, B. S., Manikandan, E., & Radha, S. (2018). A stretchable smart and highly efficient radio frequency antenna on low cost substrate. *Microwave and Optical Technology Letters*, *60*(7), 1798–1803. doi:10.1002/mop.31242

Tsaniyah, D., Aspitriani, A., & Fatmawati, F. (2013). Prevalensi dan Gambaran Histopatologi Nevus Pigmentosus di Bagian Patologi Anatomi Rumah Sakit Dr. Mohammad Hoesin Palembang Periode 1 Januari 2009-31 Desember 2013. *Majalah Kedokteran Sriwijaya*, *47*(2).

Dhanasekar, S. & Govindaraj, V., (2023). Low-power test pattern generator using modified LFSR. *Aerospace Systems*. doi:10.1007/s42401-022-00191-5

Dhanasekar, S., Malin Bruntha, P., & Martin Sagayam, K. (2019). An Improved Area Efficient 16-QAM Transceiver Design using Vedic Multiplier for Wireless Applications. *International Journal of Recent Technology and Engineering*, *8*(3), 4419–4425. doi:10.35940/ijrte.C5535.098319

Dhanasekar, S., & Ramesh, J. (2015). FPGA Implementation of Variable Bit Rate 16 QAM Transceiver System. *International Journal of Applied Engineering Research: IJAER*, *10*, 26479–26507.

Dildar, M., Akram, S., Irfan, M., Khan, H. U., Ramzan, M., Mahmood, A. R., Alsaiari, S. A., Saeed, A. H. M., Alraddadi, M. O., & Mahnashi, M. H. (2021). Skin Cancer Detection: A Review Using Deep Learning Techniques. *International Journal of Environmental Research and Public Health*, *18*(10), 5479. doi:10.3390/ijerph18105479 PMID:34065430

Duchi, Hasan, & Singer. (2011). Subgradient Methods for Online Learning and Stochastic Optimization. *J. of Machine Learning Research*.

Estava, A. (2015). *Deep Networks for Early Stage Disease and Skin Care Classification*. Stanford University.

Esteva, A., Kuprel, B., Novoa, R. A., Ko, J., Swetter, S. M., Blau, H. M., & Thrun, S. (2017, January 25). Dermatologist-level classification of skin cancer with deep neural networks. *Nature, 542*(7639), 115–118. doi:10.1038/nature21056 PMID:28117445

Goyal, M., Knackstedt, T., Yan, S., & Hassanpour, S. (2020). Artificial Intelligence-Based Image Classification for Diagnosis of Skin Cancer: Challenges and Opportunities. *Computers in Biology and Medicine, 127*, 104065. doi:10.1016/j.compbiomed.2020.104065 PMID:33246265

Haggenmüller, S., Maron, R. C., Hekler, A., Utikal, J. S., Barata, C., Barnhill, R. L., Beltraminelli, H., Berking, C., Betz-Stablein, B., Blum, A., Braun, S. A., Carr, R., Combalia, M., Fernandez-Figueras, M.-T., Ferrara, G., Fraitag, S., French, L. E., Gellrich, F. F., Ghoreschi, K., & Brinker, T. J. (2021). Skin Cancer Classification via Convolutional Neural Networks: Systematic Review of Studies Involving Human Experts. *European Journal of Cancer (Oxford, England), 156*, 202–216. doi:10.1016/j.ejca.2021.06.049 PMID:34509059

Höhn, J., Hekler, A., Krieghoff-Henning, E., Kather, J. N., Utikal, J. S., Meier, F., Gellrich, F. F., Hauschild, A., French, L., Schlager, J. G., Ghoreschi, K., Wilhelm, T., Kutzner, H., Heppt, M., Haferkamp, S., Sondermann, W., Schadendorf, D., Schilling, B., Maron, R. C., & Brinker, T. J. (2021). Integrating Patient Data Into Skin Cancer Classification Using Convolutional Neural Networks: Systematic Review. *Journal of Medical Internet Research, 23*(7), e20708. doi:10.2196/20708 PMID:34255646

J., J., C., S., R., B., & S., D. (2023). *Design and Analysis of CNN based Residue Number System for Performance Enhancement*. 2023 Third International Conference on Artificial Intelligence and Smart Energy (ICAIS), Coimbatore, India. 10.1109/ICAIS56108.2023.10073805

Kaur, R., Gholam, H., & Sinha, R. (2021). Synthetic Images Generation Using Conditional Generative Adversarial Network for Skin Cancer Classification. In TENCON 2021-2021 IEEE Region 10 Conference (TENCON). Institute of Electrical and Electronics Engineers (IEEE).

Khan, S., Rahmani, H., Shah, S. A. A., Bennamoun, M., Medioni, G., & Dickinson, S. (2018). *A Guide to Convolutional Neural Networks for Computer Vision*. Morgan Claypool. https: //ieeexplore.ieee.org/document/8295029

Kim, P. (2017). *MATLAB Deep Learning: With Machine Learning*. Neural Networks, and Artificial Intelligence. doi:10.1007/978-1-4842-2845-6

Le, D. N., Le, H. X., Ngo, L. T., & Ngo, H. T. Transfer Learning With Class Weighted and Focal Loss Function for Automatic Skin Cancer Classification. ArXiv (2020) abs/2009.05977:arXiv:2009.05977. doi:10.48550/arXiv.2009.05977

Lee, K. W., & Chin, R. K. Y. (2020). The Effectiveness of Data Augmentation for Melanoma Skin Cancer Prediction Using Convolutional Neural Networks. In *IEEE 2nd International Conference on Artificial Intelligence in Engineering and Technology (IICAIET)*. Institute of Electrical and Electronics Engineers. 10.1109/IICAIET49801.2020.9257859

Manne, R., Kantheti, S., & Kantheti, S. (2020). Classification of Skin Cancer Using Deep Learning, Convolutionalneural Networks-Opportunities and Vulnerabilities-a Systematic Review. *Int J Modern Trends Sci Technol*, *6*(11), 2455–3778. doi:10.46501/IJMTST061118

Nachbar, F., Stolz, W., Merkle, T., Cognetta, A. B., Vogt, T., Landthalerv, M., Bilek, P., Braun-Falco, O., & Plewig, G. (1994). The abcd rule of dermatoscopy: High prospective value in the diagnosis of doubtful melanocytic skin lesions. *Journal of the American Academy of Dermatology*, *30*(4), 551–559. doi:10.1016/S0190-9622(94)70061-3 PMID:8157780

Nivethika, S. D., Sreeja, B. S., Manikandan, E., Radha, S., & Senthilpandian, M. (2020). Dynamic frequency analysis of stress–strain-dependent reversibly deformable broadband RF antenna over unevenly made elastomeric substrate. *Pramana*, *94*(1), 122. doi:10.100712043-020-01992-z

Pathan, S., Prabhu, K. G., & Siddalingaswamy, P. (2018). Techniques and Algorithms for Computer Aided Diagnosis of Pigmented Skin Lesions—A Review. *Biomedical Signal Processing and Control*, *39*, 237–262. doi:10.1016/j.bspc.2017.07.010

Pham, T.C., Doucet, A., Luong, C.M., Tran, C.T., Hoang, V.D. (2020). *Improving SkinDisease Classification Based on Customized Loss Function Combined With Balanced Mini-Batch Logic and Real-Time Image Augmentation*. IEEE. doi:10.1109/ACCESS.2020.3016653

Nivethika, S., Sreeja, B., Radha, M. (2020). Polymer resin coating over dielecric elastomer for effective stretchable RF devices. *Journal of Optoelectronics and Advanced Materials*.

Qin, Z., Liu, Z., Zhu, P., & Xue, Y. (2020). A Gan-Based Image Synthesis Method for Skin Lesion Classification. *Computer Methods and Programs in Biomedicine*, *95*, 105568. doi:10.1016/j.cmpb.2020.105568 PMID:32526536

Robbins, H. & Monro, S. (1985). *A Stochastic Approximation Method.* Springer.

Roy, M. (2016). Dermatofibroma: Atypical Presentations. *Indian Journal of Dermatology.* PMID:26955137

Nivethika, S. (2018). Lycra fabric as an effective stretchable substrate for a compact highly efficient reversibly deformable broadband patch antenna. *Journal of Optoelectronics and Advanced Materials*, *20*(11-12), 634–641.

V., S., V., J., Srinivasan, D., & M., P. (2023). *A Concept-based Ontology Mapping Method for Effective Retrieval of Bio-Medical Documents.* 2023 9th International Conference on Advanced Computing and Communication Systems (ICACCS), Coimbatore, India. 10.1109/ICACCS57279.2023.10113073

Shen, S., Xu, M., Zhang, F., Shao, P., Liu, H., Xu, L. (2021). Low-Cost and HighPerformance Data Augmentation for Deep-Learning-Based Skin Lesion Classification. doi:10.34133/2022/9765307

Soyer, H. P. (2004). Three-point checklist of dermoscopy. Dermatology, 208(1), 27-31. doi:10.1159/000075042

Srinivasan, D., & Gopalakrishnan, M. (2019). Breast Cancer Detection Using Adaptable Textile Antenna Design. *Journal of Medical Systems*, *43*(6), 177. doi:10.100710916-019-1314-5 PMID:31073787

Syril Keena, T. (n.d.). Cutaneous squamous cell carcinoma. *Journal of The American Academy of Dermatology, 78*(2), 237-432.

WHO. (n.d.). *Statistics on skin cancer.* WHO. http//www.who.int/uv/faq/skincancer/ en/ /index1.html

Xiang, K., Peng, L., Yang, H., Li, M., Cao, Z., Jiang, S., & Qu, G. (2021). A Novel Weight Pruning Strategy for Light Weight Neural Networks With Application to the Diagnosis of Skin Disease. *Applied Soft Computing*, *111*, 107707. doi:10.1016/j. asoc.2021.107707

Yunlong, Y., & Fuxian, L. (2019). Effective Neural Network Training with a New Weighting Mechanism-Based Optimition Algorithm. *IEEE Access: Practical Innovations, Open Solutions.*

Chapter 6

Energy and Performance Analysis of Robotic Applications Using Artificial Neural Network

Ramesh A.
Sri Eshwar College of Engineering, India

P. Sivakumar
PSG College of Technology, Coimbatore, India

E. Venugopal
Sri Eshwar College of Engineering, Coimbatore, India

Ahmed Elngar
Beni-Suef University, Egypt

ABSTRACT

Many robotic applications require autonomous decision making. The obstacles may be uncertain in nature. Because of the mobility, most robots might be battery operated. This chapter briefs the energy and performance analysis of robotic applications using artificial neural networks. This chapter is designed to understand the operation of robots from understanding sensor data (training), processing (testing) the data in an efficient manner, and respond (prediction) to the dynamic situation using self-learning and adaptability.

DOI: 10.4018/978-1-6684-6596-7.ch006

INTRODUCTION TO ARTIFICIAL NEURAL NETWORK

Human brain study has a long history. In advancement of technology, it's rational in attempting and managing the style of thinking. ANN was established in late 1943 with the publication of a study on the potential uses of neurons by Warren McCulloch (neurophysiologist) and Walter Pitts (mathematician) (ANNs). They created a subtle model using electric circuits. Thanks to the amazing capability ofinferring the meaning of complex and irrelevant data, neural networks can be used to uncover patterns and discern trends from data that is too complex for either people or other computer systems to pick up on. A trained neural network could be considered an "expert" in the area of the data to be analysed.

A different approach of solving a problem by using an algorithmic approach, Traditional computers handle issues by following a set of instructions, which includes the computer. The computer is unable to resolve the issue without knowing the precise procedures that must be followed.Because of this, only issues that humans can currently understand and be familiar with may be solved by conventional computers. However, computers would be so much more useful if they could carry out activities that we are unclear of how to do. Neural networks process information in a manner akin to that of the human brain. The network is made up of many processing units that are closely connected to one another and work together to solve a certain problem simultaneously. Neural networks can learn from examples. They can't be forced to complete a pre-planned assignment. To avoid wasting time or, worse yet, having the network behave poorly, the examples must be carefully picked.

The network determines on fixing the problem by itself, its behaviour is unpredictable. Traditional computers, use a cognitive approach in problem solving; the answer is known and provided in a few simple, understandable steps. Once these instructions have been converted into a high-level language programme, the computer can comprehend them. These devices will only have hardware or software problems, if any.

These devices are entirely foreseeable. The usage of classic algorithmic computers and neural networks complements rather than competes with each other. There are tasks that are suited for neural networks, whereas arithmetic operations, are suited for algorithmic approaches. In addition, many activities require a combination of the two techniques in order for systems to operate at their best (often, a traditional computers require to oversee the neural network) (Maind et.al, 2014).

ANN: Characteristics

The characteristics of ANN are as follows.

Parallel Processing Capability

ANN is only beginning to learn about the concept of parallel preparing in the realm of computers. Human neurons perform parallel processing, which is incredibly unpredictable, but by using basic parallel preparation techniques, like matrix and some lattice estimations, we can mimic this in ANN.

Distributed Memory

We must therefore store data atweight lattice, sort of long-lasting memory, data is stored as examples throughout the system arrangement because ANN is a very large system and particular location memory or unified memory cannot satisfy ANN system's needs.

Capability for Fault Tolerance

Because ANN is a very complicated system, fault tolerance is a must. Because even if one component fails, the system as a whole won't be affected as much; nevertheless, if every component fails at once, the system will entirely malfunction.

Collective Solution

Because ANN is a networked system, the system's result is a summation of total inputs it has processed, or a combined output of those inputs. The incomplete response is useless to any ANN System user.

Learning Capability

Most learning rules used in ANNs are used to simulate processes, adjust the network to its changing environment, and gather useful data. Unsupervised, supervised, and reinforcement are these learning techniques.

Activation Mechanism

The transfer function that comes from an artificial neuron and send signals to other neuron is what activation functions are essentially. The various types of activation functions are each of the four models - Piecewise linear, threshold, Gaussian, and sigmoid is distinct from the others. ANN operation is continued in the next section.

ARTIFICIAL NEURAL NETWORK OPERATION

The numerous ways that individual neurons might be gathered andorganisedto make up the other aspects of the skill of engaging neural networks. The clustering that takes place in the human brain allows for dynamic, interactive, and self-organizing information processing. In the biological world, minute parts are assembled into three-dimensional brain networks. The connection potential of these neurons seems to be nearly infinite. This does not apply to any network that is currently being developed or proposed. Combined circuits are 2D objects withlimited number of interconnecting layers at present technology.This physical limitation limits the types and scope of ANN that can be implemented in silicon. At the moment, neural networks are only a simple grouping of artificially rudimentary neurons. By building layers and connecting them, this clustering takes place. How these levels connect is another element of the "art" of developing networks to address issues in the real world.

In essence, every simulated neural system has a similar topology or structure. A fraction of the neurons in such structure interface with the current world to obtain their information sources. This current reality is provided by several neurons in the system. A specific character or image that the system believes to have been confirmed could be the output in this case. Whole fragments of the neurons have been shown to elude capture. However, a neurological system is made up of surplus than a collection of neurons. Early researchers made several unsuccessful attempts to simply merge neurons in random ways. A neurological system cannot function without the layering of these neurons, the connectivity between each layers, and the summation and exchange processes.

The universalexpressions used to define these traits are common to all structures. The majority of applications require systems to at the very least contain the three most frequent categories of layers: (i) input, (ii) covered up, and (iii) yield, while there are effective systems that only have one layer or even just one component. The layers of information neurons may directly access information from electronic sensors or through information records. Data is sent specifically to external devices by the output layer, such asan additional computer handle.

Figure 1. Structure of neural network

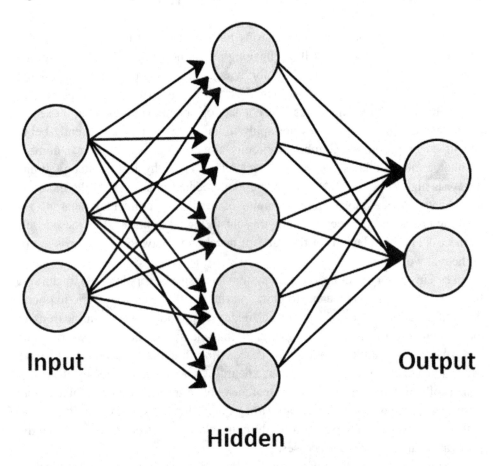

There are multiple layers in a neural network, including (i) input layer and (ii) output layer as shown in figure 1. Between the input and output layers there are several hidden layers. Each contain a hugequantity of interrelated neurons. The input and output of everyunknown neurons only go to another neurons, and in many systems, every neuron in aunknown layer obtains input from most of the neurons in the layer beyond it, which is typically the input layer. Following completion of its task, a neuron sends its output to the majority of the neurons in the layer beneath it, establishing a feed forward path for the output.Because they give the input in a brain network a variable strength, connections between neurons are crucial.

These connections come in two varieties: those that add to the following neuron's summing function and those that remove from it. One stimulates, whereas the other inhibits, to use more human language. Parallel inhibition is a requirement in some systems where a neuron must impede other neurons located in the alike layer.

Competition is yet another name for this idea.In a feedback link, the output of one layer is transmitted back to a lower layer. An example of this is shown in figure 2.

Figure 2. Neural network with feedback and competition

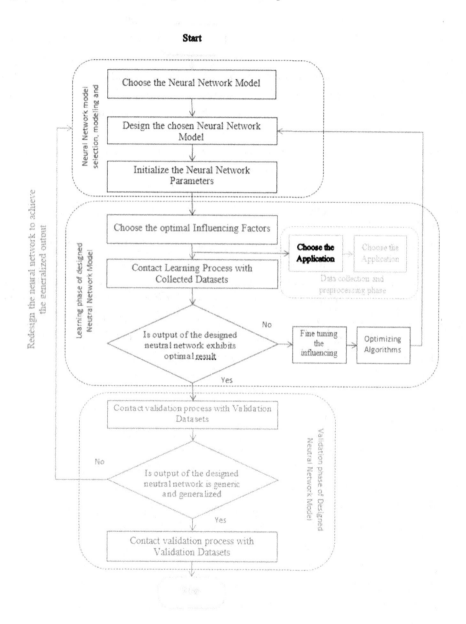

Properties of Artificial Neural Networks

ANNs are a type of machine learning procedure that are modelled after the construction and role of the human intelligence. They are particularly good at distinguishing patterns and taking decisions from large and somewhat fuzzy input data, and they are commonly used for responsibilities such as pattern identification, decision-making, and classification. ANNs are particularly effective at solving nonlinear problems, which are characterized by functions that do not follow the conditions of linearity, such as the equations $f(ay) = af(y)$ and $f(y1+y2) = f(y1) + f(y2)$. Nonlinear systems can be more challenging to understand and model using traditional methods, but ANNs are well-suited to this task due to their ability to distinguish patterns and take choices based on complex and ambiguous data.

In real life, the association between different variables is often more complex than a simple linear relationship. For example, as shown in figure 3, the relationship between money and happiness may not be straightforward. While it is true that having more money can generally lead to an increase in happiness, there may also be other factors that influence this relationship.

For example, an increase in earning may also lead to doubts of dropping money or suspicions about how to invest it, which can reduce happiness. In situations like this, where the relationship between variables is more complex and nonlinear, it can be more difficult to infer the underlying rules governing the behaviour of the system. In these cases, using an ANN can be a valuable utensil for analysing and considerate the data, as ANNs are particularly good at distinguishing patterns and taking decisions from complex and ambiguous data.

Figure 3. Association between happiness and money

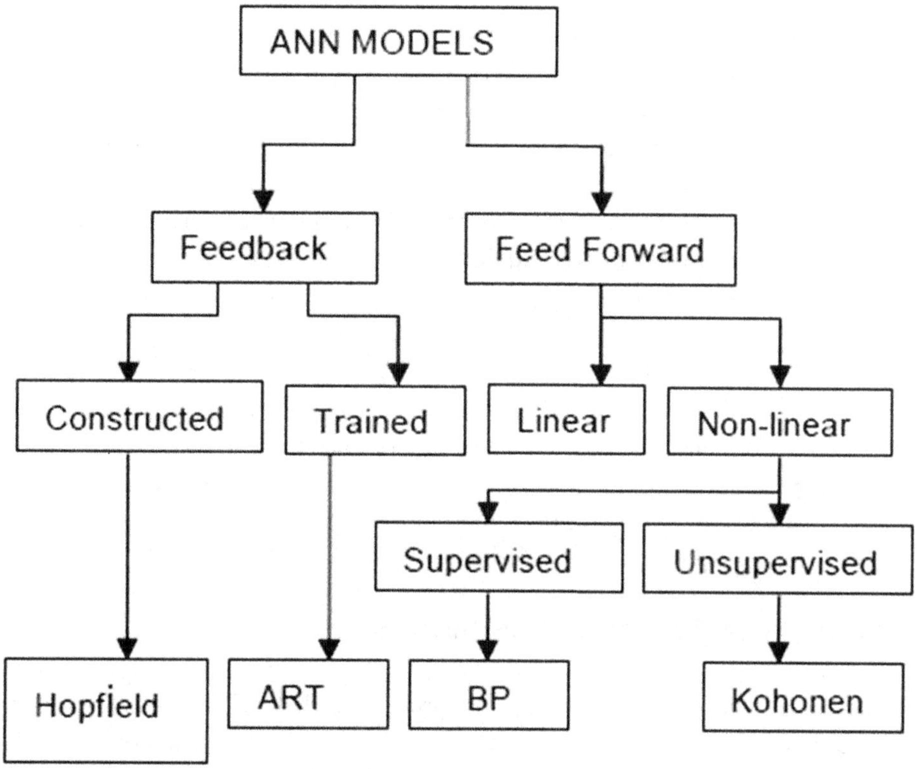

ANN Exposes the Unseen Guidelines of a Problem

Artificial neural networks are machine learning algorithms that are intended to distinguish patterns and take decisions created on complex and ambiguous records. They do not follow preciseguidelines to process information, but rather use the information they obtain to discover the guidelines prevailing the problem at hand.

COMPREHENSIVE ARTIFICIAL NEURAL NETWORK STEPS

The general algorithm for an artificial neural network contains of the subsequentphases as shown in figure 4:

1. Begin the strategy phase of the neural system, then select the best neural network model (such as feed forward or feedback model).

2.   Create the proposed model, taking into account the amount of input considerations, unknown layers, and hidden neurons.

3.Initialize the proposed model.

4.   Gather the data set and normalize it for the application of choice, splitting it into aexercise set and a testing set.

5.   Use the working data to train the suggested neural network prototypical.

6.   Assess the model's performance during the training phase to make sure it satisfies the required standards. Moving on to the testing phase is appropriate if the performance is adequate. In the event that the performance is subpar, go back to step 2 and rethink the model.

7.Test the proposed model using the testing set (unseen raw data).

8.Consider how effectively the model generalizes to new data by assessing its performance throughout the testing phase. Note the results if the model generalizes properly. Redesign the model and go through the training and testing processes once more if the model does not generalize well.

9.   Stop the process (Madhiarasan et.al, 2022).

General Classification of ANN Models

ANNs are a type of machine learning procedure that are modelled after the construction and role of the human intelligence. They are composed of individual neurons connected to each other through a network of connections, and they are proficient of learning and familiarizing to novel information over time through the use of a learning algorithm.

Some ANNs, such as perceptrons and linear associators, have a feedforward architecture, meaning that the result from solitary layer of neurons is only allowed to activate neurons in the next layer. Other ANNs, such as Kohonen nets and Hopfield models, allow the signal to activate neurons in the same layer. Still other ANNs, such as self-organizing feature maps, have a more complex architecture that connects a vector of inputs to a 2D grid of resultant neurons. Figure 5 shows a universal classification of ANN models based on their architecture and learning algorithm (Malik 2005).

Figure 4. Generalized algorithm for artificial neural network

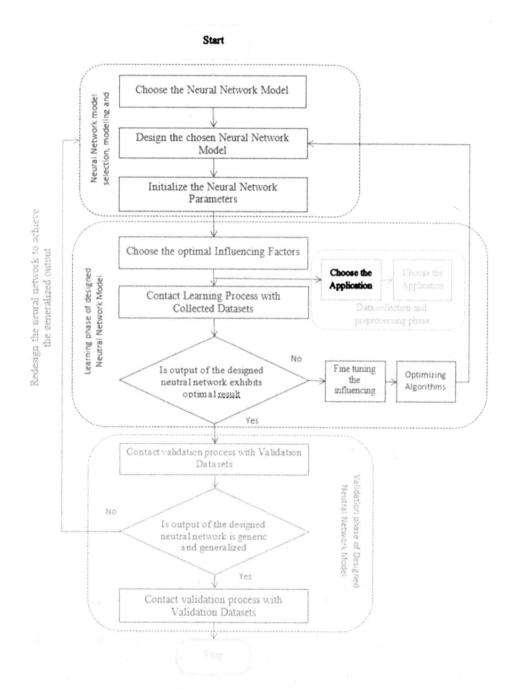

Figure 5. General classification of ANN models

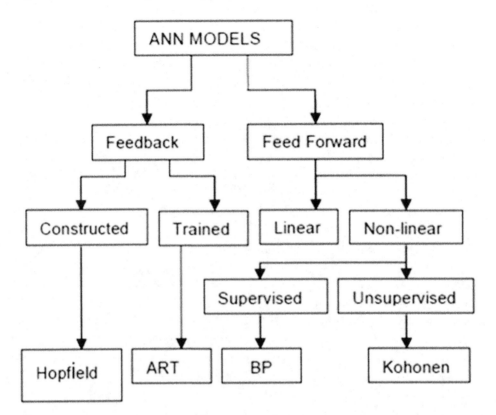

Training Neural Network Models

An ANN is trained by changing the relationsamong its neurons in an effort to reduce the faultamong the network's projected result and the desired result. Usually, a training algorithm is used for this procedure, which modifies the connection weights according to the mistakes calculated when each record in a dataset is processed by the system.

The joining weights among neurons are altered during an ANN's training phase to reduce the faultamong the system's anticipated result and the desired output. As every data in a dataset is processed through the system, the connection weights are often adjusted using a training technique, which employs gradient descent to do so.

The first derivative of the activation function of the recipient neuron, the raw signal flowing through the connection, and the output error of the net, which is properly weighted by all the joining weights foremost back to the neuron it gives, are combined to calculate the update to any given connection weight. The network's traversal of the gradient can be sped up or slowed down using a multiplicative constant known as the learning rate.

Large changes in connection weights from iteration to iteration can result from a strong learning rate, but it can also result in the network's inability to resolve the global minimum. On the other hand, complex models with many of local minima can have issues with low learning rates since the network might not be able to break free of a local minimum with slight weight changes. This can be solved by adding a momentum component to the error correction term. This enables the network to build momentum in its corrections if they continue in the same or general direction for a number of iterations, which can aid in the network's ability to exit local minima and enter global minima.

Automatic Training

- Input: The model receives a collection of training data. Each record is examined by the algorithm, which then iteratively adjusts the link weights across the network.
- Training errors:The training error is reduced during this process. The difference between the model's output and the outputs in the training dataset is known as the training error. Any implicit connections between input and resultant patterns are incorporated into the neural network once the training error is minimized.
- Training optimization: Neural system models that have undergone the best training describe a relationship that accurately depicts the overall correlation between the parameters of input and output. A model's collection of connection weights may not be able to preciselydenote the general relationship if it has not received enough training.

Figure 6. Training within a neural network

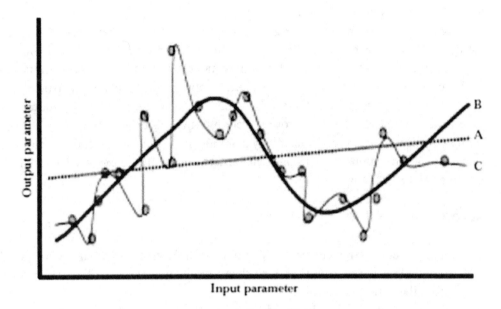

Avoiding over fitting the model to the training data is crucial while training an ANN. When a model is over fitted, the training set of data is fit too tightly to the model, which results in poor generalization to new data. This can be graphically demonstrated by looking at the figure 6, which displays plotted data points. The data can contain unwanted data and is consequently not accurate. If the prototypical is over fitted, a complex, developed order association may develop that turns the instance training data well but may source issues when it is put on to other examples that are anticipated to apply to this prototypical. A smooth line (B) may be the best representation of the general relationship of this data.

It is typically advised to employ a direct model arrangement with a negligible number of unknown layers and nodes per layer to prevent over fitting. This can ensure that the model stays manageable and has good generalizability to new data. On the other hand, less complicated relationships in the data might not be well captured by simpler model structures. Depending on the type of training data being used, it may take some experimentation to discover the proper balance between model complexity and generalization capability.

ANN Process in MATLAB

The fundamental ANN MATLAB process phases are listed here.

a. Gathering input-output data
b. Pre-processing the data
c. Designing and training a neural system
d. Assessing the network's activity.

Gathering of the Output and Input Data Sets

The first stage in using an ANN is to gather a dataset of input and output data. This dataset will be used to train the neural system to identifydesigns and relationsamong the input and result data. It is important to carefully select the input and resultant data to ensure that the neural system can accurately learn and generalize to new data.

Pre-Processing of Input-Output Dataset

When the dataset has been composed, it is often essential to process in advance the data to ensure that it is in aappropriatearrangement for the neural network. This may involve scrubbing the data to eliminate any faults or discrepancies, normalizing the data to scale it to a consistent range, and excruciating the data into exercise, authentication, and testing sets.

Neural Network Design and Training

The subsequentstage is to design and train the neural system. This includes choosing the construction of the neural network, such as the numeral of layers and the numeral of neurons in each layer, and selecting a suitable training algorithm to optimize the weights and biases of the system. The neural network is then skilled using the training dataset, and the performance is assessed using the authentication dataset to ensure that the network is learning accurately.

Performance Evaluation of the Neural Network

Using the testing dataset, the neural network's performance may be assessed once it has been trained. This enables you to assess the neural network's learning of the designs and correlations in the data and its generalizability to fresh data. Accuracy, precision, and recall are just a few of the measures that may be used to assess a neural network's performance.

$$R2 = 1 - \left[\frac{\Sigma \left(t_j - O_j \right)^2}{\Sigma \left(O_j \right)^2} \right]$$

t_j = Threshold value, O_j = Result, R = Determination coefficient, j = elements

Training of ANN

It is essential to plan and implement the input data collection in order for the ANN to create the appropriate output (either directly or through the use of a relaxation procedure). The strengths of the linkages can be determined in a number of ways. As an alternative, the solution can be modified to include learning patterns, and the net is then allowed to update or adjust the weights in line with some learning rule.

Following are some categories for learning-based solutions:

Associative or Guided Learning

Where the net is taught by comparing output patterns and quantifying input. The net itself, sometimes known as the self-supervised technique, or an external instructional component both supply these input/output pairings.

Learning Without Supervision

Unsupervised learning (self-organizing paradigm) trains the net (output) unit to answer to bunches of designs within the input framework. This paradigm states that the system should find properties of the input population that are statistically significant. No defined set of groups into which the designs are to be categorized, unlike the supervised learning approach, therefore the system must construct its own representation of the incoming stimuli.

Reinforcement Learning

In this strategy, the learning machine makes a change to the environment and then responds to it by receiving feedback. Based on the response from the environment, the learning component assigns a grade to its activity and modifies its settings accordingly. In general, parameter adjustments are made repeatedly until an equilibrium condition develops when they are no longer required.

ANNs are particularly useful for solving problems where the associationsamong the input and resultant are not well understood or are too complex to be modelled by traditional methods. They have been applied to extensive range of jobs, including predictive modelling, speech and imagerecognition, and processing of natural language. However, they can be subtle to the excellence and size of the training data, and may need careful design and tuning to achieve good performance (Mhatre et.al, 2015).

Neural systems have been applied in a widespread fields, including recognition of speech, signature, character, fingerprint, and face. It is also applicable for prediction of stock market, diagnosis of medical treatment, process control, quality control, data sorting and classification, sales and marketing, operational analysis, retail inventory optimization, employee retention, pattern recognition, chemical formulation optimization, ecosystem estimation, college student performance prediction, electrical load prediction, energy demand prediction, weather prediction, games development, optimization problems, routing, agricultural production, engine performance prediction, reactive power allocation, fuzzy intelligent systems, robot kinematics, battery charge estimation, food and fermentation technology, meat production, and materials science. These are just a few examples of the many areas in which neural networks have been applied successfully (Manickam et.al, 2017).

APPLICATIONS OF AN ARTIFICIAL NEURAL NETWORK IN ROBOTICS APPLICATIONS

To navigate and navigate autonomously, mobile robots need to be equipped with sensors that can collect data about their environment and location. The selection of these sensors depends on the tasks that the robot will perform and the accuracy and type of obstacles it will encounter. Commonly used sensors for this purpose include ultrasonic sensors, infrared sensors, cameras, and microphones. Ultrasonic sensors, while low cost, have some limitations such as angle restrictions and sensitivity to the material of the detected surface. Infrared sensors can also be used for obstacle detection and recognition, but they work best with certain types of obstacles. In combination, these sensors can provide complementary information about the atmosphere and increase the correctness of the mobile robot's navigation. Other sensors such as LiDAR, GPS, and vision-based systems such as Microsoft Kinect can also be used for autonomous navigation, depending on the preciseneeds of the application.

Since the Earth is not an ideal sphere, the Global Positioning System (GPS) uses geodetic coordinates, such as geodetic latitude and longitude and ellipsoidal height, or geographic coordinates, such as longitude and latitude, to locate receivers by calculating their distance from satellites (at least three) in which they are located. The GPS system is made to find objects at greater distances, measured in kilometres (square kilo meters). Due to the fact that it can forecast a vehicle's location by superimposing the vehicle's direction of movement onto a map, it works well with vehicles that can travel long distances in a short amount of time and move much faster than mobile robots. Robot displacements are much smaller and therefore require greater accuracy.

LiDAR sensors are utilised to produce maps of the surrounding area. By sensing laser pulses that are proportionate to an item's distance from the source, they enable object detection. For instance, positioning and orienting the mobile robot in 3D space using a laser head measuring the position relative to photoelectric reference points deployed in the room, determining the position of a robot by measuring distance and angle relative to another robot, using measurements obtained from raw data provided by two laser rangefinders in a 2D plane, or using an industrial laser navigation system to gather information about the distance between two objects.

The Microsoft Kinect system, an add-on for the Xbox game console, has become one of the most widely utilised tools for controlling mobile robots. The system is vision-based. A common navigational tool for mobile robots is Kinect, which allows them to avoid obstacles while sending data, for example, to an artificial neural network that deals with environmental detection and decides which course to take. The development of simultaneous localization and map-building algorithms like Simultaneous Localization and Mapping and all related techniques like SLAM - Parallel Tracking and Mapping) is another benefit of vision systems.

Any mutual radio communications between mobile robots or reference locations can be used as a basis for locating robots in constrained spaces. The sample signal vector and references contained in the database can be located using straightforward location techniques over a local wireless network. A wireless network can also be used to find an object by assessing signal intensity using a compressive sampling method, which makes it possible to effectively reconstruct signals from sparse data. The many methods of acquiring location data have been taken into account so far while thinking about how mobile robots should navigate.

Popular space location and orientation systems like GPS display decreased interior efficiency, as was previously mentioned. Solutions based on established reference points, however, restrict the robot to exclusively operating in that space. They give place to other information-based solutions from magnetometers, accelerometers, and gyroscopes, particularly while working indoors. These sensors' data can balance out each other's faults, and inertial navigation may be useful in some circumstances. It is based on a continual evaluation of the object's position in relation to the original position utilising input from sensitive sensors (such a gyroscope and an accelerometer). The method for controlling the motor drives in line with the topographical environment is equally important.

Artificial neural network implementation in machine vision and navigation tasks for mobile robots is essential for the advancement of modern robotics. The image that is captured can be used by the robot to avoid obstacles, follow the marker, and offer navigational data all at once. For these kinds of jobs, artificial intelligence techniques are ideal, such as the multilayer perceptron.

The suggested system's autonomous movable trolley in warehouses is one example of its utilisation. A cargo label is scanned by the robot controller, who then moves the cargo along a designated path to its destination. The network's design made it possible to achieve the desired path recognition outcomes.

Digitalization will include the popular of engineering arenas, with a better influence over wide-area communication network connecting fast data communication (Dhanasekar et.al, 2020).

Another research discussed trial design generator with least switching activity for high speed circuits (Govindaraj et.al, 2023). For reducing random valued impulse noise for neumorphic circuits, the switching median filter with L2 norm-based auto-tuning function was discussed (Bruntha et.al, 2023).

Another work used the Gravitational Search Algorithm to explain modeling a classification system based on fuzzy logic (Jubair et.al, 2022).

Industrial robots are typically programmed to select parts from conveyors for assembly tasks. However, there are frequent introductions of new designs and frequent component changes in the industrial sector. Robots should be reprogrammed in such circumstances. The time required to establish a new assembly programme increases noticeably after a company instals a new manufacturing unit. The lead time has increased as a result. Robots need to perceive their surroundings, make judgements, and take appropriate action in order to avoid situations like this. Artificial intelligence and robot vision are crucial for achieving this goal. The process of acquiring an image, having it processed by a computer, and then interpreting it for a specific purpose is known as machine vision.

Machine vision applications in industry can offer answers for a range of issues relating to the online component recognition. The cameras can be used to give the robots this vision.

On the conveyor, a variety of items that are frequently utilised in actual industrial applications are moved. The necessary object is provided to the neural network that has previously received training. As soon as it receives input, it begins taking pictures of the components moving through a conveyor.

After processing the collected image, ANN recognises that component as shown in figure 7. Once the component has been identified, the robot will move and push it off the conveyor and deposit it in the bin that is located behind the conveyor. The robot then returns to its starting location. Up until we stop the robot, it continues to look for the input element (Prasad et.al, 2012).

Figure 7. Components identification by two wires

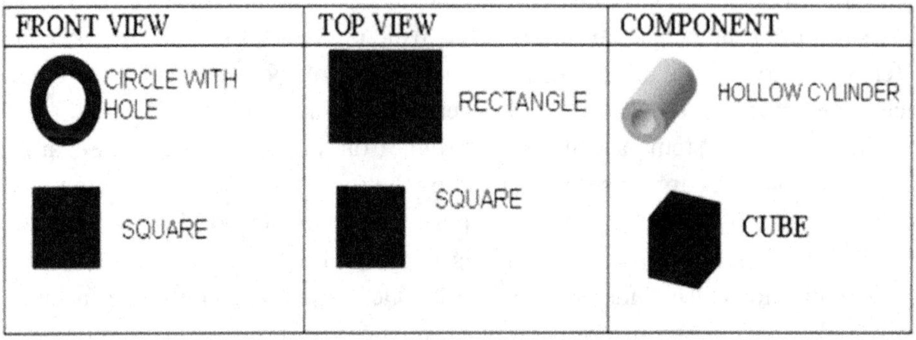

FRONT VIEW	TOP VIEW	COMPONENT
⬤ CIRCLE WITH HOLE	⬛ RECTANGLE	HOLLOW CYLINDER
⬛ SQUARE	⬛ SQUARE	CUBE

In order to overcome the difficulties of complex assembly movements and unpredictable component shape, the use of ANNs for automatic assembly of deformable components is recommended. These difficulties can be overcome by sensor-guided or compliant robots, albeit at the expense of a larger parameter space for the assembly process. To find the best parameter settings for this procedure, ANNs can be utilized.

ANNs can be used to aid automate the assembly of deformable components by acting as a model or controller for the assembly process. Two uses of ANNs are the parameter of the assemblage robot's trajectory and the approximation of assembly. ANNs were employed to learn the assembly trajectory and calculate the assembly offsets in a case study involving the assembly of automotive wheel arch liners. Comparing the approach based on ANNs to conventional position-controlled and impedance-controlled systems, it was discovered that the ANNs approach was less forgiving of loose gripping of the wheel arch liner. For complicated handling and assembly procedures, such as those involving deformable components, ANNs have the ability to produce an ever-improving assembly system.

The assembly usually failed because of extremely powerful torques in the positive Y-direction, whilst in the negative direction, it was difficult to construct the assembly configuration. Since the confirmed assembly gestures for constructing the ANNs training set assume that the component is positioned optimally in relation to the handlers, the missed placements were not picked up on. To improve strength, a fresh training set that trains the ANNs utilizing varied gripper positions might be created. All three techniques can correct sufficiently serious misplacements (Heyn et.al, 2019).

Industrial robots significantly increase efficiency and quicken the engineeringprocedure. In order to accomplish this, several investigators have focussed on optimizing robotic prototypes utilizing AI techniques during the past ten years.

Due of their adaptable mechanical benefits, particularly when they are designed to have extremely small motions, gimbal joints have been examined as a potential standby for conventional revolute joints. The result shows that when selecting the appropriate gimbal joint settings, the anticipated ANN model can be used in its place of the intricate and time wasting evolutionary approach.

Figure 8. Flowchart

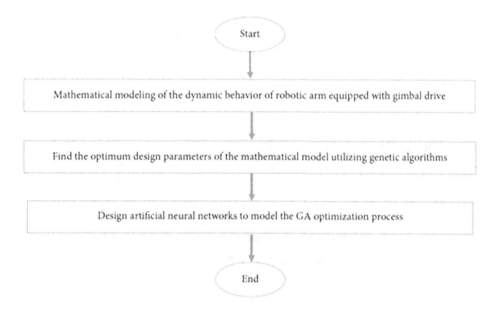

The final objective of this experimentation is to improve an ANN prototypical that can approximate a function and depict the vibrantperformance of a GA optimizer as it seeks out the most effective gimbal driving configurations for robotic arms.

As opposed to past research, which used overalltake out data from the robotic arm scientific model as its reference model, the suggested ANN makes use of the GA as the gimbal-furnished robotic arm model's parameter optimizer. This suggests that the planned ANN will perform as a function optimizer, eliminating the necessity for the use of optimization methods.

To do this, a mathematical model describing the activity of the gimbal drive must first be created. The newly created gimbal drive will then be used with three different well-known robotic arms, and the accompanying scientific models will be shown. In the third stage, the ideal design parameters are chosen using GA, one of the renowned AI evolutionary procedures. The new component of this research is the final stage, which involves designing and training an ANN to take the role of the optimization algorithm, GA. Figure 8 displays a flowchart of the suggested approach (Azizi 2020).

In order to maximize tolerance for robot kinematic parameters, artificial neural networks are deployed. To remove performance uncertainty, the robotic arm must be able to manipulate objects with extreme precision and consistency. The signal to noise ratio has a significant impact on kinematic parameters, which directly affect cost and performance with reference to application. The ANN is a technique for selecting the ideal tolerance range and identifying the crucial parameters. ANNs and biological neural systems function and have benefits in many ways that are similar. Artificial neural networks may generalize based on a limited amount of data, are fault-tolerant, and learn from new experiences. In the end, ANN is a tool for identifying the crucial variables and selecting the ideal tolerance range. The methodology is developed and illustrated using the Scorbot 5u plus planar manipulator.

The main focus neural network of this study is feed forward model. The system in this model is subjected to a set of inputs and a set of joining weights. The weighted data to the neuron are combined together, and the resulting total is subsequently activated. Level of activation that the neuron reaches becomes its output, and it can either act as input for more neurons or as a systemresult. This network learns (input and related desired output) by altering the link weights depending on training vectors. When a neural network receives a training vector, the joining weights are modified to lessen the alterationamong the expected and actual result. An effective output match for the inputs should be produced by a network after it has been trained using a set of training vectors (Anand et.al, 2007).

In the first phases of the manipulator's control design phase, the active model of the arrangement and associated structure parameters must be exactly represented while building the organizer. You could accomplish a noble control outcome through a control strategy methods like control of computational torque and control of inverse dynamics, which are both well-organized, by computing the robot arm's torque and developing your dynamic equation. This, however, is predicated on the ability to acquire a correct data prototypical. It is hard to establish a precise scientific model of a robot because of how it is actually built and used. Finding appropriate model-based solutions may also be difficult because of the effects of different payloads.

In order to increase the capabilities of robotic manipulator regulatorschemes, neural network computers have been used recently. CNC systems can substitute a neural system interpolator of robot link routes for the spline interpolator.

This technique is utilized to teach compensators using neural systems without accurate starting data and for numerical control systems of robotic manipulators. The adaptive neural network compensator is used in place of the PID controller and other approaches to correct the lively error brought on by the torsional weight in the robot connection drive (Yan et.al, 2022).

Such devices can be designed in a number of ways to maximize application efficiency while using less power and space. Spiky Neuromorphic Computing is a new example that can be used to a range of cutting-edge applications in devices with constrained resources. SNC helps reduce energy use while providing the benefits of machine learning. For instance, memristors are a type of low energy memory device that are widely used to achieve low power operation while also helping to save system space. We forestall that SNC will, overall, use low-power, resource-constrained devices to provide computational efficiency that is nearly as good as deep learning.

Such devices can be designed in a number of ways to maximize application efficiency while using less power and space. SNC is a new example that can be used to a range of cutting-edge applications in devices with constrained resources. SNC helps reduce energy use while providing the benefits of machine learning. For instance, memristors are a type of short energy memory device that are widely used to attainshort power task while also helping to save system space. We anticipate that SNC will, overall, use low-power, resource-constrained devices to provide computational efficiency that is nearly as good as deep learning.

To test how successfully the network can direct the robot avoiding obstacles, a series of specified room configurations are specifically used. The building and training of networks is done via evolutionary optimization. Simulate the neuromorphic system, the robot, and the environments it travels through during the evolutionary optimization rather of teaching it in real-world scenarios as shown in figure 9.

Despite the simulator's relative primitiveness, the network may be trained through evolutionary optimization onto alternative design- DANNA. This network has since been used to effectively operate the real robot in new situations. We are assured in its success since the robot will use the resulting mrDANNA network to navigate unexpected environments.

Figure 9. Simulator visualization for robot navigation

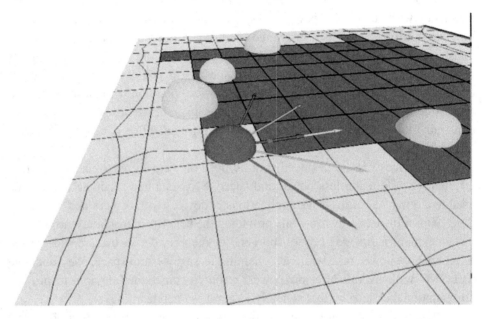

The example network designed by the evolutionary optimization is composed of 119 synapses, thirteen neurons, including eighteen hidden neurons, four output neurons, and nine input neurons, to operate the robot. The nine input neurons receive five inputs from the LIDAR sensor, two inputs from the limit switches of robot, random value and a bias value that aids in driving activity. Forright and left motors, the four outputs correspond to forward and backward motion.

A system for a neuromorphic constructionusing incipient devices can be built through evolutionary procedures to fulfil an independent robot navigation task. The resulting system is compact and sparse related to the majority of deep learning networks, maximizing space efficiency while maintaining power efficiency (Chakma et.al, 2018).

Currently, mobile robots are used in industrial settings, such as warehouses, that are typically designed to favour straight line movements. Intersections serve as turning points, and the robots' potential paths are marked by some kind of guiding line, whether it be physical, radio frequency, or another. Therefore, for the purposes of this study, we identified a test situation based on a 2D grid in which an iRobot Create 2 robot explores the grid by moving from intersection to intersection while only being able to move in one of four directions: up, down, left, or right, as depicted in figures 10 a, b. A colored square on the floor serves as the objective, and the robot is initially unaware of where it is.

The subsequent variables are used to set up the grid: ID dimension, objective scene, quantity of impediments and their scenes, and examination method. The robots' fixed vantage point is in the upper-left corner of the grid.

Arduino Nano and Raspberry Pi 3 are added to the Create 2 and connected through a communication cable to the robot's inner controller in order to increase the number of sensors and computing capability. An Arduino Nano is connected to a colour sensor to assess if the target square is present at the junction the robot has reached right now. When the target is located, the Arduino sends the Raspberry Pi a signal outlining its location. Two optical-reflective sensors are also connected to the Raspberry Pi computer to produce a line-following capability. Given the actual measurements, square grids of numerous sizes, such as 7 x 7, 5 x 6, 4 x 4, and 3 x 3 are selected.

Figure 10. Experimental set-up. (a) Routes; (b) Real situation with a 7 × 7 grid

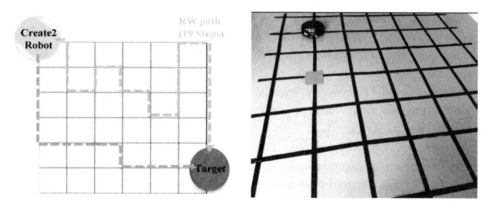

The Raspbian operating system, which is loaded on the Raspberry Pi, was used to do the examinationprocedures, communicate, regulate, and sense on the robot. The PyCreate2 module, which makes it simpler to develop the exploration algorithms on Raspberry Pi and interface with the robot, is one reason why Python was chosen. Similar to that, an Arduino program is used to bring the algorithm for finding the target square into practice.On the other hand, the neural networks and optimization techniques were implemented using MATLAB.The data processing did not require any special memory for a small database.

A PC with Intel Core i7 processing device running at 1.8 GHz, 8 GB of RAM, and a 64-bit operating system can be used to finish the neural network training in 20 hours. It should be noted that system training is a single-time procedure. After the model has been obtained, a prediction can be made in around one to two seconds.

An artificial neural network, a kind of computer model, is a collection of artificial neurons associated to one another to send signals. Every neuron is associated to other neurons by connections. These connections multiply the preceding neuron's output value by a weight cost, which can either rise or lessen the neighbouring neurons' activity levels.

Similar to this, the neuron's output may have a non-linear activation task that alters the outcome data or enforces a boundary that cannot be surpassedformerly spreading to next neurons. These schemes are skilled by lessening a loss function that relates well-known results with the network's existing results. The weights of the neurons are modified to try and reduce the loss function's value. In sectors where it is difficult to express the discovery of solutions using conventional programming, these methods are commonly utilized. The results demonstrate that a structure based on machine learning that employs ANN with Bayesian regularization can predict arrangement of exploratory techniques used in mobile robotics with high accuracy.

An ANN model of this type, for example, can forecast the maximum quantity of stages the robot will need to go in a 2D grid in order to locate the target based on the size of the grid, the quantity of hindrances, and the target's position. Using two specially designed datasets, an ANN model with supervised learning is skilled, validated, and evaluated.

Figure 11 and 12 shows the block diagram illustrates our suggested approach for predicting how much energy a robot would need while doing an exploratory job using the previously discussed ANN model.

In STAGE 2, a battery-operated electrical discharge model is utilized to estimate the amount of energy essential to effectively finish the hunt job based on the forecasts made by the trained model for a specific test situation.

Figure 11. Training the nonlinear model for the exploration performance prediction

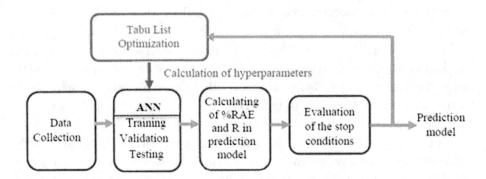

Figure 12. Estimation model for energy

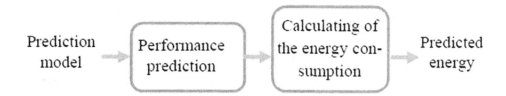

The amount of stages took by the robot to get there varies each time non-deterministic methods are applied. Since the exploration algorithm's worst-case expected performance is predicted by the ANN prediction model, it is useless to try to predict the exact amount of energy the robot will use for a specific run. Instead, one should make an estimation of the utmostquantity of energy the robot will essential (Caballero et.al, 2021).

CONCLUSION

Artificial Neural Networks are introduced in this chapter. For robotic applications, there are numerous ANN techniques available. Numerous real-time applications were used to discuss the functions of artificial neural networks in energy and performance assessments of robotic applications. The performance of ANN-implemented robots is higher to that of classical robots. Due to the incorporation of ANN, the robot's energy consumption is also reduced. To make a viable robot, it is essential to have knowledge in neoscience, electronics, and computer science. Neuromorphic robot system can be built using software and hardware chips. Understanding the architecture and computational capabilities of various neuromorphic chips is important. Various software tools are available to understand neural network architecture, and computational model for fast prototyping and product design. The energy and performance optimization is the major part any robotic applications.

REFERENCES

Anand, M. D., Selvaraj, T., & Kumanan, S. (2007). Parameter identification of robot arm using artificial neural networks. In *National Conference on Computational Intelligence* (p. 1). IEEE.

Arunkumar, N., Senathipathi, N., Dhanasekar, S., Malin Bruntha, P., & Priya, C. (2020). An ultra-low-power static random-access memory cell using tunneling field effect transistor. *International Journal of Engineering, 33*(11), 2215–2221. doi:10.5829/ije.2020.33.11b.13

Azizi, A. (2020). Applications of artificial intelligence techniques to enhance sustainability of industry 4.0: Design of an artificial neural network model as dynamic behavior optimizer of robotic arms. *Complexity, 2020*, 1–10. doi:10.1155/2020/8564140

Bruntha, P. M., Dhanasekar, S., Hepsiba, D., Sagayam, K. M., Neebha, T. M., Pandey, D., & Pandey, B. K. (2023). Application of switching median filter with L 2 norm-based auto-tuning function for removing random valued impulse noise. *Aerospace Systems, 6*(1), 53–59. doi:10.100742401-022-00160-y

Caballero, L., Perafan, Á., Rinaldy, M., & Percybrooks, W. (2021). Predicting the energy consumption of a robot in an exploration task using optimized neural networks. *Electronics (Basel), 10*(8), 920. doi:10.3390/electronics10080920

Chakma, G., Skuda, N. D., Schuman, C. D., Plank, J. S., Dean, M. E., & Rose, G. S. (2018, May). Energy and area efficiency in neuromorphic computing for resource constrained devices. In *Proceedings of the 2018 on Great Lakes Symposium on VLSI* (pp. 379-383). GLSVLSI. https://www.glsvlsi.org/

Dhanasekar, S., Bruntha, P. M., Madhuvappan, C., & Sagayam, K. (2019). An improved area efficient 16-QAM transceiver design using Vedic multiplier for wireless applications. *International Journal of Recent Technology and Engineering, 8*(3), 4419–4425. doi:10.35940/ijrte.C5535.098319

Dhanasekar, S., & Ramesh, J. (2015). FPGA implementation of variable bit rate 16 QAM transceiver system. *International Journal of Applied Engineering Research: IJAER, 10*(10), 26497–26507.

Govindaraj, V., Dhanasekar, S., Martinsagayam, K., Pandey, D., Pandey, B. K., & Nassa, V. K. (2023). Low-power test pattern generator using modified LFSR. *Aerospace Systems,* 1-8. Springer. doi:10.1007/s42401-022-00191-5

Heyn, J., Gümbel, P., Bobka, P., Dietrich, F., & Dröder, K. (2019). Application of artificial neural networks in force-controlled automated assembly of complex shaped deformable components. *Procedia CIRP, 79*, 131–136. doi:10.1016/j.procir.2019.02.027

Jubair Ahmed, L., Anish Fathima, B., Dhanasekar, S., & Martin Sagayam, K. (2022). Modeling of Fuzzy Logic-Based Classification System Using the Gravitational Search Algorithm. In *Multimedia Technologies in the Internet of Things Environment* (Vol. 3, pp. 79–94). Springer Singapore. doi:10.1007/978-981-19-0924-5_5

Madhiarasan, M., & Louzazni, M. (2022). Analysis of artificial neural network: Architecture, types, and forecasting applications. *Journal of Electrical and Computer Engineering*, *2022*, 1–23. doi:10.1155/2022/5416722

Maind, S. B., & Wankar, P. (2014). Research paper on basic of artificial neural network. *International Journal on Recent and Innovation Trends in Computing and Communication*, *2*(1), 96–100. doi:10.17762/ijritcc.v2i1.2920

Malik, N. (2005). *Artificial neural networks and their applications.* arXiv preprint cs/0505019. https://doi.org/ doi:10.48550/arXiv.cs/0505019

Manickam, M. V., Mohanapriya, M., Kale, S., Uday, M., Kulkarni, P., Khandagale, Y., & Patil, S. P. (2017). Research study on applications of artificial neural networks and E-learning personalization. *International Journal of Civil Engineering and Technology*, *8*(8), 1422–1432.

Mhatre, M. S., Siddiqui, F., Dongre, M., & Thakur, P. (2015). A review paper on artificial neural network: A prediction technique. *International Journal of Scientific and Engineering Research*, *6*(12), 161–163.

Prasad, M. M., & Kumar, T. V. (2012). Intelligent robot used in the field of practical application of artificial neural network & machine vision. *Int. J. Lean Thinking*, *3*(2), 38–46.

Yan, Z., Klochkov, Y., & Xi, L. (2022). Improving the Accuracy of a Robot by Using Neural Networks (Neural Compensators and Nonlinear Dynamics). *Robotics (Basel, Switzerland)*, *11*(4), 83. doi:10.3390/robotics11040083

Chapter 7

Strategies for Automated Bike-Sharing Systems Leveraging ML and VLSI Approaches

Jagrat Shukla
Vellore Institute of Technology, India

Numburi Rishikha
Vellore Institute of Technology, India

Janhavi Chaturvedi
Vellore Institute of Technology, India

Sumathi Gokulanathan
Vellore Institute of Technology, India

Srihari priya Krishnan Chandrasekaran
Vellore Institute of Technology, India

Konguvel Elango
Vellore Institute of Technology, India

Sathishkumar Selvaperumal
Asia Pacific University of Technology and Innovation, Malaysia

ABSTRACT

Machine learning has had an impact in the area of microchip design and was initially used in automation. This development could result in a tremendous change in the realm of hardware computation and AI's powerful analysis tools. Traffic is a pressing issue in densely populated cities. Governments worldwide are attempting to address this problem by introducing various forms of public transportation, including metro. However, these solutions require significant investment and implementation time. Despite the high cost and inherent flaws of the system, many people still prefer to use their personal vehicles rather than public transportation. To address this issue, the authors propose a bike-sharing solution in which all processes from membership registration to bike rental and return are automated. Bagging is an ensemble learning method that can be used for base models with a low bias and high variance. It uses randomization of the dataset to reduce the variance of the base models, while keeping the bias low.

DOI: 10.4018/978-1-6684-6596-7.ch007

INTRODUCTION

Machine learning and Artificial Intelligence (AI) have resulted in significant advancements in various fields, including microchip design and revolutionizing traditional VLSI design concepts. Initially used for automation, machine-learning techniques are gradually replacing time-consuming manual processes. By automating design creation, machine learning eliminates the need for extensive human intervention and expert knowledge. This transformative development has the potential to bring about a remarkable shift in hardware computation and leverage AI's powerful analysis tools.

Traffic congestion is one of the most pressing challenges facing densely populated cities. Governments worldwide have been striving to address this issue by introducing different forms of public transportation such as metro systems. However, these solutions often require substantial investment and implementation time. Despite these flaws, many individuals still opt for personal vehicles over public transportation. To address this problem, the implementation of an automated bike-sharing system is proposed. This system aims to streamline all processes from membership registration to bike rental and return through automation. By offering a convenient and efficient alternative to private vehicles, automated bike-sharing endeavours can reduce traffic congestion.

Bagging is an effective ensemble learning method for machine-learning algorithms. It is particularly suitable for base models characterized by low bias and high variance. Bagging reduces the variance of these models by randomizing the dataset while maintaining a low bias. Bagging enhances the performance and accuracy of machine-learning algorithms by mitigating the trade-off between bias and variance. This technique finds valuable application in addressing complex problems, such as traffic prediction and optimization, where reliable and precise models are crucial.

Moreover, the integration of machine learning and AI in bike-sharing systems has several advantages. Automating the entire process, from registration to payment, enhances the overall user experience. With online payments, users can conveniently rent bikes without the need for third-party vendors. This streamlined approach not only saves time, but also ensures a trustworthy and efficient bike-sharing service. By leveraging the power of machine learning and AI, bike-sharing systems can operate seamlessly, reducing traffic congestion while promoting sustainable transportation options. Automation in microchip design driven by machine-learning techniques has the potential to transform the hardware computation landscape. Automated bike-sharing systems offer an effective alternative to private vehicles in addressing traffic congestion. Furthermore, techniques such as bagging enhance the accuracy and performance of machine-learning algorithms, enabling better traffic prediction and optimization. By incorporating machine learning and AI into bike-sharing systems, the overall user experience is improved, facilitating efficient and reliable rental processes.

Bike renting systems have emerged as the latest trend, replacing the traditional methods of renting bikes. These systems offer a quick and convenient way for customers to rent bikes within seconds, with easy pick-up and drop-off services. Unlike other transportation services, bike-sharing systems utilize a virtual sensor network to accurately record travel duration as well as the arrival and departure positions of bikes throughout the city. This advanced technology allows for precise tracking of bike locations, ensuring efficient management of the system.

The main objective of this study is to predict the hourly bike count based on various attributes, such as weather conditions, specific hours of the day, and overall daily information. The analysis begin with a descriptive analysis that provides insights into the characteristics and distribution of the dataset. Subsequently, a missing-value analysis will be conducted to handle any incomplete or null data. Outlier analysis is then performed to identify and handle any extreme or abnormal values that could affect the accuracy of the predictions. Correlation analysis is an essential step in understanding the relationships between different attributes and hourly bike count. This analysis helps identify any significant factors that may influence bike demand. Once the preliminary steps are completed, the focus shifts to selecting an appropriate model for prediction. In this case, the analysis revealed that Random Forest regression is the best model for the given dataset and scenario. The Random Forest model is then applied to make accurate predictions based on the selected attributes. Finally, a graph of feature importance is plotted to visualize the significance of each attribute in determining the hourly bike count. This graphical representation provides valuable insights into the key factors that contribute to bike rental demand. By analyzing this information, it is possible to draw conclusions and identify the necessary attributes that should be considered when predicting bike counts in similar scenarios.

In conclusion, bike renting systems have revolutionized the way bikes are rented, offering customers convenient and efficient service. The prediction of hourly bike counts can be achieved through a step-by-step process that includes descriptive analysis, missing value analysis, outlier analysis, correlation analysis, model selection, and the application of the Random Forest model. The resulting feature importance graph aids in understanding the significant attributes that influence bike rental demand. These analyses and predictions provide valuable insights into optimizing bike-sharing systems and effectively meeting the transportation needs of users.

RELATED WORKS

Permitasari and Sahara (2018) presented an implementation of a Bike Sharing and Bike Rental application. The objective of their work was divided into two main categories: Bike Sharing and Bike Rentals. To address the major challenges encountered during the development of this application, the researchers utilized the PIECES Analysis framework. This framework involved various analyses such as System Performance Analysis, Information Analysis, Economic Analysis, Control Analysis, Efficiency Analysis and Service Analysis. Based on the findings from the PIECES Analysis, a spiral model was devised for the application's development. The Spiral Model encompassed key stages including Communication, Planning, Modelling, Construction and Development. This approach ensured a systematic and well-structured process for creating the application. The web-based technology employed in this application enables visitors to easily and swiftly rent a bike when visiting tourist destinations. Additionally, the application offers a secure and convenient payment method, eliminating the need for cash transactions. Moreover, the application provides accurate and prompt reporting based on the bicycle data, including comprehensive financial statements. These reports cater to the company's further operational requirements and contribute to efficient decision-making processes. This study showcased the successful implementation of a Bike Sharing and Bike Rental application. By employing the PIECES Analysis framework and the Spiral Model, the researchers were able to address critical challenges and create a user-friendly, web-based solution. This application not only facilitates easy bike rentals but also offers secure payment methods and comprehensive data reporting for effective company management.

Thoa Pham Thi et al. (2017) conducted an analysis of Dublin bike data to gain insights into bike usage patterns. Their study involved clustering analysis, which led to the identification of intriguing clusters at both the busiest and quietest bike stations. By examining the availability of bikes every 10 minutes, the research revealed noteworthy variations in bike usage between weekends and weekdays, as well as during business hours and after work. These distinct patterns observed in the results can be attributed to geographical factors and knowledge of the specific locations. Furthermore, the consistency of these patterns was confirmed through testing with new data.

An analysis focusing on the emerging social practices within Bike Rental Systems, which serve as an alternative form of urban mobility is discussed in Normark et al. (2018). The primary objective of their study was to facilitate the transition from pedestrians to cyclists by utilizing bike sharing services as an intermediary device. This approach aimed to bridge the gap between pedestrians and bike sharing services, while also ensuring technical standardization and highlighting the disparities between individuals familiar and unfamiliar with the bike rental system. The key aspects discussed in their analysis encompass self-service bicycles, inter-modality, transportation, the bike rental system itself, and the modal shift.

The significance of land as a crucial factor in predicting the model of a bike rental system is highlighted in Zhang et al. (2018). The authors focused on predicting an appropriate model by initially collecting data on the walking distance riders covered from a rental station to their respective destinations when returning public bicycles. This data was then utilized, with 85% considered as a statistical value, to determine the influence factor for those stations. Subsequently, a relationship model was constructed based on these findings. To assess the effectiveness of the new model, a comparison was made between the old rental model and the newly proposed one through rigorous testing. The final outcome of the study revealed the daily rental demand as a significant result.

Xu et al. (2018) explore the growing trend of bicycle sharing systems in both developed and some developing countries. Despite their popularity, these systems face numerous challenges such as shortages of docking stations and bicycles' unavailability. The primary objective of the paper is to develop a prediction model that can effectively balance the operational needs of bicycle sharing systems with the increasing demands of customers. The researchers propose various methods to process and collect the necessary rental data. They analyze bicycle usage patterns from both a station-based and trip-based perspective to offer guidance for predicting user demand. The study employs back propagation neural network models to predict demand across different stations and utilizes cluster analysis to identify various services offered at different stations. Comparative analysis is performed to assess the impact of factors such as working and non-working days and distinctions between stations on the accuracy of prediction models. By combining these approaches, the researchers are able to predict customer demand effectively. Through a case study evaluation, they demonstrate the performance of their proposed methodologies and conclude that factors such as working and non-working days, as well as distinctions between stations, contribute to improved prediction model accuracy.

Mooney et al. (2010) tackled a significant challenge faced by a public bike rental application, focusing on the effective planning of resource usage. The researchers examined the Dublin bike rental scheme, employing statistical and data mining methods to analyse the system. Initially, they collected relevant data and conducted an exploratory analysis to identify bike stations and rental patterns within specific areas. By mapping these areas, they gained insights into the spatial distribution of bike rentals. Furthermore, they analysed bike usage patterns over time and performed cluster analysis to identify groups of rentals with similar characteristics. The results obtained from these analyses served as an initialization step for developing a robust prediction analysis. In summary, Authors addressed the challenge of resource planning in a public bike rental application. They collected data and employed statistical and data mining techniques to analyse the Dublin bike rental scheme. Through exploratory analysis, they mapped bike stations and rental patterns, providing a spatial understanding of the system. Time-based analysis and cluster analysis were conducted to identify temporal patterns and group rentals with similar characteristics. These findings formed the foundation for developing an accurate prediction analysis for resource usage in the bike rental application.

An application designed to assist individuals in utilizing a bike sharing system for transportation purposes is proposed in Yoon et al. (2012). This application aims to identify the two closest bike stations to a user's location, enabling them to conveniently pick up or drop off a city bike. By optimizing the probability of finding available bikes and minimizing walking distances, the application enhances the overall user experience. The researchers developed this application using a Spatio-temporal prediction algorithm, which estimates bike availability and outperforms existing solutions. They constructed a spatial underlying network among different bike stations, incorporating various temporal patterns. To validate their application, they tested it using the real-time dataset from the Dublin Bike Sharing System.

Pan et al. (2019) emphasized the significance of predicting bike sharing demand to optimize bike location and ensure efficient bike movement for users. The authors introduced a real-time method in their paper that predicts bike rentals and returns across different locations within a city. They collected data based on specific periods, considering features such as time, weather, and historical patterns. By constructing a network of bike trips using this data, they performed community detection to identify two communities comprising various stations. The researchers utilized a two-layer LSTM (Long Short-Term Memory) model for training and predicting bike sharing patterns. They employed a gating mechanism to process the sequential data within the neural recurrent network. By assessing the Root Mean Squared Error (RMSE), they evaluated the performance of their proposed model and compared it with other deep learning models. Their proposed model outperformed the other models in terms of RMSE, indicating its superior predictive accuracy.

Yang et al. (2018) introduced a predictive model and analysed the usage of a bike sharing system. They employed deep learning techniques, specifically utilizing a convolutional neural network (CNN), to predict the daily usage of bike sharing at both the station and city levels. The CNN model was trained using various parameters such as the nearest neighbourhood station, patch size, temporal window, and learning rate. By incorporating these factors, the researchers successfully predicted the bike sharing system's usage patterns.

Wang (2019) focused on visualizing data using visualization technology to identify factors that impact the number of users utilizing a bike sharing service. Through data analysis, the study identified important factors such as feeling temperature, season, wind speed, weather situation, and humidity that directly influence the number of users. The study employed various models including the NN model, DELM model, Regression Model and ELM model to predict the expected number of users for the bike sharing system based on these factors.

Digitalization will encompass the majority of engineering fields, with a bigger impact over wide-area communication network involving fast data transmission (Arunkumar & Dhanasekar, 2020; Dhanasekar et al., 2019; Dhanasekar & Ramesh, 2015). Test pattern generator with minimum switching activity for high speed circuits was discussed in Dhanasekar and Govindaraj (2023). The switching median Filter with L2 norm-based auto-tuning function for removing random valued impulse noise for neumorphic circuits were discussed (Bruntha et al., 2022). The modelling of Fuzzy Logic-Based Classification System using the Gravitational Search Algorithm were discussed in Jubair Ahmed et al. (2022). Several approaches and strategies in microcontroller, FPGA and VLSI implementation are discussed in Konguvel, Hariharan, Sujatha et al. (2022), Konguvel and Kannan (2022), Konguvel, Nithiyameenatchi, and Rachel (2022), Thirumal et al. (2022), and Vineeth Reddy et al. (2022).

METHODOLOGY

In the initial phase of the analysis, the given dataset undergoes several steps to gain a comprehensive understanding. Descriptive analysis is performed, involving the splitting of the dataset into validation, training, and testing sets. This division allows for proper evaluation and assessment of the performance of the model. Next, a missing value analysis is conducted to identify and handle any NULL values present in the data. This step ensures the dataset is complete and reliable for further analysis.

An outlier analysis is performed to identify and address any extreme values that may adversely affect the analysis. Box plots are utilized to visually detect outliers, which are then removed from the dataset. A correlation analysis was then conducted to explore the relationships between the different attributes. This analysis provides insights into the interdependencies among variables and assists in determining the attribute relevance.

Following correlation analysis, a model selection process was conducted. Based on the obtained results, certain attributes that show a weak correlation with the target variable are dismissed, as they are deemed less influential in predicting the desired outcome. The next crucial step involves implementing Random Forest regression model. This can be achieved using different approaches. In this particular case, two methods were employed.

The first method involved applying the Random Forest Regression model to the training, validation, and testing datasets. This allowed for a comprehensive assessment of the performance of the model on different data subsets. The second method involves utilizing the K-fold cross-validation technique, with K set to three in this scenario. Through three-fold cross-validation, the dataset was divided into three subsets, and Random Forest Regression was performed on each split.

Finally, the feature importance of the attributes was evaluated for both the methods. This analysis identified the most significant and influential attributes that have a notable impact on the target or response variables. By considering the results of feature importance, valuable insights were gained, guiding the understanding of the key factors affecting the desired outcome.

In conclusion, the detailed analysis process involved descriptive analysis, missing value analysis, outlier analysis, correlation analysis, model selection, and Random Forest Regression using different data division approaches, which is shown in Figure 1. The identification of prominent attributes through feature importance analysis enhances the understanding of the key factors that influence the target attribute or response variable.

Figure 1. Flow diagram

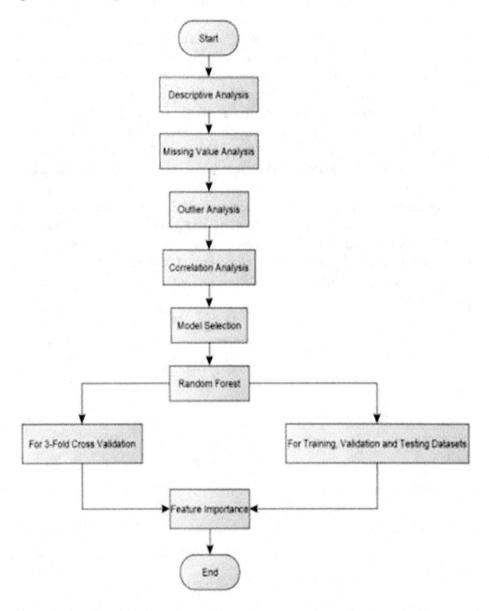

PERFORMANCE ANALYSIS

Descriptive Analysis

Descriptive analysis is a statistical method used to summarize and describe the main characteristics of a dataset. It involves organizing, analyzing, and presenting data in a meaningful way to gain insights and understand patterns or trends within the data. Descriptive analysis focuses on providing a clear and concise summary of the data, without making inferences or drawing conclusions beyond what the data presents. In the context of Very Large-Scale Integration (VLSI) implementation of bike count prediction using machine learning (ML), descriptive analysis can still be applied to understand and analyze the dataset before proceeding with the VLSI design.

Data Exploration: Perform descriptive analysis to explore the dataset specific to bike count prediction. This may involve examining the structure of the dataset, checking for missing values, understanding the data types, and identifying any outliers or anomalies relevant to the VLSI implementation.

Summary Statistics: Calculate summary statistics for the variables that are important for bike count prediction. This could include statistics related to the inputs (e.g., weather conditions and time of day), as well as the output (i.e., bike count). Understanding the statistical characteristics of data can guide design decisions during VLSI implementation.

Visualization: Create visualizations tailored to the VLSI context. For example, one might visualize the distribution of input variables or analyze the correlation between inputs and bike count outputs. These visualizations can help identify patterns or trends that could be relevant for designing an efficient VLSI implementation.

Pre-Processing Considerations: Analyze the dataset for any preprocessing steps that might be necessary to prepare the data for ML modeling and VLSI implementation. This could involve handling missing values, normalizing or scaling variables, or dealing with categorical variables, depending on the requirements of ML algorithms and VLSI design constraints.

By applying descriptive analysis techniques in the VLSI implementation of bike count prediction, insights about the dataset's characteristics will be gained and informed decisions will be made for the subsequent steps of ML modeling and VLSI design. This helps in understanding the dataset and ensures that the VLSI implementation is tailored to the specific requirements of the bike count prediction task.

The first step is to load the dataset from a CSV file. Once loaded, the attributes within the dataset can be divided based on their features, distinguishing between categorical attributes and integer attributes. This division serves as a foundation for subsequent tasks such as validation, testing, and training.

For the integer attributes, statistical information can be computed. This includes calculating measures such as mean, median, mode, standard deviation, minimum, maximum, and quartiles for each column. These statistics provide valuable insights into the distribution and central tendencies of the numerical data, allowing a better understanding of their characteristics.

Moving on to the categorical attributes, an analysis can be performed on each column individually. For each categorical column, several variables are extracted. These variables include the count of occurrences for each unique value, the number of distinct values, the most frequent value (top value), and its corresponding frequency. This information provides an overview of the categorical data and allows for an understanding of its distribution and dominant categories.

By conducting this descriptive analysis, the dataset can be thoroughly explored and statistical summaries can be obtained for both integer and categorical attributes. This aids in identifying patterns, outliers and potential pre-processing steps required to prepare the data for ML modelling and VLSI implementation. Moreover, the division of attributes based on their features facilitates subsequent tasks such as data validation, testing, and training, as it allows for proper handling and manipulation of the dataset during these stages. The data statistics and categorical attributes are shown in Figures 2 and 3.

Figure 2. Data statistics

	temp	atemp	hum	windspeed
count	17379.000000	17379.000000	17379.000000	17379.000000
mean	0.496987	0.475775	0.627229	0.190098
std	0.192556	0.171850	0.192930	0.122340
min	0.020000	0.000000	0.000000	0.000000
25%	0.340000	0.333300	0.480000	0.104500
50%	0.500000	0.484800	0.630000	0.194000
75%	0.660000	0.621200	0.780000	0.253700
max	1.000000	1.000000	1.000000	0.850700

Figure 3. Categorical attributes

	season	holiday	mnth	hr	weekday	workingday	weathersit
count	17379	17379	17379	17379	17379	17379	17379
unique	4	2	12	24	7	2	4
top	3	0	7	17	6	1	1
freq	4496	16879	1488	730	2512	11865	11413

Missing Value Analysis

The missing value analysis is performed to determine whether the dataset contains any null values, which are values that are undefined or missing. This analysis helps identify if any attribute in the dataset has missing data that needs to be addressed before proceeding with VLSI implementation and ML modelling.

In the case of bike count prediction using ML, it is crucial to examine the dataset for the presence of null values. Null values can arise due to various reasons, such as data entry errors or missing sensor readings. These missing values can potentially impact the accuracy and reliability of the prediction model. During the missing value analysis, the dataset is thoroughly checked for any null values or "not a number" (NaN) kind of values. If any null values are found, appropriate steps must be taken to handle them before proceeding with the VLSI implementation and ML modelling.

However, in the specific case of the given data attributes for bike count prediction, it is mentioned that there are no null values present. This means that the dataset is complete, and there is no missing data that requires replacement or imputation. Having a dataset without null values is beneficial as it eliminates the need for additional pre-processing steps to handle missing data. It allows for a more straightforward VLSI implementation and ML modelling process since the data is complete and can be directly utilized for further analysis.

Figure 4. Missing value analysis

```
instant        False
dteday         False
season         False
yr             False
mnth           False
hr             False
holiday        False
weekday        False
workingday     False
weathersit     False
temp           False
atemp          False
hum            False
windspeed      False
casual         False
registered     False
cnt            False
dtype: bool
```

Outlier Analysis

Outlier analysis is a statistical method used to identify and understand observations or data points that significantly deviate from the normal or expected behaviour of the dataset. Outliers are data points that lie outside the typical range or pattern exhibited by the majority of the data. Outlier analysis helps in detecting these exceptional observations and determining their potential impact on the analysis or modelling process. In VLSI implementation of bike count prediction using machine learning (ML), outlier analysis plays a crucial role in ensuring the quality and reliability of the dataset before proceeding with the implementation.

Data Examination: Conduct a thorough examination of the dataset to identify any data points that appear to be significantly different from the rest. This can involve visual inspection, summary statistics, or data visualization techniques.

Statistical Methods: Utilize various statistical methods to detect outliers. Common approaches include the use of measures such as z-scores, interquartile range (IQR), or Mahalanobis distance to identify observations that deviate significantly from the mean or median of the dataset.

Visualization Techniques: Create visualizations, such as box plots, scatter plots, or histograms, to visually represent the distribution of the data and identify potential outliers. Outliers may appear as data points that lie far away from the main cluster or exhibit unusual patterns in the plot.

Domain Knowledge: Apply domain knowledge or contextual understanding to determine whether the identified outliers are genuine anomalies or if they are caused by data collection errors or other factors. This step helps in distinguishing between valid outliers and erroneous data points.

Outlier Treatment: Based on the analysis, decide on the appropriate treatment for outliers. This could involve removing the outliers if they are deemed to be erroneous or irrelevant to the analysis. Alternatively, if the outliers represent significant but valid observations, they may be retained and handled differently during the subsequent modelling or implementation stages.

By performing outlier analysis in the VLSI implementation of bike count prediction, you can identify and understand any exceptional observations in the dataset that could potentially impact the accuracy and reliability of the model. Handling outliers appropriately ensures that the implemented VLSI system is robust and capable of accurately predicting bike counts under normal operating conditions.

Box Plots

In VLSI implementation of bike count prediction using machine learning (ML), box plots can be created to visualize the relationship between the count of bike rides and various other factors. These box plots provide a clear representation of the distribution of the bike count data across different categories.

To analyse the relationship between the count of bike rides and different variables, we create box plots. In these box plots, the y-axis represents the count of bike rides, while the x-axis displays various data categories such as Month, Weather Situation, Working Day, Hour of the Day, and Temperature. By utilizing box plots, we can visually observe the distribution of bike counts within each category. The boxes in the plot indicate the interquartile range (IQR), with the horizontal line inside the box representing the median. The whiskers extending from the box display the range of the data, excluding any outliers. Analysing the box plots allows us to gain insights into how the count of bike rides varies across different factors. For example, we can determine if there are variations in bike counts based on the month of the year, different weather situations, working days versus non-working days, specific hours of the day, or temperature levels.

By examining the box plots, we can identify any potential patterns or trends in the bike count data. For instance, we may observe higher median bike counts during certain months or specific weather conditions. Additionally, the presence of outliers beyond the whiskers can indicate exceptional or extreme observations that might require further investigation. The box plots are shown across month-wise, hour-wise and across the temperature in Figures 5, 6, and 7.

Figure 5. Box plot: Month-wise

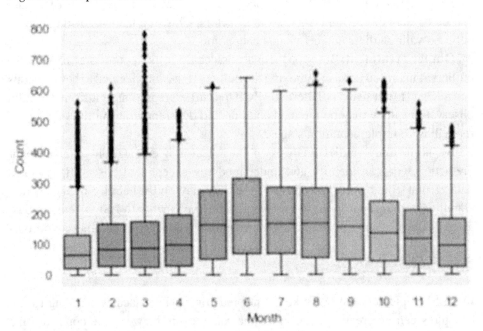

Figure 6. Box plot: Hour-wise

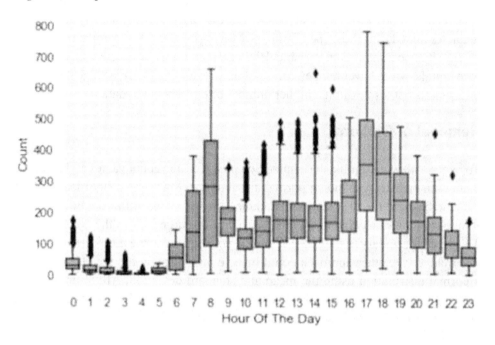

Figure 7. Box plot: Temperature

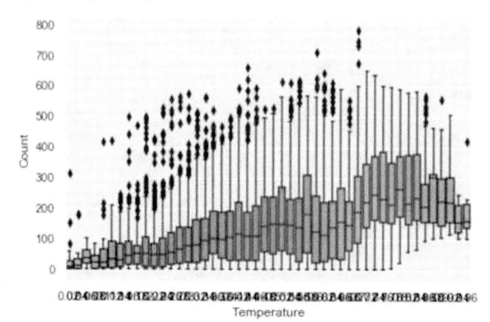

By analyzing the hourly box plot, it becomes apparent that there are two distinct peaks at 8 AM and 5 PM. This observation suggests that customers heavily utilize bike rental services during those specific hours. Moving on to another factor, temperature, we find it to be a significant variable. Higher temperatures correlate with increased bike rentals, while lower temperatures not only result in a lower average number of bike rentals but also exhibit a higher number of outliers in the data.

Removal of Outliers

To begin with, we examine the distribution plot of all the count values and compare them with their corresponding normal distribution. However, no significant match is found between the two. In order to address this issue, we utilize the Interquartile Range (IQR) and median to identify and remove outliers from the count values. This step is necessary as the count values do not conform to the normal distribution. Alternatively, another approach could involve transforming the target values into a normal distribution using the mean and standard deviation. After applying the outlier removal process, we observe a reduction in the number of samples from 10,151 to 10,427 in the dataset. The data with and without outliers are shown in Figures 8 and 9.

Figure 8. Data with outliers

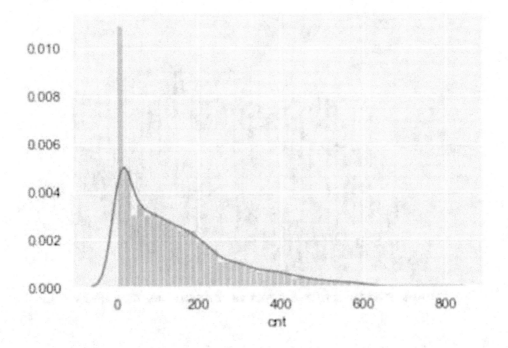

Figure 9. Data without outliers

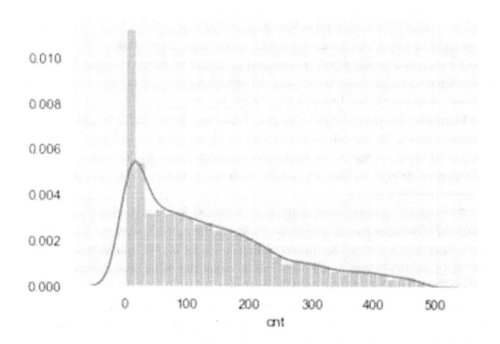

```
Samples in train set with outliers: 10427
Samples in train set without outliers: 10151
```

Correlation Analysis

Correlation analysis is a statistical technique used to measure the strength and direction of the relationship between two variables. It helps to identify the degree to which changes in one variable are associated with changes in another variable. In correlation analysis, the correlation coefficient is calculated, which quantifies the strength and direction of the relationship. In VLSI implementation of bike count prediction using machine learning (ML), correlation analysis can be applied to understand the relationships between different variables in the dataset and their impact on the bike count.

Data Preparation: Prepare the dataset by selecting the relevant variables for analysis. In the case of bike count prediction, this may include factors such as weather conditions, time of day, temperature, and any other variables that could potentially influence the bike count.

Correlation Calculation: Calculate the correlation coefficient between each pair of variables. Commonly used correlation coefficients include Pearson's correlation coefficient, which measures linear relationships, and Spearman's rank correlation coefficient, which captures monotonic relationships. These coefficients will range from -1 to +1, indicating the strength and direction of the correlation.

Interpretation of Correlation: Analyze the correlation coefficients to understand the relationships between variables. A positive correlation coefficient close to +1 indicates a strong positive relationship, meaning that an increase in one variable is associated with an increase in the other. A negative correlation coefficient close to -1 indicates a strong negative relationship, where an increase in one variable is associated with a decrease in the other. A correlation coefficient close to 0 indicates a weak or no correlation between the variables.

Feature Selection: Utilize the correlation analysis results to guide feature selection for the ML model. Variables with strong correlations to the bike count can be considered as important features for the prediction model. Variables with weak correlations or high collinearity may be excluded to reduce model complexity and improve interpretability.

By performing correlation analysis in the VLSI implementation of bike count prediction, the variables that have the strongest relationship with the bike count is identified. This helps in selecting relevant features for the ML model and designing an efficient VLSI system that takes into account the influential factors affecting bike counts. Displayed below in Figure 10 is a correlation matrix showcasing the relationships between the numerical features in the bike sharing dataset. From the matrix, it is evident that temperature ("temp") and hour ("hr") exhibit the most significant correlations, indicating their potential as promising variables for the predictive model. Furthermore, both feeling temperature ("atemp") and temperature ("temp") demonstrate a strong correlation. However, to prevent collinearity, reduce dimensionality, and simplify the predictive model, we choose to exclude the variable of feeling temperature ("atemp").

Figure 10. Correlation matrix for numerical features

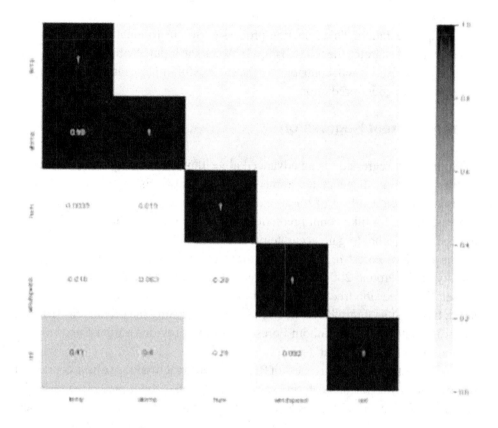

Model Selection

To predict the count value based on categorical and numerical attributes in the VLSI implementation of bike count prediction using machine learning (ML), a regression algorithm is required. Despite having a relatively small dataset with less than 20,000 samples, we can still extract meaningful insights by following the analysis steps. Through this process, we can identify significant variables or attributes that strongly influence the bike count.

Considering the dataset's characteristics, we can select suitable regression algorithms. Initially, we can explore algorithms such as Support Vector Regression with various kernel options, Lasso regression, Random Forest regression, Elastic Net regression, and Ridge regression. By employing these algorithms, we can evaluate their performance using metrics like Mean Square Error and R-squared score. These metrics provide insights into the accuracy and goodness of fit of the regression models.

By applying regression algorithms and assessing their performance metrics, we can determine the most appropriate algorithm for the bike count prediction in the VLSI implementation. This selection process allows us to identify the regression model that best captures the relationships between the input attributes and the count value. Ultimately, this will contribute to the successful implementation of the VLSI system for bike count prediction.

Random Forest Regression

Random Forest regression is an advanced algorithm that leverages the concept of ensemble learning. It generates numerous individual decision trees, where each tree is trained on a subset of observations from the dataset. In the case of VLSI implementation for bike count prediction using ML, we apply the Random Forest regression algorithm to gain accurate predictions.

The Random Forest regression algorithm constructs an ensemble of decision trees, typically around 200 in our case, by utilizing different sub-samples from the dataset. Each decision tree receives a set of observations as input and generates an output based on its internal decision rules. By aggregating the predictions from all the individual trees, the Random Forest algorithm provides a robust and reliable prediction for the bike count.

To demonstrate the effectiveness of Random Forest regression, we have conducted experiments using various datasets specific to the bike count prediction task. We have defined a Random Forest Regression function that incorporates these datasets and trained the algorithm accordingly. In evaluating the performance of the Random Forest regression, we have calculated metrics such as Mean Square Error (MSE), Mean Absolute Error (MAE), R-Squared score, and Root Mean Squared Logarithmic Error (RMSLE).

These metrics provide valuable insights into the accuracy and reliability of the Random Forest regression model. The MSE measures the average squared difference between the predicted and actual values, while the MAE calculates the average absolute difference. The R-Squared score indicates the proportion of the variance in the bike count that can be explained by the model. Additionally, the RMSLE measures the accuracy of the logarithmic predictions.

By applying Random Forest regression and analyzing these metrics, we can assess the performance and suitability of the algorithm for bike count prediction in VLSI implementation. This allows us to make informed decisions about the model's effectiveness and refine the implementation process accordingly shown in Figure 11.

Figure 11. Random forest regression for training, validation, and testing datasets

Model	Dataset	MSE	MAE	RMSLE	R^2 score
RandomForestRegressor	training	291.74	10.80	0.21	0.98
RandomForestRegressor	validation	18910.27	96.29	0.47	0.59
RandomForestRegressor	testing	19852.06	96.14	0.51	0.59

We observe the results of the random forest regression analysis, which includes metrics such as MSE, MAE, RMSLE, and R-Squared score for the Training, Validation, and Testing datasets. Upon examination, we note that the values of MSE, MAE, and RMSLE are relatively small, while the R-Squared score is higher for the Training dataset. This finding leads us to conclude that the Training dataset exhibits the highest accuracy compared to the Validation and Testing datasets.

The small values of MSE, MAE, and RMSLE indicate that the predictions made by the random forest regression model are close to the actual values in the Training dataset. These metrics measure the error and difference between predicted and actual values, with lower values suggesting higher accuracy. Furthermore, the higher R-Squared score for the Training dataset signifies that a larger proportion of the variance in the bike count can be explained by the model compared to the Validation and Testing datasets. The R-Squared score indicates the goodness of fit of the regression model, with values closer to 1 representing a better fit.

Based on these observations, we can infer that the Training dataset provides the most accurate predictions and has a better overall performance compared to the Validation and Testing datasets. This insight helps us evaluate the effectiveness of the random forest regression model and make informed decisions about its application in the VLSI implementation for bike count prediction.

Random Forest Regression Using K-Fold Cross Validation

An alternative approach to solving Random Forest Regression is by utilizing K-Fold Cross Validation, where we set the value of K to 3 for illustration purposes. This technique involves dividing the dataset into three equal parts or folds. For each split, we perform the Training, Validation, and Testing steps, and evaluate the metrics including MSE, MAE, RMSLE, and R-Squared score for each split.

By employing K-Fold Cross Validation, we aim to enhance the accuracy of our predictions. The dataset is split into K parts, and the model is trained and evaluated K times, with each part serving as the Validation set once while the remaining K-1 parts are used for Training. This process ensures that every data point has the opportunity to be part of the Validation set, enabling a comprehensive assessment of the model's performance.

To improve the accuracy further, we consider averaging the evaluation metrics obtained from each split. Averaging the metrics provides a more robust estimation of the model's overall performance and reduces the impact of any specific split's peculiarities. Moreover, implementing this averaging technique helps control overfitting, a phenomenon where the model performs exceptionally well on the Training data but fails to generalize to unseen data. By averaging the metrics across the different splits, we obtain a more balanced assessment of the model's performance and mitigate the risk of overfitting.

In summary, utilizing K-Fold Cross Validation with a value of K equal to 3 allows us to perform Training, Validation, and Testing on different subsets of the dataset. By calculating metrics such as MSE, MAE, RMSLE, and R-Squared score for each split and averaging the results, we obtain a comprehensive evaluation of the model's accuracy and improve its ability to generalize to unseen data. This technique proves useful in VLSI implementation for bike count prediction, enhancing the reliability of the predictions and addressing potential overfitting concerns.

Figure 12. Random forest regression for three-fold classification dataset

Model	Split	Mean Squared Error	Mean Absolute Error	RMSLE	R^2 score
RandomForestRegressor	1	4489.95	43.72	0.41	0.86
RandomForestRegressor	2	4636.60	44.60	0.41	0.86
RandomForestRegressor	3	4691.67	44.57	0.41	0.86
RandomForestRegressor	Mean	4606.07	44.30	0.41	0.85

In Figure 12, we observe the results of the final model obtained through Three-Fold Cross Validation. The Mean Absolute Error (MAE) for the model is calculated as 44.30, which represents the average of the MAE values obtained from all three splits. By employing Three-Fold Cross Validation, we split the dataset into three equal parts and perform the Training, Validation and testing steps on each split. This approach allows us to evaluate the performance of the model across different subsets of the data and provides a more comprehensive understanding of its accuracy.

In the case of identifying the best split, we determine that split 1 yields the most favorable results. The best split is determined based on various factors such as the performance metrics, model convergence, or specific characteristics of the dataset. In this particular analysis, split 1 exhibits the most desirable outcome. Hence, in Figure 16, the final model achieves an average MAE of 44.30, calculated by averaging the MAE values from all three splits obtained through Three-Fold Cross Validation.

Additionally, upon evaluating the performance across the splits, split 1 emerges as the most favorable choice. These findings contribute to the selection of an optimized model and guide decision-making processes in the VLSI implementation for bike count prediction.

Feature Importance

Feature importance is a crucial step in understanding the relevance and contribution of different features or attributes within a dataset. To determine feature importance, we assign rankings to all features except for the 'count' attribute. This process can be divided into two parts. In the first part, we employ the Random Forest Regression technique for Training, Validation, and Testing. During this process, we specifically focus on the validation dataset to derive the feature rankings. By analyzing the model's performance on the validation dataset, we gain insights into the importance of each feature in predicting the target variable. Using the derived feature rankings, we then create a bar graph to visualize the feature importance. This graph provides a clear representation of the relative significance of each feature in the prediction process.

Figure 13. Feature importance in validating dataset

```
Feature ranking:
1. feature hr (0.631562)
2. feature atemp (0.095735)
3. feature temp (0.073585)
4. feature workingday (0.047627)
5. feature hum (0.046196)
6. feature weathersit (0.026882)
7. feature windspeed (0.023634)
8. feature weekday (0.019906)
9. feature mnth (0.019243)
10. feature season (0.012421)
11. feature holiday (0.003210)
```

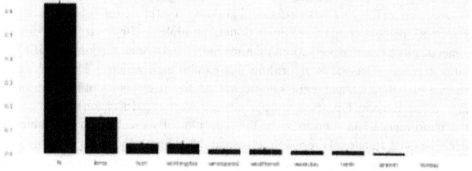

By examining the feature importance graph, we can identify the most influential features that strongly affect the prediction of the target variable. This information is valuable for feature selection, model refinement, and gaining insights into the underlying relationships between the features and the predicted outcome. The process of feature importance involves ranking the features based on their relevance, plotting the feature importance graph, and assessing the significance of each feature in the context of the VLSI implementation for bike count prediction using ML. We can also determine the feature rankings and feature importance for Three Fold Cross Validation by following a similar process. By analyzing the data from each split, we can assess the importance of different features in predicting the bike count. Let's focus on Split 1 and examine the feature rankings and feature importance specifically for this split.

Based on the analysis, we find that the feature values of 'hr' (Hour) and 'temp' (Temperature) hold the highest importance in predicting the bike count. These features exhibit a strong correlation with the target variable, indicating their significant role in influencing the bike rental demand. On the other hand, the remaining features demonstrate negligible importance and have a comparatively lower impact on the bike count prediction. By understanding the feature importance in each split of the Three Fold Cross Validation, we can gain insights into the key factors that contribute to the accuracy of the prediction model. These findings help us identify the most influential features and guide decision-making processes related to feature selection and model refinement for VLSI implementation in bike count prediction using ML.

Ensemble Learning: Bagging

Random Forest is a highly renowned and effective machine learning algorithm that belongs to the family of ensemble learning techniques known as Bootstrap Aggregation or bagging. In statistics, the bootstrap method is a robust approach for estimating various quantities based on a sample of data. It is particularly useful when estimating descriptive statistics such as means or standard deviations. Bootstrap Aggregation, or Bagging for short, is a straightforward yet powerful ensemble method. Ensemble methods combine the predictions of multiple machine learning models to generate more accurate predictions than any individual model. Bagging specifically aims to reduce variance in algorithms that exhibit high variance. Decision trees, such as classification and regression trees (CART), are examples of high-variance algorithms. Random Forests, as an improvement over bagged decision trees, enhance the performance and robustness of the algorithm. By creating an ensemble of decision trees, Random Forests introduce additional randomness and diversity into the model. This diversity, combined with the averaging or voting mechanism used in Random Forests, leads to more reliable and accurate predictions. The power of

Random Forest lies in its ability to handle complex problems and provide reliable predictions by leveraging the collective wisdom of multiple decision trees. The algorithm's effectiveness has made it a popular choice in various domains, including VLSI implementation for tasks such as bike count prediction using machine learning techniques.

One drawback of decision trees, such as CART, is their greedy nature. They select variables for splitting based on a greedy algorithm that aims to minimize error. Consequently, even with Bagging, decision trees can exhibit structural similarities, leading to high correlation in their predictions. In ensemble methods, combining predictions from sub-models is most effective when the predictions are uncorrelated or weakly correlated. Random Forest addresses this issue by modifying the way sub-trees are learned, resulting in less correlation among their predictions. This modification is a simple tweak to the algorithm. In CART, when selecting a split point, the learning algorithm considers all variables and their values to choose the optimal split. In contrast, the random forest algorithm restricts the learning algorithm to randomly sample a subset of features for the search. By introducing this randomization, Random Forest reduces the correlation among sub-models and improves the ensemble's predictive performance.

During the construction of Bagged decision trees, we can evaluate how much the error function decreases for each variable at every split point. This measure can be the drop in sum squared error for regression problems or the Gini score for classification tasks. By averaging these error drops across all decision trees, we obtain an estimate of the importance of each input variable. A greater drop in error when a variable is chosen indicates its higher importance in the prediction process. These outputs provide insights into the relevance of different input variables and can guide feature selection experiments by suggesting which variables may be most or least relevant to the problem. This information allows for possible dataset refinement by removing irrelevant features. Additionally, when constructing Bagged decision trees, some samples from the training data are left out in each bootstrap sample. These left-out samples are known as Out-Of-Bag (OOB) samples. The performance of each model on its respective OOB samples, when averaged, provides an estimated accuracy of the bagged models. This estimate, known as the OOB estimate of performance, serves as a reliable indicator of test error and correlates well with estimates obtained through cross-validation. The mean squared error and R2 score for different models are shown in Figure 15.

Figure 15. Model comparison

Model	Mean Squared Error	R² score
SGDRegressor	42616.39	0.08
Lasso	43103.36	0.07
ElasticNet	54155.92	-0.17
Ridge	42963.88	0.07
SVR	50794.62	-0.09
SVR	41659.68	0.10
BaggingRegressor	19513.18	0.58
BaggingRegressor	47600.05	-0.03
NuSVR	41517.67	0.11
RandomForestRegressor	18949.93	0.59

In the process of bagging, we evaluate and compare multiple models to identify the ones that contribute the most to the overall prediction performance. These highly contributing models are given greater preference in the bagging ensemble. By assessing the performance of individual models, we can determine their effectiveness in making accurate predictions. Models that exhibit superior performance, such as lower error rates or higher accuracy, are considered more influential and valuable. These models demonstrate a greater understanding of the underlying patterns and relationships in the data.

When constructing the bagging ensemble, we prioritize the inclusion of these highly contributing models. Their predictions carry more weight and influence the final aggregated prediction. By emphasizing the models that exhibit stronger performance, we aim to enhance the overall predictive power and accuracy of the bagging ensemble. This selective approach in bagging ensures that the most valuable models play a more prominent role in the ensemble, leading to improved predictions and more reliable outcomes. Figure 16 shows the test accuracy for difference estimators.

Figure 16. Test accuracy

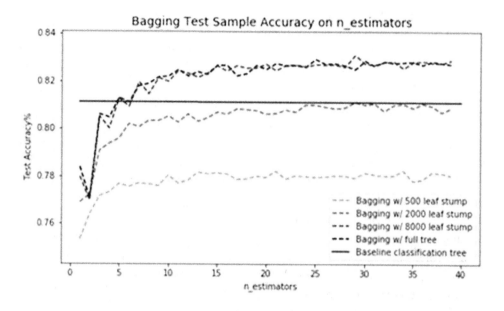

In our analysis, we set the number of estimators (n_estimators) to 10 based on the results shown in Figure 16. The figure clearly illustrates that with 10 estimators, we achieve a higher level of accuracy. Moreover, we observed that increasing the number of estimators beyond this point does not significantly improve the accuracy. Therefore, 10 estimators provide a good balance between accuracy and computational efficiency. Additionally, we recommend utilizing bagging with 2000 leaf stumps to further enhance the accuracy of the model. By employing 2000 leaf stumps, we aim to capture a more comprehensive representation of the data and leverage the power of ensemble learning. This configuration is selected to maximize accuracy while considering computational resources and model complexity. By choosing an optimal combination of 10 estimators and 2000 leaf stumps, we aim to strike a balance between accuracy and computational efficiency, ensuring that the model delivers robust predictions while remaining practical for implementation.

VLSI Implementation Strategies

The rapid advancement of AI/ML techniques has brought dynamic changes to VLSI architecture design. With the integration of neural network algorithms and advancements in high-performance semiconductor designs, hardware implementations for real-time applications have become more efficient. VLSI technology has evolved over the years, driven by the need for high-speed processing, improved reliability, cost-effective solutions, and shorter time-to-market windows in edge applications.

The progress in computing and semiconductor technologies has made AI and deep learning feasible in various hardware applications. System-on-Chip (SoC) architectures have undergone significant modifications to incorporate deep learning capabilities. To operate within memory-constrained architectures in edge applications such as mobile, communications, automotive, and IoT devices, AI-SoC models are often compressed. Field-Programmable Gate Arrays (FPGAs) are widely used to enhance AI computing power on hardware, while Application-Specific Integrated Circuits (ASICs) are preferred for specialized applications.

The physical design of VLSI chips poses challenges due to complex combinatorial problems and the impact of semiconductor technology scaling. The introduction of design rules and design for manufacturing (DFM) constraints has increased design complexity and made it harder to achieve optimal solutions. The VLSI chip design flow involves multiple abstraction levels, from circuit design to chip fabrication and testing. Each level requires different models that relate inputs to outputs, generating massive amounts of data that flows across billions of integrated devices or components on the chip.

AI/ML algorithms can be employed to explore the intricate input-output relationships between components, processes, and abstraction levels. By leveraging information gathered from various simulations and analyses, these algorithms can analyze data streams associated with file operations and improve application performance through clustering algorithms. AI/ML solutions can also optimize the VLSI-CAD design flow by automating tasks such as design rule checking, physical verification, placement and routing, timing closure, and test pattern generation. By learning from historical data, identifying patterns, making predictions, and generating new ideas, AI/ML algorithms enhance the accuracy and efficiency of VLSI-CAD tools. The integration of AI/ML in VLSI-CAD has the potential to significantly enhance the design process, leading to faster time-to-market, reduced costs, and higher-quality chips.

CONCLUSION

In the context of VLSI implementation of Bike Sharing/Count Prediction using ML, we have determined that the hour and temperature variables hold significant influence over the bike sharing count dataset. These findings can guide us in designing efficient VLSI architectures to accurately predict the impact of different attributes. Among the various ML algorithms, Random Forest proves to be the most suitable choice for this type of dataset, allowing us to identify the relative importance of attributes. However, when dealing with large datasets exceeding 10 million samples, the implementation of Random Forest using sklearn may encounter performance challenges. The computational cost and memory constraints can hinder its efficiency. In such scenarios, it is recommended to explore alternative solutions, such as leveraging the Python Woodley implementation. This implementation utilizes top tree pre-classification and distributed sampling, optimizing the VLSI hardware implementation by employing C programming.

To further enhance scalability and performance, machine learning frameworks like Apache Spark ML can be employed. This allows for distributed computation utilizing computer clustering and accessing data from popular Apache databases like Apache Cassandra. Leveraging the power of Spark ML on frameworks such as Kubernetes, Apache Mesos, or Hadoop can significantly accelerate the processing speed, enabling efficient VLSI implementation for large-scale datasets. Additionally, to improve the performance of the data model, it is crucial to address the distribution of the target variable. Some predictive models assume a normal distribution, which might not be optimal for accurate predictions. By applying appropriate data pre-processing techniques, such as transformation methods, we can align the target variable's distribution with the model's assumptions. This adjustment enhances the overall performance of the VLSI-based ML algorithms for Bike Sharing/Count Prediction applications, resulting in faster time-to-market, reduced costs, and high-quality chips.

REFERENCES

Arunkumar, N., & Dhanasekar, S. (2020, November). An Ultra-Low-Power Static Random-Access Memory Cell Using Tunneling Field Effect Transistor. *International Journal of Engineering*, *33*(11). Advance online publication. doi:10.5829/ije.2020.33.11b.13

Bruntha, P. M., Dhanasekar, S., Hepsiba, D., Sagayam, K. M., Neebha, T. M., Pandey, D., & Pandey, B. K. (2022). Application of switching median filter with L2 norm-based auto-tuning function for removing random valued impulse noise. *Aerospace Systems*, *6*(1), 53–59. doi:10.100742401-022-00160-y

Dhanasekar, S., Malin Bruntha, P., & Martin Sagayam, K. (2019). An Improved Area Efficient 16-QAM Transceiver Design using Vedic Multiplier for Wireless Applications. *International Journal of Recent Technology and Engineering*, *8*(3), 4419–4425. doi:10.35940/ijrte.C5535.098319

Dhanasekar, S., & Ramesh, J. (2015). FPGA Implementation of Variable Bit Rate 16 QAM Transceiver System. *International Journal of Applied Engineering Research, 10*, 26479–26507.

Govindaraj, V., Dhanasekar, S., Martinsagayam, K., Pandey, D., Pandey, B. K., & Nassa, V. K. (2023). Low-power test pattern generator using modified LFSR. Aerospace Systems, 1-8.

Jubair Ahmed, L., Anish Fathima, B., Dhanasekar, S., & Martin Sagayam, K. (2022). Modeling of Fuzzy Logic-Based Classification System Using the Gravitational Search Algorithm. In Multimedia Technologies in the Internet of Things Environment, Volume 3. Studies in Big Data. Springer. doi:10.1007/978-981-19-0924-5_5

Konguvel, Hariharan, Sujatha, & Kannan. (2022). Hardware implementation of approximate multipliers for signal processing applications. *International Journal of Wireless and Mobile Computing, 23*(3-4), 302-309. doi:10.1504/IJWMC.2022.10052548

Konguvel & Kannan. (2022). A Novel Digital Logic for Bit Reversal and Address Generations in FFT Computations. *Wireless Personal Communications, 128*(3), 1827-1838. doi:. doi:10.1007/s11277-022-10021-8

Konguvel, E., Nithiyameenatchi, N., & Rachel, L. (2022). IoT-enabled ECG Monitoring System for Remote Cardiac Patients. *Proc. of 2022 IEEE International Conference on Augmented Intelligence and Sustainable Systems (ICAISS – 2022),* 1146 – 1151. doi:10.1109/ICAISS55157.2022.10010849

Mooney, P., Corcoran, P., & Winstanley, A. C. (2010). *Preliminary results of a spatial analysis of Dublin city's bike rental scheme.* Academic Press.

Normark, D., Cochoy, F., Hagberg, J., & Ducourant, H. (2018). Mundane intermodality: A comparative analysis of bike-renting practices. *Mobilities, 13*(6), 791–807. doi:10.1080/17450101.2018.1504651

Pan, Y., Zheng, R. C., Zhang, J., & Yao, X. (2019). Predicting bike sharing demand using recurrent neural networks. *Procedia Computer Science, 147,* 562–566. doi:10.1016/j.procs.2019.01.217

Permitasari, R. I., & Sahara, R. (2018). Implementation of Web–Based Bike Renting Application "Bike–Sharing.". *International Journal Computer Science and Mobile Computing, 7*(12), 6–13.

Thirumal, R., Rahul, B. R., Rahulpriyesh, B., Konguvel, E., & Sumathi, G. (2022). EVMFFR: Electronic Voting Machine with Fingerprint and Facial Recognition. *Proc. of 2022 IEEE Second International Conference on Next Generation Intelligent Systems (ICNGIS – 2022),* 1–6. 10.1109/ICNGIS54955.2022.10079752

Thoa Pham Thi, T., Timoney, J., Ravichandran, S., Mooney, P., & Winstanley, A. (2017). *Bike Renting Data Analysis: The Case of Dublin City.* arXiv e-prints, arXiv-1704.

Vineeth Reddy, C., Lohitt Venkata Saai, N., Konguvel, E., Sumathi, G., & Sujatha, R. (2022). Emergency Alert System for Women Safety using Raspberry Pi. *Proc. of 2022 IEEE Second International Conference on Next Generation Intelligent Systems (ICNGIS – 2022),* 1–4. doi:10.1109/ICNGIS54955.2022.10079823

Wang, Z. (2019). Regression Model for Bike-Sharing Service by Using Machine Learning. *Asian Journal of Social Science Studies, 4*(4), 16. doi:10.20849/ajsss.v4i4.666

Xu, X., Ye, Z., Li, J., & Xu, M. (2018). Understanding the usage patterns of bicycle-sharing systems to predict users' demand: A case study in Wenzhou, China. *Computational Intelligence and Neuroscience, 2018,* 2018. doi:10.1155/2018/9892134 PMID:30254667

Yang, H., Xie, K., Ozbay, K., Ma, Y., & Wang, Z. (2018). Use of deep learning to predict daily usage of bike sharing systems. *Transportation Research Record: Journal of the Transportation Research Board, 2672*(36), 92–102. doi:10.1177/0361198118801354

Yoon, J. W., Pinelli, F., & Calabrese, F. (2012, July). Cityride: A predictive bike sharing journey advisor. In *2012 IEEE 13th International Conference on Mobile Data Management* (pp. 306-311). IEEE. 10.1109/MDM.2012.16

Zhang, S., Zhou, Z., Hao, H., & Zhou, J. (2018). Prediction model of demand for public bicycle rental based on land use. *Advances in Mechanical Engineering, 10*(12). doi:10.1177/1687814018818977

Chapter 8
ML–Based Finger–Vein Biometric Authentication and Hardware Implementation Strategies

Nayan Keshri
Vellore Institute of Technology, India

Sumathi Gokulanathan
Vellore Institute of Technology, India

Swapnadeep Sarkar
Vellore Institute of Technology, India

Konguvel Elango
Vellore Institute of Technology, India

Yash Raj Singh
Vellore Institute of Technology, India

Sivakumar Ponnusamy
Capital One, USA

ABSTRACT

The industrial world is facing swiftly changing challenges, including technical fluctuations, swings in global markets, and climate change. Digitalization and automation are the game changers to meet these challenges. Machine learning has made an impact on the area attributed to microchips, and it is initially used in automation. These practices will ultimately succeed the current VLSI design. A biometric authentication system is a form of biometric verification system that uses finger vein detection for biometric check framework. Consumer electronics development necessitates high security, high accuracy, and fast authentication speed. Since it presents the elements inside the human body, finger vein validation is a prominent technique in terms of security. Furthermore, it has a fair advantage over other personal authentication methods because to its contactless aspect. The main goal of the chapter is to provide a solution using machine learning for finger vein authentication and implementation using VLSI design.

DOI: 10.4018/978-1-6684-6596-7.ch008

INTRODUCTION

Biometrics refers to a person's distinguishing characteristics. Biometric recognition is the process of automatically recognising people in view of element vectors acquired from physiological and additionally social attributes. Biometric advances for far off human ID have forever been sought after in an assortment of significant applications. The quick threat of malicious actions is one of the key issues that biometric systems face today. To overcome biometric systems, the majority of hostile actors use a common sort of presentation attack known as "spoofing."

For identity identification, biometrics utilizes at least one physiological (veins, iris, faces, and fingerprints) or social (signature and gait) traits of humans. Finger vein acknowledgment innovation, which utilizes the vein structure design underneath the finger surface as proof, has started to assume a significant part in the field of biometrics since 1) it is hard to manufacture since it utilizes the vascular construction design underneath the skin as proof; 2) it can work under contactless or slight contact procurement boundaries, which are easy to understand elements; and 3) it is powerless against obstruction since it is less defenceless against scars, oil or sweat on the finger's surface.

A late examination into the turn of events and execution of finger vein acknowledgment has supported the innovation's quick and promising development, showing its colossal market potential.

RELATED WORKS

A proposed method on convolutional-neural-network-(CNN) based finger vein recognizable proof framework and research the capacities of the planned organization over freely accessible data sets. The outcomes show that it is feasible to accomplish a position 1 recognizable proof exactness more prominent than 95% for every one of the four data sets, utilizing our proposed CNN design (Das et al., 2018). Another framework incorporates a product and equipment stage that gathers a full perspective on the vein design data from entire fingers with three cameras, because of CNN calculation. This paper portrays a starter investigation of a 3D finger vein check framework. Albeit the proposed approach accomplishes a promising presentation for finger vein check, a significant measure of work stays to further develop the confirmation exactness and diminish time utilization (Kang et al., 2019).

A technique proposed where they embrace seven layers of CNN which incorporate 5 convolution layers and 2 completely associated layers. This organization acquires an acknowledgment pace of 95.53%, which ends up being preferred performing over conventional calculation. The right acknowledgment pace of our proposed strategy can reach 95.53%. It shows that the exhibition of utilizing CNN is superior to utilizing conventional calculations (Liu et al., 2017). The method in Yang and Li (2010) first localizes the region of interest (ROI) of vein images using the inter-phalangeal joint prior. Then, vein images are characterized as a series of energy features through steerable filters. Finally, the vein features are used to identify the human vein. Experimental results show that the proposed method achieves promising performance.

Working on the current frameworks in light of a CNN utilize two strategies: utilizing a distinction picture as the contribution to the organization and ascertaining the distance between highlight vectors extricated from the CNN and DenseNet sometimes vein designs were not obviously caught with concealing, and a serious level of misalignment happened vein designs were somewhat caught and there were issues of similitude in the examples and concealing (Song et al., 2019). A framework that all the while obtains the finger-vein and low-goal finger impression pictures and joins and tests utilizing Gabor Filters. Introduced a calculation for the finger-vein recognizable proof, which can all the more dependably separate the finger-vein shape includes and accomplish a lot higher precision than the recently proposed finger-vein ID draws near (Kumar & Zhou, 2011).

Out of all the acknowledgment qualities present inside the human body, finger veins can be considered safer than other biometric ascribes zeroed in on the hands, for example, fingerprints and palm prints. Another surface descriptor called nearby line parallel example (LLBP) is utilized as a component extraction instrument in the recommended strategy. We propose utilizing the nearby line paired design (LLBP) as an element extraction strategy rather than LBP and LDP. LLBP's straight-line shape permits it to extricate hearty highlights from photographs with questionable veins. The equivalent blunder rate (EER) for the LLBP is a lot of lower than the LBP and LDP, as indicated by trial results from 204 fingers taken from our own model gadget (Lee et al., 2009).

Technique where Vein pictures are portrayed as a progression of energy highlights through steerable channels and eliminating uninformative vein symbolism in view of the between phalangeal joint earlier. Resolved the issues of FV restriction and acknowledgment. The distal between phalangeal joint is utilized to pinpoint vein pattern and confine vein ROI. Steerable channels are additionally taken advantage of to extricate measurable vein energy qualities (Yang & Li, 2010). The double sliding window approach for finding the phalangeal joint is created in this review to separate an additional steady ROI, which can oppose the impact of lopsided lighting, and to mitigate the issue of light awareness in earlier phalangeal joint limitation techniques (Qiu et al., 2016).

To start, they separate the vein examples' highlights to remember them. Second, the vein examples' minuscule components, for example, bifurcation focuses and ending focuses, are recovered for acknowledgment. These component focuses are utilized to delineate the state of vein designs mathematically. At long last, the altered Hausdorff distance method is accommodated deciding the separation between all conceivable relative places of vein design shape. The equivalent mistake rate (EER) arrives at 0.761 percent in exploratory information, with a limit worth of 0.43 for the distance measure HD (Yu et al., 2009). On the UTFVP finger-vein informational collection, a trial examination integrating different component extraction draws near and different combination methodologies are being directed. The outcomes recommend that element-level combination further develops acknowledgment precision over single component extraction methodologies regarding EER. They exhibited that melding highlights at the element level can further develop acknowledgment execution regarding EER (Kauba et al., 2016).

Digitalization will encompass the majority of engineering fields, with a bigger impact over wide-area communication network involving fast data transmission (Arunkumar & Dhanasekar, 2020; Dhanasekar et al., 2019; Dhanasekar & Ramesh, 2015). Govindaraj et al. (2023) discussed test pattern generator with minimum switching activity for high speed circuits. The switching median Filter with L2 norm-based auto-tuning function for removing random valued impulse noise for neumorphic circuits were discussed Bruntha et al. (2022). Jubair et al. (2022) discussed the modeling of Fuzzy Logic-Based Classification System Using the Gravitational Search Algorithm. Several approaches and strategies in microcontroller, FPGA and VLSI implementation are discussed in Konguvel, Hariharan, Sujatha et al. (2022), Konguvel and Kannan (2022), Konguvel, Nithiyameenatchi, and Rachel (2022), Thirumal et al. (2022), and Vineeth Reddy et al. (2022).

METHODOLOGY

Input Image

The input images are taken from the Kaggle data set. This dataset contains images of more than 100 people. The images are MRI scans of finger veins of index, middle and ring fingers of both the hands. Each folder contains various images of the finger veins and are unique to a person. The overall flow is shown in Figure 1. Figure 2 shows the images of different persons with veins of different fingers.

Figure 1. Stepwise process flow diagram of the project

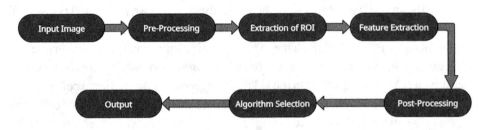

Figure 2. Kaggle image datasets

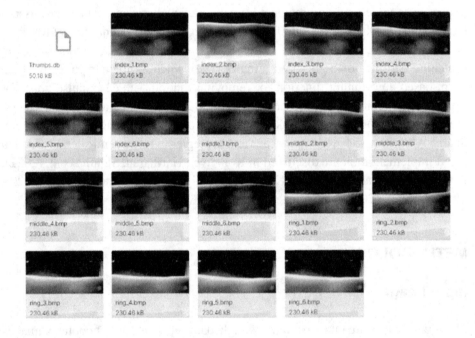

Pre-processing

Data pre-processing is a step in the data mining and analysis process of transforming unprocessed data in a form that computers and machine learning can comprehend and analyse. Text, images, videos, and other real information are disorganised. It is typically inadequate and lacks a coherent design, not to mention faults and contradictions. Computers read input as 1s and 0s in order to handle information in a neat and tidy manner. Calculating structured data, such as whole numbers and statistics, is so straightforward. Before even being analysed, unstructured data such as text and photographs should be cleaned and processed. The data preprocessing steps are shown in Figure 3. The reason for which pre-processed data required is:

1. Enhance our database's authenticity. As a result of human mistake or issues, we erase any entries that are incorrect or lacking.
2. It is necessary to increase consistency. Because there are data inconsistencies or duplicates, the accuracy of the outcomes suffers.
3. Complete the database as much as practicable. We can fill up the remaining information if necessary. The data should have a nice flow to it. This method makes it much easy to use and comprehend.

Figure 3. Data preprocessing

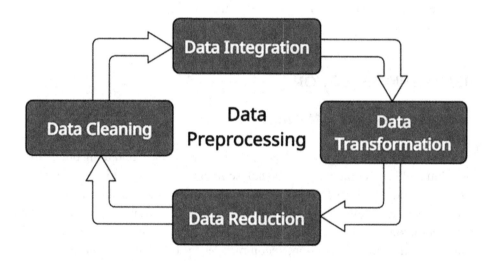

Extraction of RoI

A region of interest (ROI) is a section of a photograph or database that has been chosen for a particular purpose. Any of the datasets listed below might be used:

1. **Waveform or 1D Dataset:** The ROI is a time or frequency interval (a graph of some quantity displayed against time) on the waveform.
2. **Two-Dimensional Dataset or Image:** The ROI is defined by the limits on an image of an item or a drawing. Volume datasets, also known as three-dimensional datasets: The ROI refers to the curves or surfaces that characterize a physical

item. Whenever it relates to the altering 3D dataset of an item changing form with time, the ROI is the 3D data within a certain period of time.

GLCM Feature Extraction

It is the technique of obtaining higher-level features of an image, like texture, colour, and contrast. In actuality, texture analysis is an important part of both human and machine sensory acuity. It is effectively used to boost the reliability of the diagnostics system by identifying significant features. Feature extraction is a method for minimising the size of a picture by removing relevant sections as a compressed feature vector. This approach is utilised when the picture size is large and a simplified feature map is required to complete a job quickly, such as depth images and retrieval. A highlight extractor feature called Gray Level Co-event Matrix requires observing a surface and presenting the spatial configurations of each pixel. Entropy (E) - Entropy is calculated to characterize the randomness of the textural image.

ALGORITHM SELECTION

Convolutional Neural Network

Convolutional neural networks (CNNs) are neural networks containing one or more convolutional layers that are used to analyse images, classify data, and segment it. The bulk of contemporary Deep Learning models involve artificial neural networks, particularly CNNs. A convolutional neural network is a sort of deep neural network that is commonly used to analyse images. They may be utilised in domains like as image and video recognition, recommender systems, image analysis, image segmentation, medical image analysis, natural language processing, brain-computer interfaces, and financial time series, to name a few. Convolutional neural networks outperform traditional neural networks using visual, voice, or audio signal inputs due to their superior performance. The CNN flow diagram is shown in Figure 4.

Main Layers present are:

1. Convolution Layer
2. Pooling Layer
3. Fully Connected Layer

Figure 4. CNN flow diagram

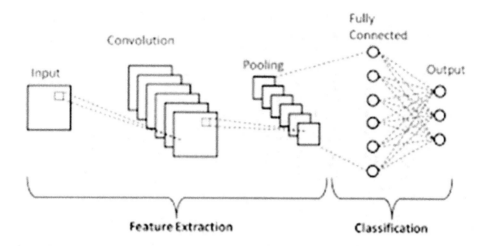

Since the Convolution Layer is where the majority of the processing takes place, the convolutional layer is by far the most significant component of a CNN, which is shown in Figure 5. It requires, among other things, input data, a filter, and a feature map. Assume that the input is a colour picture composed of a 3D matrix of pixels. This implies the input will have three elements: height, width, and depth, all of which correspond to a picture's RGB colour space. A feature detector, also referred as a kernel or a filter, will identify the presence of the feature all across image's visual field. This method is known as convolution.

Figure 5. Convolutional layer

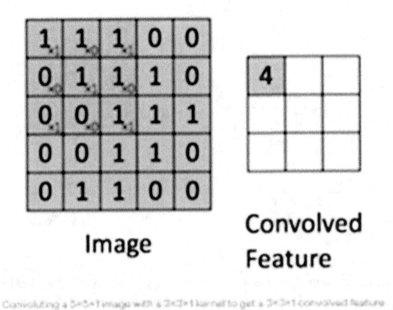

Image

Convolved Feature

Convoluting a 5×5×1 image with a 3×3×1 kernel to get a 3×3×1 convolved feature

A CNN adds a Rectified Linear Unit (ReLU) adjustment to the feature map after every convolution operation, imparting nonlinearity to the model, shown in Figure 6a and 6b.

Figure 6. a and b show the Relu function

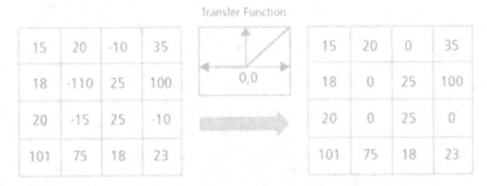

A pooling layer reduces the number of learnable parameters by performing a traditional down sampling operation on the feature maps, lowering their in-plane dimensionality and introducing translation invariance to minor shifts and distortions. Whereas filter size, stride, and padding are parameters in pooling operations, similar to convolution processes, neither of the pooling layers have graspable parameters. The different categories of pooling layer is shown in Figure 7.

Figure 7. Two types of pooling

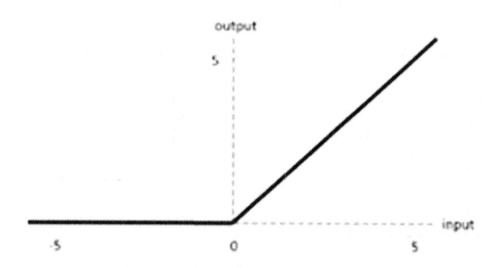

The output feature maps from the the last convolution or pooling layer are usually flattened, or converted into a (1-dimensional) array of numbers, and connected with one or even more fully - connected layer, also identified as dense layers, wherein every input is connected to every outcome by a trainable weight. A subset of fully connected layers transfers the characteristics retrieved by convolution layers and down sampled by the pooling layers towards the network's final outputs, like the probability for each class in classifiication. In the final fully linked layer, the number of output nodes is generally equivalent to the number of classes. Each entirely linked layer is followed by a nonlinear function. The CNN output layers are shown in Figure 8.

Figure 8. CNN output layer

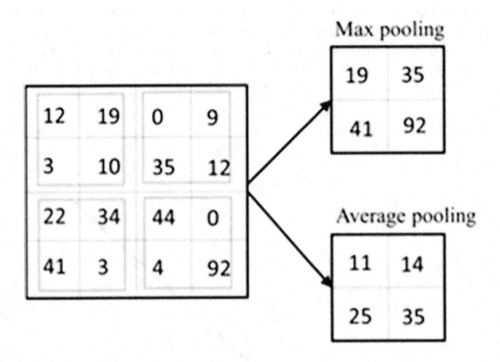

Gradient Boosting

Gradient boosting is an approach that distinguishes out for its precision and speed, particularly when working with large, complex datasets. This algorithm has provided the best results in everything from Kaggle competitions to machine learning solutions for businesses. In any machine learning method, errors play a significant role. The primary idea behind this technique is to develop models in a sequential manner, with each model attempting to reduce the mistakes of the previous model. Figure 8 shows the working of Gradient Boosting Algorithm. The two most prevalent forms of mistake are bias and variance error. We may use the gradient boosting method to minimise the model's bias error.

Figure 9. Boosting algo model

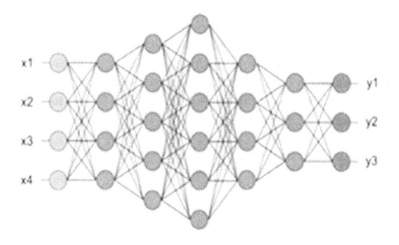

K-Means Clustering

The vector quantization method which divides N observations into K clusters is called K-means clustering. Here, each observation belonging to the cluster with the closest mean (cluster centres or cluster centroid), which serves as the cluster's prototype. As a result, Voronoi cells are created in the data space. Within-cluster variances (squared Euclidean distances) are reduced by k-means clustering, but regular Euclidean distances are not, making the Weber problem more difficult: the mean optimises squared errors, while only the geometric median decreases Euclidean distances. Better Euclidean solutions can be obtained by using k-medians and k-medoids. Despite the fact that the problem is computationally difficult (NP-hard), effective heuristic strategies quickly reach at a local optimum. Both k-means and Gaussian mixture modelling adopt an iterative refining process similar to the expectation-maximization procedure for Gaussian mixtures. Both use cluster centres to represent the data; however, k-means clustering tends to discover clusters with comparable spatial extents, whereas the Gaussian mixture model allows for a variety of cluster shapes.

The supervised k-nearest neighbour classifier, a well-known supervised machine learning technique for classification that is frequently confused with k-means due to nomenclature, is connected to the unsupervised k-means algorithm. When fresh data is classified into existing clusters, the 1-nearest neighbour classifier is applied to the cluster centres acquired using k-means. This is also known as the Rocchio algorithm or nearest centroid classifier.

In data mining, the K-means technique begins with a set of randomly chosen centroids that serve as the starting points for each cluster, and then performs iterative (repetitive) calculations to optimise the centroids' placements. However, because minor changes in the data can produce significant variance, its performance is typically inferior to that of other complicated clustering techniques. Furthermore, clusters are thought to be spherical and homogenous in size, which may reduce the precision of the K-means clustering Python results. Before and after applying K-means clustering is shown in Figure 10.

Figure 10. K-means cluster formation

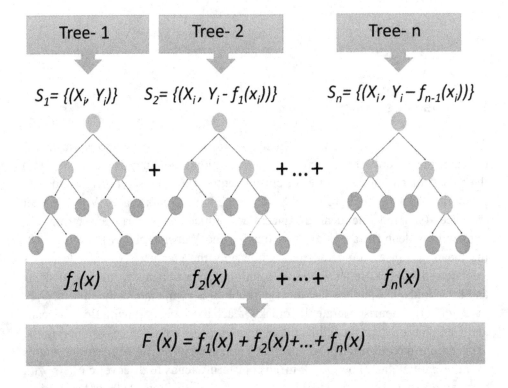

AI/ML in VLSI: Strategies

The design of VLSI architectures has become more dynamic with the evolution of AI/ML techniques. Advances in neural network algorithms and innovations in high-bandwidth and high-performance semiconductor designs have opened up new ways to address the challenges of hardware implementations for advanced real-time applications. Over the past few decades, different architectures have inspired the advancement of VLSI technology. Most design developments and improvements have been motivated by the need for edge applications with high processing speeds, improved reliability, low implementation cost, and short time-to-market windows.

AI and deep learning are now feasible in most hardware applications due to advancements in computing and semiconductor technologies. Several critical modifications have been made to SoC architectures to incorporate deep learning capabilities. AI-SoC models must be compressed to ensure their operation at constrained memory architectures in mobile, communications, automobile, and IoT edge applications. FPGAs are one of the most widespread and commercially available programmable logic devices to accelerate the computing power of AI on hardware. ASICs are best for implementing specialized applications.

VLSI physical design is a challenging task due to the numerous combinatorial problems that require many iterations to converge. Semiconductor technology scaling has increased the complexity of these design problems by introducing complex design rules and design for manufacturing (DFM) constraints. As a result, it is difficult to achieve optimal solutions.

The design flow for VLSI chips involves multiple abstraction levels, from circuit design to chip fabrication and testing. Each abstraction level has its own set of models that relate inputs to outputs. An enormous amount of data flows across billions of devices or components integrated or to be integrated on the chip.

AI/ML algorithms can be used to explore the complex I/O relationships between the components, processes and various abstraction levels within each abstraction level. This can be done by using the information accumulated during different kinds of simulations and analyses. Additionally, AI/ML algorithms can be used to analyse data streams associated with file operations. This can be done by using clustering algorithms to deliver high application performance. AI/ML solutions can be employed in VLSI–CAD for design-flow optimization. This can be done by using AI/ML algorithms to automate tasks such as Design rule checking, Physical verification, Placement and routing, Timing closure and Test pattern generation. AI/ML solutions can also be used to improve the accuracy and efficiency of VLSI–CAD tools by Learn from historical data, Identify patterns in data, Make predictions and Generate new ideas. The use of AI/ML in VLSI–CAD has the potential to significantly improve the design process. This can lead to faster time to market, lower costs, and better quality chips.

Results and Discussions

The Algorithms implemented in this proposed paper are (1) CNN, (2) Gradient Boosting, (3) K-Means. In the main recognition processes of picture acquisition, pre-processing, feature extraction, and matching, algorithms were evaluated. The dataset was taken from kaggle; dataset of finger vein scanned images. In this paper, the results of two-person finger vein images taken from database is shown. First, we select an image from the database, which is then pre-processed to produce an enhanced image. The Binary and Gray segments of the input Original image are then extracted from the ROI of the enhanced image. As a result, the picture ROI extraction method is simplified, and the Feature extraction technique is used to extract the desired features, in this case GLCM features for the required Finger-vein image. The CNN algorithm classifies and recognizes the person from the dataset photos using these features retrieved from the finger-vein image, and matches the finger-vein image to the needed individual of that finger-vein pattern. As a result, this experiment yielded accurate results; the results for the detected Person 3 and Person 10 from the input finger-vein images are shown below. The user interface is shown in Figure 11. The extraction of RoI is shown in Figure 12.

Figure 11. User interface

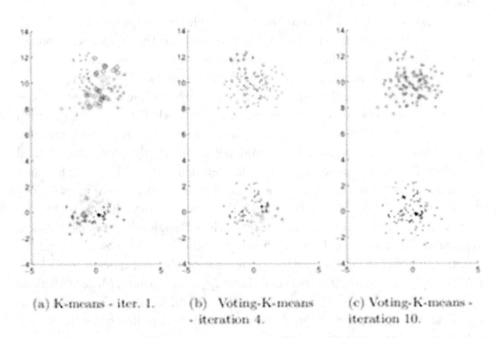

(a) K-means - iter. 1.   (b) Voting-K-means   (c) Voting-K-means -
                          - iteration 4.   iteration 10.

Figure 12. Extraction of ROI

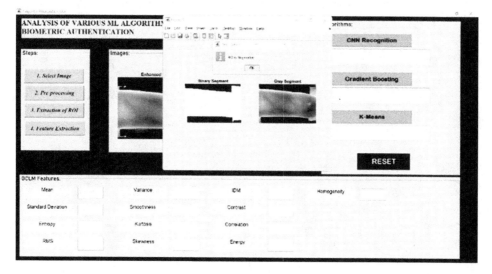

The enhanced image is set to ROI extraction of the image, which gives the gray segment and Binary segment of the image. Figure 13 shows the GLCM feature extraction of the selected image. From the Binary image as the input we can extract the GLCM features for the input original image. GLCM Features are now extracted for the input image and the summary is shown in the Table 1. The accuracy of different algorithms are summarized in Table 2. The receiver output characteristics curves are shown for different algorithms against two different samples in Figures 14 and 15.

Figure 13. GLCM feature extraction

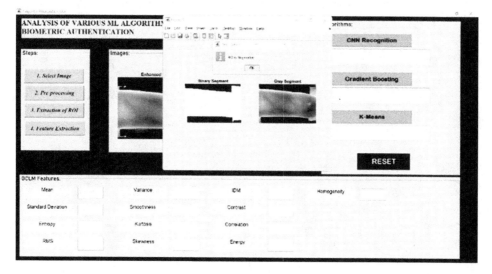

Table 1. Gray level co-occurrence matrix features of two different persons

GLCM Features	Person 1	Person 2
Mean	99.5765	116.07
Standard Deviation	69.4047	63.5473
Entropy	6.18403	7.13431
RMS	13.6587	14.9061
Variance	4559.75	2814.45
Smoothness	0.999999	1.0
Kurtosis	2.06928	2.66508
Skewness	-0.22367	-0.235
IDM	255	255
Contrast	0.986384	0.963071
Correlation	0.10688	0.118855
Energy	0.189122	0.136669
Homogeneity	0.963468	0.947838

Table 2. Accuracy % of different algorithms

Algorithm	Person 1	Person 2
CNN	96.5	97.5
Gradient Boosting	98.7	96.8
K-means clustering	93.8	94.8

Figure 14. RoC curves of three algorithms for Person 1

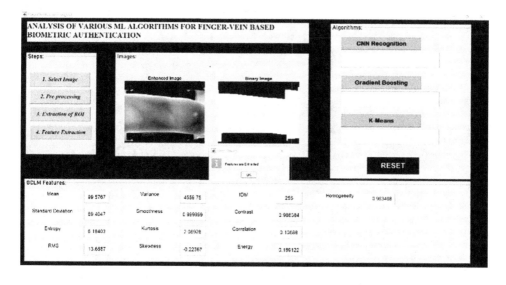

Figure 15. RoC curves of three algorithms for Person 2

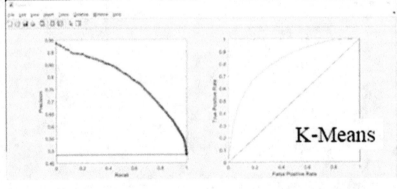

CONCLUSION

In this study, the suggested CNN-based finger-vein authentication technique is compared to previously existing conventional based methods for accurate recognition, and it comes out on top, proving that the new approach surpasses the present method in this regard. On the basis of MATLAB software, we created a Finger-vein

Recognition system using CNN. Despite the hurdles that must be overcome, the paper offers the most current scientific breakthroughs in the domain of finger-vein identification in recent times. Three algorithms were implemented in this study (CNN, Gradient boosting, K-means). Other than implementing three algorithms for finger vein based biometric identification, an image's GLCM features were also extracted. It is the technique of obtaining higher-level features of an image, like texture, colour, and contrast. In actuality, texture analysis is an important part of both human and machine sensory acuity. It is effectively used to boost the reliability of the diagnostics system by identifying significant features.

REFERENCES

Arunkumar, N., & Dhanasekar, S. (2020, November). An Ultra-Low-Power Static Random-Access Memory Cell Using Tunneling Field Effect Transistor. *International Journal of Engineering*, *33*(11). doi:10.5829/ije.2020.33.11b.13

Bruntha, Malin, Dhanasekar, Hepsiba, Sagayam, Neebha, Pandey, & Kumar Pandey. (2022). Application of Switching Median Filter with L2 Norm-Based Auto-Tuning Function for Removing Random Valued Impulse Noise. *Aerospace Systems*. . doi:10.1007/s42401-022-00160-y

Das, R., Piciucco, E., Maiorana, E., & Campisi, P. (2018). Convolutional neural network for finger-vein-based biometric identification. *IEEE Transactions on Information Forensics and Security*, *14*(2), 360–373. doi:10.1109/TIFS.2018.2850320

Dhanasekar, S., & Govindaraj, V. (2023). Low-power test pattern generator using modified LFSR. *Aerospace Systems*. doi:10.1007/s42401-022-00191-5

Dhanasekar, S., Malin Bruntha, P., & Martin Sagayam, K. (2019). An Improved Area Efficient 16-QAM Transceiver Design using Vedic Multiplier for Wireless Applications. *International Journal of Recent Technology and Engineering*, *8*(3), 4419–4425. doi:10.35940/ijrte.C5535.098319

Dhanasekar, S., & Ramesh, J. (2015). FPGA Implementation of Variable Bit Rate 16 QAM Transceiver System. *International Journal of Applied Engineering Research: IJAER*, *10*, 26479–26507.

Jubair Ahmed, L., Anish Fathima, B., Dhanasekar, S., & Martin Sagayam, K. (2022). Modeling of Fuzzy Logic-Based Classification System Using the Gravitational Search Algorithm. In Multimedia Technologies in the Internet of Things Environment, 3. Springer. doi:10.1007/978-981-19-0924-5_5

Kang, W., Liu, H., Luo, W., & Deng, F. (2019). Study of a full-view 3D finger vein verification technique. *IEEE Transactions on Information Forensics and Security*, *15*, 1175–1189. doi:10.1109/TIFS.2019.2928507

Kauba, C., Piciucco, E., Maiorana, E., Campisi, P., & Uhl, A. (2016, September). Advanced variants of feature level fusion for finger vein recognition. In *2016 International Conference of the Biometrics Special Interest Group (BIOSIG)* (pp. 1-7). IEEE. 10.1109/BIOSIG.2016.7736908

Konguvel, E., Hariharan, I., Sujatha R., & Kannan, M. (2022). Hardware implementation of approximate multipliers for signal processing applications. *International Journal of Wireless and Mobile Computing*, *23*, 302-309. . doi:10.1504/IJWMC.2022.10052548

Konguvel E. & Kannan, M. (2022). A Novel Digital Logic for Bit Reversal and Address Generations in FFT Computations. *Wireless Personal Communications*. . doi:10.1007/s11277-022-10021-8

Konguvel, E., Nithiyameenatchi, N., & Rachel, L. (2022). IoT-enabled ECG Monitoring System for Remote Cardiac Patients. In *Proc. of 2022 IEEE International Conference on Augmented Intelligence and Sustainable Systems (ICAISS – 2022)* (pp. 1146 – 1151). IEEE. 10.1109/ICAISS55157.2022.10010849

Kumar, A., & Zhou, Y. (2011). Human identification using finger images. *IEEE Transactions on Image Processing*, *21*(4), 2228–2244. doi:10.1109/TIP.2011.2171697 PMID:21997267

Lee, E. C., Lee, H. C., & Park, K. R. (2009). Finger vein recognition using minutia-based alignment and local binary pattern-based feature extraction. *International Journal of Imaging Systems and Technology*, *19*(3), 179–186. doi:10.1002/ima.20193

Liu, W., Li, W., Sun, L., Zhang, L., & Chen, P. (2017, June). Finger vein recognition based on deep learning. In *2017 12th IEEE conference on industrial electronics and applications (ICIEA)* (pp. 205-210). IEEE. 10.1109/ICIEA.2017.8282842

Qiu, S., Liu, Y., Zhou, Y., Huang, J., & Nie, Y. (2016). Finger-vein recognition based on dual-sliding window localization and pseudo-elliptical transformer. *Expert Systems with Applications*, *64*, 618–632. doi:10.1016/j.eswa.2016.08.031

Song, J. M., Kim, W., & Park, K. R. (2019). Finger-vein recognition based on deep DenseNet using composite image. *IEEE Access : Practical Innovations, Open Solutions*, *7*, 66845–66863. doi:10.1109/ACCESS.2019.2918503

Thirumal, R., Rahul, B. R., Rahulpriyesh, B., Konguvel, E., & Sumathi, G. (2022). EVMFFR: Electronic Voting Machine with Fingerprint and Facial Recognition. In *Proc. of 2022 IEEE Second International Conference on Next Generation Intelligent Systems (ICNGIS – 2022)*. IEEE. 10.1109/ICNGIS54955.2022.10079752

Vineeth Reddy, C., Lohitt Venkata Saai, N., Konguvel, E., Sumathi, G., & Sujatha, R. (2022). Emergency Alert System for Women Safety using Raspberry Pi. In *Proc. of 2022 IEEE Second International Conference on Next Generation Intelligent Systems (ICNGIS – 2022)* (pp. 1–4). IEEE. 10.1109/ICNGIS54955.2022.10079823

Yang, J., & Li, X. (2010, August). Efficient finger vein localization and recognition. In *2010 20th International Conference on Pattern Recognition* (pp. 1148-1151). IEEE. 10.1109/ICPR.2010.287

Yu, C. B., Qin, H. F., Cui, Y. Z., & Hu, X. Q. (2009). Finger-vein image recognition combining modified hausdorff distance with minutiae feature matching. *Interdisciplinary Sciences, Computational Life Sciences, 1*(4), 280–289. doi:10.100712539-009-0046-5 PMID:20640806

Chapter 9
Digital Implementation of Neural Network by Partial Reconfiguration

C. Udhaya Kumar
Bodhi Computing, India

P. Saravanan
PSG College of Technology, Coimbatore, India

N. Thiyagarajan
Sri Eshwar College of Engineering, Coimbatore, India

Veena Raj
Universiti Brunei Darussalam, Brunei

ABSTRACT

Artificial Neural Networks (ANNs) are becoming increasingly important in the present technological era due to their ability to solve complex problems, adapt to new inputs, and improve decision-skills for different domains. The human brain serves as a model for Artificial Neural Networks (ANNs), a type of machine learning, as a reference for both structure and function. The existing work on ANNs supports tasks, such as regression, classification and pattern recognition separately. The discussion aims at resolving the above highlighted issues related to various ANN architectural implementations, considering the dynamic function exchange feature of FPGAs. With the aid of Zynq SOC, CNN and DNN architectures are designed in its Processing System, and the structure is accelerated using Programmable Logic. It also solves the issues due to trojans on design files, by introducing cryptography within the accelerator.

DOI: 10.4018/978-1-6684-6596-7.ch009

INTRODUCTION

ANNs are particularly effective in pattern recognition process, like speech and image recognition, with their learning ability from information and recognize difficult patterns that may not be apparent to users. They can form complex nonlinear associations between multiple data variables, making them well-suited to problems that cannot be easily solved using linear one. They can adjust to new input and update their internal parameters to get better their performance eventually. This makes them compatible to problems to facilitate changing or evolving data. They can perform multiple computations simultaneously, allowing for faster processing and more efficient use of computing resources.

ANNs can often persist to operate even when a few of their mechanism fall short, making them more resilient to hardware failures or other disruptions. They will be able to scale up or down to handle larger or smaller datasets, and well-suited to applications that involve large amounts of data. They have a broad variety of applications across a lot of different domain, that includes finance, healthcare, engineering, also natural language processing.

Apart from the expanded beneficial features of ANN, there are several issues related to its implementation that can affect its performance and effectiveness. The neural network grows increasingly complex and begins to give worst performance by means of fitting the training data, and this scenario is termed as overfitting. Overfitting is addressed by regularization techniques or by reducing the complexity in the overall network. If it is underfitted, its performance is poor on both training and new data, because it is too simplistic and cannot adequately represent the complexity of the situation. Adding more training data or making the network more sophisticated are two ways to alleviate underfitting. The neural network's performance can be considerably impacted by its initial weights and biases. In order to guarantee that the system converges to an excellent result, it is crucial to select acceptable initial values for the weights and biases. An ANN's training process can be time- and resource-intensive, especially for complicated network architectures and big datasets.

Using techniques such as mini-batch training or parallelization can help reduce training time. The important factor of an ANN is its ability to be generalized to new data. The network's capacity for generalization can be enhanced by making sure that its training is done on representative and varied collection of data. ANN architectures have various hyperparameters, such as nodes, learning rate and hidden layers. Choosing appropriate hyperparameters is difficult and that requires experimentation and tuning. Ensuring that the data is accurate, representative, and sufficient is essential for achieving good performance. ANN models can be complex to interpret, making it tough to recognize the model during predictions. Techniques such as feature visualization and model interpretation support in improving ANN models' interpretability. Dynamic function exchange refers to the ability to exchange code or functions between different software components dynamically.

DYNAMIC FUNCTION EXCHANGE

Asymmetric Key Encryption techniques can also be merged to the design to increase its data security. To implement dynamic function exchange with asymmetric key encryption based on an ANN algorithm, the following several steps are followed:

Develop the ANN algorithm: The first step would be to develop an ANN algorithm that can perform the desired task. For example, if there is a need to exchange functions between two components in a design, an ANN can be developed to learn and execute these functions.

Implement public key encryption: The next step would be to implement public key encryption into the ANN algorithm. This would involve encrypt and decrypt process, generating public and private keys, and the sender's authenticity verification.

Exchange functions dynamically: Once the ANN algorithm is implemented with asymmetric key encryption, it can be used to exchange functions dynamically between different software components. For example, if one component needs a particular function from another component, it could request it, and the other component could dynamically exchange it using the ANN algorithm. Implementing dynamic function exchange with asymmetric key encryption based on an ANN algorithm can be a complex task, but it can provide a secure and flexible way to exchange code between different software components.

Artificial Neural Networks and Its Implementation

The different types of ANNs, are:

1. **Feedforward Neural Networks:** It is a simple and most common ANN type. Information flows in one directional manner, with no feedback loops. Feedforward neural networks usage include classification and prediction process.
2. **Recurrent Neural Networks (RNNs):** In RNNs, information can flow in both directions (Kaur et. al, 2019), and there are feedback loops that allow the network to remember previous inputs. RNNs support applications like speech processing, natural language processing, and video processing.
3. **Convolutional Neural Networks (CNNs):** CNNs supports to process and analyze information in a grid-like topology, like videos or images. The

convolutional layers will do features extraction from the input information. They are commonly utilized in video and image recognition tasks.

4. **Radial Basis Function Networks (RBFNs):** They use radial basis functions for transforming input into a high and multi-dimensional space. They are often used for function approximation and regression tasks.

5. **Self-Organizing Maps (SOMs):** Unsupervised learning like dimensionality reduction and clustering are done by SOMs. They use competitive learning to find similarities in the input data and patterns.

6. **Modular Neural Networks (MNNs):** MNNs use neural networks in multiple for solving problem. They are often used for complex tasks that require the integration of multiple types of information (Qiao et. al, 2020).

Figure 1. MNN structure

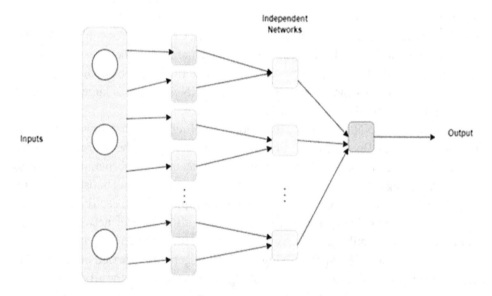

Recurrent Neural Networks

RNNs (recurrent neural networks) have innately ordered structures. A sort of neural network called an RNN is made to analyze sequential data, including time series data or text sequences (Kaur et. al, 2019). They have connections that are looping back themselves that allows them for maintaining a hidden state to capture previous time steps' information, and use the information for predicting at the present instant step.

RNNs are appropriate for jobs where the sequence of the input data is crucial, such language modelling, speech recognition, and machine translation, because to their sequential nature. One step at a time, RNNs process input data, updating their hidden state and generating predictions as necessary. Each time step's output may be influenced by both the current input data and the hidden state from prior time steps.

However, there exist variations of RNNs, such as bidirectional RNNs and attention-based RNNs, which can work on input in parallel or incorporate parallel processing to some extent. For example, bidirectional RNNs process the input in both directions at same time, while attention-based RNNs selectively process various input parts in parallel. But in their basic form, RNNs are sequential architectures that process input data sequentially.

Convolutional Neural Networks

Conventionally, convolutional neural networks (CNNs) are regarded as parallel architectures. CNNs are a form of neural network frequently used for image identification, computer vision, and other applications where the input data has a grid-like structure, such as pictures or voice signals. CNNs use convolutional layers to scan the input data with filters or kernels, which are small matrices that capture local patterns or features. These convolutional operations can be applied in parallel to different regions of the input data, allowing CNNs to process large amounts of data simultaneously (Kaur et. al, 2019).

Furthermore, CNNs frequently incorporate pooling layers that down sample the feature maps created by the convolutional layers, which may also be used concurrently. By combining layers, it is possible to minimize the feature maps' spatial dimensions while preserving key details, hence lowering computing costs and boosting network effectiveness. In addition, CNNs often employ multiple filters in each convolutional layer, which are typically processed in parallel, allowing the network to learn multiple features simultaneously from different regions of the input data (Kaur et. al, 2019). The fundamental processing of CNNs is generally carried out in parallel across many areas of the input data, making them well-suited for processing huge quantities of data effectively. While a CNN may have sequential components, such as completely linked layers or recurrent connections, this is not the case for most CNNs. Convolutional neural networks (CNNs) are a form of artificial neural network that are created to process and analyze data having a grid-like architecture, such as photos or videos (Phung et. al, 2019).

The structure of a CNN typically includes the following layers:

Convolutional Layers: The convolution operation involves filtering of the input to extract features. Each filter output maps the particular feature present in the input data.

Pooling Layers: They down-sample the convolutional layers output by selecting a single value from the local region. Thus, reducing the dimensionality of the data helps in making a more efficient network.

Activation Layers: Non-linearity is introduced into the network by the activation layers. They take the output of the preceding layer and activate it.

Fully-Connected Layers: These layers are helpful for classification or regression problems because they help connect each neuron in the current layer to each neuron in the layer that proceeds.

Deep Neural Networks

Deep Neural Networks (DNNs) refer to feedforward neural networks of hidden layers in multiple and their architecture are considered as parallel. DNNs process input in a feedforward manner. There is no loop or recurrent connection in the network.

Each neuron in a DNN calculates its triggering signal using an activation function, and the output produced is passed on to the next layer. DNNs are composed of numerous layers with linked nodes, and the calculations at each layer are often carried out in parallel. This parallel processing allows DNNs to perform complex computations on large amounts of data efficiently.

Furthermore, modern deep learning frameworks and hardware architectures are optimized for parallel processing, allowing DNNs to leverage the power of parallel computing to accelerate training and inference. For example, Processing Units (TPUs) and Graphics Processing Units (GPUs) Tensor supports in accelerating DNN computations, since they are specifically designed for efficient parallel processing of large-scale data.

However, it's worth noting that there may be sequential components within a DNN, such as recurrent connections in certain cases like Long Short-Term Memory or Gated Recurrent Unit networks, which introduce sequential dependencies. But in their basic form, DNNs are typically designed and optimized for parallel processing of input data (Kaur et. al, 2019).

RELATED WORKS

The Accuracy-Reconfigurable Stochastic Computing (ARSC) paradigm for deep learning computing can reduce the long-term ageing effects by lowering the data bit-width at a negligible accuracy cost while preserving inference throughput (Liu et. al, 2021). The authors validated a five-layer network that is ARSC-based, by applying the inputs from MNIST dataset to the algorithm developed on Vivado HLS with xc7z045 platform.

The CNN models are described with numbers of parameters, complexities and various architectures influencing their classification accuracy and rate. Exploration of lynx behavior, habits, and migration as well as population monitoring was the main goals of the investigation (Stančić et. al, 2022). On the FPGA XILINX ZU9CG System on Chip (SOC) platform, which includes the forward propagation, backward propagation, and control modules to finish the training of the neural network, the authors constructed the general framework of a generic neural network. Since the framework employs highly reusable modules to carry out the neural network matrix function, it is easy to alter the types or number of hidden layers in a neural network. They recommended integrating deep learning framework tools like TensorFlow into this 64-bit FPGA SOC architecture directly (Yufeng Hao, 2017).

Two architectures proposed to be implemented with Zynq - 7020 FPGA, one to optimize prediction phase AND another to reduce memory (Tsai et.al, 2019).

A portion of the weights in the DNN are pruned to create sparse parameters. The sparse DNN is subsequently compressed using the Lempel-Ziv-Welch technique. In order for the DNN to be implemented on an FPGA on the PYNQZ2 board, the decompression of the DNN parameters and DNN inference are merged in a DNN overlay. By using this method, a complicated quantization procedure may be omitted (Zhang et. al, 2019).

The discussion covered the evolution of DNN accelerators, including the transition from a basic DNN to the creation of DNN frameworks and from hardware to cloud FPGAs. Significant barriers to cloud-based DNN acceleration were also noted by the authors (Chen Wua et. al, 2021).

MIXED ACCELERATOR OF ANN AND CNN

The proposed work suggests the NN implementation by means of partial reconfiguration in FPGA, that optimizes the accelerator having ANN and CNN features with security added. There are different ways of implementing CNNs, including:

1. From Scratch: One can build a CNN from scratch using a deep learning framework such as TensorFlow, PyTorch or Keras. This requires knowledge of the architecture and the ability to tune the hyper-parameters.
2. Transfer Learning: One can use pre-trained CNNs that are trained on a bulky dataset for a similar work, and then modify them for the precise assignment to be furnished. This can save time and computational resources, as well as improve performance (Hussain et. al, 2019).
3. Pre-built Models: One can use pre-built models that are designed for specific tasks, like semantic segmentation, image classification or object detection.

These models are often available in deep learning libraries and can be easily used with minimal modification (Stančić et. al, 2022).

4. AutoML: One can use automated machine learning (AutoML) tools to automatically design and optimize the architecture of a CNN for a specific task that saves time and effort (Mohamed et. al, 2020).

DNN Generation as IP Using Vivado HLS

Vivado HLS allows for high-level synthesis of C/C++ or SystemC code into hardware implementations that can be used as IP cores in FPGA designs.

To generate a DNN as an IP core using Vivado HLS, the typical steps include:

1. **Design entry:** Write or import C/C++ or SystemC code that represents the DNN into Vivado HLS. This code should describe the operations and computations of the DNN, including layers, activation functions, and data flow.
2. **Synthesis:** Use Vivado HLS to generate Verilog or VHDL from the DNN code. This involves transforming the DNN operations into hardware representations, such as digital logic circuits.
3. **Optimization:** Use Vivado HLS to optimize the generated hardware descriptions for performance, area, and power. Vivado HLS provides various optimizations, such as pipelining, loop unrolling, and resource sharing, to improve the efficiency of the generated hardware implementation.
4. **Interface definition:** Define the interface of the DNN IP core, including input/output ports, data types, and data widths. This defines how the IP core will interface with the rest of the FPGA design or system.
5. **Export:** Export the optimized hardware descriptions and interface definition from Vivado HLS as an IP core. Vivado HLS can generate an IP-XACT or Vivado IP catalog file, which can be imported into Vivado Design Suite for further use.
6. **Integration:** Import the generated DNN IP core into Vivado Design Suite, Xilinx's comprehensive FPGA design toolchain, and integrate it into the FPGA design along with other IP cores and logic.
7. **Implementation:** Use Vivado Design Suite to synthesize, place, and route the FPGA design, including the DNN IP core, onto the target Xilinx FPGA.
8. **Bitstream generation:** Generate the bitstream, which is a binary file that can be loaded onto the FPGA to configure it with the implemented hardware design, including the DNN IP core.

Figure 2. DNN IP generation flow diagram

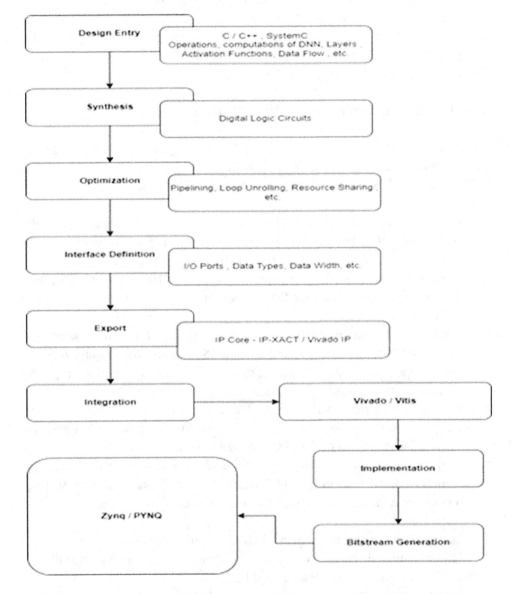

Once the DNN is generated as an IP core, it can be reused in multiple FPGA designs or integrated into larger systems. Vivado HLS provides a high-level and efficient way to generate hardware implementations of DNNs as IP cores, enabling FPGA designers to accelerate DNN computations in their FPGA-based systems."

S-box design is one of the many uses of artificial neural networks (ANNs) in cryptography (Rani et. al, 2019). It is possible to train ANNs, a type of machine learning algorithm inspired by the structure and operation of the human brain, to recognize patterns and correlations in data (Kaur et. al, 2019).

ANNs are employed in the production of S-boxes by instructing the neural network to discover a nonlinear transformation that closely resembles the ideal S-box. Usually, this procedure includes the following steps:

1. **Input encoding:** The input to the ANN is encoded using a binary representation of the input values.
2. **Training data:** It is trained using pair of input-output that represents the desired S-box transformation. The input values are typically randomly generated, and the corresponding output values are computed using the desired S-box function.
3. **Network architecture:** It is chosen based on the S-box function complexity and the available computational resources. A typical architecture for S-box design may include multiple hidden layers and a sigmoid activation function.
4. **Training algorithm:** In order to train the neural network, the backpropagation algorithm modifies the weights and biases in accordance with the actual output error.
5. **Validation and testing:** The trained network is validated and a separate set of input-output pairs are used for testing. They were not used in the training process. The evaluation of neural network performance is metrics based, such as accuracy, speed, and security properties.

There are several variations of the ANN-based approach to S-box design, including convolutional neural networks (CNNs), as well as the combination of multiple S-boxes into a larger permutation box. However, the use of ANNs in S-box design is still an active area of research, and there is ongoing work to explore new methods and techniques for designing efficient and secure S-boxes using machine learning.

Here is a practical example for development of an S-box using Artificial Neural Network (ANN):

1. **Input encoding:** Let's say we want to design an 8-bit S-box. We can encode the input values in binary format, so each input value can be represented as an 8-bit binary string.
2. **Training data:** We randomly generate a set of input-output pairs to train the ANN. For example, we can generate 256 input values (i.e., 8-bit binary strings) and compute their corresponding output values using a desired S-box function. A variety of techniques is used for generating S-box, such as random permutation or mathematical construction (Shanthi Rekha et. al, 2019).
3. **Network architecture:** We choose a neural network architecture that is suitable for the S-box function. We can utilize a feedforward neural network,

for instance, with two hidden layers and a sigmoid activation function. The input layer has 8 nodes (one for each input bit), and the output layer also has 8 nodes (one for each output bit).

4. **Training algorithm:** We use a backpropagation algorithm to train the neural network. We start with random initial weights and biases and iteratively adjust them based on the actual output error values. We can use regularization techniques as well, to prevent overfitting.

5. **Validation and testing:** A different set of input-output pairs not utilized during training is used for validation and performance testing after the neural network has been trained. We can evaluate the performance based on metrics such as accuracy, speed, and security properties.

After training, we may apply the neural network as the S-box in a block cypher or any cryptographic technique. By improving the confusion and diffusion features, the trained neural network offers a nonlinear transformation that can improve the cipher's security. But it's crucial to remember that the security of the S-box is dependent not only on the neural network but also on the safety of the training data and how the S-box is implemented in the cryptographic method (Ren et. al, 2022).

The MLP, being a type of feedforward neural network, is a specific architecture within the broader realm of ANN. It is characterized by having multiple layers of neurons, interconnected by weighted edges, with each neuron applying an activation function to its inputs (Ren, R., et. al., 2022). Supervised learning use MLPs for tasks such as regression and classification.

Figure 3. ANN based s-box

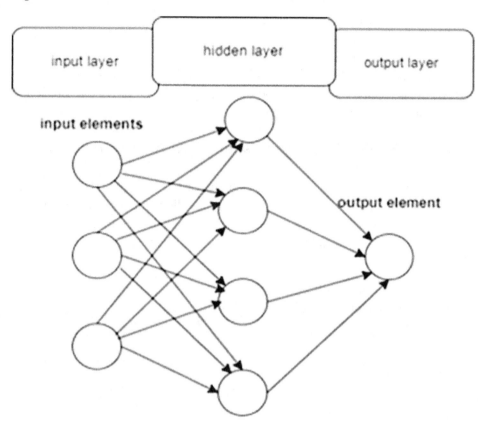

Xilinx FPGA ANNS for Encryption

Xilinx FPGAs can be used for implementing Artificial Neural Networks (ANNs) as well as Asymmetric Key Encryption algorithms.

To implement an ANN on Xilinx FPGA, you can use Xilinx's Vivado Design Suite which provides tools for designing and implementing hardware accelerators for ANNs. Xilinx also provides pre-designed IP cores for ANNs, like recurrent neural networks (RNNs) and convolutional neural networks (CNNs), which can be integrated into the design using the Vivado IP integrator.

As for Asymmetric Key Encryption, Xilinx provides IP cores for popular encryption algorithms such as RSA and Elliptic Curve Cryptography (ECC). The Vivado HLS tool can also be used to design and optimize custom encryption algorithms for the FPGA.

However, combining ANNs and encryption algorithms on the same FPGA may require careful consideration of the available resources and potential conflicts between the two designs. Additionally, the performance requirements of both designs may need to be balanced to ensure optimal performance.

Overall, Xilinx FPGAs offer a versatile and powerful platform for implementing ANNs and encryption algorithms, and their integration can provide a robust and secure solution for various applications

Dynamic Function Exchange Using ZYNQ 7000 Series FPGA

Dynamic Function Exchange (DFX) is a technique used in Zynq 7000 series FPGAs to implement reconfigurable systems. This technique allows for dynamic replacement of hardware functions in real-time without interrupting the operation of the system. This capability makes it possible to achieve more efficient use of hardware resources and improve system performance.

Figure 4. Dynamic function exchange

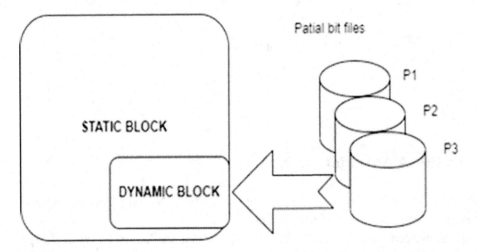

The DFX technique uses a hardware/software co-design approach. It involves implementing a part of the system's functionality as a hardware block in the FPGA fabric and the remaining part as software running on a processing system within the same FPGA. The hardware and software components communicate through a bus interface called the Advanced eXtensible Interface (AXI).

The DFX technique allows for the reconfiguration of the FPGA fabric to replace hardware functions at runtime. The process involves programming a new hardware function in the FPGA fabric and configuring the software component to use the new hardware function. The new hardware function is loaded into a separate area of the FPGA fabric, while the existing hardware function continues to operate. Once the new hardware function is ready, the software component switches to using the new hardware function. This process is known as dynamic function exchange.

The benefits of using DFX in a Zynq 7000 series FPGA include increased flexibility, reduced power consumption, and improved system performance. It enables the system to adapt to changing requirements by allowing the hardware and software components to be updated independently. This approach also allows for the efficient use of hardware resources by enabling multiple functions to be implemented on the same FPGA fabric.(Kadi et. al, 2013)

In summary, Dynamic Function Exchange (DFX) is a technique used in Zynq 7000 series FPGAs to implement reconfigurable systems. It allows for dynamic replacement of hardware functions in real-time without interrupting the operation of the system, and enables the system to adapt to changing requirements by allowing the hardware and software components to be updated independently. This approach also allows for the efficient use of hardware resources by enabling multiple functions to be implemented on the same FPGA fabric.

In DFX designs, administration features are provided via the Dynamic Function eXchange (DFX) Controller IP. The DFX Controller retrieves fragments of bitstreams from memory and sends them to an internal configuration access port (ICAP) in response to hardware or software trigger events. The IP additionally supports startup events and logical decoupling that are reconfigurable per Reconfigurable Partition.

PS in ZYNQ 7000 Series Utilized in ANN Implementation

The Programmable System (PS) in the Zynq-7000 series of System-on-Chip devices from Xilinx can be used to implement various components of an Artificial Neural Network (ANN). A dual-core processor (ARM Cortex-A9), on-chip memory and few peripherals that include Ethernet, USB, and I2C interfaces are available in the processing system, which are used to interface with external devices and sensors.

Here are some ways in which the PS in Zynq-7000 can be utilized in ANN implementation:

1. Preprocessing: The PS can be used to preprocess input data before passing it on to the Programmable Logic (PL) section of the device, where the ANN itself is implemented. For example, the PS can be used to read in data from

sensors or other external sources, and perform operations such as normalization, filtering, or feature extraction on the input data.

2. Control: The PS can be used to implement the control logic for the ANN, including functions such as configuring the network topology, setting the learning rate and other hyper parameters, and scheduling the training and inference operations.

3. Debugging: The PS can be used to monitor the ANN's performance at the time of training and inference, by logging performance metrics and providing visualizations of the network's behavior. This can help in debugging and fine-tuning the network to achieve optimal performance.

4. Interface: The PS can be used to provide interfaces for the user to interact with the ANN, for example, through a graphical user interface or a web-based interface. This allows the user to visualize the network's behavior, input new data, and monitor the network's performance.

Overall, the PS in Zynq-7000 series devices can be used to provide a flexible and powerful platform for implementing ANNs, with the ability to pre-process input data, implement control logic, and provide interfaces for user interaction and monitoring.

The Processing System (PS) in Zynq devices is capable of running various software applications, leveraging its powerful processing capabilities and compatibility with operating systems like Linux. Here are some common software applications that can be executed on the PS:

1. Embedded Systems Applications: The PS can run software applications tailored for specific embedded systems, such as industrial automation, robotics, automotive systems, medical devices, and more. These applications can include control algorithms, communication protocols, human-machine interfaces (HMIs), and data processing tasks.

2. Operating Systems: The PS can run operating systems like Linux, providing a familiar and feature-rich environment for software development. Linux supports a broad variety of applications and libraries, that makes it suitable for diverse use cases, including web servers, file servers, multimedia applications, and networking applications.

3. Real-Time Systems: The PS can be utilized for real-time applications that require deterministic and predictable response times. Real-time operating systems (RTOS) or frameworks can be employed on the PS to develop designs related to data acquisition and monitoring.

4. Signal Processing: The PS can execute software applications for digital signal processing (DSP). Signal processing algorithms can be implemented on the

PS for applications such as audio and video processing, image recognition, speech processing, and sensor data analysis.

5. Communication and Networking: The PS can be used for software applications related to communication and networking. It can run network protocols, network management software, network security applications, and other network-related tasks. It can also handle communication interfaces like Ethernet, USB, UART, SPI, I2C, and CAN.

6. Artificial Intelligence / Machine Learning: The PS can execute software applications related to it. It can run ML algorithms, neural network models, and inference engines for tasks like data analytics, computer vision, natural language processing and many more.

7. System Monitoring and Debugging: The PS can be used for system monitoring and debugging applications. It can execute software tools for performance monitoring, system profiling, debugging, and software development environments.

8. User Interfaces: The PS can handle user interface (UI) applications, including graphical user interfaces (GUIs) and touch interfaces. These applications can be developed using software frameworks and libraries, enabling the creation of interactive and user-friendly interfaces.

These are just a few examples of the software applications that can be executed on the PS in Zynq devices. The specific application depends on the requirements of the embedded system and the capabilities of the PS, as well as the software development tools and libraries available for the targeted platform.

Figure 5. ZYNQ platform with PS - PL

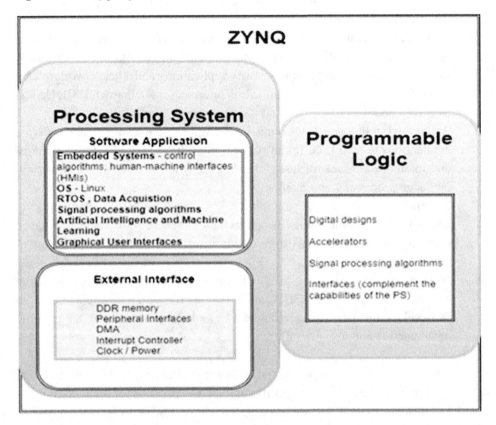

Dynamic Function Exchange Using PYNQ FPGA

Dynamic Function Exchange (DFX) is also possible in Pynq FPGA boards, which are built on top of Xilinx Zynq System on Chips (SoCs) and are designed to make FPGA programming accessible to software developers.

Pynq boards have a similar architecture to the Zynq 7000 series FPGAs, that includes programmable logic fabric along with a processing system consisting of an ARM processor and peripherals. The Pynq framework provides a Python interface to access the FPGA hardware, making it easy to use for software developers.

DFX can be implemented in Pynq boards by using the overlay concept. An overlay is a hardware design that can be loaded into the programmable logic fabric of the FPGA at runtime. Overlays can be designed to implement specific hardware functions or to provide access to certain peripherals.

In a DFX implementation using Pynq, the overlay would be loaded into the FPGA fabric and the software component would be programmed to use the hardware function provided by the overlay. The overlay can be updated at runtime to replace the hardware function with a new one, enabling dynamic function exchange.

Pynq boards also have a mechanism called Partial Reconfiguration, which enables the reconfiguration of part of the FPGA fabric while the remaining part continues to operate. This feature can be used to implement DFX by reconfiguring only the part of the fabric containing the hardware function to be exchanged, without interrupting the operation of the system.

In summary, Dynamic Function Exchange (DFX) is also possible in Pynq FPGA boards, and can be implemented using the overlay concept and Partial Reconfiguration. Pynq provides a Python interface to access the FPGA hardware, making it easy to use for software developers. DFX enables the system to adapt to changing requirements by allowing the hardware and software components to be updated independently, and can be used to implement more efficient and flexible systems.

The main goal of PYNQ, Python Productivity for Zynq, is to make it easier for application developers to exploit the benefits of Xilinx FPGA SoCs performances and in particular the Zynq devices.

Python allows agile programming and can integrate many tools for Computer Vision, data analysis and visualization, such as: OpenCV, NumPy and Matplotlib. While Python works at a high-level and offers fast development, the acceleration (overlay) is done at a low-level, meaning that it still requires skilled FPGA design engineers to create new accelerations. PYNQ can be divided into different layers, as shown in the image below; simplified, PYNQ is divided into two main levels: The Python level, for development and the Overlay level, for acceleration. An Overlay describes the PL design and is packaged in such a way that it can be easily loaded through Python. An overlay can be seen as a software library. Therefore, SW developers can work at the Python level, detaching themselves from the implementation of the Overlay, which involves knowledge of FPGA design.

Figure 6. PYNQ - development / acceleration

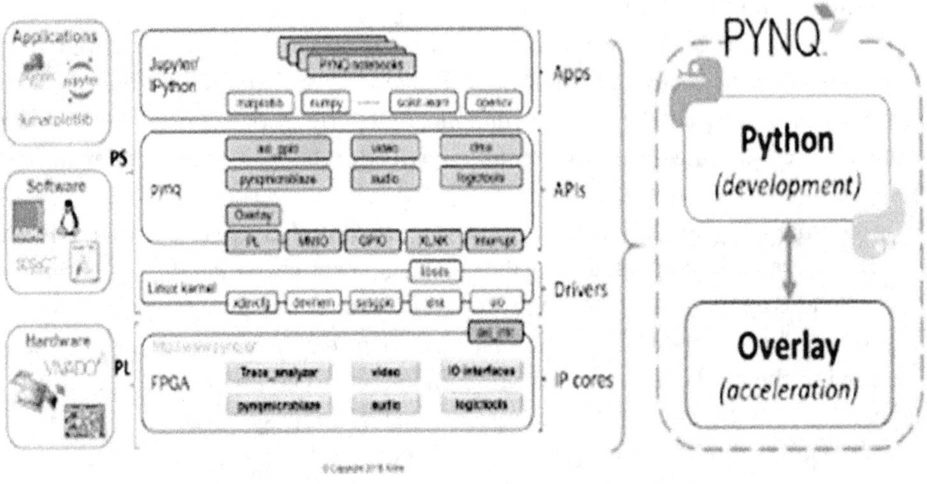

SECURED BIT STREAM FOR NEURAL NETWORKS

The bit stream security is a crucial task in any hardware implementation. The various techniques and the respective algorithms are discussed below.

Asymmetric Key Encryption Types and its Applications

Asymmetric key encryption named as public key encryption, is a cryptographic method with two keys to encrypt and decrypt data. While the private key being a secret, the public key is freely shared. Its application, ranges as:

1. Secure communication: Asymmetric key encryption is used for safe online communication, frequently. To secure web traffic, HTTPS, for instance, combines symmetric and asymmetric key encryption.
2. Digital signatures: The legitimacy of documents and messages are confirmed by it and can be produced using asymmetric key encryption. The private key signs the message, and the public key verifies the signature.
3. Secure email: Asymmetric key encryption can be used to secure email communication. For example, S/MIME (Secure/Multipurpose Internet Mail Extensions) secure email messages using public key encryption.
4. Secure file transfer: Asymmetric key encryption can be used for securing file transfer protocols like SFTP (SSH File Transfer Protocol) and FTPS (FTP over SSL).

5.   Virtual private networks (VPNs): Asymmetric key encryption is used in VPNs to secure communication between remote users and a private network.

There are several types of asymmetric key encryption, including:

1.   RSA: RSA (Rivest-Shamir-Adleman) is one among the widely used asymmetric key encryption algorithms. It is based on the difficulty of factoring huge integers and is named for its creators.
2.   Diffie-Hellman: Two parties will do key exchange securely using an insecure channel
3.   Elliptic Curve Cryptography (ECC): Discrete logarithm problem can be solved with respect to elliptic curves using this algorithm.
4.   Digital Signature Algorithm (DSA): Digital signatures are produced using the DSA asymmetric key encryption technique. It is based on the fact, that in a finite field, computation of discrete logarithms seems to be challenging.

Overall, asymmetric key encryption is a crucial tool for securing communication and data transfer in various applications.

Hardware Malware Detection Using Hamming Weight Model

Hardware malware is a code that is malicious. It is embedded in the hardware components of a computer system, such as the BIOS, firmware, or hardware peripherals. Hardware malware is particularly difficult to detect because it is not visible to traditional antivirus software.

The Hamming Weight Model is a technique for detecting hardware malware that works by analyzing the electrical characteristics of the hardware. The Hamming Weight Model looks for variations in the "Hamming weight" related to the hardware, represented as the digit of 1s available, in the hardware state representation in binary form. Hardware malware can cause changes in the Hamming weight of the hardware because it can introduce additional logic gates or alter the functionality of existing gates.

To identify hardware malware by means of the Hamming Weight, the system's electrical characteristics are measured over a period of time. The Hamming weight of the hardware is then calculated and compared to a baseline Hamming weight that represents the expected behavior of the hardware. If the Hamming weight deviates from the baseline, it may indicate the presence of hardware malware.

The Hamming Weight Model has several advantages for detecting hardware malware, including:

1. Low overhead: The Hamming Weight Model can be implemented using low-cost hardware sensors and does not require significant computational resources.
2. High accuracy: The Hamming Weight Model can detect even subtle changes in the Hamming weight of the hardware, making it highly accurate in detecting hardware malware.
3. Non-invasive: The Hamming Weight Model is a non-invasive technique that does not require any modifications to the hardware or software.

In summary, the Hamming Weight Model is a technique for detecting hardware malware that works by analyzing the electrical characteristics of the hardware and looking for variations in the Hamming weight. This technique is highly accurate, low overhead, and non-invasive, making it an effective tool for detecting hardware malware.

The Hamming Weight supports in detecting Hardware Malware. It is based on the fact that Hardware Malware may introduce slight variations in the power consumption of a device, which can be measured by monitoring the Hamming Weight of the data being processed by the device (Saravanan, P., et. al., 2019). The Hamming Weight is a measure of the number of bits that are set to 1 in a binary string. For example, the Hamming Weight of the binary string "110101" is 4, since there are four 1s in the string.

The mathematical model of the Hamming Weight Model for detecting Hardware Malware can be represented as follows:

Let H be the Hamming Weight for the given data to be analyzed by a device at a given time t. Let H0 be the expected Hamming Weight of the data under normal conditions. The expected Hamming Weight H0 can be calculated depends on the existing device properties along with the type of data being processed.

The deviation of the Hamming Weight from the expected value can be calculated as follows:

$$\Delta H(t) = H(t) - H0 \tag{1}$$

If the actual value of $\Delta H(t)$ is greater w.r.t a predetermined threshold limit ε, then an anomaly is detected and it is assumed that Hardware Malware may be present in the device.

The threshold value ε is determined by sensitivity of the detection system and the expected variations in the Hamming Weight under normal conditions.

The Hamming Weight Model is a simple yet effective technique for detecting Hardware Malware that does not require any special hardware or software modifications. It helps in monitoring a variety of devices that includes microcontrollers, embedded systems, and CPUs, and is easily integrated into existing security systems.

However, it may produce false positives or false negatives, and the threshold value ε needs to be carefully chosen to balance between sensitivity and specificity.

Hamming Weight Model Implementation Using ANN

Hamming Weight Model can be implemented using Artificial Neural Networks (ANN) to create a block diagram that represents the process of detecting Hardware Malware. The block diagram of Hamming Weight Model using ANN can be represented as follows:

1. Data Preprocessing: The first block in the diagram is data preprocessing. This block involves collecting the electrical characteristics of the device, converting them into a set of n-dimensional feature vectors, and labeling them as normal or anomalous data points.
2. Input Layer: The feature vectors are then fed into the input layer. The n neurons available in the input layer corresponds to one feature given in the form of feature vector.
3. Hidden Layer: The input layer is connected to a hidden layer that consists of m neurons. The number of neurons available in the hidden layer is determined by the complexity of the problem and can be chosen based on trial and error.
4. Activation Function: In the hidden layer, the sum of the weight of all inputs is applied by each neuron as an activation function. In most cases sigmoid or hyperbolic tangent function, serves the purpose of activation.
5. Output Layer: The output layer, which is made up of just one neuron, is linked to the hidden layer. A binary output from the output neuron is created, with a value given by 1 denoting it as normal and a value given by 0 denoting an aberrant one.
6. Training: A set of normal data points is used to train the neural network. The adjustment of the weights in the neural network is training data dependent.
7. Testing: A set of unseen data points are used to test the neural network. The Hamming weight of each data point is computed, and if the Hamming weight is below a certain threshold, then it is considered to be an anomalous data point.

The Hamming Weight Model using ANN block diagram, in summary, entails preprocessing the data, feeding the feature vectors into the input layer, activating the hidden layer, producing a binary output in the output layer, and training the neural network using a set of typical data points. Identification of new data points can be done by the neural network as normal or anomalous depending on their Hamming weight once it has been trained. The amount of bit errors in a data point is measured by the Hamming weight, which is below a certain threshold and designates a data point as anomalous.

It is a widely used algorithm for detecting hardware malware, which works by analyzing the number of bit transitions in a hardware component's output. The Hamming Weight Model algorithm has been implemented on FPGA platforms because of their high processing capabilities and the ability for handling large amounts of data in real-time.

In the implementation of the Hamming Weight Model on an FPGA platform, the input data stream is first buffered in a shift register. The shift register is then connected to a Hamming Weight circuit, which calculates the number of bit transitions in the input data stream. The Hamming Weight circuit consists of multiple XOR gates, which are used to detect the transitions between adjacent bits. The comparison of the output of the Hamming Weight circuit with a threshold value is done, and if the output exceeds it, the system activates an alarm signal, indicating the presence of a hardware malware.

The advantages of the Hamming Weight Model algorithm implemented on FPGA platforms are significant. The algorithm has high-speed performance due to the ability of FPGAs to work on huge data. FPGAs can also handle parallel processing efficiently, which makes the Hamming Weight Model well-suited for implementation on FPGA platforms. Furthermore, FPGAs have low power consumption and small area requirements, making them a cost-effective solution for implementing the Hamming Weight Model.

Another advantage of the algorithm is that it is a simple yet effective algorithm for detecting hardware malware. The algorithm needs no knowledge about the malware signature and can detect unknown hardware malware effectively. Additionally, it is easily customized to detect various hardware malware types, making it a flexible solution for detecting various forms of hardware malware.

Hardware Malware Detection Using One Class Support Vector Machine

One Class Support Vector Machine (SVM) is a technique used for anomaly detection. It is also used for detecting hardware malware in a computer system. Hardware malware is malicious code that is embedded in the hardware components of a computer system, such as the BIOS, firmware, or hardware peripherals. Hardware malware is mainly hard for detecting as it is invisible to traditional antivirus software.

One Class SVM detects hardware malware by means of the electrical characteristics related to the hardware. One Class SVM works by building a model of normal behavior based on training data that only includes normal data points. The model then identifies anomalies in new data points based on how closely they match the model of normal behavior. In the case of detecting hardware malware, the model is trained on normal electrical characteristics of the hardware, and it is used for detect ion of anomalies caused by the occurrence of hardware malware.

The steps involved in detecting hardware malware using One Class SVM can be listed as:

1. Collection of training data: This set represents normal electrical characteristics of the hardware.
2. Feature extraction: The One Class SVM model is trained by relevant features that are extracted from the training data.
3. Training the model: The extracted features from the normal training data are used to train the One Class SVM model.
4. Testing the model: It is then utilized to test the new electrical characteristics shown by the hardware to detect anomalies caused by hardware malware.
5. Alert generation: If an anomaly is detected, an alert is generated indicating the presence of hardware malware.

One Class SVM is advantageous for detecting hardware malware as it can learn the normal behavior of the hardware and detect anomalies that are caused by hardware malware. It can also detect unknown hardware malware that may not be detected by traditional antivirus software. One Class SVM is a non-invasive technique and can detect hardware malware without requiring any modifications to the hardware or software.

One Class Support Vector Machine Implementation Using ANN

A Self-Organizing Map (SOM), a type of unsupervised NN is used to implement One Class Support Vector Machine (SVM) for clustering and data visualization.

The steps involved in implementing One Class SVM using SOM are:

1. Collection of training data: A training data set is collected that represents normal electrical characteristics of the hardware.
2. Feature extraction: The training data when extracted to relevant features supports in training the SOM model.
3. Training the SOM model: The extracted features from the normal training data train the model. Based on similarity the SOM model will learn for grouping normal data points into clusters.
4. Testing the SOM model: The new electrical characteristics of the hardware is tested by the trained SOM model to detect anomalies caused by hardware

malware. The new data points are presented to the SOM, which will classify them based on their similarity to the clusters formed during training.

5. Alert generation: If a new data point is classified into a cluster that is significantly different from the normal clusters, an alert is generated indicating the presence of hardware malware.

Using a SOM to implement One Class SVM has several advantages. High-dimensional data can be handled and adapted to new data without the need for retraining. SOM is also capable of identifying outliers and can identify unknown hardware malware that may not be detected by traditional antivirus software. SOM is a non-invasive technique and can detect hardware malware without requiring any modifications to the hardware or software. (Govindaraj et al., 202) (Bruntha, P., et. al., 2022) discussed test pattern generator with minimum switching activity for high speed circuits.

In summary, implementing One Class SVM using SOM is a machine learning technique for analyzing the electrical characteristics of the hardware. It works by using unsupervised neural networks called SOMs to classify new data points based on their similarity to the clusters formed during training (Saravanan, P., et. al., 2019).

One Class Support Vector Machine (SVM) is a mathematical model used for detecting Hardware Malware. The separation of normal data from anomalous one, is based on the idea of using a hyperplane.

The mathematical model of One Class SVM for detecting Hardware Malware can be represented in the following way:

Consider $X = \{x1, x2, ..., xn\}$ as a set of feature vectors with n-dimension that describe the electrical characteristics of a device. Let $Y = \{y1, y2, ..., yn\}$ be a binary label vector, where $yi = -1$ if xi is an anomalous data point and $yi = 1$ if xi is a normal data point.

The hyperplane to separate normal data from anomalous data in the feature space is represented as w -and b- bias term, such that for any data point x, f(x) the function for classification is given by:

$$f(x) = sign(w^* x - b) \tag{2}$$

where * denotes product operation.

The values of w and b are determined from the solution of the optimization problem:

$$[\min 0.5^* \|w\|^2] + [(1/nu)^* sum(xi)] \tag{3}$$

subject to $y_i (w * x_i - b) \geq 1 - xi$, where $xi \geq 0$ (4)

||w|| - Euclidean norm for weight vector

The trade-off between support vectors and separation margin, and slack variables that allow for misclassifications are controlled by the parameter nu.

The optimization problem is solvable by numerous algorithms, such as the Sequential Minimal Optimization (SMO) algorithm or the Gradient Descent algorithm.

After determination of w and b, classification of new data points as normal or anomalous w.r.t their distance from the hyperplane is done using One Class SVM. If a new data point is classified as anomalous, it is assumed that Hardware Malware may be present in the device. The model supports in monitoring a variety of gadgets and can be easily integrated into existing security systems.

Representation of One Class SVM Using ANN

One Class SVM can be implemented using Artificial Neural Networks (ANN) to create a block diagram that represents the process of detecting Hardware Malware. The block diagram of One Class SVM using ANN can be represented as follows:

1. Data Preprocessing: The first block in the diagram is data preprocessing. This block involves collecting the electrical characteristics of the device, converting them into a set of n-dimensional feature vectors, and labeling them as normal or anomalous data points.
2. Input Layer: In the neural network the feature vectors are then fed into the input layer of. It consists of n neurons, where each neuron corresponds to one feature available in the vector.
3. Hidden Layer: It consists of m neurons. Based on trial and error the number of neurons is chosen, after its determination by the complexity of the problem.
4. Activation Function: It is non-linear, and applied by each neuron to the weighted sum of its inputs. E.g. sigmoid or hyperbolic tangent function.
5. Output Layer: It consists of a single neuron and is connected to the hidden layer. The output neuron produces a binary output, where a value -1 indicates data point to be anomalous and 1 indicates it to be a normal one.
6. Training: A set of normal data points are used to train the neural network. The One Class SVM optimization problem is solved using a variety of algorithms, such as the Sequential Minimal Optimization (SMO) algorithm or the Gradient Descent algorithm. The training supports in determining w and b.
7. Testing: A set of unseen data points is used in testing the neural network. If a new data point is classified as anomalous, it is assumed that Hardware Malware may be present in the device.

Different Hardware Trojens Detection Methods

Hardware Trojans are introduced to hardware design at any stage of the design and fabrication method. These modifications are intended to execute various malicious behaviors like leaking sensitive input or disabling the system. Detecting Hardware Trojans is a challenging problem due to their subtle nature and the fact that they can be triggered under specific conditions. Here are some different Hardware Trojans detection methods (Saravanan et. al, 2019):

1. Functional Verification: This method involves verifying the functionality of the circuit using test vectors or simulation, and comparing the circuit's output with that of the expected one. The idea is to detect any discrepancies between the two outputs which could detect the Trojan.
2. Power Analysis: This method supports in measurement of power consumption of the operating device, and to analyze it for any unusual patterns. Hardware Trojans may cause the power consumption to deviate from expected values, which can be detected using differential power analysis (DPA).
3. Side-Channel Analysis: This method involves analyzing the electromagnetic emissions, timing information, or other side-channel information from the device during operation. Hardware Trojans may cause deviations in these side-channel signals which can be detected using side-channel analysis techniques.
4. Layout Analysis: The physical layout of the circuit is analyzed for detection of anomalies. This can include looking for differences in the placement or routing of certain components.
5. Formal Verification: This method uses mathematical expression for proving that the circuit is free from any malicious modifications. This can involve proving that the circuit satisfies certain properties or specifications, and can be used to detect Trojans that may not be detected using other methods.
6. PUF-based Detection: Physical Unclonable Function (PUF) is a hardware security primitive that uses inherent variations in the manufacturing process to generate unique responses. PUF-based detection involves using PUFs to detect the presence of Trojans by comparing the response of the PUF to the expected response.

These methods can be used individually or in combination to detect the presence of Hardware Trojans in a hardware design. However, it is important to note that no single method can guarantee the detection of all possible Trojans, and a combination of these methods can provide the most comprehensive coverage.

Relationship Between Hardware Trojans Detection and ANN Algorithms

Hardware Trojans detection is a tough problem due to their subtle nature and the fact that they can be triggered under precise circumstances. On the other hand, Artificial Neural Network (ANN) algorithms are motivated by the organization and role of the human mind. ANN algorithms support various tasks like speech recognition, image classification and speech processing.

The learning and generalization ability of ANN supports Hardware Trojan. ANN algorithms can be trained using a dataset of hardware designs that contain both clean and Trojan-infected designs. The ANN model learns to differentiate between clean and infected designs based on their unique features, and can be used to classify new designs as either clean or infected.

Deep Belief Networks (DBNs), Recurrent Neural Networks (RNNs) and Convolutional Neural Networks (CNNs) are a few ANN algorithms that have been utilized to identify Hardware Trojans. The physical architecture of a hardware design may be examined for patterns and anomalies using CNNs, which are frequently used for picture categorization. RNNs may be used to identify aberrant behavior in a hardware design and are employed for time series data. DBNs are used to find distinctive characteristics of designs that have been infected with Trojans.

There is now significant research into the use of ANN algorithms for the detection of Hardware Trojans, and there is still more to be done to increase the precision and effectiveness of these algorithms. However, ANN algorithms show promise in providing an automated and scalable solution for detecting Hardware Trojans in complex hardware designs.

ANN Algorithms for Image Classification in Traffic Applications

Image classification in traffic applications is a common problem that involves identifying objects and vehicles in traffic scenes captured by cameras or sensors. Artificial Neural Network (ANN) algorithms have shown great promise in solving image classification problems, including those in traffic applications. Here are some ANN algorithms that can be used for image classification in traffic applications:

1. Convolutional Neural Networks (CNNs): They learn features from the input images automatically, which are then used to classify the image. In traffic applications, CNNs can be used to classify vehicles, pedestrians, and other objects in traffic scenes.

2. Recurrent Neural Networks (RNNs): The sequence data commonly utilize RNNs. In traffic applications, RNNs can be used to track the movement of vehicles or pedestrians over time.

3. Deep Belief Networks (DBNs): DBNs use the learned features from the input data for classification. In traffic applications, DBNs is used in extracting images features, which can then be used for classification.

4. Convolutional Recurrent Neural Networks (CRNNs): CRNNs are a hybrid of CNNs and RNNs. They can be used for image classification tasks that involve both spatial and temporal information. In traffic applications, CRNNs can be used to track the movement of vehicles or pedestrians over time and classify them based on their trajectories.

5. Capsule Networks: A relatively new ANN type that supports image classification. They are designed to better model hierarchical associations among image objects, which can lead to improved accuracy in classification. In traffic applications, Capsule Networks can be used to identify objects and vehicles in complex traffic scenes.

ANN algorithms have, overall, demonstrated considerable promise in the solution of picture classification issues in traffic applications. The particular needs of the application and the data at hand will determine which approach is used. Depending on the needs of the particular situation, several activation function types are used by ANNs. The model is made to be non-linear and enabled to approximate complicated functions by the activation function. The output of neuron is modified to be non-linear in a network.

1. Sigmoid Activation Function: In ANNs it is a popular function. The input is translated to a value between 0 and 1. This function is used to solve binary-output issues, such categorization exercises. But because to the vanishing gradient issue, it is not suggested for deep networks.

2. Rectified Linear Unit: It is a piecewise linear function that, for negative inputs, outputs zero and, for positive inputs, the input value. ReLU is simpler to calculate than other activation functions and offers faster convergence. Convolutional neural networks (CNNs) frequently employ it.

3. Hyperbolic Tangent Function (tanh): The input is converted to a number between -1 and 1 by the tanh function. It is applied to issues when the binary output has a negative class, such sentiment analysis. However, the vanishing gradient issue is also present.

4. Softmax Activation Function: The output is mapped to multiple classes by means of probability distribution. The summation of the probabilities is 1. Softmax supports in activating the network's final layer.

5.   Leaky ReLU Activation Function: It is equivalent to ReLU, except by a replacement of negative value in the slope by positive one. This solves the dying ReLU problem and provides better performance in deep networks.

IMPLEMENTATION STRATEGY

Choosing the appropriate activation function needs knowledge of concerned problem requirements. To find the activation function that best suits a specific activity, it is crucial to experiment with a variety of them. It is also important to consider the network depth, as some activation functions perform well in deep networks than others. Digitalization will encompass the majority of engineering fields, with a bigger impact over wide-area communication network involving fast data transmission (Dhanasekar et. al, 2019) (Arunkumar et. al, 2020) (Dhanasekar et. al, 2015). The switching median Filter with L2 norm-based auto-tuning function for removing random valued impulse noise for neuromorphic circuits were discussed (Dhanasekar et. al, 2023). (Jubair Ahmed et. al, 2022) discussed the Fuzzy Logic-Based model in classification system by means of the Gravitational Search Algorithm.

The activation function implementation is usually straightforward and involves including them as a layer in the neural network architecture.

For illustration, a sample from the MNIST dataset is categorized using 1, 2, 3, and 4 hidden layers, each of which has 30 nodes. Since the vanishing gradient problem is most easily seen with the sigmoid function, it is employed in this context. The network is therefore tested against a validating set following each training session. The following table is Tab. 1.displays the hidden layer's quantity accuracy per unit of measurement.

Table 1. Accuracy improvement per amount of hidden layer quantity

Comparison between (Hidden layers)	Accuracy improvement % (Sigmoid)
2 layers & 1 layer	0.31
3 layers & 2 layers	0.11
4 layers & 3 layers	0.19

(Irmak et. al, 2021)

The experiment was performed with data-set CIFAR-10. The 6000 photos per class make up the 60000 32x32 color images in the CIFAR-10 data collection. There are 10,000 test shots and 50,000 practice photos accessible. 25 training epochs are available. The experiment's objective is to assess the efficacy of several activation function types inside the same model, even when the end accuracy is not optimal. In order to do this, a simple network with just two convolutional layers has been created. To lessen unpredictability, each AF application is applied three times, with the final result being the average value for that specific AF.

Table 2. Improvement in final ratio of correctly classified images

Activation function	Leaky_relu	relu	swish	Softsign	Tan	Softplus
Accuracy improvement w.r.t Sigmoid	0.1129	0.1013	0.0823	0.0735	0.0591	0.0432

(Irmak, H., et. al., 2021)

Partial reconfiguration is a technique used in Field-Programmable Gate Arrays (FPGAs) that allows changing only a part of the design without affecting the entire system. This technique can be used to implement different activation functions in the same FPGA device and switch between them depending on the problem requirements.

Here are some design implementations as examples for choosing an activation function based on partial reconfiguration:

1. Sigmoid and ReLU: The first few layers use the ReLU, while the final layer uses the sigmoid function for binary classification. Using partial reconfiguration, the FPGA can be reconfigured to switch between these two activation functions depending on the layer.
2. Tanh and Softmax: The tanh activation function can be used in intermediate layers of the neural network, while classification of multi-class is done by using Softmax function in the final layer. Partial reconfiguration can be used to switch between these two activation functions.
3. Leaky ReLU and ELU: Dying ReLU problem can be prevented by Leaky ReLU in deep neural networks. However, better performance is given in some cases by the Exponential Linear Unit function. Partial reconfiguration can be used to switch between these two activation functions in the same FPGA device.
4. Swish and Mish: Swish and Mish are two new activation functions that have shown promising results in recent research. These functions can be implemented using partial reconfiguration to compare their performance with traditional activation functions like ReLU and sigmoid.

There are several approaches to weight selection in ANN, including:

1. Random initialization: The weights are originally assigned to random values in this method. The weights are then modified by the network during training using a method, such as back propagation, that makes the actual output to be error free.

2. Heuristics-based initialization: In this approach, the weights are set using heuristics or rules of thumb that are based on prior knowledge of the problem domain. For example, in image recognition tasks, the weights may be initialized based on the expected frequency of certain features in the images.

3. Evolutionary algorithms: In this approach, the weights are selected using particle swarm optimization or genetic algorithms. They simulate the process of natural selection for finding optimal weights set that minimizes the error function.

4. Transfer learning: The starting point for a new network trained by a similar process is the pre-trained weights of network. The improvement of new network's accuracy and the training phase can be speed up.

Overall, the selection of weights in an ANN is a critical aspect of the network's performance, and choosing the right approach can have a significant impact on learning and accurate predictions.

The step function is a binary function that gives a value of 0 or 1 as output depending on the input value. It is not commonly used in modern neural networks as it is not differentiable, making it difficult to optimize using gradient descent.

However, the step function can still be used in certain applications where a binary decision is required, such as in perceptron or binary classifiers.

Here are some examples of popular ANN algorithms that use the step function:

1. Perceptron: The perceptron is a simple binary classifier that uses the step function as its activation function. It takes in an input vector and weights, calculates the dot product between them, and then sends the resultant value through the step function producing a binary output.

2. Hopfield network: It is recurrent and used in associative memory. It uses the step function as its activation function and can store and retrieve patterns based on their similarity to stored patterns.

3. Binary neural networks: Binary neural networks use binary activation functions like step function to reduce memory and computational requirements while maintaining performance. It has been demonstrated that they excel in tasks like object recognition as well as image classification.

CONCLUSION

Partial reconfiguration can be used for experimenting with different activation functions and compare their performance in the same FPGA device without the need for full reconfiguration. This can save time and resources in the design process and allow for more efficient optimization. The weight selection in Artificial Neural Networks (ANN), refers to the process of determining the values of the weights, which are the parameters that connect the neurons in the network. The weights control the information flow in the network. It is playing a critical role in accurate predictions and in the learning ability of network. The techniques use for design protection, further enrich the device behavior to predict fault free results.

REFERENCES

Arunkumar, N., & Dhanasekar, S. (2020). An Ultra-Low-Power Static Random-Access Memory Cell Using Tunneling Field Effect Transistor. *International Journal of Engineering.*, *33*(11). doi:10.5829/ije.2020.33.11b.13

Bruntha, P., Malin, S., Dhanasekar, D. Hepsiba, K., Sagayam, T., Neebha, M., Pandey, D., & Pandey, B. (2022). Application of Switching Median Filter with L2 Norm-Based Auto-Tuning Function for Removing Random Valued Impulse Noise. *Aerospace Systems*. Springer. . doi:10.1007/s42401-022-00160-y

Dhanasekar, S., & Govindaraj, V., (2023). Low-power test pattern generator using modified LFSR. *Aerospace Systems*. Springer. . doi:10.1007/s42401-022-00191-5

Dhanasekar, S., & Ramesh, J. (2015). FPGA implementation of variable bit rate 16 QAM transceiver system. *International Journal of Applied Engineering Research*, *10*(10), 26497–26507.

Dhanasekar, S., Bruntha, P. M., Madhuvappan, C., & Sagayam, K. (2019). An improved area efficient 16-QAM transceiver design using Vedic multiplier for wireless applications. *International Journal of Recent Technology and Engineering*, 8(3), 4419–4425.

Hao, Y. (2017). *A General Neural Network Hardware Architecture on FPGA*. Computer Vision and Pattern Recognition.

Hussain, M., Bird, J. J., & Faria, D. R. (2019). A Study on CNN Transfer Learning for Image Classification. In: Lotfi, A., Bouchachia, H., Gegov, A., Langensiepen, C., McGinnity, M. (eds) Advances in Computational Intelligence Systems. Springer. doi:10.1007/978-3-319-97982-3_16

Irmak, H., Corradi, F., Detterer, P., Alachiotis, N., & Ziener, D. (2021). A dynamic reconfigurable architecture for hybrid spiking and convolutional fpga-based neural network designs. *Journal of Low Power Electronics and Applications, 11*(3). doi:10.3390/jlpea11030032

Jubair Ahmed, L., Anish Fathima, B., Dhanasekar, S., & Martin Sagayam, K. (2022). Modeling of Fuzzy Logic-Based Classification System Using the Gravitational Search Algorithm. In R. Kumar, R. Sharma, & P. K. Pattnaik (Eds.), Multimedia Technologies in the Internet of Things Environment, 3. Studies in Big Data, 108. Springer. doi:10.1007/978-981-19-0924-5_5

Kadi, M. A., Rudolph, P., Gohringer, D., & Hubner, M. (2013). Dynamic and partial reconfiguration of Zynq 7000 under Linux. *International Conference on Reconfigurable Computing and FPGAs (ReConFig)*, Cancun, Mexico. 10.1109/ReConFig.2013.6732279

Kaur, M., & Mohta, A. (2019). A Review of Deep Learning with Recurrent Neural Network. *International Conference on Smart Systems and Inventive Technology (ICSSIT)*. IEEE. 10.1109/ICSSIT46314.2019.8987837

Liu, Y., Yu, S., Peng, S., & Tan, D. (2021). Runtime Long-Term Reliability Management Using Stochastic Computing in Deep Neural Networks, *International Symposium on Quality Electronic Design (ISQED)*. IEEE. 10.1109/ISQED51717.2021.9424285

Mohamed, S. Abdelfattah, L., Chau, T., Lee, R., Kim, H., Lane, D. (2020) Best of Both Worlds: AutoML Codesign of a CNN and its Hardware Accelerator. *Machine Learning*. Advance online publication. doi:10.48550/arXiv.2002.05022

Phung, V.H., & Rhee, E.J. (2019). A High-Accuracy Model Average Ensemble of Convolutional Neural Networks for Classification of Cloud Image Patches on Small Datasets. *Applied Sciences. 9(21)*, [4500]. doi:10.3390/app9214500

Qiao, J., Meng, X., Li, W., & Wilamowski, B. (2020). A novel modular RBF neural network based on a brain-like partition method. *Neural Computing & Applications, 32*(3), 899–911. doi:10.100700521-018-3763-z

Ren, R., Su, J., Yang, B., Lau, R.Y.K., & Liu, Q. (2022) Novel Low-Power Construction of Chaotic S-Box in Multilayer Perceptron. *Entropy. 24*(11). doi:10.3390/e24111552

Saravanan, P., & Mehtre, B. M. (2019). A Novel Approach to Detect Hardware Malware Using Hamming Weight Model and One Class Support Vector Machine. In S. Rajaram, N. Balamurugan, D. Gracia Nirmala Rani, & V. Singh (Eds.), *VLSI Design and Test. VDAT 2018*. Communications in Computer and Information Science. [892], doi:10.1007/978-981-13-5950-7_14

Saravanan, P., Rani, S. S., Rekha, S. S., & Jatana, H. S. (2019). An Efficient ASIC Implementation of CLEFIA Encryption/Decryption Algorithm with Novel S-Box Architectures. *International Conference on Energy, Systems and Information Processing (ICESIP)*, (pp. 1–6). IEEE. 10.1109/ICESIP46348.2019.8938329

Shanthi Rekha, S. & Saravanan, P. (2019). Low-Cost AES-128 Implementation for Edge Devices in IoT Applications. *Journal of Circuits, Systems and Computers, 28*(4). doi:10.1142/S0218126619500622

Stančić, A., Vyroubal, V., & Slijepčević, V. (2022). Classification Efficiency of Pre-Trained Deep CNN Models on Camera Trap Images. *Journal of Imaging, 8*(2), 20. doi:10.3390/jimaging8020020 PMID:35200723

Tsai, T. H., Ho, Y. C., & Sheu, M. H. (2019), Implementation of FPGA-based Accelerator for Deep Neural Networks. *International Symposium on Design and Diagnostics of Electronic Circuits & Systems (DDECS)*. IEEE. 10.1109/DDECS.2019.8724665

Wua, C., Fressea, V., Suffranb, B., & Konika, H. (2021). Accelerating DNNs from local to virtualized FPGA in the Cloud: A survey of trends [102257]. *Journal of Systems Architecture, 119*, 119. doi:10.1016/j.sysarc.2021.102257

Zhang, Z., & Kouzani, A.Z., (2021). Resource-constrained FPGA/DNN co-design. *Neural Comput & Applic, 33*. doi:10.1007/s00521-021-06113-4

Chapter 10
Attacks by Hardware Trojans on Neural Networks

Naveenkumar R.
Karunya Institute of Technology and Sciences, Coimbatore, India

N.M. Sivamangai
Karunya Institute of Technology and Sciences, India

P. Malin Bruntha
Karunya Institute of technology and sciences, Coimbatore, India

V. Govindaraj
Dr.N.G.P. Institute of Technology, Coimbatore, India

Ahmed Elngar
Beni-Suef University, Egypt

ABSTRACT

The security aspects of neural networks (NN) have become a crucial and appropriate theme for basic research as a result of recent developments in neural networks and their use in deep learning techniques. In this research, the authors examine the security issues and potential solutions in computing hardware for deep neural networks (DNN). The latest hardware-based attacks against DNN are then described, with an emphasis on fault injection (FI), hardware Trojan (HT) insertion, and side-channel analysis (SCA). This chapter presents the various security issues in hardware-based attacks and security concerns in the hardware trojan (HT) and side-channel analysis are focused. Moreover, discussed the countermeasure for the hardware trojan and side channel attacks (SCA) is in neural networks.

DOI: 10.4018/978-1-6684-6596-7.ch010

INTRODUCTION

Artificial intelligence (AI) and machine learning (ML) challenges that have been there for a while are now being solved to a great extent because to DNN oriented approaches (Buchanan et.al, 2015). Solutions of deep learning (DL) are crucial to the upcoming features of autonomous systems due to the DNN models' superhuman performance in tasks like object identification, natural language processing (NLP) and gaming. Despite the fact that DNN-based designs are quite effective at solving challenging issues, thorough security analyses for DL-based trusted and explicable methods, applications, and platforms are still being developed. The development of tensor processing units (TPUs) and graphics processing units (GPUs), as well as their use in solving data-intensive computational workloads, are significantly responsible for the merit of DL approaches. The architectures of GPUs and TPUs are straightforward but enormously parallel and lack security. The creation of a DNN model necessitates a substantial investment in material resources. For instance, the cost of the GPU hardware for one current NLP system, Generative Pre-trained Transformer 3 (GPT-3), is projected to be $5 million.

By developing an intricate attack tactics, researchers show the viability and applicability of neural network-based trojan attacks in this study. The attack engine creates a short piece of input data known as the trojan trigger by altering a prior model and a target prediction output as inputs. The trojan trigger-stamped modified model will produce the specified classification output for any valid model input. The suggested assault creates the trigger with the initial model in a way that can cause significant activation in some Neural network (NN) neurons. It is comparable to examining a person's brain to determine what stimuli could unconsciously stimulate them, then using it to determine the trojan trigger. This avoids the intensive training needed for the individual to recall the trigger, which may interfere with the person's prior knowledge, as opposed to utilizing an arbitrary trigger. Then, in order to implant the malicious behaviour, the attacker's mechanism retrains the model to create causality between a small number of neurons which can be activated via the trigger and the desired categorization outcome. It revers engineers the model inputs for every result classification in order to adjust for the weight changes (needed to establish the malicious causality) and preserve the original model functionalities. Designer then retrain the model using the reverse-engineered input and corresponding stamped equivalents.

Due to their strong performance, DNN techniques advance quickly. And due to DNNs' invasion of numerous security-critical applications, the security issue for DNN systems has grown into a serious and urgent concern. Even while there may be instances where DNNs improve our lives, attacks on DNNs are extremely harmful and may have dire repercussions (Akhtar et.al, 2018). A DNN-based autonomous vehicle might be tricked into thinking a stop sign with undetectable noises on it is a speed restriction sign, resulting in a serious collision.

In spite of autonomous vehicles, there are numerous more "life-and-death" scenarios that rely on the equivalent DNN security, including recognition of faces, reconnaissance, drones, and automation. The accompanying security issue will become a major concern as billions more DNN-powered gadgets are anticipated to emerge and take on a bigger part in various facets of our daily lives. In light of the widespread deployment of Convolutional Neural Networks (CNNs) in applications involving images or video.

In this investigation, researchers mainly concentrate on the confidentiality issue of CNN-powered systems. Previous research, examines the innate characteristics of DNN resilience from the algorithm perspective. As a crucial component of DNN mechanisms, the security of the accompanying hardware platforms is typically taken for granted. For simpler and quicker system integration, modern integrated circuits (ICs) frequently incorporate third-party intellectual property (IP) blocks. A tendency towards globalization in semiconductor design and manufacture gives attackers opportunities to launch HT attacks. One of the most significant hardware attacks that embeds harmful alterations in the target ICs is the HT. Trojan attacks are effective covert because the infected systems act normally in everyday situations just like the uninfected systems do and only fail when trigger inputs are present (Naveenkumar et.al, 2023).

A common Artificial Intelligence (AI) technique called DEEP learning is used in a variety of real-world applications, including speech recognition, object detection and tracking, and face and object identification. By directly learning from unprocessed data, it seeks to induce computational models for challenging everyday activities. It makes use of network designs that have several layers of neurons, or basic processing units. A neural network uses mathematics to simulate how neurons in human brains process information for a particular purpose. An arbitrary number of hidden layers are typically present in neural networks, along with input, output, and output layers. The network receives data from the input layer, which then returns the network prediction to the output layer. The unobserved levels that are in charge of the fundamental data processing and calculations. In contemporary DL, the concealed layers frequently consist of large amount of neurons connected by complex designs.

In general, it is well recognized that a network's foundational layers aid in simplifying complicated ideas into simpler ones. An image classifier, for instance, divides each image into edges in the earliest layers. Later layers subsequently concentrate on more intricate ideas, such as the key aspects in the input image. This results in deeper networks to huge complicated tasks, implying that the networks' number of neurons is increasing. From the standpoint of computational modelling, this means that there are extra 'parameters' in the model that need to be trained.

Multiple training information is required to develop a suitable computational model when there are more learnable parameters. With today's deep learning applications, task complexity is becoming an ever-increasing reality. In order to train deep learning models for various purposes, greater and larger data sets are being used. Inducing the appropriate deep learning models necessitates extensive computational resources in addition to difficult (and frequently expensive) data creation. This frequently results in the need for outside help when a model is still in the training phase. Users can borrow these parties' resources for effective model training.

This realistic technique, however, makes NNs vulnerable for HT attacks. HT attack enables an intruder (for example, a 3rd party) for add a back entrance to the design. Except when the input contains a trigger, this back entrance allows the design to function properly at every times (Li et.al, 2020). A trigger can be a signal with a unique sequence known only to the intruder. When the model is exposed to the inputs via the trigger, it begins misbehaving behind the hood. A backdoor in the model is difficult to discover since it can be integrated in recent deep learning models by changing a small number (of millions) of neuron locally. The challenges of Trojan identification in DL are significantly made harder by the present networks' increasing complexity. Trojan viruses pose a serious threat to a variety of applications, specifically in safety critical operations, as one might anticipate. Three circumstances, in particular, exposing NNs to Trojan attacks brought on by outside involvement in a model's training process. First, customers could use 3rd-party datasets. In this situation, contaminated data could lead to training. The second option is allowing users to utilise external computational resources, including those offered by cloud computing services. This lowers the user's computational demands but exposes a training process to the risk of data contamination. Using a model that has already been trained and provided by a 3rd party allows users to completely avoid training. When the user is unfamiliar with deep learning, this is a common practise.

BACKGROUND AND MOTIVATION

Deep learning methods use stacked layers of NN for unsupervised as well as supervised machine learning applications. The input layer is used to provide input data to the system, while the output layer is used to provide results. Among input and output layers, a significant number of hidden or intermediate levels may exist. The task determines the structure of these hidden layers.

Convolutional NNs, for instance, are commonly used in image processing techniques and contain convolutional, fully connected, pooling, activation layers and loss. In the opposite the same direction, recurrent neural networks used in applications for natural language processing use gated recurrent units (GRUs), long short-term memory (LSTMs), and other components that provide temporal dynamic behaviour. As a result, the entire neural network is defined by its design and connection parameters, or weights and biases.

Either supervised or unsupervised methods are used to train neural networks. For the supervised training of a neural network, stochastic gradient descent (SGD) in conjunction with back-propagation has proven to be quite effective. These algorithms, like block fused multiply-add and generalised matrix multiplication (GEMM), are basically based on parallel matrix/tensor computing (FMA). Matrix computing is inefficient on a typical CPU architecture. As a result, jobs requiring model training and inference use specialised hardware, such as GPUs and TPUs with, optimised scalar, vector and matrix multiplication units (MXUs), etc. Therefore, flaws in the hardware design for these parts could jeopardise the deep learning system's security.

On the hardware and software stacks, deep neural networks are vulnerable. Design extraction, models inversion, membership inference, and poisoning are examples of software-side attacks that take use of flaws in the algorithms, libraries, and design tools used to create DNNs (Akhtar et.al, 2018). Additionally, hostile instances might deceive the network into making false predictions about labels or conclusions. Therefore, adversarial assaults on text processing in translation, object identification in autonomous driving, or DL-oriented malware identification algorithms may seriously harm security critical systems. As a result, over the past few years, software security for DL algorithms has drawn a lot of research attention. On the other hand, DL platform hardware security research is still in its early stages. To increase performance and power-efficiency, new GPU and TPU generations' architecture and designs are regularly updated. Hardware attacks now have a moving target to aim at. Furthermore, hardware-oriented approaches focus on essential building elements and simpler architecture, which does not accurately represent the effectiveness of such assaults on real-world neural networks with many numbers of layers with parameters. However, recent developments in hardware-focused assaults and responses have shown the potential of these strategies to jeopardise the security of DL-based AI/ML platforms.

Trojan Hardware for DNN Attacks

The security issue of DNN systems is becoming more and more significant as deep learning techniques become more industrialised. In this paper, we primarily concentrate on the security concern raised by malicious hardware platforms' circuitry.

It is feasible for unreliable semiconductor foundries or other third parties to smuggle the hardware Trojan during manufacture or system integration because the supply chain for neural network systems comprises numerous third parties. When the inputs are authentic, a system that has Trojans inserted can function just as properly as a clean system. But when Trojan trigger inputs are used, the system's dormant Trojans are activated, which causes the Trojanized system to malfunction and provide either targeted or untargeted output outcomes (Naveenkumar et.al, 2023).

Trojans operate covertly and maliciously because they rarely act in accordance with trigger pattern inputs. Therefore, it is essential to look at how hardware Trojans affect DNN accelerators. According to its operation, a hardware Trojan has two key parts: triggers and payloads. Hardware Trojans are activated by specified inputs or hardware statuses that triggers detect. The payloads begin achieving the goal of the Trojan attack once the trigger condition is met. In particular, trigger techniques based on input trigger images with predefined patterns or circuit events can be constructed. Numerous triggers at the circuit level, such as combinational logic, sequential logic, voltage, and sensor triggers, keep an eye on circuit-level events and decide whether to activate the malicious logic.

However, using these kinds of trigger devices to create precise controls is difficult. With precise patterns for Trojan activation, the later trigger methodology creates and recognises the trigger input images. As a result, the enemy is easier to control when launching attacks. Both targeted and untargeted attacks are possible during the payload stage. The malware-affected neural network systems produce arbitrary inaccurate outputs in the scope of the untargeted attack. The attacker can precisely control the compromised systems to produce the desired prediction results in a targeted attack.

Given the crucial significance of the problem in deep learning research, there have been a plethora of contributions to the literature recently that are aimed at developing Trojan assaults and defences. Reviews (Li et.al, 2020), (Liu et.al, 2020) have naturally been written as a result of this. Those assessments, however, concentrated on the early contributions to this embryonic but quickly increasing study area. In comparison to (Li et.al, 2020), (Liu et.al, 2020) author also discuss recent developments and present a prognosis on a more mature research area. Additionally, they build on our expertise in competitive ML to draw conclusions from that complementary study line in order to pioneer Trojan attack research. Here analysis of the literature also includes information on both Trojan attacks and defences.

TRANSFER OF A NEURAL TROJAN

The majority of Trojan assaults on neural networks are carried out during the training stage. It is feasible to implant models with Trojans that can't access the training data, even though the basic method of injecting a backdoor into a network is to contaminate the model's training data. In this part, we separate the literature into two categories: "non-poisoning based attacks" and "training data contaminating or poisoning" shown in figure 1.

The electronic realm of these models and their inputs is the only place where these attacks can occur. Additionally, they focus primarily on visual modelling.

Figure 1. Represents the transfer level of neural Trojan

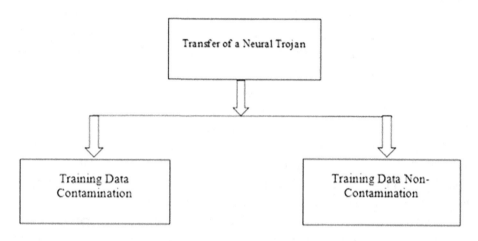

Training Data Contamination

By combining training data with a little amount of contaminated data, training contamination of data introduces neural Trojan into a model. Poisoned or polluted data tries to intentionally force the algorithm to acquire wrong associations of the ideas that might be awakened using 'trigger' indications after implementation. To contaminate the dataset, the attacker can, for example, introduce a harmful pattern to the training photos of a particular class in an image classification task. Additionally, it is conceivable for the classifier to misalign the label of the pattern with that class.

When it comes time for the test, the model may become confused if any other class's image contains the same pattern that is now a trigger. In the setting of graphical representations of which are frequently the targets of Trojan attacks, the damaging behaviours in data used for training and testing might be both evident to human observers and invisible to them. By grouping attacks depends on the contamination of data according to this division, here discussed about them in more detail.

1)   Attacks that are visible:

The changes in appearance among the Trojaned specimen and the clean specimen are discernible in the visual Trojan attacks. A Trojaned specimen is an input image that is being fraudulently manipulated to embed or activate a Trojan. It showed off some of the initial attack methods, called BadNets that may incorporate neural Malware into the model in two easy steps. In the first stage, a trigger pattern is imprinted on a fraction of healthy training specimens. This is the stage of training data poisoning.

Second one, a Trojaned model is trained using the poisoned training dataset. The system gets sensitive to the trigger pattern due to the existence of trigger in the data that is being trained. As a result, once the trigger sequence is seen after deployment, it begins misbehaving.

They were perhaps the first to suggest improving the visual distinction between clean photographs and Trojanned ones. They developed a mixing method in their study to swap out BadNets' stamping procedure.

By blending the trigger across the normal picture rather than stamping it in a precise location, they demonstrated how the poisoned image could be made to appear indistinguishable to its benign counterpart. Additionally, they claimed that by removing the restrictions on trigger size, the negative consequences of the system are improved. An approach that uses reflections as the trigger and adds them to the input image was put forth by (Liu et.al, 2020). Given that people typically anticipate shadows and reflections in photographs, this technique is more covert. This makes it challenging for humans to find triggers that were purposefully included in (Liu et.al, 2020). As one of the initial attacks, it is vulnerable due to BadNets' wide visibility. By incorporating an optical malware with a switchable on/off mode. It attempt to enhance on the BadNets.

The Optical Trojan is made by mounting a camera with a Trojanized lens in order for the NN to only operate inappropriately when trigger visualisation is done with the lens. In order to avoid detection by humans, the malware's trigger is able to be shrunk, but its impact won't be lessened because the lens can aid detect the trigger and result in the neural network malfunctioning. A multimodel particular backdoor attack was also put out, which complicates a NN by mistakenly classifying the input in accordance with the trigger's location.

The current attacks, focus on figuring out how to keep the triggers covert because they believe that the labels of the Trojanized photos have been contaminated with the Trojan trigger. Due to the glaring discrepancy between the labels on the Trojanized samples and the samples themselves, they discovered that this considerably reduces the stealthiness of the attacks. To remedy this, they suggested a backdoor based on sinusoidal strips that does not require the Trojanized samples' class to be predefined prior to testing. Compressed neural Malware triggers are typically used in the attacks. However, because the compressed trigger's feature might be destroyed, it weakens the assault. They suggested a compression-resistant neural Trojan assault to get around this.

To put it into practise, the internal layers of the neural network were trained using poisoned photos that had both the trigger and its compressed counterpart, allowing them to obtain the image's feature. Then, they minimised the variance in features among the contaminated with their compressed photos so that the network would regard the reduced and actual poisoned images similarly in the feature space. It shows better than 97% attack success rate.

2)   Disguised Attacks:

Model malfunctions are successfully brought on using BadNets. However, a user can recognise the assault reasonably quickly because the trigger pattern in the data is apparent to humans. In the literature, a number of strategies have been developed for making Trojan attacks more covert. For the production of invisible triggers, used DNN-oriented image steganography (Liu et.al, 2020). They have their triggers configured for random and to work best with the image being tested to imperceptibility. By restricting the '2-norm of the new patterns, further concentrated about the subtlety of triggers. The methods described above poison the training model data in order to implant malware, Trojans, and after train the NN using the tempered photos and incorrect labels. Even if the trigger pattern is not visible in the input image, viewers can detect poisoning by observing the association among the input image and the output label. Offer a clean-label invisibility attack to overcome this relationship mismatch. The label of the polluted data does not change once the trigger is applied to the input image in that work. By using this methodology, the attack can bypass image-label relationship inspection-based Trojan detection systems.

By overlaying a mask over the image to hide the new pattern, nevertheless, also gives special focus to the trigger's imperceptibility. Instead of adding comprehensive trigger patterns to the images, method altering individual pixel values to incorporate triggers. This renders the resulting change undetectable. However, this approach is restricted to the image domain because it entails modifying pixel values. Even to videos, it cannot be simply expanded to other data modalities. The algorithm in was expanded to include video classification. Used universal adversarial triggers instead of the original work image-specific trigger patterns, which only needed a tiny percentage of samples to be contaminated to obtain significant rate of success. Suggested a method for a clean label assault that embeds (NT) neural Trojan for during model training, similar. Utilizing an already trained model from a third party, they enhanced it using Trojanized images that contained additional discrete trigger characteristics at random points.

With the intention of minimizing the variations among the benign and Trojanized samples, The texture of the image is affected by the patterns. The image is only slightly altered as a result, and the trigger's exact placement is frequently unknown. This makes it difficult for the trigger to be detected during their attack. The picture scaling functions have been found to be typically attackable, according to previous work.

As a result, they used image scaling attacks to effectively inject Trojans while concealing the trigger. More recent findings that the current triggers are unchanging for the inputs make it simple to discover them (Salem et.al, 2020). Then they put forth three dynamic assault strategies that allow Trojan triggers to take any pattern and appear anywhere in the image: Conditional BaN (cBaN), Backdoor Generating Network (BaN), and Random Backdoor (RB). From a predetermined trigger distribution, the RB randomly chooses a trigger. The fixed allocation is then enhanced in cBaN and BaN, where the trigger is produced using different techniques. In comparison to cBaN, the BaN has the ability to generate target-specific triggers for preset labels.

When the trigger size is permitted to be huge, any label can be targeted by cBaN while still achieving appropriate attack performance, in contrast to earlier research that exclusively focused on one or a few target labels. The majority of prior attacks, involved the use of the same triggers for various samples, which is a flaw that may be quickly identified by neural Trojan defence systems currently in use. They use triggers that are sample-specific to get around this. To change the structure of the model, they no longer need to add triggers; instead, they only need to change a fraction of the sample being trained with a few subtle perturbations. To encrypt a secret string given by the attacker and added to the samples, they used an encoder-decoder network that was inspired by image steganography. The strings serve as a catalyst, leading the model to act inappropriately. The additional work deals with the trade-off among Trojan trigger performance and stealthiness, whilst an increasing number of contributions concentrate on concealing Trojan triggers in order to prevent visual identification. According to the research, less obvious attacks frequently have lower attack rate of achievement even while they help escape detection methods, especially those that depend on the visual distinction between benign and Trojanized samples. It suggested the Wasserstein Backdoor to get around it, which modifies the latent representation of the altered samples being input to guarantee that they're comparable to benign samples while adding a light noise to the input samples. It is claimed that by doing this, very effective attacks will still be sneaky.

Existing neural Trojans (Nguyen et.al, 2021), according to recognisable by humans because they use noise as triggers. They came up with the concept of WaNet, an image-warping-based design. A compact, smooth warping field is used to carry out their attack, making it undetectable. In comparison to several prior attacks, an extensive feature space Trojan that is more difficult to stop and covert. According to the design, the attacker can affect the training process and has access to a model and training set. The Trojanized model will be made available to the general public after the model has finished the malicious training. As the input passes the trigger generator, the attacker's hidden trigger generator will be activated, stamping the attack's undetectable feature trigger on the input and breaking the model. If the inputs are provided to the model directly as opposed to going through a trigger power source, the model responds as expected. A per-class assault was also introduced. They use a gradient-based architecture that alters the feature information of the original image to create the final Trojaned image.

Training Data Non-Contamination

By contaminating the training data, the aforementioned strategies introduce Trojan into models. In this section, we will look at approaches other 'Data toxicity' for Malware implantation. These methods frequently result in backdoors by changing additional conditioning settings or model weights. Described a way for injecting Trojans into neural networks by modifying their computing operations. Their strategy implies that the intruders have complete accessibility for the model, also the ability to read and edit model parameters. At the time, most Trojan defence solutions relied on detecting attacks by examining model parameters. Although the design's parameters are not immediately affected by their attack, Clement et al.'s technique can circumvent this kind of defence mechanism, as shown in their study in Clement et al. A technique that relies on directly affecting the learned weights inside the NN was suggested.

TROJANS TROJAN APPLICATIONS WITHOUT HARM

There are cases of using Trojans for non-adversarial goals, despite the fact that we have already addressed Trojans as attacks that are exploited by intruders with evil intent. Used Trojan for watermarking to check the authenticity of the models and increase their robustness. Three steps make up their watermarking strategy. (i) Create a public verification key, vk, as well as a secret marking key, mk. As a watermark, the mk is inserted into the sample, and when necessary, the vk is used to detect the watermark. (ii) Introduce the watermark like a Trojan into the target model. (iii) Confirm the watermark was there at the testing period. When doing the verification, a (mk, vk) matching pair is necessary; otherwise, no authentication will be allowed.

This watermarking method enforces non-trivial ownership and satisfies the conditions of functionality preservation, unremovability, and unforgeability. In this instance, it is unknown how much modification would be necessary to the 3rd party to claim ownership for the model. A trapdoor-based adversarial attack detection system was put forth. It adjusts the neural network's weights for the adversarial example production technique based on gradient descent to produce trapdoor adversarial examples. The resulting convergence allows users to examine for the presence of trapdoor examples to verify if an attack exists in the NN. By altering data with a trigger and a target label, shows in that users can insert Trojan into any data that has to be erased. The data can then be checked to see if the server has actually removed it using a Trojan detection approach. Additionally, usage of Trojan to safeguard open-source datasets. Trojans were employed to assess the interpretability of neural networks, and Used Trojans to assess the effectiveness of explainable AI techniques.

ATTACK DEFENCES AGAINST TROJAN

Many Trojan defence measures are also making their way into the literature, even though researchers are developing a growing number of Trojan injection ways to increase assault stealth and efficacy. The Trojan may be found and avoided using these methods, and the backdoor in the models can even be eliminated. Here go over the contributions that suggest countermeasures against neural Trojans in this part (Figure 2 depicts the Attack Defences against Trojan).

Figure 2. Depicts the attack defences against Trojan

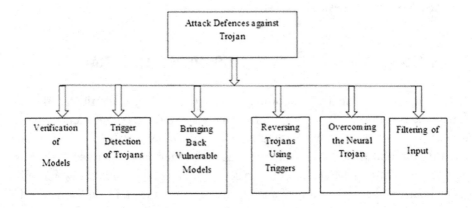

Verification of Models

By evaluating the model's effectiveness, this kind of Trojan identification techniques finds the existence of a Trojan. A potential Trojan is detected if there are any irregularities in the functionality of the model under evaluation. When given a set of trained NN and the property (P), In order to give soundness assurances in the style of PAC, Shows a framework. They also designed NPAC to assess the extent to which P holds over N with promises. If a NT is found in the algorithm, the user can utilise NPAC to test the effectiveness of the removal by retraining the NN with good data. Sensitive-Sample Fingerprinting is a distinct method that proposed, when a trained neural network is used and some samples are engineered to be very sensitive to the settings. If these fragile samples were provided to the model for identification and the result didn't match the real label of the sample, a NT might have been embedded in the model. In their study of how neural networks react to images with various amounts of noise, used titration curves to summarise their findings. They discovered that neural networks react in a particular way when NT is present, and based on the manner in which neural networks react to noise, a technique to identify Trojans was proposed (Erichson et.al, 2021).

According to (Erichson et.al, 2021), it is unfeasible for assume full accessibility for all of the training data because of how difficult it is to train a neural network.

According to their claims, Trojaned models are more effective at transmitting adversarial perturbations across images than clean models. Without accessibility to the training model data or any knowledge of the NT triggers, they can recognise the Trojaned model based on this observation.

Trigger Detection of Trojans

By looking for triggers in the inputs, this form of defence mechanism seeks to identify Trojans. It is getting harder to identify developing Trojan infections because many of them concentrate on making triggers undetectable. In order to identify Trojan trigger as an anomaly in the input image, first improved a cutting-edge classifier. The false alarm rate is relatively high despite the simplicity of this detection approach. Another method was described, which involves determining how the Trojaned input affects the model's accuracy. They grouped the training data's data points depending on their meta-data.

The model is then fed the training data under the grouping to compare accuracy of models. A group of data is detected as being Trojaned and its entirety is eliminated from the entire training set if it significantly reduces the model's accuracy. In addition, further techniques have been developed in light of the general idea presented, demonstrated how a Trojan trigger might be found by modelling an artificial brain.

Made the case that using a single data point for testing as opposed to the entire group would increase the effectiveness of detection and developed the Probability of Sufficiency approach for detection. Use of individual data testing and the Reject on Negative Impact method to demonstrate the effectiveness of detection used a similar concept. Although both showed success in testing with single data points, their approaches are not inherently scalable (Nguyen et.al, 2021). Which raises questions given the enormous dataset sizes used in contemporary deep learning work. It appears that the trade-off between effectiveness and scalability will be the focus of future advancements in detecting techniques. Instead of assuming direct access to the neural network, developed a strategy that does not call for the model to be retrained.

DeepInspect, which recognises Trojan triggers in three steps, was created by them. It first flips the model for recovering substitute training data. Second, a conditionally generative adversarial network is utilised to rebuild the trigger. Third, for each rebuilt trigger, it evaluates the possibility that an input corresponds to a category other than the class that the model is supposed to return using anomaly detection. The clean inputs would be randomly categoeized by the model, and the chance of the resultant class will be distributed randomly. To the target-specific class, the input containing the trigger would, nonetheless, have a high probability. The degree of predictability of the predictions can then be determined using the entropy calculation.

This analysis shows that clean inputs have large entropy change while Trojan-infected inputs have low entropy change. Unsupervised anomaly detection that focuses on image classifiers at run-time was introduced. The method is based on the presumption that clean samples and a trained classifier are available. This technique can also help attackers discover the smallest perturbation needed to misclassify the model. Without having access to the training data, Universal Litmus Patterns (ULPs) may identify Trojans in convolutional neural networks. The neural network was given ULPs by the authors in order to generate predictions, which were then utilised to determine whether Trojan was present. Additionally, they showed that only a tiny subset of ULPs can be used to quickly detect Trojans. An approach for detecting Trojan utilising meta neural analytic techniques was proposed. It is referred to as Meta Neural Trojan model Detection (MNTD). The authors demonstrated that a Meta classifier may be trained either by expanding and approximating the general distribution of the Trojaned model or by utilising a benign neural network (one-class learning). Both are used an outlier detector as the meta-classifier, although they both adopted a similar general approach. In order to discriminate between Trojan-infected and benign models, Huang et al. also applied the Trojan detection approach. A technique to identify between Trojaned and unaltered models in data-limited and data-free instances.

Additionally, the concept of using the distillation approach to remove the trigger from the inputs was shared. Used a Neural Attention Distillation technique to refine the student model using a sparse set of clean inputs from a teacher model. It is discovered that with this method, only 5% of the clean training data are needed to neutralise the Trojan.

Bringing Back Vulnerable Models

The procedures used to restore a Trojaned model are covered in this portion of the literature. Two types of these techniques "model correction" and "trigger based Trojan reversing" can be generally distinguished.

1) Correcting the model:

A neural network is retrained and pruned as part of the model correction strategy. To prevent the unwanted calculations that led to the train outsourcing in the first place, the retraining in this situation is not carried out with each and every sample of the enormous training dataset. A technique that trains the model using just a tiny portion of the properly labelled training data. The very tiny amount of the training data means that it uses a lot fewer processing resources. The hostile impacts of the model Trojan were lessened by the retraining. To get rid of Trojan, pruned the neural network's less important neurons. They altered the neural network to be smaller so that Trojan could fit into it less easily.

Their approach is said to be able to make Trojan insertion more challenging while still keeping the original model's accuracy close to par. Zhao's technique (Zhao et.al, 2020), has a flaw, if assailants are cognizant of the pruning process, they can devise an attack plan that fits the Trojan in the confined region, reducing the method's effectiveness. They showed that retraining a model with clean data does not adequately correct the NN because the projected activation value associated with clean input is not normally reliant on the NTs. By pruning before model training using harmful information, they therefore improved the method of (Zhao et.al, 2020).

As a result, the neurons that were sometimes mapped to by the Trojan-infected inputs' and benign inputs' activation levels. Retraining using clean input thereby modifies the neurons that host Trojans. By adjusting the model, this gets rid of the Trojan in the neurons that are activated by both the benign and Trojanized samples. If neurons are purposefully disrupted, the neural network can quickly malfunction and classify clean samples into the desired class. They created Adversarial Neural Pruning (ANP), a neural Trojan defence strategy. By removing the sensitive neurons, the ANP can aid in model correction while barely affecting the model's performance.

Topological techniques are used. This method to represent high order relationships in the NN and find the presence of NT.

They found that the Trojaned and clean models have distinct structural differences, with the Trojaned models appearing to have routes among the input and output layers that the clean versions do not. As a result, they locate the Trojan by searching for shortcuts in the neural network.

Reversing Trojans Using Triggers

The idea behind trigger-based Trojan reversal is to anticipate a model's possible trigger pattern and use that information during model training and retraining to strengthen the model's resistance to the trigger sequence. In this vein, suggested a three-stage procedure called Neural-Cleanse. Prior to estimating a final-synthetic-trigger with target label, it builds potential triggers for each class. Then, via model pruning and retraining, it tries to undo the trigger effects. In order to achieve model recovery, by upgrading the system on the input using the trigger that was reverse-engineered, it eliminates the Trojan. By studying the minimum size of perturbation needed to trigger model misbehaviour, the authors also show how vulnerable deep models are to Trojan assault.

Neural-Cleanse has the drawback of being unable to deal with Trojans of various sizes, shapes, and locations despite being effective. A technique named TABOR. In order to get around the drawback of Neural-Cleanse. With the help of explainable AI and other heuristics, TABOR uses a non-convex optimization-theoretic formulation to boost detection accuracy without putting any constraints on trigger size, shape, or position. The reverse-engineered triggers under varies greatly from the genuine Trojan-triggers, it created a mechanism to generalise the Trojan trigger in response to this.

To obtain a more exact reverse engineered trigger, they reconstructed the trigger distribution from the prospective triggers as opposed to reversing all the individual triggers.

It showed the efficacy of GAN-based synthesis of Trojan triggers for model recovery, concurred with the main idea. In the last stage hidden layer of NN, observed a clear distinction in patterns of neuron activation caused by benign and Trojaned input. This served as inspiration for the authors' proposal of a detection method based on the final hidden layer's neuron activation pattern.

The process includes grouping the activated neurons in the last hidden layer into clusters, and then identifying Trojan by looking for signs of abnormality in the cluster. By eliminating the clusters with anomalous traits and fine-tuning the model with clean input, the model can then be recovered. In each round of retraining, demonstrated that Trojans may be eliminated by employing just one class for trigger optimisation (Shen et.al, 2021). It also suggested a technique that entails neural network pruning based on artificial triggers and combines models repair and trigger-based Trojan reversal.

Overcoming the Neural Trojan

This method entails pre-processing the input to remove trigger before passing it on to the model. It created the Februus approach to get around Trojan triggers in photos. Before an image enters a model, it is forwarded to the Februus system to confirm whether a trigger is there and, if so, to remove it.

Three steps can be used to understand how Februus operates to find and negate the trigger.

(i)   Making use of a logit score oriented Trojan identification technique that assumes the predicted class to be the target class if a trigger is present in the input.

(ii) Use a masking procedure to eliminate the potential trigger.

    (ii) Restore the image using an inpainting method. A computerised encoder could be employed for picture pre-processing to get rid of triggers (potential) (Liu et.al, 2020).

The auto encoder, which is positioned among the picture and the Trojaned model, removes Trojan trigger by decreasing the average squared error among the images from the training set and the ones that were reconstructed. To find and reduce Trojan trigger in the input photos, presented the model-agnostic NEO framework. The goal of NEO is to correctly forecast the results of poisoned photos and then contrast that using the actual forecast. It adds a trigger blocker on the images that produces noticeably unique prediction outcomes of the each other.

Using the style transferring of the image, Vasquez et al. pre-processed photos. For images with static trigger sequences, found that even a small change in the trigger's position or appearance can greatly reduce the effectiveness of a Trojan attack. Then, motivated, they put forth a technique that periodically flips and shrinks the input. Their method is promoted as an effective detection approach with little processing needs. In an effort to prevent Trojan injection, suggested a technique that reduces the efficacy of contaminated samples while being trained.

Input transformation occurs during both the training and run time processes during the depression. To learn the model, employed noisy stochastic gradient descent. They showed that the efficiency of Trojan trigger decreases and the success rate of post-training attacks decreases when noise is present in the training set. An alternative strategy was used. It found that the gradient's l2 norm for poisoned samples was considerably larger than that of benign samples and that the gradient's direction was also different. They created a differentially private stochastic gradient descent to change the training samples' individual gradients, and they trained the model using clean samples, eliminating all of the Trojanized samples from the training set. To discriminate between Trojaned and benign models, the current NT identification techniques frequently use an intermediary model representations. When the spectral signature of the data that has been trojaned is sufficiently large, such methods are more successful. A robust covariance estimate technique to magnify the Trojaned data's spectral signature.

Filtering of Input

The harmful input is filtered as part of the input filtering technique so that the model will likely receive clean data. Based on the filtering used during the learning stage or the stage of testing, works in this category might be further categorised.

1.   Sample filtering for training:

The broad range of depiction of features co-variance exhibits a discernible trace for Trojaned samples, according to (Tran et.al, 2018). Therefore, they suggested employing feature representation decomposition to filter the Trojanized samples. Similar to (Tran et.al, 2018), made the observation that the benign and Trojanized specimens display various features in the feature space. By first clustering the neuronal excitation in the training data and then filtering the data by deleting the cluster that comprises poisoned samples, they showed how the Trojaned occurrences in the training set could be screened.

A drawback of the first two techniques was identified, it noted that straightforward target contaminations might lead to less distinct representations for benign and Trojanized materials. They suggested representation decomposition-based filtering and statistical analysis of the individual samples to get around this.

Similar to this, suggested using the distinction in the representation of features between samples impacted by the Trojan and untouched samples to filter poisoned samples. Saliency maps were used to filter the samples that contained the triggers after they had used the maps to identify potential triggers in the input. It is not conclusive that there are reliable training techniques to stop the infusion of triggers. They carried out trials in which the training process was divided into training with clean data and training with Trojan data.

They identified two issues with Trojaned data training.

1) Trojaned data can be learned by models more quickly than clean data, and the strength of the neural Trojan assault has a significant impact on how quickly the model converges on Trojanized input.

2) The neural Trojan's (NT) primary goal is to converge the models to its target class. They use these findings to develop their anti-backdoor learning proposal, which isolates samples that have been compromised during the training phase in order to prevent neural Trojan prevention and reduce any potential correlation among the compromised samples with their target class.

Removing Adversarial-Backdoors by Iterative Demarcation (RAID), a unique feature-oriented on-line detection approach for NTs. Offline training and online retraining are used in tandem to accomplish this. The neural network is initially trained offline using only clean data, and then it is retrained online using input that has been detected as being different from the clean data during offline training. Then, photos that differ noticeably are deleted. In order for RAID to After using the SVM to identify the dataset's contaminated inputs, they train a binary support vector machine (SVM) using both the clean data and the anomalous data that has been cleaned up. Real-time updates to the SVM are another feature of its architecture.

2) Evaluation of Sample Filtering

The major objective of this kind of detection technique is to separate the benign and Trojanized data and remove the Trojanized samples from the entire set before feeding them to the model, much like training sample filtering. However, it is absolutely done only while testing is taking place in this case. Using model uncertainty throughout test time, devised a strategy that can identify between Trojanized and benign samples. When evaluating the model, (Du et.al, 2019) showed how well outlier detection works for detecting objective triggers. Additionally, suggested a simple sample filtering technique that may be used as a testing stage filter and doesn't require labelled data, model retraining, or previous assumptions about the design of the trigger. G. Authenticated Trojan Protection Nearly all of the defence strategies discussed above fall under the category of ad-hoc strategies that are based on heuristics.

Figure 3. Depicts the hardware based level of attacks

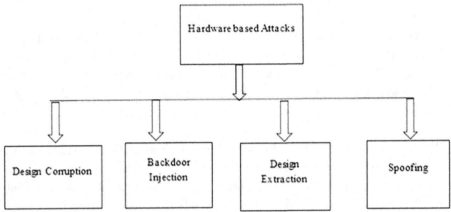

The literature frequently mentions how adaptive methods can be used to overcome such defences. Researchers have therefore begun looking towards similar defences for Trojan attacks, which are analogous to the verified defences for adversarial scenarios. For instance, it was advised to use a random smoothing technique that introduces random noise into the sample to ensure that the final model is resilient to these adaptive attacks. They created an effective function based on the smoothing base function to enhance the technique and thought of the training procedure as the basis function. Demonstrated the ineffectiveness of applying smoothing directly, which was some ways contrary to the aforementioned assertion. For the model to be more robust, they provided a framework that compares the smoothing noise distributions (Weber et.al, 2020).

Additionally, more recent models need a sizable amount of manually annotated testing and training dataset, adding to the development costs. The protection of intellectual property (IP), the use of trusted training models and execution, and verifiable and explicable computation are of the utmost importance for the correct integration of DNNs in security-critical learning activities. Research on computer security's hardware security subfield focuses on the hardware's weaknesses. Deep learning hardware platforms contain significant vulnerabilities that have been disclosed by hardware based attack methods like HT, injection of fault, and SCA. As a result, we concentrate on the following goals in this work to examine the hardware-based security of neural networks at the moment.

The hardware based Significance attacks are shown in figure 3. Design Corruption: alter the model's memory-stored parameters so that it performs poorly on all tasks. Backdoor Injection: Adjust the model in memory so that it only fails on a portion of the jobs. Design Extraction: During operation or by demonstrating non-volatile memory, remove the model from the device. Spoofing: altering the surroundings or the input sensors to corrupt the input data.

RECENT APPROACH ON CHIP AND IC LEVELS

Once the assault objectives have been determined, many hardware-based strategies can be used to accomplish them. The most popular methods include fault injection, side-channel, and hardware trojan attacks.

Hardware Trojan (HT)

A neural network is modified maliciously by Trojan assaults so that incorrect outputs may only be produced with purposefully created inputs. Both software and hardware have the potential to introduce Trojan. By contaminating the data during the training phase, software trojans typically embed themselves into the neural network parameters, creating a back door that only functions when inputs contain trojan triggers. On the other hand, malevolent designers or fabrication companies introduce HT into the integrated circuits circuitry. A trigger and related payload are typically carefully crafted into hardware trojans in order to compromise the integrity of the NN.

Bit triggers, combinational triggers, and sequential triggers are the three main categories of HT triggers. In order to govern the transition between the normal and triggered modes, a hidden extra pin is added to the circuit by Bit Trigger. Combinatorial trigger concentrates on the input being delivered to the hacked neural network right now. The trigger could be the complete input, partial input, or even an intermediate calculation result that was impacted by the input. A series of inputs with attributes created by the attacker, such as a specific arrangement of labels, can activate the sequential trigger. Overall, HT triggers could be created using an additional pin or secret information in inputs. There are four parts of the neural network that can be vulnerable with regard to the payload location: input, processing block, intermediate data, and output. Providing illicit input data saved independently from the genuine ones and setting the entered input information to zero are two methods used to compromise inputs. Some payloads entail changing the computing block, either by adding gates to change the activation function or by pruning multiply-accumulate (MAC) (Naveenkumar et.al, 2021).

Bit width reduction and perturbation introduction are two methods that can be used to compromise the intermediate computation outcome. Targeted erroneous labels are typically concealed in the triggers to directly contaminate the output, and a multiplexer is used to make changes (Jemimah Rinsy et.al, 2022). To sum up, each link in the neural network hierarchy can accept the payload.

Table 1. Represents the security issues from the side channel attacks (SCA)

S,No	SCA Parameters	Design architecture	Design parameter	Input	Ref
1	Memory access	Y	Y	N	(Hua et.al, 2018)
2	Cache	Y	N	N	(Hua et.al, 2018)
3	Timing	Y	N	Y	(Dong et.al, 2019)
4	EM/ Power	Y	Y	Y	(Xiang et.al, 2019)
5	GPU	Y	N	N	(Naghibijouybari et.al, 2018), (Wei et.al, 2020)

Side-Channel Attack (SCA)

The physical data generated by implementing computer systems is used in a SCA on a neural network to violate privacy. Memory access patterns, cache information, electromagnetic leaks, timing information, platform-specific leaks and power usage, etc. are a few physical information examples that attackers are likely to overhear. With this knowledge, the attacker might determine the parameters and design of the neural network, as well as the inputs used during inference. Cache-based attacks often take advantage of the fact Thus, in order to steal private data, the attack process and the victim process share an instruction cache. Traditional SCA approaches like Prime+Probe and Flush+Reload are used to monitor GEMM functions in order to deduce the network architecture. When more target functions that reflect the network architecture are seen, a meta-model is trained to comprehend this relationship and predict victim network architecture later. In conclusion, security experts have serious concerns about memory-based pattern leakage.

The timing attack, which takes advantage of how long a certain sequence of calculations takes to complete in order to uncover hidden information from a neural network, is another often utilised side-channel attack. (Hua et.al, 2018) Investigates the victim network's execution time for a certain input and uses it to determine the network depth and condense the architectural search space. A time attack could be used to deduce model inputs in addition to architecture.

(Dong et.al, 2019) Suggests using the first hidden layer's floating-point multipliers' running times to recover the input. In essence, the architecture and the inputs were gained through timing assaults.

The computer system's EM/power leakage is used by EM and power-based side-channel assaults to access network architecture, network characteristics, or inputs. One intriguing finding is that network inputs and parameters cannot be inferred simultaneously; instead, researchers make the assumption that one of them is known and use EM/power data to infer the other. For instance, using a known network and EM traces or power traces, input information might be retrieved.

On the other hand, using a known input and EM or power traces, it was possible to determine network characteristics. Furthermore, (Xiang et.al, 2019) also infer network architecture using EM/power leakage. In conclusion, EM/power side-channel attacks are effective at jeopardising privacy. Several general-purpose attacks (GPU) have been presented in light of the fact that the majority of neural networks are trained and assessed on GPU platforms. Recent studies, for instance, suggested using the CUDA spy application to track the evolution of hardware performance counter values (Naghibijouybari et.al, 2018) and the Context-switching penalty on the GPU (Wei et.al, 2020) to determine architectures network there has never been any investigation on attacks on edge devices and other platforms like TPU, except from side-channel assaults on GPU platforms.

COUNTERMEASURES

Some countermeasures are offered to either identify or mitigate the adverse effects of the assaults outlined in the preceding section, which have the potential to seriously damage the integrity and privacy of the neural network.

Prevention from the HT

Despite the fact that a number of software Trojan (ST) detection and elimination strategies have been put out, HT defences have not been thoroughly studied. By identifying the least inputs (Jemimah Rinsy et.al, 2022) or least input changes that could result in misunderstanding, Trojan detection can be carried out for ST, It is typically integrated with in the networks during the training cycle. These optimization problem-solving methods, however, are not effective at finding hardware trojans.

This is due to the fact that after the models have been trained, hardware malware is typically integrated within a network through the addition of new circuits or functions. Temporary inputs satisfying the trigger won't cause the categorization result to change to the incorrect tag; the trojan can only be activated when the inputs exactly match the attacker's defined ones. Trigger identification by input feature evaluation is the only anti-trojan defence that can combat HTs.

This method, however, remains ineffective for some HT triggers, particularly for sequential triggers and even combinational triggers coupled to a very narrow sample of inputs (Naveenkumar et.al, 2021).

Prevention from SCA

There have been some suggested countermeasures for SCA that get memory-access patterns, electromagnetic (EM) leaks and power. (Yan et.al, 2017) Suggests a safe hierarchy-aware cache replacement policy to stop attackers from learning the victim process's access behaviour, and employs an unaware scramble of the memory location to prevent the neural network's architecture from being discovered.

Fully-masked neural networks (Dubey et.al, 2019) are suggested in order to combat the assaults' fundamental flaw, which assumes that attackers are aware of the inputs, and for further protection the NN from (EM) leaks and power of SCA. Blinding and multi-party computation are employed to keep the secret inputs concealed from attackers. Security measures of this type concentrate on eradicating the assaults basics, the knowledge intruders are presumptively aware of, for safeguard the privacy of the neural network.

Prevention from FI

As previously stated, errors might enter into the function or parameters by undesired physical conditions such as low voltage and clock glitch.

While voltage and clock signal detectors can detect the second form of attack, the first type, which uses bit flips to generate unexpected outputs, is more difficult to detect. Different strategies have been useful in defending against the former type.

On the one hand, redundant neurons are added to the important data path (Li et.al, 2019). (Hong et.al, 2019) to identify bit flips and big changes in the values of parameters, and each weight's binary representation includes a verification bit inserted to it to do the same. On the other hand, uses activation magnitude limitation and low precision values via quantized or the binarization process to mitigate the impact of substantial value changes.

A selective latch hardening strategy is also recommended (Li et.al, 2017) in order to render the data path less sensitive to bit-flip errors. More over some of the other preventive measure are Physical Unclonable function (PUF) (Naveenkumar et.al, 2022), (Shariffuddin et.al, 2022), Logical locking (Ashika et.al, 2023), (Naveenkumar et.al, 2022), (Naveenkumar et.al, 2023), and Obfuscation techniques (Naveenkumar et.al, 2022).

Moreover, Digitalization will encompass the majority of engineering fields, with a bigger impact over wide-area communication network involving fast data transmission (Dhanasekar et.al, 2019) – (Dhanasekar et.al, 2023), so the above suggested parameters based easily prevent the HT in Digital circuits.

CONCLUSION

In this paper examined recent advancements in NNs and with their application In DL techniques, the security features of NNs have become an essential and accepted problem for basic study. The most recent hardware-based attacks against DNN are then discussed, with a focus on side-channel analysis (SCA), fault injection, and hardware Trojan insertion (HT). The numerous security concerns in hardware trojan (HT) and side channel analyses are highlighted in this research, which also provides the various security difficulties in hardware-based assaults. More often than not, neural networks are used as a defence against hardware Trojans and Side Channel Attacks (SCA).

REFERENCES

Akhtar, N., & Mian, A. S. (2018). Threat of Adversarial Attacks on Deep Learning in Computer Vision: A Survey. *IEEE Access : Practical Innovations, Open Solutions*, *6*, 14410–14430. doi:10.1109/ACCESS.2018.2807385

Arunkumar, N., Senathipathi, N., Dhanasekar, S., Malin Bruntha, P., & Priya, C. (2020). An ultra-low-power static random-access memory cell using tunneling field effect transistor. *International Journal of Engineering*, *33*(11), 2215–2221.

Ashika, S. V., Sivamangai, N. M., Naveenkumar, R., & Napolean, A. (2023). Importance of Logic Locking Attacks in Hardware Security. *2023 International Conference on Intelligent Data Communication Technologies and Internet of Things (IDCIoT)*, (pp. 156-160). IEEE. 10.1109/IDCIoT56793.2023.10052782

Buchanan, M. (2015). Depths of learning. *Nature Physics*, *11*, 798–798.

Dhanasekar, S., Malin Bruntha, P., & Martin Sagayam, K. (2019). An Improved Area Efficient 16-QAM Transceiver Design using Vedic Multiplier for Wireless Applications. *International Journal of Recent Technology and Engineering*, *8*(3), 4419–4425. doi:10.35940/ijrte.C5535.098319

Dhanasekar, S., & Ramesh, J. (2015). FPGA Implementation of Variable Bit Rate 16 QAM Transceiver System. *International Journal of Applied Engineering Research: IJAER*, *10*, 26479–26507.

Dong, G., Wang, P., Chen, P., Gu, R., & Hu, H. (2019). Floating-Point Multiplication Timing Attack on Deep Neural Network. *2019 IEEE International Conference on Smart Internet of Things (SmartIoT)*, (pp. 155-161). IEEE.

Dubey, A., Cammarota, R., & Aysu, A. (2019). MaskedNet: The First Hardware Inference Engine Aiming Power Side-Channel Protection. *2020 IEEE International Symposium on Hardware Oriented Security and Trust (HOST)*, (pp. 197-208). IEEE.

Erichson, N., Taylor, D., Wu, Q., & Mahoney, M. W. (2021). *Noise-Response Analysis of Deep Neural Networks Quantifies Robustness and Fingerprints Structural Malware*. SDM.

Hong, S., Frigo, P., Kaya, Y., Giuffrida, C., & Dumitras, T. (2019). *Terminal Brain Damage: Exposing the Graceless Degradation in Deep Neural Networks Under Hardware Fault Attacks*. ArXiv, abs/1906.01017.

Hua, W., Zhang, Z., & Suh, G. E. (2018). Reverse Engineering Convolutional Neural Networks Through Side-channel Information Leaks. *2018 55th ACM/ESDA/IEEE Design Automation Conference (DAC)*, (pp. 1-6). ACM.

Jemimah Rinsy, J., Sivamangai, N. M., Naveenkumar, R., Napolean, A., Puviarasu, A., & Janani, V. (2022). *Review on Logic Locking Attacks in Hardware Security*. 2022 6th International Conference on Devices, Circuits and Systems (ICDCS), Coimbatore, India. 10.1109/ICDCS54290.2022.9780725

LI., Y., Liu, Y., Li, M., Tian, Y., Luo, B., & Xu, Q. (2019). D2NN: a fine-grained dual modular redundancy framework for deep neural networks. *Proceedings of the 35th Annual Computer Security Applications Conference*. ACM.

Li, G., Hari, S. K., Sullivan, M. B., Tsai, T., Pattabiraman, K., Emer, J. S., & Keckler, S. W. (2017). Understanding Error Propagation in Deep Learning Neural Network (DNN) Accelerators and Applications. SC17. *International Conference for High Performance Computing, Networking, Storage and Analysis: [proceedings]. SC (Conference : Supercomputing)*, 1–12.

Li, Y., Wu, B., Jiang, Y., Li, Z., & Xia, S. (2020). Backdoor Learning: A Survey. *IEEE transactions on neural networks and learning systems*. IEEE. https://arxiv.org/abs/2007.08745

Liu, Y., Ma, X., Bailey, J., & Lu, F. (2020). *Reflection Backdoor: A Natural Backdoor Attack on Deep Neural Networks*. ArXiv, abs/2007.02343.

Liu, Y., Mondal, A., Chakraborty, A., Zuzak, M., Jacobsen, N. L., Xing, D., & Srivastava, A. (2020). A Survey on Neural Trojans. *2020 21st International Symposium on Quality Electronic Design (ISQED)*, (pp. 33-39). IEEE.

Naghibijouybari, H., Neupane, A., Qian, Z., & Abu-Ghazaleh, N. B. (2018). Rendered Insecure: GPU Side Channel Attacks are Practical. *Proceedings of the 2018 ACM SIGSAC Conference on Computer and Communications Security*. ACM. 10.1145/3243734.3243831

Naveenkumar, R., & Sivamangai, N. M. (2022). Hardware Obfuscation for IP Protection of DSP Applications. *Journal of Electronic Testing*, *38*(1), 9–20. doi:10.100710836-022-05984-2

Naveenkumar, R., Sivamangai, N. M., Napolean, A., & Janani, V. (2021). A Survey on Recent Detection Methods of the Hardware Trojans. *2021 3rd International Conference on Signal Processing and Communication (ICPSC)*, (pp. 139-143). IEEE. 10.1109/ICSPC51351.2021.9451682

Naveenkumar, R., Sivamangai, N. M., Napolean, A., & Priya, S. S. (2022). Design and Evaluation of XOR Arbiter Physical Unclonable Function and its Implementation on FPGA in Hardware Security Applications. *Journal of Electronic Testing*, *38*(6), 653–666. doi:10.100710836-022-06034-7

Naveenkumar, R., Sivamangai, N. M., Napolean, A., Priya, S. S. S., & Ashika, S. V. (2023). Design of INV/BUFF Logic Locking For Enhancing the Hardware Security. *Journal of Electronic Testing*. doi:10.100710836-023-06061-y

Naveenkumar, R., Sivamangai, N. M., Napolean, A., Puviarasu, A., & Saranya, G. (2022). Preventive Measure of SAT Attack by Integrating Anti-SAT on Locked Circuit for Improving Hardware Security. *2022 7th International Conference on Communication and Electronics Systems (ICCES)*, Coimbatore, India. 10.1109/ICCES54183.2022.9835923

Naveenkumar, R., Sivamangai, N. M., Napolean, A., & Sridevi Sathayapriya, S. (2023). Review on Hardware Trojan Detection Techniques. *National Academy Science Letters*. doi:10.100740009-023-01247-6

Nguyen, A., & Tran, A. (2021). *WaNet - Imperceptible Warping-based Backdoor Attack*. ArXiv, abs/2102.10369.

Salem, A., Wen, R., Backes, M., Ma, S., & Zhang, Y. (2020). Dynamic Backdoor Attacks Against Machine Learning Models. *2022 IEEE 7th European Symposium on Security and Privacy (EuroS&P)*, 703-718.

Shariffuddin, S., Sivamangai, N. M., Napolean, A., Naveenkumar, R., Kamalnath, S., & Saranya, G. (2022). Review on Arbiter Physical Unclonable Function and its Implementation in FPGA for IoT Security Applications. *2022 6th International Conference on Devices, Circuits and Systems (ICDCS),* (pp. 369-374). IEEE.

Shen, G., Liu, Y., Tao, G., An, S., Xu, Q., Cheng, S., Ma, S., & Zhang, X. (2021). Backdoor Scanning for Deep Neural Networks through K-Arm Optimization. *International Conference on Machine Learning.* IEEE.

Tran, B., Li, J., & Madry, A. (2018). Spectral Signatures in Backdoor Attacks. *Neural Information Processing Systems.*

Weber, M., Xu, X., Karlas, B., Zhang, C., & Li, B. (2020). *RAB: Provable Robustness Against Backdoor Attacks.* ArXiv, abs/2003.08904.

Wei, J., Zhang, Y., Zhou, Z., Li, Z., & Faruque, M. A. (2020). Leaky DNN: Stealing Deep-Learning Model Secret with GPU Context-Switching Side-Channel. *2020 50th Annual IEEE/IFIP International Conference on Dependable Systems and Networks (DSN),* (pp. 125-137). IEEE.

Xiang, Y., Chen, Z., Chen, Z., Fang, Z., Hao, H., Chen, J., Liu, Y., Wu, Z., Xuan, Q., & Yang, X. (2019). Open DNN Box by Power Side-Channel Attack. *IEEE Transactions on Circuits and Wystems. II, Express Briefs, 67*(11), 2717–2721. doi:10.1109/TCSII.2020.2973007

Yan, M., Gopireddy, B., Shull, T., & Torrellas, J. (2017). Secure hierarchy-aware cache replacement policy (SHARP): Defending against cache-based side channel attacks. *2017 ACM/IEEE 44th Annual International Symposium on Computer Architecture (ISCA),* (pp. 347-360). IEEE.

Zhao, P., Chen, P., Das, P., Ramamurthy, K.N., & Lin, X. (2020). *Bridging Mode Connectivity in Loss Landscapes and Adversarial Robustness.* ArXiv, abs/2005.00060.

Chapter 11
Biologically Inspired SNN for Robot Control

S. Ganeshkumar
Sri Eshwar College of Engineering, Coimbatore, India

J. Maniraj
KalaignarKarunanidhi Institute of Technology, Coimbatore, India

S. Gokul
Sri Eshwar College of Engineering, Coimbatore, India

Krishnaraj Ramaswamy
College of Engineering and Technology, Ethiopia

ABSTRACT

In recent years, there has been a trend towards more sophisticated robot control. This has been driven by advances in artificial intelligence (AI) and machine learning, which have enabled robots to become more autonomous and effective in completing tasks. One trend is towards using AI for robot control. This involves teaching robots how to carry out tasks by providing them with data and letting them learn from it. This approach can be used for tasks such as object recognition and navigation. Another trend is towards using machine learning for robot control. This involves using algorithms to learn from data and improve the performance of the robot. This approach can be used for tasks such as object recognition and navigation. A third trend is towards using more sophisticated sensors for robot control. This includes using sensors that can detect things such as temperature, humidity, and pressure.

DOI: 10.4018/978-1-6684-6596-7.ch011

INTRODUCTION

Bioinspired and biomimicry are both approaches to design and innovation that seek to learn from and imitate nature. Both approaches have their roots in observations of the natural world and the belief that nature is a source of inspiration for solving problems. Bioinspired design is inspired by the structure, function, or behavior of a biological system. The goal of bioinspired design is to create new technologies and products that mimic the best features of nature. One example of a bioinspired technology is the use of Velcro, which was inspired by the way burrs cling to fur. Biomimicry is a more specific type of bioinspired design. Biomimicry is the imitation of a specific biological system or process in order to solve a human problem. One example of biomimicry is the development of self-cleaning surfaces, which were inspired by the way lotus leaves repel water. Both bioinspired design and biomimicry are based on the observation of nature and the belief that nature can be a source of inspiration for human innovation, (Zahra et al., 2022). However, biomimicry is more focused on the imitation of specific biological systems, while bioinspired design is more general and can be inspired by a variety of features in nature. Neural networks are a type of artificial intelligence that is modeled after the way the human brain processes information. Neural networks are composed of an input layer, hidden layer, and output layer. The input layer consists of neurons that receive input from outside the network. The hidden layer consists of neurons that process the input from the input layer and generate output for the output layer. The output layer consists of neurons that receive input from the hidden layer and generate an output. Neural networks are used for a variety of tasks including pattern recognition, classification, and prediction. Neural networks have been used to create models of the human brain, to simulate the workings of the human brain, and to create artificial intelligence, (Ding et al., 2022). The first neural networks were created in the 1950s. The first neural networks were composed of only a few neurons and were used to solve simple problems. Neural networks have evolved over the years to become more complex and to be able to solve more complex problems. Today, neural networks are composed of millions of neurons and are used for a variety of tasks including pattern recognition, classification, and prediction, (Casanueva-Morato et al., 2022).

A neural network is a computer system that is designed to mimic the workings of the human brain. Neural networks are used to process and interpret data, and to make predictions based on that data. There are two main types of neural networks: artificial neural networks and biological neural networks. Artificial neural networks are computer systems that are designed to mimic the workings of the human brain. These systems are composed of a large number of interconnected processing nodes, or neurons, that work together to perform a task. Artificial neural networks are used for a variety of tasks, including pattern recognition, data classification, and prediction. Biological neural networks are the networks of neurons that make up the human brain. These networks are composed of billions of interconnected neurons that work together to perform all of the tasks that the brain is capable of. Biological neural networks are responsible for everything from basic motor control to higher-level cognitive functions. An artificial neural network is a computer program that is modeled after the brain. It is designed to recognize patterns and to learn from experience. Just as the brain learns from experience, the artificial neural network can be trained to recognize patterns of input and to respond in a certain way (Fang et al., 2022). The artificial neural network is made up of a number of interconnected processing nodes, or neurons, that work together to solve a problem. Each node is connected to several other nodes, and the connections between nodes can be adjusted. This allows the artificial neural network to learn by modifying the connections between nodes. The vast majority of artificial neural networks are used for supervised learning. This means that the network is presented with a set of training data, and the desired output for each data point is known. The network then adjusts the connections between nodes so that it can produce the desired output for future data points. There are many different types of artificial neural networks, and they can be used for a variety of tasks. Some common applications for artificial neural networks include image recognition, facial recognition, and speech recognition (Safa et al., 2022). An Industrial Mitsubishi robot is exhibited in Figure 1.

Figure 1. Mitsubishi pick and place robot arm

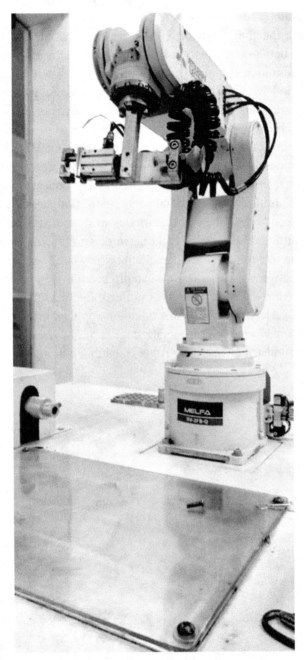

A convolutional neural network (CNN) is a type of artificial neural network used in image recognition and processing that is specifically designed to process data that has a grid-like topology. CNNs are similar to other types of neural networks but they are distinguished by their architecture, which is designed to take advantage of the 2D structure of images. CNNs are made up of a series of layers, each of which consists of a set of neurons. The first layer is the input layer, which is where the data (in the form of an image) is fed into the network. The second layer is the convolutional layer, which is where the convolutional operations are performed. The third layer is the pooling layer, which is where the data is down sampled. The fourth layer is the fully connected layer, which is where the final classification is made. The convolutional layer is the key to CNN. This is where the convolutional operations are performed. These operations are designed to extract features from the data that are relevant for the task at hand. For example, if we were trying to detect edges in an image, the convolutional layer would be responsible for extracting the edge features from the data. Spike neural networks are a type of neural network that uses spikes, or brief bursts of electrical activity, to communicate information, (Hashem, 2022). These networks are designed to emulate the way the brain processes information, and they have the potential to be much more efficient than traditional neural networks. Spike neural networks were first proposed in the early 1990s, and they have been under development ever since. The first commercial product to use a spike neural network was the TrueNorth chip, developed by IBM in 2014. This chip is capable of emulating a million neurons and 10 billion synapses, and it consumes only 70 mW of power. The TrueNorth chip is just one example of the potential of spike neural networks. These networks hold promise for a wide range of applications, from smart cars and homes to brain-machine interfaces. As research on spike neural networks continues, we can expect to see even more amazing applications for this technology (Massari et al., 2022).

Robots are increasingly being used in a variety of settings, including homes, factories, and hospitals. In many cases, it is desirable for robots to be able to learn new skills from humans. For example, a robot might need to learn how to open a door or pick up a cup. There are several ways in which a robot can learn from humans. One approach is to have a human demonstrate the task to the robot. The robot can then try to imitate the human motion. However, this approach can be difficult, because the robot might not be able to accurately reproduce the human motion. A second approach is to have the human provide explicit instructions to the robot. For example, the human might tell the robot to "move its arm to the left by 10 centimeters". This approach can be difficult, because it can be hard for the human to know exactly what the robot needs to do. A third approach is to have the human provide feedback to the robot. For example, the human might tell the robot whether its motion is correct or not. This approach can be difficult, because the human might need to have a lot of expertise in the task. Robots are increasingly becoming a staple in many industries as their accuracy, speed, and efficiency continue to improve. In many cases, they are even surpassing the abilities of their human counterparts. This ever-growing dependence on robots has led to the development of new methods for controlling them. One of the most common methods of controlling robots is through the use of sensors. Sensors allow the robot to detect its surroundings and make decisions based on that information. For example, a robot arm in a factory might be equipped with sensors that detect the presence of an object in its path. The arm would then adjust its position to avoid collision (D'Angelo et al., 2022). Another common method of controlling robots is through the use of computer programs. These programs can be written to specifically control the actions of a robot. For example, a program might be written to tell a robot arm to pick up a specific object and place it in a specific location. The most advanced method of controlling robots is through the use of artificial intelligence. This allows the robot to think and act for itself, making decisions based on its own experience and learning. This type of control is still in its early stages, but it has the potential to revolutionize the way that robots are used. Robot control techniques can vary depending on the type of robot and the application. For example, some robots may be controlled using direct remote control, while others may be controlled using a computer program. One common technique for controlling robots is using a computer program. This can be done using a variety of programming languages, such as C++ or Java. The program is typically written to control the robot's movements and actions. The program is then typically downloaded onto the robot, and the robot is controlled by executing the program (Nadizar et al., 2022). Another common technique for controlling robots is via remote control. This can be done using a variety of methods, such as infrared or radio signals. The remote control is used to send signals to the robot, which the robot uses to control its movements and actions. There are a variety of other techniques that can be used to control robots. For example, some robots may be controlled using sensors, such as sonar or GPS. Additionally, some robots may be controlled using artificial intelligence, such as by learning to recognize patterns or by making decisions based on data. A neural network is a computer system that is designed to simulate the workings of the human brain. This technology is used in a wide variety of applications, including robot control. Neural networks are used in robot control because they are able to learn and adapt to new situations, (Sun et al., 2022). This is important for robots because they need to be able to deal with unexpected situations that they may encounter during their work. Neural networks are also good at dealing with complex tasks that would be difficult for a human to program a robot to do. There are a few different ways that neural networks can be used in robot control. One is to use the neural network to directly control the robot. This can be done by using the neural network to calculate the best way for the robot to move in order to achieve its goal. Another way to use neural networks in robot control is to use them to learn a set of rules that can then be used to control the robot. This is often done by training the neural network on a set of data that includes the desired outcome of the robot's actions. Neural networks are a powerful tool that can be used to improve the performance of robots. Neural networks are used in a variety of applications, including robot control, (Kondoyanni et al., 2022). Robots are often controlled by a computer system that is programmed to carry out specific tasks. However, this can be limiting, as the robot is only able to do what it has been programmed to do. Using a neural network to control a robot gives the robot the ability to learn and adapt, just like a human. For example, a robot that is used to clean floors might be equipped with sensors that tell it when it has reached the edge of a room. A neural network can be used to learn the pattern of the room so that the robot can clean it more efficiently. The neural network would learn the size and shape of the room and the placement of furniture, so that the robot can clean the floor without bumping into things. As another example, a robot that is used to assemble products might be equipped with sensors that tell it when a part is in the correct position. A neural network can be used to learn the assembly process so that the robot can do it more quickly and accurately. The neural network would learn the sequence of steps and the placement of parts. Spike neural networks are a type of neural network that uses spikes, or short bursts of electrical activity, to communicate information, (Meng et al., 2022). These networks are similar to the way the brain processes information, and they have been shown to be very efficient at controlling robotic systems. There are many potential applications for spike neural networks in robotics. For example, they could be used to control the movement of a robotic arm or to process sensor data from a robot's environment. Spike neural networks could also be used to improve the accuracy of robot navigation, or to help a robot learn new tasks. The use of spike neural networks in robotics is a relatively new field, and there is still much research to be done in order to fully exploit their potential. However, the early results are very promising, and it is likely that spike neural networks will play an increasingly important role in the control of robotic systems in the future. Spike neural networks are gaining popularity in the area of robot control due to their ability to learn and adapt to changes in the environment. Spike neural networks are composed of neurons that fire action potentials (spikes) in response to input stimuli. The timing of the spikes is used to encode information about the stimulus, which can be used for learning and pattern recognition. Spike neural networks have several advantages over traditional artificial neural networks (ANNs). First, spike neural networks can learn in an unsupervised manner, which is more efficient than the supervised learning required by ANNs. Second, spike neural networks are more robust to changes in the environment and can continue to learn and adapt even when the environment is changing. Finally, spike neural networks have the ability to perform online learning, which is not possible with ANNs (Bercea et al., 2022). There are several different types of spike neural networks, but the most popular type for robot control is the liquid state machine (LSM). LSMs are composed of neurons that are interconnected by synapses. The strength of the synapses can be modified by the neuron that fires first, which allows the network to learn and adapt (Li et al., 2022). The neural networks of programming techniques are achieved for industrial robots along with Teach pendant device programming methods. A Typical Mitsubishi Teach pendant device is exhibited in Figure 2.

Figure 2. Teach pendant device for robot programming

BIO-INSPIRED MECHANISMS FOR LEARNING ROBOT MOTION

The article discusses a bio-inspired mechanism for learning robot motion from mirrored human demonstrations. The mechanism is based on the mirror neuron system in the brain, which is responsible for observed actions being mapped onto motor representations in the brain. The authors demonstrate how their system can be used to learn a variety of different robotic motions, including reaching and grasping, from human demonstrations. They also show how the system can be used to improve the performance of a robot in a task by fine-tuning the robot's motions to match those of the human demonstrator. The article discusses the use of dynamic thresholds for spiking neural networks. The authors describe how they were inspired by biology to develop a new type of threshold that can be adapted to changing conditions. They believe that this will allow neural networks to more closely mimic the brain's ability to learn and adapt. The article includes several simulations to demonstrate the efficacy of the dynamic thresholds. Overall, the article provides a detailed look at a promising new approach to spiking neural networks. Spike-based computational models of bio-inspired memories in the hippocampal CA3 region on SpiNNaker have the potential to provide a detailed understanding of how the brain stores and retrieves memories. These models can also be used to develop new and more efficient algorithms for artificial intelligence and machine learning. The hippocampus is a region of the brain that is critical for memory formation and retrieval (Niu et al., 2022). The CA3 region of the hippocampus is thought to be particularly important for storing memories of events that have happened in the past. SpiNNaker is a massively parallel computing platform that is designed to simulate the workings of the brain. SpiNNaker is an ideal platform for running spike-based computational models of the brain because it can simulate the high levels of parallelism that are found in the brain. Spike-based computational models of the hippocampal CA3 region have been used to simulate the formation and retrieval of memories. These models have shown that the CA3 region can store memories of events that have happened in the past, and that these memories can be retrieved when needed. The use of SpiNNaker to simulate spike-based computational models of the brain is a powerful tool for understanding how the brain works, (Kim et al., 2022). The article discusses the use of a spike-based computational model to simulate bio-inspired memories in the hippocampal CA3 region. The model is based on the SpiNNaker platform, which is a powerful tool for simulating neural networks. The article describes how the model works and how it can be used to simulate different kinds of memories. The article also discusses the potential applications of the model in the future. EMG signals are electrical signals that are produced by the contraction of muscles. They can be used to control prosthetic devices, such as robotic arms or legs. A bio-inspired neural network is used to model EMG-driven wrist movements.

The neural network will be inspired by the structure of the human nervous system. It will be made up of neurons that are connected to each other. The neurons will receive input from the EMG signals and will output a signal that will control the movement of the wrist. The neural network will be trained using a dataset of EMG signals. The dataset will be used to teach the network how to map the EMG signals to the desired wrist movements. The neural network will be able to learn how to control the wrist movements by itself, (Mohseni et al., 2022). The bio-inspired neural network will be able to model the EMG-driven wrist movements more accurately than traditional methods. This is because the neural network will be able to learn the complex relationships between the EMG signals and the wrist movements. traditional methods would not be able to learn these relationships. The bio-inspired neural network will be able to provide a more natural control of the prosthetic device. The article discusses a bio-inspired neural network that can model EMG-driven wrist movements. The network consists of two populations of neurons, one that encodes the position of the wrist and the other that encodes the velocity of the wrist. The neurons are interconnected and the network is trained using a reinforcement learning algorithm. The authors show that the network is able to accurately model the EMG-driven wrist movements of a human subject. Most drones are equipped with visual sensors that allow them to detect and avoid obstacles in their environment (Zhang et al., 2022). However, these sensors are not designed to detect people, which can pose a serious safety hazard. In order to address this problem, a team of researchers from the University of Zurich have developed a bio-inspired event-based visual system that allows drones to detect people on the fly. The system is inspired by the way in which insects detect movement. The system consists of a camera that is equipped with special sensors that can detect changes in the intensity of light. These changes are then used to generate a representation of the scene that is similar to the way in which insects see the world. The system has been tested on a number of different drones and has proven to be effective at detecting people in a variety of different scenarios. The system is also very efficient, using very little power, which is important for drones that need to be able to fly for long periods of time. Overall, this bio-inspired event-based visual system shows promise for improving the safety of drones by allowing them to detect people in their environment. The article discusses a bio-inspired event-based visual system for drones that can detect people on the fly. The system is based on the visual system of the dragonfly, which is able to detect small movements with high temporal resolution. The system is composed of an event-based camera, a microcontroller, and a neuromorphic chip. The event-based camera is used to capture images at high frame rates, and the microcontroller is used to process the events and extract information about the movement of objects in the scene. The neuromorphic chip is used to implement a spiking neural network that can learn to detect people in the scene. The system is evaluated on a dataset of real-world images, and the results show that the system is able to detect people with high accuracy (Hussaini et al., 2022).

The rapid development of Internet and computer technology has led to a dramatic increase in the number of network attacks in recent years. In order to protect computer networks from these attacks, it is necessary to develop effective intrusion detection systems. Traditional intrusion detection systems (IDSs) use rule-based methods to detect attacks, which are often unable to keep up with the pace of change in attack methods. Deep learning is a machine learning technique that has shown promise in a variety of applications. A bio-inspired hybrid deep learning model was proposed for network intrusion detection. The model combines the strengths of deep learning and rule-based methods to develop a more effective IDS. The proposed model consists of two main components: a deep learning component and a rule-based component. The deep learning component is responsible for learning the general characteristics of normal and abnormal traffic, (Yudanov et al., 2012). The rule-based component is responsible for detecting specific attacks based on a set of predefined rules. The two components are integrated in a hybrid manner, such that the deep learning component provides the general characteristics of traffic to the rule-based component. This information is used by the rule-based component to generate specific rules for detecting different types of attacks. The article presents a bio-inspired hybrid deep learning model for network intrusion detection. The model is composed of a deep neural network (DNN) and a support vector machine (SVM). The DNN is used to learn high-level features from network data, while the SVM is used to learn low-level features. The two models are combined to form a hybrid model that can detect both known and unknown attacks. The hybrid model is evaluated on the KDD Cup 99 dataset and the NSL-KDD dataset. The results show that the hybrid model outperforms the DNN and SVM alone and is able to detect both known and unknown attacks. The hybrid model presented appears to be a promising approach for network intrusion detection, (Yamazaki et al., 2022). A biologically inspired ring-shaped soft pneumatic actuator (BRSA) is a novel type of pneumatic actuator that is capable of large deformations. The BRSA is inspired by the ring-shaped muscle of cephalopods, such as squid and octopuses. These creatures are able to generate large forces and achieve remarkable feats of dexterity and strength. The BRSA is composed of a ring of elastomeric material with an embedded pneumatic chamber. When the chamber is inflated, the ring expands in diameter and contracts in circumference. This results in a large net deformation of the ring. The BRSA can be used for a variety of applications, including robotics, prosthetics, and biomechanical research. The BRSA has a number of advantages over traditional pneumatic actuators. First, the BRSA is much more compact than conventional pneumatic actuators. Second, the BRSA can generate large forces and achieve large deformations. Third, the BRSA is relatively simple to fabricate. Fourth, the BRSA is biocompatible and can be implanted in living tissue, (Juárez-Lora et al., 2022). This article presents a new type of soft pneumatic actuator that is inspired by biological systems. The actuator is made from a silicone elastomer and has a ring shape. It is filled with a gas, which can be either air or nitrogen. The actuator is capable of large deformations, due to the fact that it is made from a silicone elastomer. The actuator can be used for a variety of applications, such as robotics, prosthetics, and medical devices. Functional mimicry of Ruffini receptors with fibre Bragg gratings and deep neural networks enables a bio-inspired large-area tactile-sensitive skin. Ruffini receptors are slowly adapting mechanoreceptors that are found in the skin. They are responsible for detecting deep pressure and slow, sustained stretch. Fibre Bragg gratings are optical fibre devices that can reflect or transmit light depending on the wavelength of the light. Deep neural networks are artificial intelligence systems that are designed to mimic the workings of the human brain. The combination of these three technologies has resulted in the development of a bio-inspired large-area tactile-sensitive skin. This skin is able to detect deep pressure and slow, sustained stretch, just like the Ruffini receptors in human skin. The skin is also able to transmit this information to a computer system, which can then be used to control a robotic hand or other device. This technology has a number of potential applications. For example, it could be used to develop robotic hands that are able to replicate the sense of touch of human hand, (Zhang et al., 2022). This would allow robots to handle delicate objects without damaging them. The article discusses the use of fibre Bragg gratings and deep neural networks to create a bio-inspired large-area tactile-sensitive skin. The skin is designed to mimic the function of Ruffini receptors, which are pressure-sensitive receptors found in the skin. The skin is made up of a network of sensors that are connected to an artificial neural network. The neural network is trained to recognize patterns of pressure that are applied to the skin. The skin is designed to be used in robotics and prosthetics, and the authors demonstrate its use in a robotic hand. The skin is shown to be able to recognize a variety of different objects and can provide information about the shape, size and hardness of the object. The authors conclude that the skin has the potential to be used in a variety of applications where tactile information is required. The iCub is a humanoid robot developed by the RobotCub Consortium with the aim of providing a platform for research in cognitive robotics. The iCub has been designed to be as similar as possible to a human child in terms of size, appearance and cognitive abilities. One of the key features of the iCub is its ability to learn from experience and interact with its environment in a natural way. In order to endow the iCub with these capabilities, the RobotCub Consortium has developed a bio-inspired architecture called the Event-Driven Attention System (EDAS). The EDAS is based on the premise that the brain is an event-driven system that constantly filters and processes information from the environment in order to guide behaviour. The EDAS architecture has been implemented on the SpiNNaker platform, which is a massively parallel computing platform designed for real-time applications. The SpiNNaker platform is well suited to the implementation of the EDAS architecture as it is able to handle the high-speed, event-driven data streams that are generated by the iCub's sensors (Guan et al., 2022). The iCub is a humanoid robot developed by the RobotCub Consortium with the aim of providing a platform for research in cognitive robotics. The iCub has been designed to be as close as possible to a human child in terms of physical and cognitive abilities. One of the key features of the iCub is its event-driven bio-inspired attentive system (EDBAS). The EDBAS is based on the principle that the brain is constantly bombarded with sensory information but only attends to a small fraction of it. The EDBAS aims to replicate this by constantly monitoring the iCub's sensors and only attending to events that are deemed important. This allows the iCub to focus its attention on relevant information and ignore irrelevant information. The EDBAS is composed of two main components: the Event Detection Module (EDM) and the Attention Selection Module (ASM). The EDM is responsible for detecting events in the iCub's environment, (Hussaini, 2022). The article discusses a bio-inspired attentive system for the iCub humanoid robot that is event-driven. The system is designed to provide the robot with the ability to focus its attention on specific events that are relevant to its current task. The system is based on the principle of selective attention in humans, which allows us to filtering out unimportant information in order to focus on what is most relevant. The system consists of two main components: an event detector and an attention controller. The event detector is responsible for detecting relevant events in the environment and generating an attention signal. The attention controller uses this attention signal to modulate the activity of the robot's sensors and actuators, so that the robot can focus its resources on the event that is most relevant to its current task. The article describes the design of the system and its implementation on the SpiNNaker platform (Volinski et al., 2022). The system is evaluated in a simulated environment and shown to be effective at detecting and responding to events that are relevant to the robot's current task. A modular soft robot is a robot made up of many small, identical modules that can be connected together to form a larger robot. These modules are often made of a soft, flexible material, such as silicone, and are equipped with simple sensors and actuators. One advantage of using modular soft robots is that they can be easily reconfigured to perform different tasks. Embodied Spiking Neural Cellular Automata (eSNCA) is a computational model that can be used to control modular soft robots. This model is inspired by the way that biological nervous systems control the body. In eSNCA, each module is represented by a neuron, and the connections between neurons represent the connections between modules (Xie et al., 2022). The strength of these connections can be adjusted to control the behavior of the robot. eSNCA has been used to control modular soft robots in a variety of tasks, including locomotion, object manipulation, and environmental exploration. In each of these tasks, the eSNCA controller is able to adapt the robot's behavior to the specific task at hand. For example, when the robot is required to move quickly, the eSNCA controller will increase the strength of the connections between the modules that are responsible for locomotion. A method for controlling modular soft robot is presented using a spiking neural cellular automaton (SNCA). The SNCA is a neural network that can be used to control robotic systems. The authors demonstrated how the SNCA can be used to control a modular soft robot. The modular soft robot is made up of multiple modules that can be controlled independently (Jia et al., 2022). The SNCA is used to control the modules in a coordinated manner. The authors showed how the SNCA can be used to control the robot's motion, including its speed and direction and how the SNCA can be used to control the robot's grippers, allowing it to pick up and move objects. In the past decade, there has been significant progress in the modelling and control of bio-inspired fish robots. Inspired by the swimming of real fish, these robots have the potential to be used for a variety of applications, including underwater exploration, environmental monitoring, and search and rescue missions. One of the challenges in designing fish robots is to create a control system that can replicate the complex and efficient swimming motions of real fish. Researchers have made progress in this area by developing control algorithms that take into account the hydrodynamic interactions between the robot and its environment. These algorithms have been used to successfully control the swimming of fish robots in a variety of different environments. In addition to their use in underwater applications, fish robots are also being developed for use in terrestrial environments (Zeglen et al., 2022). For example, researchers are working on designs for fish robots that can be used to monitor agricultural crops or to assist in search and rescue operations. The recent progress in the modelling and control of bio-inspired fish robots has opened up a number of new possibilities for their use in a variety of applications. With further research and development, these robots have the potential to revolutionize the way we interact with our underwater environment. The article discusses recent progress in modelling and control of bio-inspired fish robots. The authors presented a review of the current state of the art in this field, including a discussion of the challenges associated with modelling and control of these types of robots. The article describes several successful applications of bio-inspired fish robots and provides an overview of the current state of research in this area (Azimirad et al., 2022).

APPLICATIONS OF BIO-INSPIRED ROBOTS

There are many potential applications for bio-inspired robots. Some of the most promising applications include search and rescue missions, environmental monitoring, and healthcare. One area where bio-inspired robots could be particularly useful is in search and rescue missions. Traditional search and rescue methods often prove to be unsuccessful, especially in large and complex environments. Bio-inspired robots, with their advanced sensors and locomotion abilities, could provide a much needed boost to search and rescue efforts. They could be used to search for survivors in disaster zones, or to locate missing persons in large and difficult to search areas. Another area where bio-inspired robots could be put to good use is in environmental monitoring. There are many areas of the world where it is difficult or impossible for humans to access, but where bio-inspired robots could easily go. For example, they could be used to monitor the health of coral reefs, to track the movements of wildlife, or to monitor pollution levels in difficult to reach areas, (Zhong et al., 2022). Finally, bio-inspired robots could also have a place in healthcare. They could be used for tasks such as delivering drugs to specific parts of the body, or for performing surgery in difficult to reach areas. Additionally, they could be used for rehabilitation purposes. The agricultural industry is in dire need of modernization in order to meet the ever-growing demand for food. However, the industry has been slow to change, largely due to the high cost of new technology and the reluctance of farmers to adopt new methods. One way to overcome these obstacles is to develop bio-inspired robots and structures that can help to increase efficiency and productivity in agriculture. There are many potential applications for bio-inspired robots in agriculture. For example, robots could be used for tasks such as planting, watering, and harvesting crops. They could also be used to transport goods or to provide information about conditions in the field. In addition, bio-inspired structures could be used to create more efficient and effective irrigation systems or to provide shelter for crops. The development of bio-inspired robots and structures could have a significant impact on the agricultural industry. By increasing efficiency and productivity, these technologies could help to reduce the cost of food production and make it more accessible to people around the world. In addition, the adoption of new technologies would help to modernize the agricultural industry, making it more competitive in the global economy. There are many challenges that need to be addressed in order to make these technologies a reality (Rueckauer et al., 2022). The article discusses the use of bio-inspired robots and structures to modernize agriculture. The author describes how robots can be used to improve crop yields and reduce pesticide use. The author also discusses how bio-inspired structures can be used to create more efficient and environmentally friendly farms. In recent years, there has been an increasing interest in developing bio-inspired robotic fish. These robots are designed to mimic the appearance and swimming behaviors of real fish, and they have potential applications in underwater exploration, environmental monitoring, and search and rescue missions. One of the challenges in designing robotic fish is to stabilize their videos in real time. This is because robotic fish are often subjected to underwater currents and turbulence, which can cause their videos to be shaky and difficult to interpret. There are several methods that have been proposed for stabilizing digital videos in real time. One popular method is the estimation-and-prediction framework, which is based on the idea of predicting the future motion of objects in the video and then using this information to stabilize the video. This framework has been used successfully in a number of applications, including video stabilization, object tracking, and activity recognition. The Real-Time Digital Video Stabilization of Bioinspired Robotic Fish Using Estimation-and-Prediction Framework is a research paper that discusses the development of a new digital video stabilization algorithm that can be used to stabilize the video footage of a bio-inspired robotic fish. The algorithm is based on an estimation-and-prediction framework, and it is designed to work in real-time. The paper describes the algorithm in detail and provides experimental results that demonstrate its effectiveness. Hydrogels are a type of biomaterial that have been designed to mimic the natural extracellular matrix (ECM). They are composed of hydrophilic polymers that can absorb and retain large amounts of water, and have the ability to swell and deform in response to changes in their environment. This makes them an attractive option for a variety of life-science applications, including tissue engineering, drug delivery, and biosensing. One of the main challenges associated with hydrogels is their lack of mechanical strength. This limits their use in load-bearing applications, such as in the repair of large tissue defects, (Rueckauer et al., 2022). To address this issue, research has focused on the development of stronger and more resilient hydrogels. This has involved the incorporation of reinforcement materials, such as nanofibers and graphene, into the hydrogel structure. Another challenge that must be addressed is the issue of biocompatibility. In order for hydrogels to be used in vivo, they must be compatible with the body's tissues and fluids. This includes being non-toxic and having the ability to support the growth of cells. Research is ongoing to develop hydrogels that meet these criteria. The article discusses the potential for using hydrogels as platforms for life-science applications. The authors note that hydrogels have several attractive features, including biocompatibility, biodegradability, and the ability to control their physical and chemical properties. However, the authors also note that there are challenges associated with using hydrogels for life-science applications, including the need to design hydrogels that are specifically tailored for the application, the difficulty of fabricating hydrogels with complex shapes, and the potential for immunogenicity. The field of bio-inspired intelligence (BI) is rapidly evolving, with new applications being found in a variety of domains. In particular, the use of BI in robotics is an area of active research, with a number of successful applications already being developed. In this essay, we survey the state of the art in BI for robotics, focusing on recent advances and applications (Luo et al., 2022). BI is concerned with the study of natural systems and the development of artificial systems that exhibit similar behaviours. This is motivated by the belief that nature provides a wealth of examples of successful behaviours and systems that can be adapted for use in artificial systems. The use of BI in robotics is motivated by the fact that robots are required to operate in unstructured environments, and must therefore be able to adapt to changing conditions. There are a number of approaches to BI, each with its own strengths and weaknesses. For robotics applications, the most relevant approaches are evolutionary computation, artificial neural networks, and fuzzy logic. Evolutionary computation is a BI approach that is based on the principles of natural selection. In this approach, a population of potential solutions (called a "generation") is subjected to a series of tests (called "evaluations"). The article discusses the various approaches to bio-inspired intelligence and their applications to robotics. It provides an overview of the field and describes the different approaches that have been taken. The article discusses the advantages and disadvantages of each approach and provides examples of where each has been successfully used. In recent years, there has been an increasing interest in the development of soft actuators with electrically responsive and photoresponsive deformations. These actuators offer a number of advantages over traditional rigid actuators, including improved compliance, lower weight, and lower power consumption. In addition, they are well suited for use in soft robots, which are becoming increasingly popular for a variety of applications. One type of soft actuator that has been developed is based on shape memory alloys (SMAs) (Zhong et al., 2022). These actuators can be actuated by applying an electric current, which causes the SMA to heat up and contract. This contraction can be used to generate a force or to deform the shape of the actuator. Additionally, the actuator can be returned to its original shape by cooling the SMA. SMAs have a number of advantages over other types of soft actuators. For example, they are relatively simple to fabricate and can be made from a variety of materials. In addition, they are highly responsive, with deformations occurring on the order of milliseconds. However, one disadvantage of SMAs is that they require a power source in order to function. The article discusses the use of SMA-based soft actuators in soft robots. The actuators are electrically responsive and photoresponsive, meaning they can change shape in response to an electric current or light. The article describes how the actuators can be used to create soft robotic devices that are compliant and adaptable (Obo et al., 2022). The actuators are also said to be energy efficient and have a long lifetime. In recent years, there has been increasing interest in developing soft robots. These robots are made of deformable materials and are capable of performing complex tasks in unstructured environments. One of the challenges in developing soft robots is powering them. Batteries are typically bulky and rigid, which limits their use in soft robots. Researchers at Harvard University have developed a new type of battery that is inspired by the scales of a fish. The battery is made up of individual scales that can change shape and attach to the robot. The scales are made of a flexible polymer and contain a thin film of lithium. When the battery is connected to a power source, the lithium film produces an electric current. The battery is still in the early stages of development, but the researchers believe that it has the potential to be used in a variety of applications, including untethered soft robots. The battery is lightweight, flexible, and scalable, which makes it well-suited for use in soft robots. In addition, the battery is self-contained and does not require an external power source, which makes it ideal for use in untethered robots. The development of this new type of battery is an important step forward in the development of soft robots. The use of legged robots has been increasing in a variety of applications, from search and rescue missions to delivering goods. With the increasing popularity of legged robots comes the need for more effective methods of control. One method that has been shown to be effective is blended physical and virtual impedance control. This method utilizes both the physical properties of the legged robot and the virtual world in which it is moving. The physical properties are used to calculate the desired trajectory of the robot, while the virtual world is used to provide feedback about the robot's actual position and orientation. This method has been shown to be effective in a variety of applications, including legged robot design (Silvestrini et al., 2022). This is due to the fact that the blended physical and virtual impedance control can provide a more natural and effective way of controlling the robot. Additionally, this method can be used to control a variety of legged robots, including those with different numbers of legs and those with different gaits. Designing robots that can effectively navigate their environments is a challenge that has long puzzled engineers. One approach that has been proposed is to design robots that are inspired by living creatures, such as animals. This approach has the advantage of drawing on the millions of years of evolution that have resulted in animals that are very effective at moving through their environments. A recent study has proposed a new method for designing legged robots that combines the best features of both physical and virtual impedance control. This method, which the authors refer to as blended physical and virtual impedance control, makes use of a physical robot platform that is used to generate data that is then used to train a virtual robot model. The authors believe that this approach has the potential to result in robot designs that are more effective than those that are based solely on either physical or virtual impedance control, (Wan et al., 2022). This article describes a new method for designing legged robots that combines the best features of both physical and virtual impedance control. This method, which the authors refer to as blended physical and virtual impedance control, makes use of a physical robot platform that is used to generate data that is then used to train a virtual robot model.

SPIKING NEURAL NETWORK PROGRAMMING FOR ROBOTS:

A spiking neural network (SNN) is a neural network that uses discrete digital events to communicate information between artificial neurons. The events, called "spikes", are generated by the neurons in response to either external stimuli or internal calculations. The advantage of using spikes over traditional artificial neural networks is that spikes can provide more information about the timing and intensity of the input signal. This can be useful for tasks that require real-time response, such as robotics or image recognition. Spiking neural networks are still in the early stages of development, and there are many challenges to programming them for use in real-world applications. One of the biggest challenges is designing algorithms that can effectively use the information provided by the spikes. Another challenge is designing hardware that can efficiently implement a spiking neural network. Despite the challenges, there is potential for spiking neural networks to be used in a variety of applications, including robotics, image recognition, and real-time control systems. With continued research and development, spiking neural networks may become a powerful tool for artificial intelligence and machine learning (Vicol et al., 2022). The introduction of spiking neural networks (SNNs) has shown promise in the area of place recognition, due to their ability to learn and store spatial representations in a manner similar to the brain. However, SNNs have typically been large and resource-intensive, making them impractical for many real-world applications. In recent years, a number of studies have demonstrated that ensembles of compact, region-specific SNNs can achieve high levels of place recognition accuracy with relatively few resources. These ensembles are composed of a number of smaller SNNs, each of which is trained to recognize a specific region of the environment. By combining the outputs of the individual SNNs, the ensemble is able to achieve high levels of accuracy while remaining compact and resource-efficient. In addition to being compact and resource-efficient, ensembles of region-specific SNNs have a number of other advantages. First, they are scalable, meaning that they can be easily extended to cover larger environments. Second, they are robust, meaning that they are less likely to be affected by changes in the environment (such as lighting changes or objects being moved). The article describes a new approach to place recognition using spiking neural networks (SNNs) (Guo et al., 2023). The proposed system, called an "ensemble of compact, region-specific, and regularized SNNs", is designed to be scalable and efficient. The system is tested on a variety of datasets, including the MNIST handwritten digit dataset and the KITTI odometry dataset. The results show that the proposed system outperforms other SNN-based place recognition systems, and is able to achieve high accuracy with low computational cost. Neural networks are computational models that are inspired by the way the brain processes information. These models are composed of interconnected processing units, or neurons, that can learn to recognize patterns of input. Spiking neural networks (SNNs) are a type of neural network that uses spikes, or brief bursts of electrical activity, to communicate information. SNNs are a promising approach for energy-efficient robot learning and control because they can take advantage of the brain's natural neural processes. The brain is very efficient at processing information and requires far less energy than traditional computer algorithms. SNNs can also learn in an unsupervised manner, which is important for robot applications where data is often scarce (Jiang et al., 2022). There are many challenges that need to be addressed before SNNs can be used for real-world applications. One challenge is that SNNs are not yet well-understood and there is much research that needs to be done to improve their performance. Another challenge is that SNNs require specialized hardware that is not yet widely available. Despite these challenges, SNNs offer a promising approach for energy-efficient robot learning and control. This article explores the potential for using spiking neural networks (SNNs) to create more energy-efficient robots. The authors noted that current methods for robot learning and control consume a lot of energy, which limits the viability of robots for long-term use. SNNs offer a more energy-efficient alternative, as they are based on the brain's own neural network structure. The authors discussed how SNNs could be used to create robots that are more efficient in their energy consumption, and thus more viable for long-term use. Spiking neural networks (SNNs) are a type of neural network that can simulate the firing of neurons in the brain. They are a relatively new type of neural network, but they have already shown promise in a number of applications. SNNs are well suited for modelling brain activity because they can capture the temporal aspects of neural firing. This is important because the timing of neural firing can carry a lot of information. SNNs can also handle a large number of inputs and outputs, which is important for modelling the complex activity of the brain (Zheng et al., 2022). There are a number of potential applications for SNNs. They could be used to develop more efficient algorithms for pattern recognition and classification. They could also be used to develop better models of brain activity. Additionally, SNNs could be used to develop new types of neural prosthetics. Overall, SNNs show a lot of promise as a tool for understanding and modeling brain activity. They also have the potential to be used in a number of practical applications. Kalman filtering is a popular technique for estimating the state of a system from noisy measurements. It has been shown that Kalman filtering can be implemented using spiking neural networks, which offer a number of advantages over traditional methods. Spiking neural networks are well suited for implementing Kalman filtering because they can perform online learning and are highly parallelizable. In addition, spiking neural networks can be used to implement nonlinear Kalman filters, which are more effective than traditional linear filters in many applications. There are a few challenges associated with implementing Kalman filtering with spiking neural networks. First, it is difficult to design spiking neural networks that accurately estimate the state of a system. Second, spiking neural networks tend to be slower than traditional Kalman filters, due to the time required for spikes to propagate through the network. Despite these challenges, Kalman filtering with spiking neural networks is a promising approach that has the potential to improve the accuracy of state estimation in many applications. Deep neural networks have been shown to be successful for various visual recognition tasks. However, they are typically limited to supervised learning, requiring large amounts of labelled data. Spiking neural networks (SNNs), on the other hand, are powerful computational models that can learn from unlabelled data. A method for visual place recognition is proposed using SNNs that does not require labels. It is based on the idea of weighted neuronal assignments, where each neuron is assigned a weight that corresponds to its importance for the task at hand (George et al., 2023). The network was trained on a dataset of place images and evaluated it on a standard place recognition benchmark. The results showed that the method outperforms the state-of-the-art unsupervised place recognition method and is comparable to the state-of-the-art supervised place recognition methods. Event-based sensors are a new type of vision sensor that only outputs information when there is a change in the scene. This makes them well suited for robotics applications, where power consumption and data bandwidth are important considerations. Radar is another type of sensor that has been used in robotics, but it is not as commonly used as vision sensors. However, radar has some advantages over vision sensors, such as the ability to penetrate fog and other obscurants. A recent trend in robotics is to use event-based sensors in combination with traditional sensors, such as cameras and radar. This approach has the potential to combine the best features of both sensor types. For example, event-based sensors can be used for SLAM (simultaneous localization and mapping) applications, while radar can be used to provide long-range sensing. Spiking neural networks (SNNs) are a type of neural network that can be used to process event-based data. SNNs are well suited for event-based data because they can handle asynchronous inputs and have a lower power consumption than traditional neural networks. Continual learning is a type of learning that allows a neural network to learn new tasks without forgetting how to perform previously learned tasks. The article discusses how a spiking neural network can be used to fuse event-based camera and radar data for SLAM (simultaneous localization and mapping). The network is trained using continual STDP (spike-timing-dependent plasticity), which allows it to learn continuously from incoming data streams. The article describes how the network can be used to improve the accuracy of SLAM algorithms and provides experimental results that show the benefits of using the network (Stasenko et al., 2022).

SCOPE FOR FUTURE RESEARCH IN SPIKE NEURAL NETWORK FOR ROBOT PROGRAMMING

The potential for future research in Spike neural networks for robot programming is considerable. This technology has already shown great promise in terms of its ability to enable robots to learn and adapt to their environment. Additionally, the potential for using Spike neural networks to improve the performance of robots in tasks such as navigation, object manipulation, and search is considerable. There are a number of different directions that future research in this area could take. One possibility would be to continue to develop the technology so that it can be used to control more complex robots (Nguyen et al., 2022). Additionally, research could focus on how to best integrate Spike neural networks into existing robot programming frameworks. Additionally, further research could focus on how to use Spike neural networks to improve the performance of robots in tasks such as navigation, object manipulation, and search. The spike neural network is a relatively new area of research and there is still much to be explored in terms of its potential for programming robots. Some future research directions that could be taken include (Han et al., 2022):

1. Investigating ways to improve the accuracy of spike timing-based computations. This could involve exploring new ways to encode information in spikes, or developing new methods for decoding spike patterns.
2. Developing new methods for training spike neural networks. This could involve exploiting the temporal nature of spikes to develop more efficient training algorithms.
3. Investigating the use of spike neural networks for more complex tasks such as navigation and object recognition. This could involve developing new methods for incorporating spatiotemporal information into spike-based computations.
4. Exploring the use of spike neural networks in hardware. This could involve designing custom hardware that is optimized for spike-based computations, or developing new ways to implement spike neural networks on existing hardware platforms.
5. Investigating the potential of spike neural networks for real-time applications. This could involve developing new methods for running spike neural networks in real-time on embedded devices or developing new ways to use spike neural networks for online learning tasks.

CONCLUSION

A biologically inspired spiking neural network (SNN) is a powerful tool for robot control. In this paper, we have presented a new SNN architecture for robot control that is inspired by the mammalian brain. This architecture is composed of an input layer, a hidden layer, and an output layer. The input layer receives input spike trains from sensors, the hidden layer performs computations on these inputs, and the output layer produces motor commands. This architecture is capable of performing a variety of tasks, including obstacle avoidance, path planning, and navigation. We have reviewed the feasibility of this approach by implementing it on a robot platform. This architecture has the potential to be used in a wide range of applications, including autonomous vehicles, service robots, and prosthetic devices. After studying the feasibility of using a spiking neural network (SNN) for robot control, it was concluded that SNN is a promising approach for this application. The SNN was found to be able to learn the desired control task and produce accurate and robust control signals. The main advantage of using SNN is its ability to process information in a more efficient way than traditional neural networks (Ganeshkumar et al., 2019). This makes SNN a promising candidate for real-time applications such as robot control. Biological systems have demonstrated many efficient ways to process and control information. One example is the spiking neural network (SNN), which has shown great promise for efficient information processing and control. In this article, we reviewed the application of SNNs to robot control and discuss some of the challenges associated with this approach. Overall, we believe that SNN-based robot control has great potential and could lead to more efficient and effective robot control systems (Dhanasekar et al., 2015).

REFERENCES

Arunkumar, N., Senathipathi, N., Dhanasekar, S., Malin Bruntha, P., & Priya, C. (2020). An ultra-low-power static random-access memory cell using tunneling field effect transistor. *International Journal of Engineering*, *33*(11), 2215–2221.

Azimirad, V., Ramezanlou, M. T., Sotubadi, S. V., & Janabi-Sharifi, F. (2022). A consecutive hybrid spiking-convolutional (CHSC) neural controller for sequential decision making in robots. *Neurocomputing*, *490*, 319–336. doi:10.1016/j. neucom.2021.11.097

Bercea, M. (2022). Bioinspired hydrogels as platforms for Life-Science applications: Challenges and opportunities. *Polymers*, *14*(12), 2365. doi:10.3390/polym14122365 PMID:35745941

Bruntha, P. M., Dhanasekar, S., Hepsiba, D., Sagayam, K. M., Neebha, T. M., Pandey, D., & Pandey, B. K. (2022). Application of switching median filter with L2 norm-based auto-tuning function for removing random valued impulse noise. *Aerospace Systems*, *6*(1), 53–59. doi:10.100742401-022-00160-y

Casanueva-Morato, D., Ayuso-Martinez, A., Dominguez-Morales, J. P., Jimenez-Fernandez, A., & Jimenez-Moreno, G. (2022). *Spike-based computational models of bio-inspired memories in the hippocampal CA3 region on SpiNNaker.* arXiv preprint arXiv:2205.04782.

D'Angelo, G., Perrett, A., Iacono, M., Furber, S., & Bartolozzi, C. (2022). Event driven bio-inspired attentive system for the iCub humanoid robot on SpiNNaker. *Neuromorphic Computing and Engineering*, *2*(2), 024008. doi:10.1088/2634-4386/ac6b50

Dhanasekar, S., Malin Bruntha, P., Jubair Ahmed, L., Valarmathi, G., Govindaraj, V., & Priya, C. (2022). An Area Efficient FFT Processor using Modified Compressor adder based Vedic Multiplier. *Proceedings of the 2022 6th International Conference on Devices, Circuits and Systems (ICDCS)*. 10.1109/ICDCS54290.2022.9780676

Dhanasekar, S., Malin Bruntha, P., & Martin Sagayam, K. (2019). An Improved Area Efficient 16-QAM Transceiver Design using Vedic Multiplier for Wireless Applications. *International Journal of Recent Technology and Engineering*, *8*(3), 4419–4425. doi:10.35940/ijrte.C5535.098319

Dhanasekar, S., & Ramesh, J. (2015). FPGA Implementation of Variable Bit Rate 16 QAM Transceiver System. *International Journal of Applied Engineering Research*, *10*, 26479–26507.

Ding, J., Dong, B., Heide, F., Ding, Y., Zhou, Y., Yin, B., & Yang, X. (2022). *Biologically Inspired Dynamic Thresholds for Spiking Neural Networks.* arXiv preprint arXiv:2206.04426.

Fang, Y., Yang, J., Zhou, D., & Ju, Z. (2022). Modelling EMG driven wrist movements using a bio-inspired neural network. *Neurocomputing*, *470*, 89–98. doi:10.1016/j.neucom.2021.10.104

Ganeshkumar, S. (2023). Exploring the Potential of Integrating Machine Tool Wear Monitoring and ML for Predictive Maintenance-A Review. *Journal of Advanced Mechanical Sciences*, *2*(1), 10–20.

Ganeshkumar, S., Kumar, S. D., Magarajan, U., Rajkumar, S., Arulmurugan, B., Sharma, S., Li, C., Ilyas, R. A., & Badran, M. F. (2022). Investigation of tensile properties of different infill pattern structures of 3D-printed PLA polymers: Analysis and validation using finite element analysis in ANSYS. *Materials (Basel)*, *15*(15), 5142. doi:10.3390/ma15155142 PMID:35897575

Ganeshkumar, S., Singh, B. K., Kumar, S. D., Gokulkumar, S., Sharma, S., Mausam, K., Li, C., Zhang, Y., & Tag Eldin, E. M. (2022). Study of Wear, Stress and Vibration Characteristics of Silicon Carbide Tool Inserts and Nano Multi-Layered Titanium Nitride-Coated Cutting Tool Inserts in Turning of SS304 Steels. *Materials (Basel)*, *15*(22), 7994. doi:10.3390/ma15227994 PMID:36431481

Ganeshkumar, S., Sureshkumar, R., Sureshbabu, Y., & Balasubramani, S. (2019). A numerical approach to cutting tool stress in CNC turning of EN8 steel with silicon carbide tool insert. *International Journal of Scientific & Technology Research*, *8*(12), 3227–3231.

Ganeshkumar, S., Sureshkumar, R., Sureshbabu, Y., & Balasubramani, S. (2020). A review on cutting tool measurement in turning tools by cloud computing systems in industry 4.0 and IoT. *GIS Science Journal, 7*(8), 1-7.

Ganeshkumar, S., Thirunavukkarasu, V., Sureshkumar, R., Venkatesh, S., & Ramakrishnan, T. (2019). Investigation of wear behaviour of silicon carbide tool inserts and titanium nitride coated tool inserts in machining of en8 steel. *International Journal of Mechanical Engineering and Technology*, *10*(01), 1862–1873.

Ganeshkumar, S., & Venkatesh, S. (2022). Manufacturing Techniques and Applications of Multifunctional Metal Matrix Composites. Functional Composite Materials: Manufacturing Technology and Experimental Application, 157.

Ganeshkumar, Venkatesh, Paranthaman, Arulmurugan, Arunprakash, Manickam, Venkatesh, & Rajendiran. (2022). Performance of Multilayered Nanocoated Cutting Tools in High-Speed Machining: A Review. *International Journal of Photoenergy*. doi:10.1155/2022/5996061

George, A. M., Dey, S., Banerjee, D., Mukherjee, A., & Suri, M. (2022). Online Time-Series Forecasting using Spiking Reservoir. *Neurocomputing*.

Gokilakrishnan, G., Ganeshkumar, S., Anandakumar, H., & Vigneshkumar, M. (2021, March). A Critical Review of Production Distribution Planning Models. In *2021 7th International Conference on Advanced Computing and Communication Systems (ICACCS)* (Vol. 1, pp. 2047-2051). IEEE. 10.1109/ICACCS51430.2021.9441879

Govindaraj, V., Dhanasekar, S., Martinsagayam, K., Pandey, D., Pandey, B. K., & Nassa, V. K. (2023). Low-power test pattern generator using modified LFSR. Aerospace Systems, 1-8.

Guan, Y., Shang, Z., & Li, C. (2022, May). Analysis of Spiking Neural Network trends based on CiteSpace. In *International Symposium on Computer Applications and Information Systems (ISCAIS 2022)* (Vol. 12250, pp. 38-51). SPIE. 10.1117/12.2639578

Guo, L., Song, Y., Wu, Y., & Xu, G. (2022). Anti-interference of a small-world spiking neural network against pulse noise. *Applied Intelligence*, 1–19.

Han, J. K., Yun, S. Y., Lee, S. W., Yu, J. M., & Choi, Y. K. (2022). A review of artificial spiking neuron devices for neural processing and sensing. *Advanced Functional Materials*, *32*(33), 2204102. doi:10.1002/adfm.202204102

Hashem, R., Kazemi, S., Stommel, M., Cheng, L. K., & Xu, W. (2022). A biologically inspired ring-shaped soft pneumatic actuator for large deformations. *Soft Robotics*, *9*(4), 807–819. doi:10.1089oro.2021.0013 PMID:34704835

Hussaini, S., Milford, M., & Fischer, T. (2022). *Ensembles of Compact, Region-specific & Regularized Spiking Neural Networks for Scalable Place Recognition.* arXiv preprint arXiv:2209.08723.

Hussaini, S., Milford, M., & Fischer, T. (2022). Spiking Neural Networks for Visual Place Recognition via Weighted Neuronal Assignments. *IEEE Robotics and Automation Letters*, *7*(2), 4094–4101. doi:10.1109/LRA.2022.3149030

Jia, Z., Ji, J., Zhou, X., & Zhou, Y. (2022). Hybrid spiking neural network for sleep electroencephalogram signals. *Science China. Information Sciences*, *65*(4), 1–10. doi:10.100711432-021-3380-1

Jiang, S., Liu, Y., Xu, B., Sun, J., & Wang, Y. (2022). Asynchronous numerical spiking neural P systems. *Information Sciences*, *605*, 1–14. doi:10.1016/j.ins.2022.04.054

Juárez-Lora, A., García-Sebastián, L. M., Ponce-Ponce, V. H., Rubio-Espino, E., Molina-Lozano, H., & Sossa, H. (2022). Implementation of Kalman Filtering with Spiking Neural Networks. *Sensors (Basel)*, *22*(22), 8845. doi:10.339022228845 PMID:36433442

Kim, M. H., Nam, S., Oh, M., Lee, H. J., Jang, B., & Hyun, S. (2022). Bioinspired, shape-morphing scale battery for untethered soft robots. *Soft Robotics*, *9*(3), 486–496. doi:10.1089oro.2020.0175 PMID:34402653

Kondoyanni, M., Loukatos, D., Maraveas, C., Drosos, C., & Arvanitis, K. G. (2022). Bio-Inspired Robots and Structures toward Fostering the Modernization of Agriculture. *Biomimetics*, *7*(2), 69. doi:10.3390/biomimetics7020069 PMID:35735585

Kumar, S. G., & Thirunavukkarasu, V. (2016). Investigation of tool wear and optimization of process parameters in turning of EN8 and EN 36 steels. *Asian Journal of Research in Social Sciences and Humanities*, *6*(11), 237–243. doi:10.5958/2249-7315.2016.01188.6

Li, J., Xu, Z., Zhu, D., Dong, K., Yan, T., Zeng, Z., & Yang, S. X. (2022). *Bio-inspired intelligence with applications to robotics: a survey*. arXiv preprint arXiv:2206.08544.

Luo, Y., Shen, H., Cao, X., Wang, T., Feng, Q., & Tan, Z. (2022). Conversion of Siamese networks to spiking neural networks for energy-efficient object tracking. *Neural Computing & Applications*, *34*(12), 9967–9982. doi:10.100700521-022-06984-1

Massari, L., Fransvea, G., D'Abbraccio, J., Filosa, M., Terruso, G., Aliperta, A., D'Alesio, G., Zaltieri, M., Schena, E., Palermo, E., Sinibaldi, E., & Oddo, C. M. (2022). Functional mimicry of Ruffini receptors with fibre Bragg gratings and deep neural networks enables a bio-inspired large-area tactile-sensitive skin. *Nature Machine Intelligence*, *4*(5), 425–435. doi:10.103842256-022-00487-3

Meng, Y., Wu, Z., Zhang, P., Wang, J., & Yu, J. (2022). Real-Time Digital Video Stabilization of Bioinspired Robotic Fish Using Estimation-and-Prediction Framework. *IEEE/ASME Transactions on Mechatronics*, *27*(6), 4281–4292. doi:10.1109/TMECH.2022.3155696

Mohseni, O., Rashty, A. M. N., Seyfarth, A., Hosoda, K., & Sharbafi, M. A. (2022). Bioinspired legged robot design via blended physical and virtual impedance control. *Journal of Intelligent & Robotic Systems*, *105*(1), 1–15. doi:10.100710846-022-01631-2

N. V. H. S., B. K. S, G. K. S, A. U., & J. B. (2023). Controlling Gate Valves with Wi-Fi: An Overview of Available Technologies and Applications. *2023 9th International Conference on Advanced Computing and Communication Systems (ICACCS)*, 1396-1400. doi: 10.1109/ICACCS57279.2023.10112698

Nadizar, G., Medvet, E., Nichele, S., & Pontes-Filho, S. (2022). *Collective control of modular soft robots via embodied Spiking Neural Cellular Automata*. arXiv preprint arXiv:2204.02099.

Nguyen, D. A., Tran, X. T., Dang, K. N., & Iacopi, F. (2022). A low-power, high-accuracy with fully on-chip ternary weight hardware architecture for Deep Spiking Neural Networks. *Microprocessors and Microsystems*, *90*, 104458. doi:10.1016/j.micpro.2022.104458

Niu, D., Li, D., Chen, J., Zhang, M., Lei, B., Jiang, W., Chen, J., & Liu, H. (2022). SMA-based soft actuators with electrically responsive and photoresponsive deformations applied in soft robots. *Sensors and Actuators. A, Physical*, *341*, 113516. doi:10.1016/j.sna.2022.113516

Obo, T., & Takizawa, K. (2022, July). Gesture Learning Based on A Topological Approach for Human-Robot Interaction. In *2022 International Joint Conference on Neural Networks (IJCNN)* (pp. 1-6). IEEE. 10.1109/IJCNN55064.2022.9892731

Rueckauer, B., Bybee, C., Goettsche, R., Singh, Y., Mishra, J., & Wild, A. (2022). NxTF: An API and compiler for deep spiking neural networks on Intel Loihi. *ACM Journal on Emerging Technologies in Computing Systems*, *18*(3), 1–22. doi:10.1145/3501770

Rueckauer, B., Bybee, C., Goettsche, R., Singh, Y., Mishra, J., & Wild, A. (2022). NxTF: An API and compiler for deep spiking neural networks on Intel Loihi. *ACM Journal on Emerging Technologies in Computing Systems*, *18*(3), 1–22. doi:10.1145/3501770

S, G., T, D., & Haldorai, A. (2022). A Supervised Machine Learning Model for Tool Condition Monitoring in Smart Manufacturing. *Defence Science Journal*, *72*(5), 712-720. doi:10.14429/dsj.72.17533

Safa, A., Ocket, I., Bourdoux, A., Sahli, H., Catthoor, F., & Gielen, G. (2022). *Learning to Detect People on the Fly: A Bio-inspired Event-based Visual System for Drones*. arXiv preprint arXiv:2202.08023.

Silvestrini, S., & Lavagna, M. (2022). Deep Learning and Artificial Neural Networks for Spacecraft Dynamics, Navigation and Control. *Drones*, *6*(10), 270. doi:10.3390/drones6100270

Stasenko, S., & Kazantsev, V. (2023). Astrocytes Enhance Image Representation Encoded in Spiking Neural Network. In *International Conference on Neuroinformatics* (pp. 200-206). Springer. 10.1007/978-3-031-19032-2_20

Sun, B., Li, W., Wang, Z., Zhu, Y., He, Q., Guan, X., Dai, G., Yuan, D., Li, A., Cui, W., & Fan, D. (2022). Recent Progress in Modeling and Control of Bio-Inspired Fish Robots. *Journal of Marine Science and Engineering*, *10*(6), 773. doi:10.3390/jmse10060773

Venkatesh, S., Sivapirakasam, S. P., Sakthivel, M., Ganeshkumar, S., Prabhu, M. M., & Naveenkumar, M. (2021). Experimental and numerical investigation in the series arrangement square cyclone separator. *Powder Technology*, *383*, 93–103. doi:10.1016/j.powtec.2021.01.031

Vicol, A. D., Yin, B., & Bohté, S. M. (2022, July). Real-time classification of LIDAR data using discrete-time Recurrent Spiking Neural Networks. In *2022 International Joint Conference on Neural Networks (IJCNN)* (pp. 1-9). IEEE. 10.1109/IJCNN55064.2022.9892006

Volinski, A., Zaidel, Y., Shalumov, A., DeWolf, T., Supic, L., & Tsur, E. E. (2022). Data-driven artificial and spiking neural networks for inverse kinematics in neurorobotics. *Patterns*, *3*(1), 100391. doi:10.1016/j.patter.2021.100391 PMID:35079712

Wan, Z., Lele, A. S., & Raychowdhury, A. (2022, January). Circuit and system technologies for energy-efficient edge robotics. In *2022 27th Asia and South Pacific Design Automation Conference (ASP-DAC)* (pp. 275-280). IEEE.

Xie, K., Zhang, Z., Li, B., Kang, J., Niyato, D., Xie, S., & Wu, Y. (2022). Efficient federated learning with spike neural networks for traffic sign recognition. *IEEE Transactions on Vehicular Technology*, *71*(9), 9980–9992. doi:10.1109/TVT.2022.3178808

Yamazaki, K., Vo-Ho, V. K., Bulsara, D., & Le, N. (2022). Spiking neural networks and their applications: A Review. *Brain Sciences*, *12*(7), 863. doi:10.3390/brainsci12070863 PMID:35884670

Zahra, O., Tolu, S., Zhou, P., Duan, A., & Navarro-Alarcon, D. (2022). A Bio-Inspired Mechanism for Learning Robot Motion from Mirrored Human Demonstrations. *Frontiers in Neurorobotics*, *16*, 16. doi:10.3389/fnbot.2022.826410 PMID:35360830

Zelgen, M. A. (2022). *Amygdala Modeling with Context and Motivation Using Spiking Neural Networks for Robotics Applications*. Wright State University.

Zhang, D., Zhang, T., Jia, S., Wang, Q., & Xu, B. (2022). *Recent Advances and New Frontiers in Spiking Neural Networks*. arXiv preprint arXiv:2204.07050.

Zhang, R., Li, J., Zheng, P., Lu, Y., Bao, J., & Sun, X. (2022). A fusion-based spiking neural network approach for predicting collaboration request in human-robot collaboration. *Robotics and Computer-integrated Manufacturing*, *78*, 102383. doi:10.1016/j.rcim.2022.102383

Zheng, S., Qian, L., Li, P., He, C., Qin, X., & Li, X. (2022). *An Introductory Review of Spiking Neural Network and Artificial Neural Network: From Biological Intelligence to Artificial Intelligence.* arXiv preprint arXiv:2204.07519.

Zhong, S., Zhang, Y., Zheng, H., Yu, F., & Zhao, R. (2022). *Spike-Based Spatiotemporal Processing Enabled by Oscillation Neuron for Energy-Efficient Artificial Sensory Systems.* Advanced Intelligent Systems. doi:10.1002/aisy.202200076

Zhong, X., & Pan, H. (2022). A spike neural network model for lateral suppression of spike-timing-dependent plasticity with adaptive threshold. *Applied Sciences (Basel, Switzerland), 12*(12), 5980. doi:10.3390/app12125980

Chapter 12
Spiking Neural Networks for Robotic Applications

J. Dhanasekar
Sri Eshwar College of Engineering, India

K S. Tamilselvan
KPR Institute of Engineering and Technology, Coimbatore, India

R. Monisha
KPR Institute of Engineering and Technology, Coimbatore, India

V. Seethalakshmi
KPR Institute of Engineering and Technology, Coimbatore, India

Gokul Basavaraj G
Central Queensland University, Melbourne, Australia

ABSTRACT

The biologically inspired spiking neural network can be said to mimic the most neural network models in existence that is evolved from artificial neural networks. This concept was derived from the nervous system and was able to generate electric impulses, commonly known as spikes or action impulses. Here the neural models try to replicate the biological neurons almost accurately and can be considered to be more powerful than its peers as it was able to integrate temporal information. As such they can said to have great potential in several complex applications like classification, mapping, and pattern recognition, etc. Out of the available spiking neuron models, Leaky-Integrate-and-Fire is very frequently applied. Spiking neural networks are gaining rapid importance in the last few years following the sharp incline in artificial intelligence field. In this modern era robots are incorporated in our daily life, and said to have the potential to increase economic growth and productivity.

DOI: 10.4018/978-1-6684-6596-7.ch012

INTRODUCTION

Deep learning, often referred to as training and interpreting using deep neural networks (DNN), has been a major factor in numerous remarkable accomplishments in Artificial Intelligence (AI) field as suggested by LeCun et al. (2015), Schmidhuber (2015), and Goodfellow et al. (2016). Starting from perceptron, a model for brain cells, i.e., multi-layer perceptrons until the various cutting-edge approaches regarding current-era DNNs, they have become more and more capable. This success heavily depends on the availability of a lot of databases, high-performance computers, and a Graphics Processing Unit.

Neuroscientific models of cortical structures have been a major source of inspiration for the design principles of Deep Neural Networks as described in Fukushima (1988) and Riesenhuber et al. (1999), however, there are very few implementation-level analogies between brain computation and artificial neural network (ANN) employed in AI applications. Although artificial neural network has generally been modeled after the brain, they fundamentally differ from biological neural network (BNN) considering their morphology, learning algorithms, and computation methods. While neurons in a neural network are often non-linear yet continuous and work with a universal clock, biological neurons operate via asynchronous pulses one which digitally communicate the presence of distinct event. Moreover, ANNs are less effective at using energy and are less capable of dynamic learning than biological neural networks. Conventional deep learning model's power usage has also been reduced through numerous efforts.

This discovery gave rise to spiking neural network (SNN), which was almost able to solve the problems with existing bottlenecks. Researchers have been attempting to reduce the gap between SNN and DNN for AI projects during the last decade. These researchers' field of interests include embedded systems, machine learning, neuromorphic science, and VLSI (Maass, 1997; Ponulak et al., 2011; Grüning & Bohte, 2014). Similar to biological neural networks, SNN operate continuously and use discrete electrical signals called spikes for communication between neurons. SNN adapts to the sparseness inherent in BNNas well as consistent with spatiotemporal programming because they behave similarly to biological neural networks (Kasabov, 2019).

The positive characteristics of SNN, such as analog computation, quick inference, dynamic learning, parallelism, and low power circuit design are demonstrated in actual neural systems (brain like). In addition, Lichtsteiner et al. (2018) showed that they have great potential for processing inputs from audio sensors more effectively Its applications on neuromorphic hardware are also noteworthy. The performance gap between SNNs and DNNs is closing on several tasks, despite the fact that SNNs typically need a lot less energy to operate. Training is challenging in SNNs, mostly because of the non-differentiable characteristics of spiking activities and the complicated dynamics of their neuronal populations.

In order to complete challenging real-world tasks, autonomous robots with uninterrupted HD (High Definition) surveillance & activity zones have been used increasingly. It is vital to develop energy effective options in order to supervise such independent robot uninterrupted due to their resource limitation. Biological systems have served as an inspiration for several robotics domains, including locomotor systems. Biology demonstrates that the events related pattern can be applied for controlling as well as perception and inference. Robotic perception and action are provided by SNNs, that imitates behaviors seen in nature. SNNs are most often hand-crafted and tuned specifically for the task at hand in robotic applications. Several approaches have been put out in the modern era to enable mobility robots. Central Pattern Generator (CPG), a type of NN which produces oscillatory, rhythmic outputs without specific periodic inputs thanks to coupled inhibitory and excitatory neurons. While SNN research is still in its beginning stage, most current studies focus on ANNs built on non-spiking neurons.

In this chapter, we brief (i) the theory of biological neurons; (ii) connection between biological and artificial neurons; (iii) existing spiking neuron models; (iv) use of SNNs in robotics.

Biological Neurons Theory

The brain is the central nervous system's command centre for all living things, and it is made up of several components that regulate hearing, vision, movement, and other senses. A sophisticated nerve network links the brain to the remainder of the body's sensors and actuators. The central nervous system of a live organism is made up primarily of roughly 10^{11} neurons found in the brain.

Figure 1. Model of a biological neuron

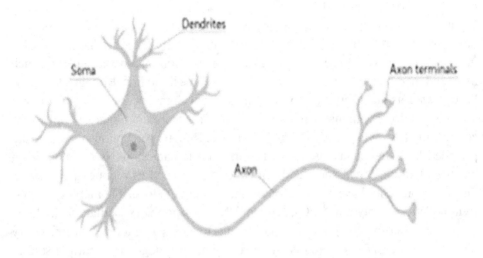

Figure 1 shows the biological neuron structure in living beings referred from Medical Xpress (2018). The fundamental unit of neural networks is the neuron. In biological systems, neuron is much like every other cell in the body. It has a DNA code and develops similarly to other cells. All creatures perform the same function, while having distinct DNA. Soma, which is cell body, dendrite, and axon are three main components that make up a neuron. The many cells in that group are joined by dendrites, which resemble threads that have been branched in different directions. The signals from neighbouring neurons are picked up by dendrites, and they are then sent to the other neurons via the axon. The axon's terminating terminal has a synapse that connects it to the dendrite. The output signal is carried along the length of the axon as electric impulses. One axon exists in each neuron. Axons act as a domino effect, sending impulses from one neuron to another. Theoretical investigation of biological neural networks is crucial because of its strong association to the development of mathematical models for artificial neural networks. Furthermore, this comprehension of brain NNs has paved the way to create artificial neural network systems and adaptive systems that can learn from their environment and modify themselves in response to inputs and circumstances.

Biologically Inspired SNN

ANN that nearly matches biology based neural networks are called spiking neural networks initially specified in Maass (1997). They embed the time notion in their working model in addition to neural and synapse state. Unlike the multi-layer perceptrons where the neurons relay information in every layer, SNNs send information if e_{mp} (membrane potential) exceeds the thresholding value. The neuron is activated simultaneously, sending a signal to nearby neurons that cause those neurons to change their membrane potentials in response to the signal. Figure 2. shows a spiking neural network with their interconnections taken from Mohamed et al. (2019).

Figure 2. Spiking neural networks and their connections
Source: Mohamed et al. (2019)

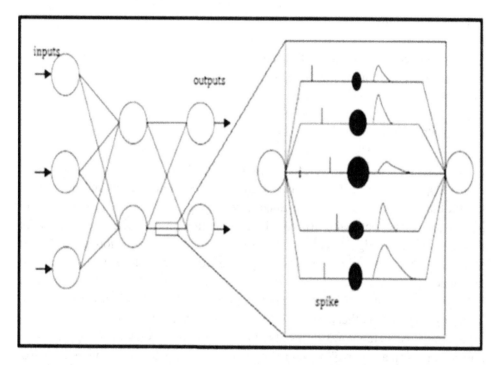

Membrane Potential

Membrane potential, which is derived from Goldman–Hodgkin–Katz equation is also known as transmembrane potential or membrane voltage. It refers to the variation in electric potential between the inside and outside of a biological cell. As long as there is no kinetic energy gain or radiation production, there is a difference in the energy needed for electric charges to flow from the interior to the outside cellular surroundings and vice versa. Numerous factors can affect the membrane potential in neurons. They contain a wide variety of ion channel types, some of which are voltage gated and chemically gated. It regulates voltage-gated ion channels, and these channels also have an impact on it and vice versa, creating feedback loops that then enable complex dynamic changes, including oscillations and regenerative events like action potentials as specified by Strickholm (1981).

$$V_{mp} = \frac{RT}{F} \ln \frac{pK[K+]op + pNa[Na+]op + pCl[Cl-]ip}{pK[K+]ip + pNa[Na+]ip + pCl[Cl-]op} \quad (1)$$

where R $= 8.3144598(48)$ J·mol^{-1}·K^{-1};

T = absolute temperature;
F $= 96,485$ C.mol^{-1};
Y_{op} = ion concentration outside the cell Y;
Y_{ip} = ion concentration inside the cellY;
pY= membrane permeability of ion Y;

Action Potential

Action potentials, frequently referred to as 'neural spikes' or 'nerve impulses', can be arranged into electrical impulses or coordinated waves of brain function, are the way that the brain expresses information. Specific voltage gated ion channels produce them by activation. It happens when a particular cell location's membrane potential rapidly rises and lowers (Hodgkin et al., 1952). Following this depolarization, nearby areas also experience depolarization. Assisting in transmission of information along the axon leading towards synapses located in the axon terminals, which will subsequently link with its contemporaries, they play a crucial role in cell-cell communication. Their primary role in other cell types is to initiate intracellular activities. A neuron's "spike train" is the temporal series of action potentials it produces. It's common to refer to a neuron as "firing" when it releases an action potential or nerve impulse. Specialized voltage-gated ion channel subtypes implanted in the plasma membrane of a cell produce action potentials brought by Barnett et al. (2007).

Determining if neurons interact using temporal pattern or rate is a crucial challenge in neuroscience (Gerstner, 2001). According to temporal encoding, a solitary spike neuron in a network with sigmoid function can take the role of thousands of hidden units (Gerstner, 2001). In contrast to discrete computation, an SNN operates in the continuous domain. As mentioned before, neurons may only check for activation when V_{mp} reaches the threshold, rather than every time they propagate. A signal generated by an active neuron is transmitted to other neurons that are linked, changing the e_{mp} of those neurons. The e_{mp} of a neuron determines its present state in a SNN (possibly modelled like differential equation). The membrane potential rises briefly after an input pulse and then starts to fall over time. These pulse sequences can be translated into numbers using encoding systems that account for both frequency and pulse duration. A NN utilizes additional data and provide superior processing capabilities by using the precise moment of the pulse occurrence. The output of the SNN method is continuous as opposed to the conventional ANN outputs, which are binary. Because pulse trains are difficult to read, encoding techniques like the ones mentioned above are required. However, van Wezel (2020) showed processing spatiotemporal data may be better served by a pulse train representation. By selectively linking nearby neurons, SNNs take into account space as they evaluate inputs independently. In order to avoid information loss during binary encoding, they take time into consideration by encoding data as pulse trains. This prevents the recurrent neural network's added complexity. It turns out that compared to conventional artificial neurons, pulse neurons discussed by Maass (1997) are more potent processors.

Existing Spiking Neuron Models

Spiking neuron model is a term used to describe a neuron model that fire right the instant of thresholding. In this section we discuss some existing neuron models.

Hodgkin-Huxley Model

A mathematical model which depicts the formation and propagation of action potential in neurons is the Hodgkin et al. (1952) model, often known as the conductance-based model. An approximate representation of the electrical properties of excitable cells is provided by a set of nonlinear differential equations. For understanding ionic mechanisms behind the start and spread of them, Alan Hodgkin and Andrew Huxley developed the model in 1952.

Figure 3. Fundamental constituents of Hodgkin-Huxley model

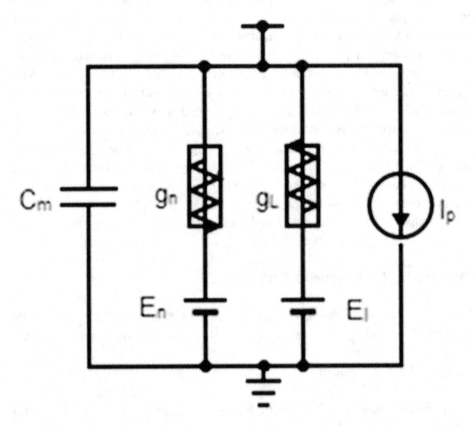

The basic components in the model are described in Figure 3. Here capacitance C_m is the lipid bilayer. The two channels are (i) voltage gated ion channels; (ii) leaky channels, which is represented by g_n (electrical conductance) and g_1 (linear conductance) respectively. E_n and E_1 are the voltage sources representing electrochemical gradients that direct the flow of ions. I_p is the current source representing ion pumps. With reference to above context, V_{mp} is the membrane potential. Mathematically, the passing current in lipid bilayer is given by

$$I_c = C_m (dV_{mp}/dt) \tag{2}$$

and current for a specific ion channel will be the multiplication of conductance of the ion channel with driving potential

$$I_i = g_i (V_{mp} - V_i) \tag{3}$$

{\displaystyle I_{i}={g_{i}}(V_{m}-V_{i})\;}

where V_i = reversal potential. The total current passing the membrane for Na and K channels is given by

$$I_{tot} = C_m \, (dV_{mp}/dt) + g_K \, (V_{mp} - V_K) + g_{Na} \, (V_{mp} - V_{Na}) + g_l \, (V_{mp} - V_l) \tag{4}$$

where I_{tot} = total membrane current per unit area;

C_m = membrane capacitance per unit area;
g_K and g_{Na} = conductance per unit area for potassium and sodium;
V_K and V_{Na} = reversal potential of potassium and sodium;
g_l and V_l = leak conductance per unit area and leak reversal potential.

Perfect Integrate and Fire

This model, also known as the non-leaky integrate-and-fire model, was initially studied by Abbott (1999). This neuron model is among the earliest ones. The membrane voltage V_m of a neuron, which changes over time when stimulated by an input current I_t according to

$$I_t = C(dV_{mp}/dt) \tag{5}$$

Eqn. (5) id derivative of capacitance law with respect to time, $Q = CV$. Initially input is fed trough then the e_{mp} rises gradually for a time period tillthe value exceeds the constant threshold V_{th}, at that point the model resumes operation after a spike in the delta function resets the voltage to its resting potential. Thus, increase in input current, rises the model's firing frequency linearly and without bound.

The addition of a refractory period t_{ref}, which prevents neurons from firing during that time, can improve the model's accuracy by limiting each neuron's firing frequency. The threshold voltage is attained for constant input $I_t = I$ after an integration time $t_{int} = CV_{th}/I$ following a zero start. The refractory period introduces a dead time after a reset, making the total duration until the subsequent firing $t_{ref} + t_{int}$. The firing frequency in reference to steady input current is given by

$$f(I) = \frac{I}{CVth + trefI} \tag{6}$$

This model's limitation is that it does not account for either adaptation or leakage. Suppose this approach ever encounters lower threshold brief current spike, it holds onto that voltage boost indefinitely, waiting till some other input causes it to ignite later. Said trait obviously doesn't correspond to observable neural behaviour. The integrate-and-fire paradigm is strengthened by the ensuing expansions, which increase its biological plausibility.

Leaky Integrate and Fire Model

The Abbott (1999) model is one where input current is integrated with respect to time till membrane potential exceeds a threshold without accounting for the behaviour of biological ion channels. This model adds a "leak" term to the IF model to reflect the ion diffusion that takes place via the membrane when a certain level of cell equilibrium is not reached. The LIF model and its variations are one of the most popular applications of the spiking neuron model due to its simplicity and low processing cost. The model is given by Gerstner et al. (2002) in the corresponding equation:

$$C_m (dv_m/dt) = I_t - v_m (t)/ R_m \qquad (7)$$

where v_m = voltage across the cell membrane;
R_m = membrane resistance.

Until a threshold V_{th} is reached, the model equation holds true for any time-dependent input; beyond that, the e_{mp} is reset. $I_{th} = V_{th} / R_m$ is the minimal input required to pass the threshold for constant input. Assume zero reset, the firing frequency is given by Koch et al. (1998):

$$f(I) = \begin{cases} 0, & I \leq I_{th} \\ \left[t_{ref} - R_m C_m \log\left(1 - \dfrac{V_{th}}{IR_m}\right)\right]^{-1}, & I > I_{th} \end{cases} \qquad (8)$$

The model's major drawback is that it lacks neural adaptation, making it unable to explain an experimentally measured spike pattern in response to constant input current. This drawback is eliminated in Fuortes et al. (1962) generalised integrate-and-fire models that can accurately forecast the spike timings of cortical neurons under current injection and also include one or more adaptation-variables.

Adaptive Integrate and Fire

Neuronal adaptation is the process through which the intervals between output spikes lengthen when a steady current flows to soma. The leaky assimilation of voltage together with more than one adaptation variables w_k lay the foundation forGerstner, W. et al. (2014) adaptive integrate-and-fire neuron model.

$$\tau_m (dV_m(t)/dt) = RI_t - [V_m(t) - E_m] - R\sum_k \alpha_k \quad (9)$$

$$\tau_k (d\alpha_k(t)/dt) = -a_k[V_m(t) - E_m] - \alpha_k + b_k\alpha_k\sum_f \delta(t - t^f) \quad (10)$$

where τ_m = membrane time constant;

α_k = adaptation current number, where k = index;
τ_k = time constant of adaptation current w_k;
E_m = resting potential;
t^f = firing time of the neuron;
δ = Dirac delta function.

Whenever the voltage reaches the firing threshold the voltage is reset to a value V_r below the firing threshold.

Fractional-Order Leaky Integrate and Fire

A whole new category of approach recognised as fractional-order leaky integrate-and-fire has emerged as a result of significant progress in theoretical and computational fractional calculus. It's advantageous that this approach can account for adaption effects using just one variable. It is given by Teka et al. (2014):

$$I(t) - \frac{V_m(t)}{R_m} = C_m \frac{d^\alpha V_m(t)}{d^\alpha t} \quad (11)$$

SNN in Robotic Applications

Locomotion/Pattern Generation

Donati et al. (2014) investigated whether the sCPG modules might be implemented on a VLSI system with FPGA. This neural model was connected to the lamprey robot's robotic actuator. This research demonstrated how to give robot locomotion control that is both reliable and decentralized. They examined the model's software as well as its real-time application. Here, the idea of sensor feedback was not used. Future works could be implemented in Printed Circuit Board. A SpiNNaker hardware circuit was used to develop, test and validate the sCPG with PyNeural Network software by Cuevas-Arteaga et al. (2017). The model was designed for three different methods of locomotion for hexapod robot. Spatial-temporal effectiveness and energy usage were enhanced and in the future the work could be extended to other robotic types. Similar to the Cuevas-Arteaga et al. (2017), Gutierrez-Galan et al. (2020) also implemented sCPGusing the same hardware board for hexapod robots in real time with the same locomotive gaits as in Gutierrez-Galan et al. (2020). They used only 30 neurons in their work. Future works include using an audio sensor or voice commands to change the locomotive gait. The same hexapod robot was used by Strohmer et al. (2020) to simulate the results in NEST. This research demonstrated that a steady gait may be maintained with a design that does not require receptive feedback. Additionally, it made it possible to study on how high-level control signals and sensor input affect how gait types evolve. The implementation of a SCPG using neuromorphic hardware to imitate swimming and control the lamprey robot in this work Angelidis et al. (2021) depended on SpiNNaker and Loihi. Linares-Barranco et al. (2022) demonstrated a Winner Take All circuit that has been integrated into an SNN to generate real-time patterns for operating a robotic arm. A commanded joint position is maintained by the robotic arm using SPID (spike-based proportional integrative derivative) controllers using the winners among the neurons. Observational study showed that robotic control via spiking circuits in response to brain inspiration is possible. In Pardo-Cabrera et al. (2022), a virtual hexapod robot was guided and controlled by a system that draws inspiration from biology employed in ROS simulated through Gazebo. Their navigation and exploration system's modules handled the robot's orientation adjustment, path interoperability, action selection, and actuation. By mimicking brain to acquire feedback signals and produce motion control directives, Lopez-Osorio et al. (2022) proposed a sCPG to operate aquatic robots. Consequently, the hybrid locomotion control system performed well. Wang et al. (2022) created various locomotor patterns that were influenced by an outside input, such as the output of an FSR sensor that provides feedback. Employing the SpiNNaker and Brian 2, its adaptation has been quantitatively confirmed at both the hardware and software levels. Implementations had similar behaviour, as indicated by a 0.905 Pearson correlation coefficient.

Localization

Tang et al. (2018) designed an autonomous robot named gridbot, that used neurons from leaky integrate and fire synaptic model. Particularly, the developed SNN generated motorized orders to govern the robot's movement and maps to encode sensory data collected from arbitrary locations in ROS (Robotic Operating System). These maps were for designing effective routes to objectives in the coming days, in addition to helping the robot navigate its surroundings without running into obstacles. Bing et al. (2019) feed the controlling technique for model as a database for training the SNN in the hardware, for moulding the required behaviour of the gridbot. It one of the quickest ways to SNN controller for robot applications. By merely changing the inputs sent into the network and slightly changing how the prize was allocated for output neurons, two SNNs learned to show the target outcome, and the robot was capable of traveling to a previously set target region while avoiding obstacles. The effect of increasing the number of hidden layers on training and performance has not yet been thoroughly investigated in our study using more output neurons. Tang et al. (2019) put out a SNN architecture modelled after the human brain that linked their GMapping algorithm with Loihi's Gazebo simulation. While having similar accuracy for localization and map construction, the prescribed model used 100% less energy than when performed on a CPU. Alternative to deep reinforcement learning (DRL), Tang et al. (2020) proposed an integrated approach of SNN with DRL, SDDPG. Loihi processor was employed for validation and achieved 1% to 4.2% navigation. Tang (2022) created an SNN, that built real time maps, and contributed to research on the interconnectedness of neurons and cognitive processes. They used 140 time less energy when compared to the existing methods.

Motor Control

Stagsted et al. (2020) realized a modified PID controller on Loihi chip and was validated using a drone. Here both the sensing and controlling signals were passed in a single spike. The frequency and latency of the PID was increased by the modification. Dupeyroux et al. (2021) demonstrated a fully embedded Loihi hardware application embedded inside a flying robot using PySNN simulation and Loihi processor implementation. There was 99.8% sequence matching for spikes in hidden layer, along with a 99.7% matching in the output layer, the root mean square error value was 0.005 g. Table 1 summarizes the literature done over the past few years.

Table 1. Some application of SNN in robotics

Ref	Robot Type	Application	Hardware	Software	Synaptic Model
26	lamprey	Locomotion/ Pattern generator	FPGA	-	Adaptive Exponential Integrate and Fire
27	hexapod		SpiNNaker	PyNN	Leaky integrate and fire
28	neuropod/ hexapod		SpiNNaker	-	Leaky integrate and fire
29	tripod		-	NEST	-
30	lamprey		SpiNNaker, Loihi	Nengo	-
31	-		FPGA	-	Exponential or linear Integrate and Fire
32	virtual hexapod		ROS	Gazebo	-
34	-		SpiNNaker	Brian 2	Leaky integrate and fire
35	gridbot	Navigation	ROS	Gazebo	Leaky integrate and fire
36	-		Kapoho-Bay USB chipset	-	Leaky integrate and fire
37	-		Loihi	Gazebo	-
38	SDDPG		Loihi	Pytorch	Leaky integrate and fire
40	Modified PID controller	Controller	Loihi	Nengo	-
41	Flying robot		Loihi	PySNN	-

CONCLUSION

Spiking neural networks have demonstrated considerable promise for reaching improved robotic intelligence by more accurately simulating the inner workings of the brain. The multi-layer training of spiking networks has advanced significantly. The selection of benchmark data sources used to test deep SNN is a good indicator of success. Therefore, we provide the literature about robotic applications such as locomotion/ pattern generator, localization, and motor control. We present the necessary fundamental theory on biological neurons. Then we discuss the background of biologically inspired spiking neural networks. Then some light was shed on some of the existing neuron models applicable for SNN. Finally, we provide a literature summary on the popular works carried out in the past few years.

REFERENCES

Abbott, L. F. (1999). Lapicque's introduction of the integrate-and-fire model neuron (1907). *Brain Research Bulletin, 50*(5-6), 303–304. doi:10.1016/S0361-9230(99)00161-6 PMID:10643408

Angelidis, E., Buchholz, E., Arreguit, J., Rougé, A., Stewart, T., von Arnim, A., Knoll, A., & Ijspeert, A. (2021). A spiking central pattern generator for the control of a simulated lamprey robot running on SpiNNaker and Loihi neuromorphic boards. *Neuromorphic Computing and Engineering, 1*(1), 014005. doi:10.1088/2634-4386/ac1b76

Barnett, M. W., & Larkman, P. M. (2007). The action potential. *Practical Neurology, 7*(3), 192–197. doi:10.1136/jnnp.2006.104982 PMID:17515599

Bing, Z., Baumann, I., Jiang, Z., Huang, K., Cai, C., & Knoll, A. (2019). Supervised learning in SNN via reward-modulated spike-timing-dependent plasticity for a target reaching vehicle. *Frontiers in Neurorobotics, 13*, 18. doi:10.3389/fnbot.2019.00018 PMID:31130854

Cuevas-Arteaga, B., Dominguez-Morales, J. P., Rostro-Gonzalez, H., Espinal, A., Jimenez-Fernandez, A. F., Gomez-Rodriguez, F., & Linares-Barranco, A. (2017). A SpiNNaker application: design, implementation and validation of SCPGs. In *International work-conference on artificial neural networks* (pp. 548–559). Springer. doi:10.1007/978-3-319-59153-7_50

Donati, E., Corradi, F., Stefanini, C., & Indiveri, G. (2014). A spiking implementation of the lamprey's Central Pattern Generator in neuromorphic VLSI. In 2014 IEEE Biomedical Circuits and Systems Conference (BioCAS) Proceedings (pp. 512-515). IEEE. https://doi.org/10.1109/BioCAS.2014.6981775

Dupeyroux, J., Hagenaars, J. J., Paredes-Vallés, F., & de Croon, G. C. (2021, May). Neuromorphic control for optic-flow-based landing of MAVs using the Loihi processor. In *2021 IEEE International Conference on Robotics and Automation (ICRA)* (pp. 96-102). IEEE. 10.1109/ICRA48506.2021.9560937

Fukushima, K. (1988). Neocognitron: A hierarchical neural network capable of visual pattern recognition. *Neural Networks, 1*(2), 119–130. doi:10.1016/0893-6080(88)90014-7

Fuortes, M. G. F., & Mantegazzini, F. (1962). Interpretation of the repetitive firing of nerve cells. *The Journal of General Physiology, 45*(6), 1163–1179. doi:10.1085/jgp.45.6.1163 PMID:13895926

Gerstner, W. (2001). What is different with spiking neurons? In W. Gerstner, A. Germond, M. Hasler, & J.-D. Nicoud (Eds.), *Plausible neural networks for biological modelling* (pp. 23–48). Springer. doi:10.1007/978-94-010-0674-3_2

Gerstner, W., & Kistler, W. M. (2002). *Spiking neuron models: Single neurons, populations, plasticity*. Cambridge University Press. doi:10.1017/CBO9780511815706

Gerstner, W., Kistler, W. M., Naud, R., & Paninski, L. (2014). *Neuronal dynamics: From single neurons to networks and models of cognition*. Cambridge University Press. doi:10.1017/CBO9781107447615

Goodfellow, I., Bengio, Y., & Courville, A. (2016). *Deep learning*. MIT Press.

Grüning, A., & Bohte, S. M. (2014). Spiking neural networks: Principles and challenges. In ESANN.

Gutierrez-Galan, D., Dominguez-Morales, J. P., Perez-Peña, F., Jimenez-Fernandez, A., & Linares-Barranco, A. (2020). NeuroPod: A real-time neuromorphic spiking CPG applied to robotics. *Neurocomputing*, *381*, 10–19. doi:10.1016/j.neucom.2019.11.007

Hodgkin, A. L., & Huxley, A. F. (1952). A quantitative description of membrane current and its application to conduction and excitation in nerve. *The Journal of Physiology*, *117*(4), 500–544. doi:10.1113/jphysiol.1952.sp004764 PMID:12991237

Koch, C., & Segev, I. (Eds.). (1998). *Methods in neuronal modeling: From ions to networks*. MIT Press.

LeCun, Y., Bengio, Y., & Hinton, G. (2015). Deep learning. *Nature*, *521*(7553), 436–444. doi:10.1038/nature14539 PMID:26017442

Lichtsteiner, P., Posch, C., & Delbruck, T. (2008). A 128×128 120 dB 15 μs latency asynchronous temporal contrast vision sensor. *IEEE Journal of Solid-State Circuits*, *43*(2), 566–576. doi:10.1109/JSSC.2007.914337

Linares-Barranco, A., Pinero-Fuentes, E., Canas-Moreno, S., Rios-Navarro, A., Wu, C., Zhao, J., & Indiveri, G. (2022). *Towards hardware Implementation of WTA for CPG-based control of a Spiking Robotic Arm*. arXiv preprint arXiv:2202.07064. doi:10.1109/ISCAS48785.2022.9937845

Lopez-Osorio, P., Patiño-Saucedo, A., Dominguez-Morales, J. P., Rostro-Gonzalez, H., & Perez-Peña, F. (2022). Neuromorphic adaptive spiking CPG towards bio-inspired locomotion. *Neurocomputing*, *502*, 57–70. doi:10.1016/j.neucom.2022.06.085

Maass, W. (1997). Networks of spiking neurons: The third generation of neural network models. *Neural Networks, 10*(9), 1659–1671. doi:10.1016/S0893-6080(97)00011-7

Medical Xpress. (2018). Neuron axons are so spindly, they're optimizing for speed. *Medical Xpress.* https://medicalxpress.com/news/2018-07-neuron-axons-spindly-theyre-optimizing.html

Mohamed, S. A., Othman, M., & Afifi, M. H. (2019). A review on data clustering using spiking neural network (SNN) models. *Indonesian Journal of Electrical Engineering and Computer Science, 15*(3), 1392. doi:10.11591/ijeecs.v15.i3.pp1392-1400

Pardo-Cabrera, J., Rivero-Ortega, J. D., Hurtado-López, J., & Ramírez-Moreno, D. F. (2022). Bio-inspired navigation and exploration system for a hexapod robotic platform. *Engineering Research Express, 4*(2), 025019. doi:10.1088/2631-8695/ac6bde

Ponulak, F., & Kasinski, A. (2011). Introduction to spiking neural networks: Information processing, learning and applications. *Acta Neurobiologiae Experimentalis, 71*(4), 409–433. PMID:22237491

Riesenhuber, M., & Poggio, T. (1999). Hierarchical models of object recognition in cortex. *Nature Neuroscience, 2*(11), 1019–1025. doi:10.1038/14819 PMID:10526343

Schmidhuber, J. (2015). Deep learning in neural networks: An overview. *Neural Networks, 61*, 85–117. doi:10.1016/j.neunet.2014.09.003 PMID:25462637

Stagsted, R. K., Vitale, A., Renner, A., Larsen, L. B., Christensen, A. L., & Sandamirskaya, Y. (2020, October). Event-based PID controller fully realized in neuromorphic hardware: a one DoF study. In *2020 IEEE/RSJ International Conference on Intelligent Robots and Systems (IROS)* (pp. 10939-10944). IEEE. 10.1109/IROS45743.2020.9340861

Strickholm, A. ((1981). Ionic permeability of K, Na, and Cl in potassium-depolarized nerve. Dependency on pH, cooperative effects, and action of tetrodotoxin. *Biophysical Journal, 35*(3), 677–697. doi:10.1016/S0006-3495(81)84820-5 PMID:7272457

Strohmer, B., Manoonpong, P., & Larsen, L. B. (2020). Flexible spiking cpgs for online manipulation during hexapod walking. *Frontiers in Neurorobotics, 14*, 41. doi:10.3389/fnbot.2020.00041 PMID:32676022

Tang, G. (2022). *Biologically Inspired Spiking Neural Networks for Energy-Efficient Robot Learning and Control* [Doctoral dissertation, School of Graduate Studies Rutgers, The State University of New Jersey]. ProQuest Dissertations Publishing. (15295701)

Tang, G., Kumar, N., & Michmizos, K. P. (2020, October). Reinforcement co-learning of deep and spiking neural networks for energy-efficient mapless navigation with neuromorphic hardware. In *2020 IEEE/RSJ International Conference on Intelligent Robots and Systems (IROS)* (pp. 6090-6097). IEEE. 10.1109/IROS45743.2020.9340948

Tang, G., & Michmizos, K. P. (2018, July). Gridbot: An autonomous robot controlled by a spiking neural network mimicking the brain's navigational system. In *Proceedings of the International Conference on Neuromorphic Systems* (pp. 1-8). IEEE. 10.1145/3229884.3229888

Tang, G., Shah, A., & Michmizos, K. P. (2019, November). Spiking neural network on neuromorphic hardware for energy-efficient unidimensional slam. In *2019 IEEE/RSJ International Conference on Intelligent Robots and Systems (IROS)* (pp. 4176-4181). IEEE. 10.1109/IROS40897.2019.8967864

Teka, W., Marinov, T. M., & Santamaria, F. (2014). Neuronal spike timing adaptation described with a fractional leaky integrate-and-fire model. *PLoS Computational Biology*, *10*(3), e1003526. doi:10.1371/journal.pcbi.1003526 PMID:24675903

van Wezel, M. (2020). A robust modular spiking neural networks training methodology for time-series datasets: With a focus on gesture control. https://doi.org/ doi:10.31234/osf.io/x7v3q

Wang, M., Zhang, Y., & Yu, J. (2022). An SNN-CPG Hybrid Locomotion Control for Biomimetic Robotic Fish. *Journal of Intelligent & Robotic Systems*, *105*(2), 1–25. doi:10.100710846-022-01664-7

Conclusion

The book *Neuromorphic Computing Systems for Industry 4.0* explores the applications and implications of neuromorphic computing in the context of the fourth industrial revolution, commonly referred to as Industry 4.0. The book provides a comprehensive overview of neuromorphic computing, which is a branch of artificial intelligence (AI) that mimics the structure and functionality of the human brain.

Throughout the book, the authors delve into the various ways in which neuromorphic computing can revolutionize Industry 4.0. They highlight the potential of this technology to enable advanced automation, intelligent decision-making, and enhanced efficiency in industrial processes. By leveraging the parallel and distributed computing capabilities of neuromorphic systems, industries can optimize resource allocation, improve predictive maintenance, and streamline their operations.

Moreover, the book discusses the integration of neuromorphic computing with other emerging technologies, such as the Internet of Things (IoT), big data analytics, and robotics. It explores the synergy between these technologies and the transformative impact they can have on Industry 4.0. The authors emphasize the potential of neuromorphic systems to process large volumes of data in real-time, enabling intelligent and adaptive systems that can continuously learn and improve.

Chapter 1 discusses the overview of neuromorphic computing, including emerging memory devices and emerging technologies used in neuromorphic circuits. Although much of the effort in neuromorphic computing has focused on hardware development and emerging technologies will be critical for the growth of computing. The extensive study shows that deep learning transforms the job at a dynamic speed with a vision to produce intelligent software that can replicate it and work like a human brain.

Chapter 2 explored the multifaceted aspects of neuromorphic computing, from the fundamental understanding of materials properties to the practical considerations of manufacturability. The development of materials properties has been instrumental in creating novel materials with desired electrical and synaptic properties, enabling the realization of efficient and reliable neuromorphic devices. The understanding of device physics has deepened our knowledge of the underlying mechanisms and behaviours of these devices, facilitating their optimized design and operation.

Chapter 3 discusses the hardware accelerator for identifying human emotions through audio data. By employing the potential memory candidate RRAM as the computation unit, the performance of the accelerator has been improved significantly. The result shows that with swish activation and the FDSOI technology, the training efficiency and acceleration has increased when compared with other memristor based neuromorphic accelerators and off-shelf CPU device. However, the misclassification rate of the proposed model is 20.7% for the trained samples which can further be reduced by running rigorous training for multiple epochs. This accelerator can further be employed to test different speech-based applications.

Chapter 4 provides a concise review of digital and pulsed neuro hardware. The work presented discusses the unique strategy for optimum multi-objective optimization for VLSI implementation of Artificial Neural Network (ANN). It has been noticed that the software implementation of ANN requires a significant amount of time in order to learn a specific example owing to the nature of recurrent training. The implementation of NN in hardware, on the other hand, may speed up the training by many orders of magnitude, which is why VLSI implementation receives the attention it does. The presented work indicates that t it is possible to create integrated BNN by making use of APSoC in FPGA. Even if the system operates well, there is always space for advancement in terms of throughput as well as energy efficiency. The goal of this research is to find the sweet spot where area, speed, and power may all be optimised in a very large scale integration (VLSI) implementation of a neural network (NN). The design should also allow for the dynamic reconfiguration of weight, and it should be very precise. We also use a 65-nm CMOS fabrication method to produce the circuits, and our results show that the suggested integral stochastic design may reduce energy consumption by up to 21% compared to the binary radix implementation, without sacrificing accuracy.

Chapter 5 presents the approach to detect the skin diseases based upon the VLSI implementation on image processing as well as machine learning techniques i.e., Convolutional Neural Networks (CNN). CNN is a specific type of neural network model that allows us to extract higher depictions for the image content. This work represents a better edge catching technique along with a low complex sharp filter. The hardware complexity was reduced with the help of bilinear interpolation equation. The edges of the targeted spot were reduced with the help of adaptive edge enhancing technique. The study show that deep learning approach can handle both generative and descriptive tasks. Machine learning makes it possible to make both batch and real-time predictions. Instead of starting with the raw pixel data from the image and heavily training the model, as is required by conventional image recognition techniques, CNN starts with the raw pixel data from the image and unintentionally extracts features for better organisation.

Chapter 6 briefs the energy and performance analysis of robotic applications using Artificial Neural Network (ANN). Existing Artificial Intelligence focuses on either computation performance improvement or energy consumption minimization. . To make a viable robot, it is essential to have knowledge in neoscience, electronics, and computer science. Neuromorphic robot system can be built using software and hardware chips. Understanding the architecture and computational capabilities of various neuromorphic chips is important.

Chapter 7 propose a bike-sharing solution in which all processes from membership registration to bike rental and return are automated. These findings represents that designing efficient VLSI architectures to accurately predict the impact of different attributes. Among the various ML algorithms, Random Forest proves to be the most suitable choice for this type of dataset, allowing us to identify the relative importance of attributes. However, when dealing with large datasets exceeding 10 million samples, the implementation of Random Forest using sklearn may encounter performance challenges. The computational cost and memory constraints can hinder its efficiency. In such scenarios, it is recommended to explore alternative solutions, such as leveraging the Python Woodley implementation. This implementation utilizes top tree pre-classification and distributed sampling, optimizing the VLSI hardware implementation by employing C programming. To further enhance scalability and performance, machine learning frameworks like Apache Spark ML can be employed. This allows for distributed computation utilizing computer clustering and accessing data from popular Apache databases like Apache Cassandra. Leveraging the power of Spark ML on frameworks such as Kubernetes, Apache Mesos, or Hadoop can significantly accelerate the processing speed, enabling efficient VLSI implementation for large-scale datasets.

Chapter 8 indicates the CNN-based finger-vein authentication technique. The method is compared to previously existing conventional based methods for accurate recognition. Three algorithms were implemented in this study (CNN, Gradient boosting, K-means). Other than implementing three algorithms for finger vein based biometric identification, an image's GLCM features were also extracted. It is the technique of obtaining higher-level features of an image, like texture, colour, and contrast. In actuality, texture analysis is an important part of both human and machine sensory acuity. It is effectively used to boost the reliability of the diagnostics system by identifying significant features.

Chapter 9, partial reconfiguration refers to the ability to dynamically modify a portion of a Field-Programmable Gate Array (FPGA) design while the remaining portions continue to operate. This capability can be leveraged to implement neural networks in a digital system, allowing for flexibility and efficient use of FPGA resources. In the context of neural networks, partial reconfiguration enables the dynamic modification of network architectures or parameters to adapt to changing requirements or input data. Partial reconfiguration can be used for experimenting with different activation functions and compare their performance in the same FPGA device without the need for full reconfiguration. This can save time and resources in the design process and allow for more efficient optimization. The weight selection in Artificial Neural Networks (ANN), refers to the process of determining the values of the weights, which are the parameters that connect the neurons in the network. The weights control the information flow in the network. It is playing a critical role in accurate predictions and in the learning ability of network. The techniques use for design protection, further enrich the device behavior to predict fault free results.

Chapter 10 examine the security issues and potential solutions in the computing hardware for deep neural networks (DNN). The most recent hardware-based attacks against DNN are discussed, with a focus on side-channel analysis (SCA), fault injection, and hardware Trojan insertion (HT). In conclusion, attacks by hardware Trojans pose serious risks to the security and reliability of neural networks. These malicious modifications or additions in the hardware can undermine the functionality, introduce biases, compromise data integrity, and provide unauthorized access to sensitive information. As neural networks become increasingly prevalent in critical applications, it is crucial to develop robust security measures to detect and mitigate hardware Trojan attacks. Hardware authentication, verification techniques, and trust management mechanisms are essential to ensure the integrity and trustworthiness of the hardware platforms hosting neural networks.

Chapter 11 presented a new SNN architecture for robot control that is inspired by the mammalian brain. This architecture is composed of an input layer, a hidden layer, and an output layer. The input layer receives input spike trains from sensors, the hidden layer performs computations on these inputs, and the output layer produces motor commands. This architecture is capable of performing a variety of tasks, including obstacle avoidance, path planning, and navigation. We have reviewed the feasibility of this approach by implementing it on a robot platform. This architecture has the potential to be used in a wide range of applications, including autonomous vehicles, service robots, and prosthetic devices. After studying the feasibility of using a spiking neural network (SNN) for robot control, it was concluded that SNN is a promising approach for this application. The SNN was found to be able to learn the desired control task and produce accurate and robust control signals. This makes SNN a promising candidate for real-time applications such as robot control. Biological systems have demonstrated many efficient ways to process and control information.

Chapter 12 demonstrated that Spiking neural networks have considerable promise for reaching improved robotic intelligence by more accurately simulating the inner workings of the brain. The multi-layer training of spiking networks has advanced significantly. The selection of benchmark data sources used to test deep SNN is a good indicator of success.

The book *Neuromorphic Computing Systems for Industry 4.0* provides a comprehensive exploration of the potential applications and benefits of neuromorphic computing in the context of the fourth industrial revolution. It highlights how this technology can enable intelligent and adaptive systems, revolutionize industrial processes, and pave the way for a more efficient and productive future in various industries. The book serves as a valuable resource for researchers, practitioners, and decision-makers interested in understanding and harnessing the power of neuromorphic computing for Industry 4.0.

Compilation of References

Abayomi-Alli, O. O., Damasevicius, R., Misra, S., Maskeliunas, R., & Abayomi-Alli, A. (2021). Malignant Skin Melanoma Detection Using Image Augmentation by Oversampling in Nonlinear Lower-Dimensional Embedding Manifold. *Turkish Journal of Electrical Engineering and Computer Sciences*, *29*(SI-1), 2600–2614. doi:10.3906/elk-2101-133

Abbott, L. F. (1999). Lapicque's introduction of the integrate-and-fire model neuron (1907). *Brain Research Bulletin*, *50*(5-6), 303–304. doi:10.1016/S0361-9230(99)00161-6 PMID:10643408

Abdelhalim I.S.A., Mohamed, M.F., & Mahdy, Y.B. (2021). Data Augmentation for Skin Lesion Using Self-Attention Based Progressive Generative Adversarial Network. *Expert Syst With Appl*. doi:.2020.113922 doi:10.1016/j.eswa

Abdelwahab, M., & Busso, C. (2015). Supervised domain adaptation for emotion recognition from speech. *IEEE International Conference on Acoustics, Speech and Signal Processing (ICASSP)*, (pp. 5058-5062). IEEE. 10.1109/ICASSP.2015.7178934

Adarsh, S., & Ramachandran, K. I. (2020). Neuro-fuzzy based fusion of LiDAR and ultrasonic sensors to minimize error in range estimation for the navigation of mobile robots. *Intelligent Decision Technologies*, *14*(2), 259–267. doi:10.3233/IDT-180109

Agarap, A. F. (2008). *Deep Learning using Rectified Linear Units (ReLU) 1*. Arxiv., https://arxiv.org/abs/1803.08375

Ahmad, B., Jun, S., Palade, V., You, Q., Mao, L., & Zhongjie, M. (2021). Improving Skin Cancer Classification Using Heavy-Tailed Student T-Distribution in Generative Adversarial Networks (Ted-Gan). *Diagnostics (Basel)*, *11*(11), 2147. doi:10.3390/diagnostics11112147 PMID:34829494

Ahmed, L. J. (2022). A Survey of IoT Based Pregnancy Woman Health Monitoring System. *2022 8th International Conference on Advanced Computing and Communication Systems (ICACCS)*. IEEE. 10.1109/ICACCS54159.2022.9785324

Ahmed, L. J. (2018). Discrete Shearlet Transform Based Speckle Noise Removal in Ultrasound Images. *National Academy Science Letters*, *41*(2), 91–95. doi:10.100740009-018-0620-7

Akhtar, N., & Mian, A. S. (2018). Threat of Adversarial Attacks on Deep Learning in Computer Vision: A Survey. *IEEE Access : Practical Innovations, Open Solutions*, *6*, 14410–14430. doi:10.1109/ACCESS.2018.2807385

Alaghi, A., Li, C., & Hayes, J. P. (2013). Stochastic circuits for real-time image-processing applications. In *Proc. 50th ACM/EDAC/IEEE Design Autom. Conf. (DAC)* (pp. 1–6). ACM.

Amirany, A., Moaiyeri, M. H., & Jafari, K. (2022). Nonvolatile Associative Memory Design Based on Spintronic Synapses and CNTFET Neurons. *IEEE Transactions on Emerging Topics in Computing*, *10*(1), 428–437. doi:10.1109/TETC.2020.3026179

Anand, M. D., Selvaraj, T., & Kumanan, S. (2007). Parameter identification of robot arm using artificial neural networks. In *National Conference on Computational Intelligence* (p. 1). IEEE.

Angelidis, E., Buchholz, E., Arreguit, J., Rougé, A., Stewart, T., von Arnim, A., Knoll, A., & Ijspeert, A. (2021). A spiking central pattern generator for the control of a simulated lamprey robot running on SpiNNaker and Loihi neuromorphic boards. *Neuromorphic Computing and Engineering*, *1*(1), 014005. doi:10.1088/2634-4386/ac1b76

Arbib, M. A. (Ed.). (2002). *The Handbook of Brain Theory and Neural Networks* (2nd ed.). MIT Press. doi:10.7551/mitpress/3413.001.0001

Armando C. W., Stamatis K. & Thomas B. (2014). Towards the Next Generation of Industrial Cyber-Physical Systems. *Industrial Cloud-Based Cyber-Physical Systems*, 1–22.

Arunkumar. (2022). *A Survey on IoT-based Hand Hygiene Dispenser with Temperature and Level Monitoring Systems.* 8th International Conference on Advanced Computing and Communication Systems (ICACCS). Coimbatore, India. . doi:10.1109/ICACCS54159.2022.9785176

Arunkumar, N., & Dhanasekar, S. (2020, November). An Ultra-Low-Power Static Random-Access Memory Cell Using Tunneling Field Effect Transistor. *International Journal of Engineering*, *33*(11). Advance online publication. doi:10.5829/ije.2020.33.11b.13

Arunkumar, N., Senathipathi, N., Dhanasekar, S., Malin Bruntha, P., & Priya, C. (2020). An ultra-low-power static random-access memory cell using tunneling field effect transistor. *International Journal of Engineering*, *33*(11), 2215–2221.

Ashika, S. V., Sivamangai, N. M., Naveenkumar, R., & Napolean, A. (2023). Importance of Logic Locking Attacks in Hardware Security. *2023 International Conference on Intelligent Data Communication Technologies and Internet of Things (IDCIoT)*, (pp. 156-160). IEEE. 10.1109/IDCIoT56793.2023.10052782

Ashokkumar, N., & Pappa, C. K. (2023). *Certain Investigation of Optimization Methods of Sensor Nodes in Biomedical Recording Systems.* 2023 9th International Conference on Advanced Computing and Communication Systems (ICACCS), Coimbatore, India. 10.1109/ICACCS57279.2023.10112688

Azimirad, V., Ramezanlou, M. T., Sotubadi, S. V., & Janabi-Sharifi, F. (2022). A consecutive hybrid spiking-convolutional (CHSC) neural controller for sequential decision making in robots. *Neurocomputing*, *490*, 319–336. doi:10.1016/j.neucom.2021.11.097

Azizi, A. (2020). Applications of artificial intelligence techniques to enhance sustainability of industry 4.0: Design of an artificial neural network model as dynamic behavior optimizer of robotic arms. *Complexity*, *2020*, 1–10. doi:10.1155/2020/8564140

Barnett, M. W., & Larkman, P. M. (2007). The action potential. *Practical Neurology*, *7*(3), 192–197. doi:10.1136/jnnp.2006.104982 PMID:17515599

Ben Abdallah, A., & Dang, N. (2022). Introduction to Neuromorphic Computing Systems. Neuromorphic Computing Principles and Organization. doi:10.1007/978-3-030-92525-3_1

Bercea, M. (2022). Bioinspired hydrogels as platforms for Life-Science applications: Challenges and opportunities. *Polymers*, *14*(12), 2365. doi:10.3390/polym14122365 PMID:35745941

Bing, Z., Baumann, I., Jiang, Z., Huang, K., Cai, C., & Knoll, A. (2019). Supervised learning in SNN via reward-modulated spike-timing-dependent plasticity for a target reaching vehicle. *Frontiers in Neurorobotics*, *13*, 18. doi:10.3389/fnbot.2019.00018 PMID:31130854

Bisla, D., Choromanska, A., Berman, R. S., Stein, J. A., & Polsky, D. (2019). Towards Automated Melanoma Detection With Deep Learning. *Data Purification and Augmentation. Proc IEEE/CVF Conf Comput Vision Pattern Recognit Workshops*. 10.1109/CVPRW.2019.00330

Bosker, B. (2017). *Affectiva's Emotion Recognition Tech: When Machines Know What You're Feeling*. The Huffington Post.

Bresnahan, T. F., Brynjolfsson, E., & Hitt, L. M. (2002). Information technology, workplace organisation, and the demand for skilled labour: Firm-level evidence. *The Quarterly Journal of Economics*, *117*(1), 339–376. doi:10.1162/003355302753399526

Brinker, T. J., Hekler, A., Utikal, J. S., Grabe, N., Schadendorf, D., Klode, J., Berking, C., Steeb, T., Enk, A. H., & von Kalle, C. (2018). Skin Cancer Classification Using Convolutional Neural Networks: Systematic Review. *Journal of Medical Internet Research*, *20*(10), e11936. doi:10.2196/11936 PMID:30333097

Bruntha, P. M., Dhanasekar, S., Ahmed, L. J., Khanna, D., Pandian, S. I. A., & Abraham, S. S. (2022). Investigation of Deep Features in Lung Nodule Classification. *2022 6th International Conference on Devices, Circuits and Systems (ICDCS)*. IEEE. 10.1109/ICDCS54290.2022.9780716

Bruntha, P. M., Dhanasekar, S., Hepsiba, D., Sagayam, K. M., Neebha, T. M., Pandey, D., & Pandey, B. K. (2022, September 5). *Application of switching median filter with L2 norm-based auto-tuning function for removing random valued impulse noise - Aerospace Systems*. Springer. https://link.springer.com/article/10.1007/s42401-022-00160-y

Bruntha, P., Malin, S. Dhanasekar, D. Hepsiba, K. Martin Sagayam, T. Neebha, M., Pandey, D., & Pandey, B. (2022). *Application of Switching Median Filter with L2 Norm-Based Auto-Tuning Function for Removing Random Valued Impulse Noise*. Aerospace Systems.

Bruntha, P. M., Dhanasekar, S., Hepsiba, D., Sagayam, K. M., Neebha, T. M., Pandey, D., & Pandey, B. K. (2023). Application of switching median filter with L 2 norm-based auto-tuning function for removing random valued impulse noise. *Aerospace Systems*, *6*(1), 53–59. doi:10.100742401-022-00160-y

Buchanan, M. (2015). Depths of learning. *Nature Physics*, *11*, 798–798.

Caballero, L., Perafan, Á., Rinaldy, M., & Percybrooks, W. (2021). Predicting the energy consumption of a robot in an exploration task using optimized neural networks. *Electronics (Basel)*, *10*(8), 920. doi:10.3390/electronics10080920

Caridakis, G. (2007). Multimodal emotion recognition from expressive faces, body gestures and speech. In C. Boukis, A. Pnevmatikakis, & L. Polymenakos (Eds.), *Artificial Intelligence and Innovations 2007: from Theory to Applications. AIAI 2007. IFIP The International Federation for Information Processing* (Vol. 247). Springer. doi:10.1007/978-0-387-74161-1_41

Casanueva-Morato, D., Ayuso-Martinez, A., Dominguez-Morales, J. P., Jimenez-Fernandez, A., & Jimenez-Moreno, G. (2022). *Spike-based computational models of bio-inspired memories in the hippocampal CA3 region on SpiNNaker.* arXiv preprint arXiv:2205.04782.

Castro, P. B., Krohling, B., Pacheco, A. G., & Krohling, R. A. An App to Detect Melanoma Using Deep Learning: An Approach to Handle Imbalanced Data Based on Evolutionary Algorithms, in: *International Joint Conference on Neural Networks (IJCNN)*. Institute of Electrical and Electronics Engineers. 10.1109/IJCNN48605.2020.9207552

Catherine, G. (2019). *Use New Alexa Emotions and Speaking Styles to Create a More Natural and Intuitive Voice Experience.* Alexa Skills Kit Blog. Amazon Developer. https://developer.amazon.com/en-US/blogs/alexa/alexa-skills-kit/2019/11/new-alexa-emotions-and-speaking-styles.

Chakma, G., Skuda, N. D., Schuman, C. D., Plank, J. S., Dean, M. E., & Rose, G. S. (2018, May). Energy and area efficiency in neuromorphic computing for resource constrained devices. In *Proceedings of the 2018 on Great Lakes Symposium on VLSI* (pp. 379-383). GLSVLSI. https://www.glsvlsi.org/

Chandrakala, S., & Rajeswari, N. (2017). Representation Learning Based Speech Assistive System for Persons With Dysarthria. *IEEE Transactions on Neural Systems and Rehabilitation Engineering*, *25*(9), 1510–1517. doi:10.1109/TNSRE.2016.2638830 PMID:27992342

Chang H.Y. et al. (2019). AI hardware acceleration with analog memory: Microarchitectures for low energy at high speed. *IBM Journal of Research and Development, 63*(6), 1-14. . doi:10.1147/JRD.2019.2934050

Chan, S., Reddy, V., Myers, B., Thibodeaux, Q., Brownstone, N., & Liao, W. (2020). Machine Learning in Dermatology: Current Applications, Opportunities, and Limitations. *Dermatology and Therapy*, *10*(3), 365–386. doi:10.100713555-020-00372-0 PMID:32253623

Chen, P. Y., & Yu, S. (2015). Compact modeling of RRAM devices and its applications in 1T1R and 1S1R array design. *IEEE Transactions on Electron Devices*, *62*(12), 4022–4028. doi:10.1109/TED.2015.2492421

Christensen, D. V., Dittmann, R., Linares-Barranco, B., Sebastian, A., Le Gallo, M., Redaelli, A., Slesazeck, S., Mikolajick, T., Spiga, S., Menzel, S., Valov, I., Milano, G., Ricciardi, C., Liang, S.-J., Miao, F., Lanza, M., Quill, T. J., Keene, S. T., Salleo, A., & Pryds, N. (2022). 2022 roadmap on neuromorphic computing and engineering. *Neuromorphic Computing and Engineering*, *2*(2), 022501. doi:10.1088/2634-4386/ac4a83

Chua, L. (1971). Memristor—The missing circuit element. *IEEE Transactions on Circuit Theory*, *18*(5), 507–519. doi:10.1109/TCT.1971.1083337

Chunguang, B., Patrick, D., Guido, O., & Joseph, S. (2020). Industry 4.0 technologies assessment: A sustainability perspective. *International Journal of Production Economics*, *229*, 107776. doi:10.1016/j.ijpe.2020.107776

Ciota, Z. (2005). Emotion Recognition on the Basis of Human Speech. *18th International Conference on Applied Electromagnetics and Communications,* (pp. 1-4). IEEE. 10.1109/ICECOM.2005.205015

Colombo, A. W., Karnouskos, S., Kaynak, O., Shi, Y., & Yin, S. (2017). Industrial Cyber physical Systems: A Backbone of the Fourth Industrial Revolution. *IEEE Industrial Electronics Magazine*, *11*(1), 6–16. doi:10.1109/MIE.2017.2648857

Conrad, D. J., James, B. A., Nadine, E. M., Craig, M. V., Fredrick, H. R., Kristofor, D. C., Samuel, A. M., Timothy, J. D., Aleksandra, F., Matthew, J. M., John, H. N., & Steven, J. P. (2017). A historical survey of algorithms and hardware architectures for neural-inspired and neuromorphic computing applications. *Biologically Inspired Cognitive Architectures, 19*, 49-64. doi:10.1016/j.bica.2016.11.002

Cortes, C., & Vapnik, V. (1995). Support-vector networks. *Machine Learning*, *20*(3), 273–297. doi:10.1007/BF00994018

Cuevas-Arteaga, B., Dominguez-Morales, J. P., Rostro-Gonzalez, H., Espinal, A., Jimenez-Fernandez, A. F., Gomez-Rodriguez, F., & Linares-Barranco, A. (2017). A SpiNNaker application: design, implementation and validation of SCPGs. In *International work-conference on artificial neural networks* (pp. 548–559). Springer. doi:10.1007/978-3-319-59153-7_50

D'Angelo, G., Perrett, A., Iacono, M., Furber, S., & Bartolozzi, C. (2022). Event driven bio-inspired attentive system for the iCub humanoid robot on SpiNNaker. *Neuromorphic Computing and Engineering*, *2*(2), 024008. doi:10.1088/2634-4386/ac6b50

Dahl, G. E., Yu, D., Deng, L., & Acero, A. (2012, January). Context-dependent pretrained deep neural networks for large-vocabulary speech recognition. *IEEE Transactions on Audio, Speech, and Language Processing*, *20*(1), 30–42. doi:10.1109/TASL.2011.2134090

Das, R., Piciucco, E., Maiorana, E., & Campisi, P. (2018). Convolutional neural network for finger-vein-based biometric identification. *IEEE Transactions on Information Forensics and Security*, *14*(2), 360–373. doi:10.1109/TIFS.2018.2850320

Davies, M., Srinivasa, N., Lin, T. H., Chinya, G., Cao, Y., Choday, S. H., & Plana, L. A. (2018). Loihi: A neuromorphic manycore processor with on-chip learning. *IEEE Micro*, *38*(1), 82–99. doi:10.1109/MM.2018.112130359

De, M. (2017). Darwin: A neuromorphic hardware co-processor based on spiking neural networks. *Journal of Systems Architecture*, *77*, 43-51. doi:10.1016/j.sysarc.2017.01.003

Deepa Nivethika, S., Sreeja, B. S., Manikandan, E., & Radha, S. (2018). A stretchable smart and highly efficient radio frequency antenna on low cost substrate. *Microwave and Optical Technology Letters*, *60*(7), 1798–1803. doi:10.1002/mop.31242

DeMuth, C. Jr. (2016). *Apple Reads Your Mind*. M&A Daily. Seeking Alpha.

Dhanasekar, S. & Govindaraj, V., (2023). Low-power test pattern generator using modified LFSR. *Aerospace Systems*. doi:10.1007/s42401-022-00191-5

Dhanasekar, S., Abarna, V. K., Gayathri, V., Valarmathi, G., Madhumita, D., & Jeevitha, R. (2023). An Efficient Smart Agriculture System Based on The Internet of Things Using Aeroponics Method. 2023 9th International Conference on Advanced Computing and Communication Systems (ICACCS). https://doi.org/10.1109/icaccs57279.2023.10112884

Dhanasekar, S., Bruntha, P. M., Ahmed, L. J., Valarmathi, G., Govindaraj, V., & Priya, C. (2022). An Area Efficient FFT Processor using Modified Compressor adder based Vedic Multiplier. *2022 6th International Conference on Devices, Circuits and Systems (ICDCS)*. IEEE. 10.1109/ICDCS54290.2022.9780676

Dhanasekar, S., Bruntha, P. M., Madhuvappan, C., & Sagayam, K. (2019). An improved area efficient 16-QAM transceiver design using Vedic multiplier for wireless applications. *International Journal of Recent Technology and Engineering*, *8*(3), 4419–4425.

Dhanasekar, S., Ganesan, A. T., Rani, T. L., Vinjamuri, V. K., & Rao, M. N. (2022). Shankar., & Golie, W. M. (2022). A Comprehensive Study of Ceramic Matrix Composites for Space Applications. *Advances in Materials Science and Engineering*.

Dhanasekar, S., & Govindaraj, V. (2023). *Low-power test pattern generator using modified LFSR*. Aerospace Systems.

Dhanasekar, S., Jothy Stella, T., Thenmozhi, A., & Divya Bharathi, N. (2022). Kamatchi Thiyagarajan, Pankaj Singh, Yanala Srinivasa Reddy, Ganganagunta Srinivas, Mani Jayakumar, and Samson Jerold Samuel Chelladurai. (2022). Study of Polymer Matrix Composites for Electronics Applications. *Journal of Nanomaterials*, *2022*. doi:10.1155/2022/8605099

Dhanasekar, S., & Ramesh, J. (2015). FPGA implementation of variable bit rate 16 QAM transceiver system. *International Journal of Applied Engineering Research*, *10*(10), 26497–26507.

Dhanasekar, S., & Ramesh, J. (2015). FPGA Implementation of Variable Bit Rate 16 QAM Transceiver System. *International Journal of Applied Engineering Research, 10*, 26479–26507.

Dhanasekar, S., & Ramesh, J. (2015). FPGA implementation of variable bit rate 16 QAM transceiver system. *International Journal of Applied Engineering Research: IJAER, 10*(10), 26497–26507.

Dhanasekar, S., & Ramesh, J. (2015). FPGA Implementation of Variable Bit Rate 16 QAM Transceiver System. *International Journal of Applied Engineering Research: IJAER, 10*, 26479–26507.

Dickson, J. A., McLeod, R. D., & Card, H. C. (1993). "Stochastic arithmetic implementations of neural networks with in situ learning," in Proc. IEEE Int. Conf. *Neural Networks, 2*(Mar), 711–716.

Diehl, P. U., Pedroni, B. U., Cassidy, A., Merolla, P., Neftci, E., & Zarrella, G. (2016). TrueHappiness: Neuromorphic emotion recognition on TrueNorth. *International Joint Conference on Neural Networks (IJCNN).* (pp. 4278-4285). IEEE. 10.1109/IJCNN.2016.7727758

Dildar, M., Akram, S., Irfan, M., Khan, H. U., Ramzan, M., Mahmood, A. R., Alsaiari, S. A., Saeed, A. H. M., Alraddadi, M. O., & Mahnashi, M. H. (2021). Skin Cancer Detection: A Review Using Deep Learning Techniques. *International Journal of Environmental Research and Public Health, 18*(10), 5479. doi:10.3390/ijerph18105479 PMID:34065430

Ding, J., Dong, B., Heide, F., Ding, Y., Zhou, Y., Yin, B., & Yang, X. (2022). *Biologically Inspired Dynamic Thresholds for Spiking Neural Networks.* arXiv preprint arXiv:2206.04426.

Donati, E., Corradi, F., Stefanini, C., & Indiveri, G. (2014). A spiking implementation of the lamprey's Central Pattern Generator in neuromorphic VLSI. In 2014 IEEE Biomedical Circuits and Systems Conference (BioCAS) Proceedings (pp. 512-515). IEEE. https://doi.org/10.1109/BioCAS.2014.6981775

Dong, G., Wang, P., Chen, P., Gu, R., & Hu, H. (2019). Floating-Point Multiplication Timing Attack on Deep Neural Network. *2019 IEEE International Conference on Smart Internet of Things (SmartIoT),* (pp. 155-161). IEEE.

Dubey, A., Cammarota, R., & Aysu, A. (2019). MaskedNet: The First Hardware Inference Engine Aiming Power Side-Channel Protection. *2020 IEEE International Symposium on Hardware Oriented Security and Trust (HOST),* (pp. 197-208). IEEE.

Duchi, Hasan, & Singer. (2011). Subgradient Methods for Online Learning and Stochastic Optimization. *J. of Machine Learning Research.*

Dupeyroux, J., Hagenaars, J. J., Paredes-Vallés, F., & de Croon, G. C. (2021, May). Neuromorphic control for optic-flow-based landing of MAVs using the Loihi processor. In *2021 IEEE International Conference on Robotics and Automation (ICRA)* (pp. 96-102). IEEE. 10.1109/ICRA48506.2021.9560937

Du, Z. (2015). Neuromorphic accelerators: A comparison between neuroscience and machine-learning approaches. *48th Annual IEEE/ACM International Symposium on Microarchitecture (MICRO).* (pp. 494-507). IEEE. 10.1145/2830772.2830789

Erichson, N., Taylor, D., Wu, Q., & Mahoney, M. W. (2021). *Noise-Response Analysis of Deep Neural Networks Quantifies Robustness and Fingerprints Structural Malware*. SDM.

Esmaeilzadeh, H., Sampson, A., Ceze, L., & Burger, D. (2012). Neural Acceleration for General-Purpose Approximate Programs. *International Symposium on Microarchitecture, 3*, 1–6. 10.1109/MICRO.2012.48

Estava, A. (2015). *Deep Networks for Early Stage Disease and Skin Care Classification*. Stanford University.

Esteva, A., Kuprel, B., Novoa, R. A., Ko, J., Swetter, S. M., Blau, H. M., & Thrun, S. (2017, January 25). Dermatologist-level classification of skin cancer with deep neural networks. *Nature, 542*(7639), 115–118. doi:10.1038/nature21056 PMID:28117445

Fang, Y., Yang, J., Zhou, D., & Ju, Z. (2022). Modelling EMG driven wrist movements using a bio-inspired neural network. *Neurocomputing, 470*, 89–98. doi:10.1016/j.neucom.2021.10.104

Fatima, A., & Pethe, A. (2022a). *Implementation of RRAM based Swish Activation Function and its Derivative on 28nm FD-SOI*. International Electrical Engineering Congress (iEECON). 10.1109/iEECON53204.2022.9741701

Fatima, A., & Pethe, A. (2021). NVM Device-Based Deep Inference Architecture Using Self-gated Activation Functions (Swish). In M. K. Bajpai, K. Kumar Singh, & G. Giakos (Eds.), *Machine Vision and Augmented Intelligence—Theory and Applications. Lecture Notes in Electrical Engineering* (Vol. 796). Springer. doi:10.1007/978-981-16-5078-9_4

Fatima, A., & Pethe, A. (2022b). Periodic Analysis of Resistive Random Access Memory (RRAM)-Based Swish Activation Function. *SN Computer Science, 3*(3), 202. doi:10.100742979-022-01059-3

Fukushima, K. (1988). Neocognitron: A hierarchical neural network capable of visual pattern recognition. *Neural Networks, 1*(2), 119–130. doi:10.1016/0893-6080(88)90014-7

Fuller, E. J., Gabaly, F. E., Léonard, F., Agarwal, S., Plimpton, S. J., Jacobs-Gedrim, R. B., & Talin, A. A. (2019). Li-ion transport and electrochemistry in nanoporous Li2O. *Science, 365*(6453), 1015–1022.

Fuortes, M. G. F., & Mantegazzini, F. (1962). Interpretation of the repetitive firing of nerve cells. *The Journal of General Physiology, 45*(6), 1163–1179. doi:10.1085/jgp.45.6.1163 PMID:13895926

Ganeshkumar, S., & Venkatesh, S. (2022). Manufacturing Techniques and Applications of Multifunctional Metal Matrix Composites. Functional Composite Materials: Manufacturing Technology and Experimental Application, 157.

Ganeshkumar, S., Sureshkumar, R., Sureshbabu, Y., & Balasubramani, S. (2020). A review on cutting tool measurement in turning tools by cloud computing systems in industry 4.0 and IoT. *GIS Science Journal, 7*(8), 1-7.

Ganeshkumar, Venkatesh, Paranthaman, Arulmurugan, Arunprakash, Manickam, Venkatesh, & Rajendiran. (2022). Performance of Multilayered Nanocoated Cutting Tools in High-Speed Machining: A Review. *International Journal of Photoenergy.* doi:10.1155/2022/5996061

Ganeshkumar, S. (2023). Exploring the Potential of Integrating Machine Tool Wear Monitoring and ML for Predictive Maintenance-A Review. *Journal of Advanced Mechanical Sciences, 2*(1), 10–20.

Ganeshkumar, S., Kumar, S. D., Magarajan, U., Rajkumar, S., Arulmurugan, B., Sharma, S., Li, C., Ilyas, R. A., & Badran, M. F. (2022). Investigation of tensile properties of different infill pattern structures of 3D-printed PLA polymers: Analysis and validation using finite element analysis in ANSYS. *Materials (Basel), 15*(15), 5142. doi:10.3390/ma15155142 PMID:35897575

Ganeshkumar, S., Singh, B. K., Kumar, S. D., Gokulkumar, S., Sharma, S., Mausam, K., Li, C., Zhang, Y., & Tag Eldin, E. M. (2022). Study of Wear, Stress and Vibration Characteristics of Silicon Carbide Tool Inserts and Nano Multi-Layered Titanium Nitride-Coated Cutting Tool Inserts in Turning of SS304 Steels. *Materials (Basel), 15*(22), 7994. doi:10.3390/ma15227994 PMID:36431481

Ganeshkumar, S., Sureshkumar, R., Sureshbabu, Y., & Balasubramani, S. (2019). A numerical approach to cutting tool stress in CNC turning of EN8 steel with silicon carbide tool insert. *International Journal of Scientific & Technology Research, 8*(12), 3227–3231.

Ganeshkumar, S., Thirunavukkarasu, V., Sureshkumar, R., Venkatesh, S., & Ramakrishnan, T. (2019). Investigation of wear behaviour of silicon carbide tool inserts and titanium nitride coated tool inserts in machining of en8 steel. *International Journal of Mechanical Engineering and Technology, 10*(01), 1862–1873.

Gemma, G. L. (2018). Emotional answers from virtual assistants. *Emotional Seo.* https://emotionalseo.com/emotional-answers-from-virtual-assistants/

Geoffrey W. B., Robert M. S., Sebastian A., Kim S., Seyoung K., Sidler S., Virwani K., Masatoshi I., Pritish N., Alessandro F., Lucas L. S., Irem B., Manuel L. G., Moon K., Jiyoo W., Hwang H. & Leblebici Y. (2017). Neuromorphic computing using non-volatile memory. *Advances in Physics, 10,* 89-124. doi:10.1080/23746149.2016.1259585

George, A. M., Dey, S., Banerjee, D., Mukherjee, A., & Suri, M. (2022). Online Time-Series Forecasting using Spiking Reservoir. *Neurocomputing.*

Gerstner, W. (2001). What is different with spiking neurons? In W. Gerstner, A. Germond, M. Hasler, & J.-D. Nicoud (Eds.), *Plausible neural networks for biological modelling* (pp. 23–48). Springer. doi:10.1007/978-94-010-0674-3_2

Gerstner, W., & Kistler, W. M. (2002). *Spiking neuron models: Single neurons, populations, plasticity.* Cambridge University Press. doi:10.1017/CBO9780511815706

Gerstner, W., Kistler, W. M., Naud, R., & Paninski, L. (2014). *Neuronal dynamics: From single neurons to networks and models of cognition.* Cambridge University Press. doi:10.1017/CBO9781107447615

Ghasemzadeh, P., Banerjee, S., Hempel, M., & Sharif, H. (2020). A New Framework for Automatic Modulation Classification using Deep Belief Networks. *2020 IEEE International Conference on Communications Workshops (ICC Workshops).* IEEE. 10.1109/ICCWorkshops49005.2020.9145320

Goi, E., Zhang, Q., Chen, X., Luan, H., & Gu, M. (2020). Perspective on photonic memristive neuromorphic computing. *PhotoniX, 1*(1), 3. doi:10.118643074-020-0001-6

Gokilakrishnan, G., Ganeshkumar, S., Anandakumar, H., & Vigneshkumar, M. (2021, March). A Critical Review of Production Distribution Planning Models. In *2021 7th International Conference on Advanced Computing and Communication Systems (ICACCS)* (Vol. 1, pp. 2047-2051). IEEE. 10.1109/ICACCS51430.2021.9441879

Goodfellow, I., Bengio, Y., & Courville, A. (2016). *Deep learning.* MIT Press.

Goodfellow, I., Bengio, Y., & Courville, A. (2016). *Deep Learning.* MIT Press.

Govindaraj, V., Dhanasekar, S., Martinsagayam, K., Pandey, D., Pandey, B. K., & Nassa, V. K. (2023). Low-power test pattern generator using modified LFSR. Aerospace Systems, 1-8.

Govindaraj, V., Dhanasekar, S., Martinsagayam, K., Pandey, D., Pandey, B. K., & Nassa, V. K. (2023, January 9). *Low-power test pattern generator using modified LFSR - Aerospace Systems.* SpringerLink. https://link.springer.com/article/10.1007/s42401-022-00191-5

Goyal, M., Knackstedt, T., Yan, S., & Hassanpour, S. (2020). Artificial Intelligence-Based Image Classification for Diagnosis of Skin Cancer: Challenges and Opportunities. *Computers in Biology and Medicine, 127,* 104065. doi:10.1016/j.compbiomed.2020.104065 PMID:33246265

Grüning, A., & Bohte, S. M. (2014). Spiking neural networks: Principles and challenges. In ESANN.

Guan, Y., Shang, Z., & Li, C. (2022, May). Analysis of Spiking Neural Network trends based on CiteSpace. In *International Symposium on Computer Applications and Information Systems (ISCAIS 2022)* (Vol. 12250, pp. 38-51). SPIE. 10.1117/12.2639578

Guo, L., Song, Y., Wu, Y., & Xu, G. (2022). Anti-interference of a small-world spiking neural network against pulse noise. *Applied Intelligence,* 1–19.

Gutierrez-Galan, D., Dominguez-Morales, J. P., Perez-Peña, F., Jimenez-Fernandez, A., & Linares-Barranco, A. (2020). NeuroPod: A real-time neuromorphic spiking CPG applied to robotics. *Neurocomputing, 381,* 10–19. doi:10.1016/j.neucom.2019.11.007

Haggenmüller, S., Maron, R. C., Hekler, A., Utikal, J. S., Barata, C., Barnhill, R. L., Beltraminelli, H., Berking, C., Betz-Stablein, B., Blum, A., Braun, S. A., Carr, R., Combalia, M., Fernandez-Figueras, M.-T., Ferrara, G., Fraitag, S., French, L. E., Gellrich, F. F., Ghoreschi, K., & Brinker, T. J. (2021). Skin Cancer Classification via Convolutional Neural Networks: Systematic Review of Studies Involving Human Experts. *European Journal of Cancer (Oxford, England), 156,* 202–216. doi:10.1016/j.ejca.2021.06.049 PMID:34509059

Hagleitner, C., Hierlemann, A., Lange, D., Kerness, N., Brand, O., Baltes, H., & de Rooij, N. F. (2001). Smart single-chip gas sensor microsystem. *Nature, 414*(6861), 293–296. doi:10.1038/35104535 PMID:11713525

Han, J. K., Yun, S. Y., Lee, S. W., Yu, J. M., & Choi, Y. K. (2022). A review of artificial spiking neuron devices for neural processing and sensing. *Advanced Functional Materials, 32*(33), 2204102. doi:10.1002/adfm.202204102

Hao, Y. (2017). *A General Neural Network Hardware Architecture on FPGA*. Computer Vision and Pattern Recognition.

Harstad, S., Hunagund, S., Boekelheide, Z., Hussein, Z. A., El-Gendy, A. A., & Hadimani, R. L. (2018). Gd-Based Magnetic Nanoparticles for Biomedical Applications. In Magnetic Nanostructured Materials (pp. 137-155). Elsevier. doi:10.1016/B978-0-12-813904-2.00005-X

Hasan, R., & Taha, T. (2014). Enabling back propagation training of memristor crossbar neuromorphic processors. *International Joint Conference on Neural Networks (IJCNN)* (pp. 21-28). IEEE. 10.1109/IJCNN.2014.6889893

Hashem, R., Kazemi, S., Stommel, M., Cheng, L. K., & Xu, W. (2022). A biologically inspired ring-shaped soft pneumatic actuator for large deformations. *Soft Robotics, 9*(4), 807–819. doi:10.1089oro.2021.0013 PMID:34704835

Hazra, P., & Jinesh, K. B. (2020). Vertical limits of resistive memory scaling: The detrimental influence of interface states. *Applied Physics Letters, 116*(17), 173502. doi:10.1063/1.5139595

Heyn, J., Gümbel, P., Bobka, P., Dietrich, F., & Dröder, K. (2019). Application of artificial neural networks in force-controlled automated assembly of complex shaped deformable components. *Procedia CIRP, 79,* 131–136. doi:10.1016/j.procir.2019.02.027

Hinton, G. E., & Salakhutdinov, R. R. (2006). Reducing the dimensionality of data with neural networks. *Science, 313*(5786), 504–507. doi:10.1126cience.1127647 PMID:16873662

Hodgkin, A. L., & Huxley, A. F. (1952). A quantitative description of membrane current and its application to conduction and excitation in nerve. *The Journal of Physiology, 117*(4), 500–544. doi:10.1113/jphysiol.1952.sp004764 PMID:12991237

Höhn, J., Hekler, A., Krieghoff-Henning, E., Kather, J. N., Utikal, J. S., Meier, F., Gellrich, F. F., Hauschild, A., French, L., Schlager, J. G., Ghoreschi, K., Wilhelm, T., Kutzner, H., Heppt, M., Haferkamp, S., Sondermann, W., Schadendorf, D., Schilling, B., Maron, R. C., & Brinker, T. J. (2021). Integrating Patient Data Into Skin Cancer Classification Using Convolutional Neural Networks: Systematic Review. *Journal of Medical Internet Research*, 23(7), e20708. doi:10.2196/20708 PMID:34255646

Hong, S., Frigo, P., Kaya, Y., Giuffrida, C., & Dumitras, T. (2019). *Terminal Brain Damage: Exposing the Graceless Degradation in Deep Neural Networks Under Hardware Fault Attacks*. ArXiv, abs/1906.01017.

Hua, W., Zhang, Z., & Suh, G. E. (2018). Reverse Engineering Convolutional Neural Networks Through Side-channel Information Leaks. *2018 55th ACM/ESDA/IEEE Design Automation Conference (DAC)*, (pp. 1-6). ACM.

Hunagund, S. G., Harstad, S. M., El-Gendy, A. A., Gupta, S., Pecharsky, V. K., & Hadimani, R. L. (2018). Investigating phase transition temperatures of size separated gadolinium silicide magnetic nanoparticles. *AIP Advances*, 8(5), 056428. doi:10.1063/1.5007686

Hussain, M., Bird, J. J., & Faria, D. R. (2019). A Study on CNN Transfer Learning for Image Classification. In: Lotfi, A., Bouchachia, H., Gegov, A., Langensiepen, C., McGinnity, M. (eds) Advances in Computational Intelligence Systems. Springer. doi:10.1007/978-3-319-97982-3_16

Hussaini, S., Milford, M., & Fischer, T. (2022). *Ensembles of Compact, Region-specific & Regularized Spiking Neural Networks for Scalable Place Recognition.* arXiv preprint arXiv:2209.08723.

Hussaini, S., Milford, M., & Fischer, T. (2022). Spiking Neural Networks for Visual Place Recognition via Weighted Neuronal Assignments. *IEEE Robotics and Automation Letters*, 7(2), 4094–4101. doi:10.1109/LRA.2022.3149030

Indiveri, G., Linares-Barranco, B., Hamilton, T. J., Schaik, A., Etienne-Cummings, R., Delbruck, T., Liu, S.-C., Dudek, P., Häfliger, P., Renaud, S., Schemmel, J., Cauwenberghs, G., Arthur, J., Hynna, K., Folowosele, F., Saighi, S., Serrano-Gotarredona, T., Wijekoon, J., Wang, Y., & Boahen, K. (2011). Neuromorphic silicon neuron circuits. *Frontiers in Neuroscience*, 5, 73. doi:10.3389/fnins.2011.00073 PMID:21747754

Irmak, H., Corradi, F., Detterer, P., Alachiotis, N., & Ziener, D. (2021). A dynamic reconfigurable architecture for hybrid spiking and convolutional fpga-based neural network designs. *Journal of Low Power Electronics and Applications, 11*(3). doi:10.3390/jlpea11030032

J., J., C., S., R., B., & S., D. (2023). *Design and Analysis of CNN based Residue Number System for Performance Enhancement*. 2023 Third International Conference on Artificial Intelligence and Smart Energy (ICAIS), Coimbatore, India. 10.1109/ICAIS56108.2023.10073805

Jemimah Rinsy, J., Sivamangai, N. M., Naveenkumar, R., Napolean, A., Puviarasu, A., & Janani, V. (2022). *Review on Logic Locking Attacks in Hardware Security*. 2022 6th International Conference on Devices, Circuits and Systems (ICDCS), Coimbatore, India. 10.1109/ICDCS54290.2022.9780725

Ji, Y., Ran, F., Ma, C., & Lilja, D. J. (2015). A hardware implementation of a radial basis function neural network using stochastic logic. Proc. Design, Autom. Test Eur. Conf. Exhibit. (DATE), (pp. 880–883). IEEE. 10.7873/DATE.2015.0377

Jiang, S., Liu, Y., Xu, B., Sun, J., & Wang, Y. (2022). Asynchronous numerical spiking neural P systems. *Information Sciences*, *605*, 1–14. doi:10.1016/j.ins.2022.04.054

Jia, Z., Ji, J., Zhou, X., & Zhou, Y. (2022). Hybrid spiking neural network for sleep electroencephalogram signals. *Science China. Information Sciences*, *65*(4), 1–10. doi:10.100711432-021-3380-1

John, S. B., & John, E. B. (1998). *Modeling emotion and personality in a computer user interface.* Microsoft Technology Licensing LLC. https://patents.google.com/patent/US6185534B1/en

Jo, S. M. (2012). Nanoelectronic programmable synapses based on phase change materials for brain-inspired computing. *Nano Letters*, *12*(5), 2179–2186. doi:10.1021/nl201040y PMID:21668029

Juárez-Lora, A., García-Sebastián, L. M., Ponce-Ponce, V. H., Rubio-Espino, E., Molina-Lozano, H., & Sossa, H. (2022). Implementation of Kalman Filtering with Spiking Neural Networks. *Sensors (Basel)*, *22*(22), 8845. doi:10.339022228845 PMID:36433442

Jubair Ahmed, L., Anish Fathima, B., Dhanasekar, S., & Martin Sagayam, K. (2022). Modeling of Fuzzy Logic-Based Classification System Using the Gravitational Search Algorithm. In *Multimedia Technologies in the Internet of Things Environment* (Vol. 3, pp. 79–94). Springer Singapore. doi:10.1007/978-981-19-0924-5_5

Jubairahmed, L., Satheeskumaran, S., & Venkatesan, C. (2017). Contourlet transform based adaptive nonlinear diffusion filtering for speckle noise removal in ultrasound images. *Cluster Computing*, *22*(S5), 11237–11246. doi:10.100710586-017-1370-x

Kadi, M. A., Rudolph, P., Gohringer, D., & Hubner, M. (2013). Dynamic and partial reconfiguration of Zynq 7000 under Linux. *International Conference on Reconfigurable Computing and FPGAs (ReConFig)*, Cancun, Mexico. 10.1109/ReConFig.2013.6732279

Kang, W., Liu, H., Luo, W., & Deng, F. (2019). Study of a full-view 3D finger vein verification technique. *IEEE Transactions on Information Forensics and Security*, *15*, 1175–1189. doi:10.1109/TIFS.2019.2928507

Kauba, C., Piciucco, E., Maiorana, E., Campisi, P., & Uhl, A. (2016, September). Advanced variants of feature level fusion for finger vein recognition. In *2016 International Conference of the Biometrics Special Interest Group (BIOSIG)* (pp. 1-7). IEEE. 10.1109/BIOSIG.2016.7736908

Kaur, R., Gholam, H., & Sinha, R. (2021). Synthetic Images Generation Using Conditional Generative Adversarial Network for Skin Cancer Classification. In TENCON 2021-2021 IEEE Region 10 Conference (TENCON). Institute of Electrical and Electronics Engineers (IEEE).

Kaur, M., & Mohta, A. (2019). A Review of Deep Learning with Recurrent Neural Network. *International Conference on Smart Systems and Inventive Technology (ICSSIT)*. IEEE. 10.1109/ICSSIT46314.2019.8987837

Khan, S., Rahmani, H., Shah, S. A. A., Bennamoun, M., Medioni, G., & Dickinson, S. (2018). *A Guide to Convolutional Neural Networks for Computer Vision.* Morgan Claypool. https: // ieeexplore.ieee.org/document/8295029

Kim, K., Bang, S., & Kong, D. (2003). *System and method for recognizing user's emotional state using short-time monitoring of physiological signals.* Samsung Electronics Co. Ltd. https:// patents.google.com/patent/US7547279B2/en

Kim, L.-W., Asaad, S., & Linsker, R. (2014). A fully pipelined FPGA architecture of a factored restricted Boltzmann machine artificial neural network. *ACM Trans. Reconfigurable Technol. Syst., 7*(1).

Kim, M. (2020). Emerging materials for neuromorphic devices and systems. *Iscience 23*(12).

Kim, M. H., Nam, S., Oh, M., Lee, H. J., Jang, B., & Hyun, S. (2022). Bioinspired, shape-morphing scale battery for untethered soft robots. *Soft Robotics, 9*(3), 486–496. doi:10.1089oro.2020.0175 PMID:34402653

Kim, P. (2017). *MATLAB Deep Learning: With Machine Learning.* Neural Networks, and Artificial Intelligence. doi:10.1007/978-1-4842-2845-6

Kim, S., Kim, T. W., Lee, J., Choi, S., Choi, Y., Kim, S. J., & Hwang, S. (2019). Synaptic electronics towards neuromorphic computing. *Advanced Materials, 31*(29), 1806133.

Kim, Y., Kim, K. H., Kim, S., Park, S., Park, S., Lee, H. G., & Hwang, S. (2018). Artificial optic-neural synapse for colored and color-mixed pattern recognition. *Nature Communications, 9*(1), 5106. doi:10.103841467-018-07572-5 PMID:30504804

Klaus, S. (2015). The Fourth Industrial Revolution. *Foreign Affairs.* (https://www.foreignaffairs. com/world/fourth-industrial-revolution)

Koch, C., & Segev, I. (Eds.). (1998). *Methods in neuronal modeling: From ions to networks.* MIT Press.

Kondoyanni, M., Loukatos, D., Maraveas, C., Drosos, C., & Arvanitis, K. G. (2022). Bio-Inspired Robots and Structures toward Fostering the Modernization of Agriculture. *Biomimetics, 7*(2), 69. doi:10.3390/biomimetics7020069 PMID:35735585

Konguvel & Kannan. (2022). A Novel Digital Logic for Bit Reversal and Address Generations in FFT Computations. *Wireless Personal Communications, 128*(3), 1827-1838. doi:. doi:10.1007/ s11277-022-10021-8

Konguvel, E., Nithiyameenatchi, N., & Rachel, L. (2022). IoT-enabled ECG Monitoring System for Remote Cardiac Patients. *Proc. of 2022 IEEE International Conference on Augmented Intelligence and Sustainable Systems (ICAISS – 2022),* 1146 – 1151. doi:10.1109/ICAISS55157.2022.10010849

Konguvel, Hariharan, Sujatha, & Kannan. (2022). Hardware implementation of approximate multipliers for signal processing applications. *International Journal of Wireless and Mobile Computing, 23*(3-4), 302-309. doi:10.1504/IJWMC.2022.10052548

Kumar, A., Nagarajan, P., Selvaperumal, S., & Venkatramana, P. (2019). Design challenges for 3 dimensional network-on-chip (NoC). *International Conference on Sustainable Communication Networks and Application* (pp. 773-782). Springer, Cham.

Kumar, A., & Zhou, Y. (2011). Human identification using finger images. *IEEE Transactions on Image Processing, 21*(4), 2228–2244. doi:10.1109/TIP.2011.2171697 PMID:21997267

Kumar, S. G., & Thirunavukkarasu, V. (2016). Investigation of tool wear and optimization of process parameters in turning of EN8 and EN 36 steels. *Asian Journal of Research in Social Sciences and Humanities, 6*(11), 237–243. doi:10.5958/2249-7315.2016.01188.6

Kuzum, D. (2013). Synaptic Electronics: Materials Devices and Applications. *Nanotechnology, 24*(382001). PMID:23999572

Kvatinsky, S., Satat, G., Wald, N., Friedman, E. G., Kolodny, A., & Weiser, U. C. (2014, October). Memristor-Based Material Implication (IMPLY) Logic: Design Principles and Methodologies. *IEEE Transactions on Very Large Scale Integration (VLSI) Systems, 22*(10), 2054–2066. doi:10.1109/TVLSI.2013.2282132

Le, D. N., Le, H. X., Ngo, L. T., & Ngo, H. T. Transfer Learning With ClassWeighted and Focal Loss Function for Automatic Skin Cancer Classification. ArXiv (2020) abs/2009.05977:arX iv:2009.05977. doi:10.48550/arXiv.2009.05977

LeCun, Y., & Bengio, Y. (1995). Convolutional networks for images, speech, and time-series. In M. A. Arbib (Ed.), *The Handbook of Brain Theory and Neural Networks*. MIT Press.

LeCun, Y., Bengio, Y., & Hinton, G. (2015). Deep learning. *Nature, 521*(7553), 436–444. doi:10.1038/nature14539 PMID:26017442

Lee, M., Yun, J., Pyka, A., Won, D., Kodama, F., Schiuma, G., Park, H., Jeon, J., Park, K., Jung, K., Yan, M., Lee, S., Zhao, X. (2018). How to Respond to the Fourth Industrial Revolution, or the Second Information Technology Revolution? Dynamic New Combinations between Technology, Market, and Society through Open Innovation. *Journal of Open Innovation: Technology, Market, and Complexity, 4* (3), 21. . doi:10.3390/joitmc4030021

Lee, C. M., & Narayanan, S. S. (2005). Toward detecting emotions in spoken dialogs. *IEEE Transactions on Speech and Audio Processing, 13*(2), 293–303. doi:10.1109/TSA.2004.838534

Lee, E. C., Lee, H. C., & Park, K. R. (2009). Finger vein recognition using minutia-based alignment and local binary pattern-based feature extraction. *International Journal of Imaging Systems and Technology, 19*(3), 179–186. doi:10.1002/ima.20193

Lee, K. W., & Chin, R. K. Y. (2020). The Effectiveness of Data Augmentation for Melanoma Skin Cancer Prediction Using Convolutional Neural Networks. In *IEEE 2nd International Conference on Artificial Intelligence in Engineering and Technology (IICAIET)*. Institute of Electrical and Electronics Engineers. 10.1109/IICAIET49801.2020.9257859

Lee, S.-T., & Lee, J.-H. (2020). Neuromorphic Computing Using NAND Flash Memory Architecture With Pulse Width Modulation Scheme. *Frontiers in Neuroscience, 14*, 571292. doi:10.3389/fnins.2020.571292 PMID:33071744

Lefter, I., Rothkrantz, L., & Van-Leeuwen, D. (2011). Automatic stress detection in emergency (telephone) calls. *International Journal of Intelligent Defence Support Systems., 4*(2), 148–168. doi:10.1504/IJIDSS.2011.039547

Li, C. (2018). Recent progress of emerging synaptic devices for neuromorphic hardware. *Advanced Electronic Materials, 4*(10).

Li, J., Xu, Z., Zhu, D., Dong, K., Yan, T., Zeng, Z., & Yang, S. X. (2022). *Bio-inspired intelligence with applications to robotics: a survey.* arXiv preprint arXiv:2206.08544.

Li, P., & Lilja, D. J. (2011). Using stochastic computing to implement digital image processing algorithms. Proc. IEEE 29th Int. Conf. Comput. Design, (pp. 154–161). IEEE. 10.1109/ICCD.2011.6081391

Li, Y., Wu, B., Jiang, Y., Li, Z., & Xia, S. (2020). Backdoor Learning: A Survey. *IEEE transactions on neural networks and learning systems.* IEEE. https://arxiv.org/abs/2007.08745

LI., Y., Liu, Y., Li, M., Tian, Y., Luo, B., & Xu, Q. (2019). D2NN: a fine-grained dual modular redundancy framework for deep neural networks. *Proceedings of the 35th Annual Computer Security Applications Conference.* ACM.

Lichtsteiner, P., Posch, C., & Delbruck, T. (2008). A 128×128 120 dB 15 µs latency asynchronous temporal contrast vision sensor. *IEEE Journal of Solid-State Circuits, 43*(2), 566–576. doi:10.1109/JSSC.2007.914337

Li, G., Hari, S. K., Sullivan, M. B., Tsai, T., Pattabiraman, K., Emer, J. S., & Keckler, S. W. (2017). Understanding Error Propagation in Deep Learning Neural Network (DNN) Accelerators and Applications. SC17. *International Conference for High Performance Computing, Networking, Storage and Analysis: [proceedings]. SC (Conference : Supercomputing), 1*–12.

Linares-Barranco, A., Pinero-Fuentes, E., Canas-Moreno, S., Rios-Navarro, A., Wu, C., Zhao, J., & Indiveri, G. (2022). *Towards hardware Implementation of WTA for CPG-based control of a Spiking Robotic Arm.* arXiv preprint arXiv:2202.07064. doi:10.1109/ISCAS48785.2022.9937845

Li, P., Lilja, D. J., Qian, W., Bazargan, K., & Riedel, M. D. (2014, March). Computation on stochastic bit streams digital image processing case studies: IEEE Trans. Very Large Scale Integr. (VLSI). *Syst., 22*(3), 449–462.

Liu, M., Xia, L., Wang, Y., & Chakrabarty, K. (2018). Design of fault-tolerant neuromorphic computing systems. *2018 IEEE 23rd European Test Symposium (ETS).* IEEE. 10.1109/ETS.2018.8400693

Liu, W., Li, W., Sun, L., Zhang, L., & Chen, P. (2017, June). Finger vein recognition based on deep learning. In *2017 12th IEEE conference on industrial electronics and applications (ICIEA)* (pp. 205-210). IEEE. 10.1109/ICIEA.2017.8282842

Liu, Y., Ma, X., Bailey, J., & Lu, F. (2020). *Reflection Backdoor: A Natural Backdoor Attack on Deep Neural Networks.* ArXiv, abs/2007.02343.

Liu, Y., Mondal, A., Chakraborty, A., Zuzak, M., Jacobsen, N. L., Xing, D., & Srivastava, A. (2020). A Survey on Neural Trojans. *2020 21st International Symposium on Quality Electronic Design (ISQED),* (pp. 33-39). IEEE.

Liu, Y., & Parhi, K. K. (2016, July). Architectures for recursive digital filters using stochastic computing. *IEEE Transactions on Signal Processing, 64*(14), 3705–3718. doi:10.1109/TSP.2016.2552513

Liu, Y., Yu, S., Peng, S., & Tan, D. (2021). Runtime Long-Term Reliability Management Using Stochastic Computing in Deep Neural Networks, *International Symposium on Quality Electronic Design (ISQED).* IEEE. 10.1109/ISQED51717.2021.9424285

Livingstone, S. R., & Russo, F. A. (2018). The Ryerson Audio-Visual Database of Emotional Speech and Song (RAVDESS): A dynamic, multimodal set of facial and vocal expressions in North American English. *PLoS One, 13*(5), e0196391. doi:10.1371/journal.pone.0196391 PMID:29768426

Lopez-Osorio, P., Patiño-Saucedo, A., Dominguez-Morales, J. P., Rostro-Gonzalez, H., & Perez-Peña, F. (2022). Neuromorphic adaptive spiking CPG towards bio-inspired locomotion. *Neurocomputing, 502,* 57–70. doi:10.1016/j.neucom.2022.06.085

Luo, P., Tian, Y., Wang, X., & Tang, X. (2014). Switchable deep network for pedestrian detection. Proc. IEEE Conf. CVPR, (pp. 899–906). IEEE. 10.1109/CVPR.2014.120

Luo, Y., Shen, H., Cao, X., Wang, T., Feng, Q., & Tan, Z. (2022). Conversion of Siamese networks to spiking neural networks for energy-efficient object tracking. *Neural Computing & Applications, 34*(12), 9967–9982. doi:10.100700521-022-06984-1

Maass, W. (1997). Networks of spiking neurons: The third generation of neural network models. *Neural Networks, 10*(9), 1659–1671. doi:10.1016/S0893-6080(97)00011-7

Madhiarasan, M., & Louzazni, M. (2022). Analysis of artificial neural network: Architecture, types, and forecasting applications. *Journal of Electrical and Computer Engineering, 2022,* 1–23. doi:10.1155/2022/5416722

Maind, S. B., & Wankar, P. (2014). Research paper on basic of artificial neural network. *International Journal on Recent and Innovation Trends in Computing and Communication, 2*(1), 96–100. doi:10.17762/ijritcc.v2i1.2920

Malik, N. (2005). *Artificial neural networks and their applications.* arXiv preprint cs/0505019. https://doi.org/ doi:10.48550/arXiv.cs/0505019

Mandal, S., El-Amin, A., Alexander, K., Rajendran, B., & Jha, R. (2014). Novel synaptic memory device for neuromorphic computing. *Scientific Reports, 4*(1), 5333. doi:10.1038rep05333 PMID:24939247

Manfredi, G., & Gribaudo, C. (2008). *Virtual assistant with real-time emotions*. Kallideas S.P.A. WO2008049834A2. https://patents.google.com/patent/WO2008049834A2/en

Manickam, M. V., Mohanapriya, M., Kale, S., Uday, M., Kulkarni, P., Khandagale, Y., & Patil, S. P. (2017). Research study on applications of artificial neural networks and E-learning personalization. *International Journal of Civil Engineering and Technology, 8*(8), 1422–1432.

Manju, M. R., Ajay, K. S., & Noel, M. D'Souza, Shivakumar Hunagund, R.L. Hadimani, V. (2018). Enhancement of ferromagnetic properties in composites of BaSnO3 and CoFe2O4, *Journal of Magnetism and Magnetic Materials, 452.*

Manne, R., Kantheti, S., & Kantheti, S. (2020). Classification of Skin Cancer Using Deep Learning, Convolutionalneural Networks-Opportunities and Vulnerabilities-a Systematic Review. *Int J Modern Trends Sci Technol, 6*(11), 2455–3778. doi:10.46501/IJMTST061118

Massari, L., Fransvea, G., D'Abbraccio, J., Filosa, M., Terruso, G., Aliperta, A., D'Alesio, G., Zaltieri, M., Schena, E., Palermo, E., Sinibaldi, E., & Oddo, C. M. (2022). Functional mimicry of Ruffini receptors with fibre Bragg gratings and deep neural networks enables a bio-inspired large-area tactile-sensitive skin. *Nature Machine Intelligence, 4*(5), 425–435. doi:10.103842256-022-00487-3

Mayr, C. G., Andreou, A. G., & Rabaey, J. M. (2012). Design techniques and fault-tolerant approaches in neuromorphic engineering. *Proceedings of the IEEE, 102*(5), 717–737.

Medical Xpress. (2018). Neuron axons are so spindly, they're optimizing for speed. *Medical Xpress.* https://medicalxpress.com/news/2018-07-neuron-axons-spindly-theyre-optimizing.html

Meng, Y., Wu, Z., Zhang, P., Wang, J., & Yu, J. (2022). Real-Time Digital Video Stabilization of Bioinspired Robotic Fish Using Estimation-and-Prediction Framework. *IEEE/ASME Transactions on Mechatronics, 27*(6), 4281–4292. doi:10.1109/TMECH.2022.3155696

Mhatre, M. S., Siddiqui, F., Dongre, M., & Thakur, P. (2015). A review paper on artificial neural network: A prediction technique. *International Journal of Scientific and Engineering Research, 6*(12), 161–163.

Miyakoshi, Y., & Kato, S. (2011). Facial emotion detection considering partial occlusion of face using Bayesian network. *IEEE Symposium on Computers & Informatics*, (pp. 96-101). IEEE. 10.1109/ISCI.2011.5958891

Mohamed, S. Abdelfattah, L., Chau, T., Lee, R., Kim, H., Lane, D. (2020) Best of Both Worlds: AutoML Codesign of a CNN and its Hardware Accelerator. *Machine Learning*. Advance online publication. doi:10.48550/arXiv.2002.05022

Mohamed, S. A., Othman, M., & Afifi, M. H. (2019). A review on data clustering using spiking neural network (SNN) models. *Indonesian Journal of Electrical Engineering and Computer Science, 15*(3), 1392. doi:10.11591/ijeecs.v15.i3.pp1392-1400

Mohseni, O., Rashty, A. M. N., Seyfarth, A., Hosoda, K., & Sharbafi, M. A. (2022). Bioinspired legged robot design via blended physical and virtual impedance control. *Journal of Intelligent & Robotic Systems*, *105*(1), 1–15. doi:10.100710846-022-01631-2

Mooney, P., Corcoran, P., & Winstanley, A. C. (2010). *Preliminary results of a spatial analysis of Dublin city's bike rental scheme*. Academic Press.

Musisi-Nkambwe, M., Afshari, S., Barnaby, H., Kozicki, M., & Sanchez Esqueda, I. (2021). The Viability of Analog-based Accelerators for Neuromorphic Computing: A Survey. *Neuromorphic Computing and Engineering*, *1*(1), 012001. doi:10.1088/2634-4386/ac0242

Mustaqeem, M. Sajjad & Kwon S. (2020). Clustering-Based Speech Emotion Recognition by Incorporating Learned Features and Deep BiLSTM. In IEEE Access. (vol. 8. pp. 79861-79875). IEEE. doi:10.1109/ACCESS.2020.2990405

N. V. H. S., B. K. S, G. K. S, A. U., & J. B. (2023). Controlling Gate Valves with Wi-Fi: An Overview of Available Technologies and Applications. *2023 9th International Conference on Advanced Computing and Communication Systems (ICACCS)*, 1396-1400. doi: 10.1109/ICACCS57279.2023.10112698

Nachbar, F., Stolz, W., Merkle, T., Cognetta, A. B., Vogt, T., Landthalerv, M., Bilek, P., Braun-Falco, O., & Plewig, G. (1994). The abcd rule of dermatoscopy: High prospective value in the diagnosis of doubtful melanocytic skin lesions. *Journal of the American Academy of Dermatology*, *30*(4), 551–559. doi:10.1016/S0190-9622(94)70061-3 PMID:8157780

Nadizar, G., Medvet, E., Nichele, S., & Pontes-Filho, S. (2022). *Collective control of modular soft robots via embodied Spiking Neural Cellular Automata*. arXiv preprint arXiv:2204.02099.

Nagarajan, N., Kumar, A., Dhanraj, J., & Kumar, T. (2022). Delay Flip Flop based Phase Frequency Detector for Power Efficient Phase Locked Loop Architecture. *International Conference on Electronics and Renewable Systems*. IEEE.

Nagarajan, P., Ashokkumar, N., Arockia Dhanraj, J., Kumar T. & Sundari, M. (2022). Delay Flip Flop based Phase Frequency Detector for Power Efficient Phase Locked Loop Architecture. *2022 International Conference on Electronics and Renewable Systems (ICEARS)*, (pp. 410-414). IEEE. doi:. doi:10.1109/ICEARS53579.2022.9752249

Nagarajan, P., Ashok Kumar, N., & Venkat Ramana, P. (2020). Design of implicit pulsed-dual edge triggering flip flop for low power and high speed clocking systems. *International Journal of Wavelets, Multresolution, and Information Processing*, *18*(01), 1941009. doi:10.1142/S0219691319410091

Naghibijouybari, H., Neupane, A., Qian, Z., & Abu-Ghazaleh, N. B. (2018). Rendered Insecure: GPU Side Channel Attacks are Practical. *Proceedings of the 2018 ACM SIGSAC Conference on Computer and Communications Security*. ACM. 10.1145/3243734.3243831

Natarajan, V., Ashokkumar, N., Pandian, N., & Savithri, V.G. (2018). Low Power Design Methodology. *Very-Large-Scale Integration*. IntechOpen.

Naveenkumar, R., Sivamangai, N. M., Napolean, A., & Janani, V. (2021). A Survey on Recent Detection Methods of the Hardware Trojans. *2021 3rd International Conference on Signal Processing and Communication (ICPSC),* (pp. 139-143). IEEE. 10.1109/ICSPC51351.2021.9451682

Naveenkumar, R., Sivamangai, N. M., Napolean, A., Puviarasu, A., & Saranya, G. (2022). Preventive Measure of SAT Attack by Integrating Anti-SAT on Locked Circuit for Improving Hardware Security. *2022 7th International Conference on Communication and Electronics Systems (ICCES),* Coimbatore, India. 10.1109/ICCES54183.2022.9835923

Naveenkumar, R., & Sivamangai, N. M. (2022). Hardware Obfuscation for IP Protection of DSP Applications. *Journal of Electronic Testing, 38*(1), 9–20. doi:10.100710836-022-05984-2

Naveenkumar, R., Sivamangai, N. M., Napolean, A., & Priya, S. S. (2022). Design and Evaluation of XOR Arbiter Physical Unclonable Function and its Implementation on FPGA in Hardware Security Applications. *Journal of Electronic Testing, 38*(6), 653–666. doi:10.100710836-022-06034-7

Naveenkumar, R., Sivamangai, N. M., Napolean, A., Priya, S. S. S., & Ashika, S. V. (2023). Design of INV/BUFF Logic Locking For Enhancing the Hardware Security. *Journal of Electronic Testing.* doi:10.100710836-023-06061-y

Naveenkumar, R., Sivamangai, N. M., Napolean, A., & Sridevi Sathayapriya, S. (2023). Review on Hardware Trojan Detection Techniques. *National Academy Science Letters.* doi:10.100740009-023-01247-6

Neuromorphic Computing Market. (2020). *Industry analysis, size, share, growth, trends, and forecast, 2020-2028.* Sheer Analytics and Insights, Report Id: TECIT 127. https://www.sheeranalyticsandinsights.com/market-report-research/neuromorphic-computing-market-21

Nguyen, A., & Tran, A. (2021). *WaNet - Imperceptible Warping-based Backdoor Attack.* ArXiv, abs/2102.10369.

Nguyen, B. Y., & Nguyen, T. D. (2020). Ferroelectric transistors for neurmorphic computing. *Journal of Applied Physics, 128*(13).

Nguyen, D. A., Tran, X. T., Dang, K. N., & Iacopi, F. (2022). A low-power, high-accuracy with fully on-chip ternary weight hardware architecture for Deep Spiking Neural Networks. *Microprocessors and Microsystems, 90,* 104458. doi:10.1016/j.micpro.2022.104458

Niu, D., Li, D., Chen, J., Zhang, M., Lei, B., Jiang, W., Chen, J., & Liu, H. (2022). SMA-based soft actuators with electrically responsive and photoresponsive deformations applied in soft robots. *Sensors and Actuators. A, Physical, 341,* 113516. doi:10.1016/j.sna.2022.113516

Nivethika, S. (2018). Lycra fabric as an effective stretchable substrate for a compact highly efficient reversibly deformable broadband patch antenna. *Journal of Optoelectronics and Advanced Materials, 20*(11-12), 634–641.

Nivethika, S., Sreeja, B., Radha, M. (2020). Polymer resin coating over dielecric elastomer for effective stretchable RF devices. *Journal of Optoelectronics and Advanced Materials.*

Nivethika, S. D., Sreeja, B. S., Manikandan, E., Radha, S., & Senthilpandian, M. (2020). Dynamic frequency analysis of stress–strain-dependent reversibly deformable broadband RF antenna over unevenly made elastomeric substrate. *Pramana*, *94*(1), 122. doi:10.100712043-020-01992-z

Normark, D., Cochoy, F., Hagberg, J., & Ducourant, H. (2018). Mundane intermodality: A comparative analysis of bike-renting practices. *Mobilities*, *13*(6), 791–807. doi:10.1080/17450 101.2018.1504651

Obo, T., & Takizawa, K. (2022, July). Gesture Learning Based on A Topological Approach for Human-Robot Interaction. In *2022 International Joint Conference on Neural Networks (IJCNN)* (pp. 1-6). IEEE. 10.1109/IJCNN55064.2022.9892731

Pan, Y., Zheng, R. C., Zhang, J., & Yao, X. (2019). Predicting bike sharing demand using recurrent neural networks. *Procedia Computer Science*, *147*, 562–566. doi:10.1016/j.procs.2019.01.217

Pardo-Cabrera, J., Rivero-Ortega, J. D., Hurtado-López, J., & Ramírez-Moreno, D. F. (2022). Bio-inspired navigation and exploration system for a hexapod robotic platform. *Engineering Research Express*, *4*(2), 025019. doi:10.1088/2631-8695/ac6bde

Pathan, S., Prabhu, K. G., & Siddalingaswamy, P. (2018). Techniques and Algorithms for Computer Aided Diagnosis of Pigmented Skin Lesions—A Review. *Biomedical Signal Processing and Control*, *39*, 237–262. doi:10.1016/j.bspc.2017.07.010

Pedota M. & Piscitello L. (2021). A new perspective on technology-driven creativity enhancement in the Fourth Industrial Revolution. *Creativity and Innovation Management*. Wiley. doi:10.1111/caim.12468

Permitasari, R. I., & Sahara, R. (2018). Implementation of Web–Based Bike Renting Application "Bike–Sharing.". *International Journal Computer Science and Mobile Computing*, *7*(12), 6–13.

Pham, T.C., Doucet, A., Luong, C.M., Tran, C.T., Hoang, V.D. (2020). *Improving SkinDisease Classification Based on Customized Loss Function Combined With Balanced Mini-Batch Logic and Real-Time Image Augmentation*. IEEE. doi:10.1109/ACCESS.2020.3016653

Philbeck, T., & Davis, N. (2018). The Fourth Industrial Revolution. *Journal of International Affairs, 72* (1), 17–22.

Phung, V.H., & Rhee, E.J. (2019). A High-Accuracy Model Average Ensemble of Convolutional Neural Networks for Classification of Cloud Image Patches on Small Datasets. *Applied Sciences*. *9(21)*, [4500]. doi:10.3390/app9214500

Ponulak, F., & Kasinski, A. (2011). Introduction to spiking neural networks: Information processing, learning and applications. *Acta Neurobiologiae Experimentalis*, *71*(4), 409–433. PMID:22237491

Poon, C.-S., & Zhou, K. (2011). Neuromorphic Silicon Neurons and Large-Scale Neural Networks: Challenges and Opportunities. *Frontiers in Neuroscience*, *5*. doi:10.3389/fnins.2011.00108 PMID:21991244

Poria, S., Majumder, N., Mihalcea, R., & Hovy, E. (2019). Emotion recognition in conversation: Research challenges, datasets, and recent advances. *IEEE Access : Practical Innovations, Open Solutions*, 7, 100943–100953. doi:10.1109/ACCESS.2019.2929050

Prasad, M. M., & Kumar, T. V. (2012). Intelligent robot used in the field of practical application of artificial neural network & machine vision. *Int. J. Lean Thinking*, 3(2), 38–46.

Prezioso, M., Merrikh-Bayat, F., Hoskins, B. D., Adam, G. C., Likharev, K. K., & Strukov, D. B. (2015). Training and operation of an integrated neuromorphic network based on metal-oxide memristors. *Nature*, 521(7550), 61–64. doi:10.1038/nature14441

Prodromakis, T. (2007). A scalable high performance neural prosthesis with integrated addressable CMOS nanoscale synaptic transistors. *Nanotechnology*, 18(3).

Qiao, J., Meng, X., Li, W., & Wilamowski, B. (2020). A novel modular RBF neural network based on a brain-like partition method. *Neural Computing & Applications*, 32(3), 899–911. doi:10.100700521-018-3763-z

Qin, Z., Liu, Z., Zhu, P., & Xue, Y. (2020). A Gan-Based Image Synthesis Method for Skin Lesion Classification. *Computer Methods and Programs in Biomedicine*, 95, 105568. doi:10.1016/j.cmpb.2020.105568 PMID:32526536

Qiu, S., Liu, Y., Zhou, Y., Huang, J., & Nie, Y. (2016). Finger-vein recognition based on dual-sliding window localization and pseudo-elliptical transformer. *Expert Systems with Applications*, 64, 618–632. doi:10.1016/j.eswa.2016.08.031

Ramachandran, P., Zoph, B., & Le, Q. V. (2017). *Swish: A Self-Gated Activation Function*. Google Brain.

Ren, R., Su, J., Yang, B., Lau, R.Y.K., & Liu, Q. (2022) Novel Low-Power Construction of Chaotic S-Box in Multilayer Perceptron. *Entropy*. 24(11). doi:10.3390/e24111552

Research and Markets. (2022). The Worldwide Neuromorphic Computing Industry is Expected to Reach $225.5 Billion by 2027. *Globe News Wire*. https://www.globenewswire.com/en/news-release/2022/05/24/2449227/28124/en/The-Worldwide-Neuromorphic-Computing-Industry-is-Expected-to-Reach-225-5-Billion-by-2027.html

Riesenhuber, M., & Poggio, T. (1999). Hierarchical models of object recognition in cortex. *Nature Neuroscience*, 2(11), 1019–1025. doi:10.1038/14819 PMID:10526343

Robbins, H. & Monro, S. (1985). *A Stochastic Approximation Method*. Springer.

Robert, S. C., Jeff, F. M., Walter, R., Derek, S., & Richard, M. U. (2002). *Personal Virtual Assistant with Semantic Tagging*. Avaya Inc. https://patents.google.com/patent/US6466654B1/en?oq=US6466654B1

Rosselló, J. L., Canals, V., & Morro, A. (2010). Hardware implementation of stochastic-based neural networks. *Proc. Int. Joint Conf. Neural Netw. (IJCNN)*, (pp. 1–4). Springer.

Roy, M. (2016). Dermatofibroma: Atypical Presentations. *Indian Journal of Dermatology.* PMID:26955137

Rueckauer, B., Bybee, C., Goettsche, R., Singh, Y., Mishra, J., & Wild, A. (2022). NxTF: An API and compiler for deep spiking neural networks on Intel Loihi. *ACM Journal on Emerging Technologies in Computing Systems, 18*(3), 1–22. doi:10.1145/3501770

S, G., T, D., & Haldorai, A. (2022). A Supervised Machine Learning Model for Tool Condition Monitoring in Smart Manufacturing. *Defence Science Journal, 72*(5), 712-720. doi:10.14429/dsj.72.17533

Safa, A., Ocket, I., Bourdoux, A., Sahli, H., Catthoor, F., & Gielen, G. (2022). *Learning to Detect People on the Fly: A Bio-inspired Event-based Visual System for Drones.* arXiv preprint arXiv:2202.08023.

Salem, A., Wen, R., Backes, M., Ma, S., & Zhang, Y. (2020). Dynamic Backdoor Attacks Against Machine Learning Models. *2022 IEEE 7th European Symposium on Security and Privacy (EuroS&P),* 703-718.

Saravanan, P., & Mehtre, B. M. (2019). A Novel Approach to Detect Hardware Malware Using Hamming Weight Model and One Class Support Vector Machine. In S. Rajaram, N. Balamurugan, D. Gracia Nirmala Rani, & V. Singh (Eds.), *VLSI Design and Test. VDAT 2018.* Communications in Computer and Information Science. [892], doi:10.1007/978-981-13-5950-7_14

Saravanan, P., Rani, S. S., Rekha, S. S., & Jatana, H. S. (2019). An Efficient ASIC Implementation of CLEFIA Encryption/Decryption Algorithm with Novel S-Box Architectures. *International Conference on Energy, Systems and Information Processing (ICESIP),* (pp. 1–6). IEEE. 10.1109/ICESIP46348.2019.8938329

Saw, A. K., Channagoudra, G., Hunagund, S., Hadimani, R. L., & Dayal, V. (2020). Study of transport, magnetic and magnetocaloric properties in Sr2+ substituted praseodymium manganite. *Materials Research Express, 7*(1), 016105. doi:10.1088/2053-1591/ab636d

Schmidhuber, J. (2015). Deep learning in neural networks: An overview. *Neural Networks, 61,* 85–117. doi:10.1016/j.neunet.2014.09.003 PMID:25462637

Schmitt, M., Fabien, R., & Björn, S. (2016). At the Border of Acoustics and Linguistics. *Bag-of-Audio-Words for the Recognition of Emotions in Speech, 495-499,* 495–499. doi:10.21437/Interspeech.2016-1124

Schuller, I. (2019). *Neuromorphic Computing: From Materials to Systems Architecture Report of a Roundtable Conference.* US DoE ┃ Office of Science

Sepp, H., & Jürgen, S. (1997). Long Short-Term Memory. *Neural Computation, 9*(8), 1735–1780. doi:10.1162/neco.1997.9.8.1735 PMID:9377276

Shanthi Rekha, S. & Saravanan, P. (2019). Low-Cost AES-128 Implementation for Edge Devices in IoT Applications. *Journal of Circuits, Systems and Computers, 28*(4). doi:10.1142/S0218126619500622

Shariffuddin, S., Sivamangai, N. M., Napolean, A., Naveenkumar, R., Kamalnath, S., & Saranya, G. (2022). Review on Arbiter Physical Unclonable Function and its Implementation in FPGA for IoT Security Applications. *2022 6th International Conference on Devices, Circuits and Systems (ICDCS),* (pp. 369-374). IEEE.

Shen, S., Xu, M., Zhang, F., Shao, P., Liu, H., Xu, L. (2021). Low-Cost and HighPerformance Data Augmentation for Deep-Learning-Based Skin Lesion Classification. doi:10.34133/2022/9765307

Shen, G., Liu, Y., Tao, G., An, S., Xu, Q., Cheng, S., Ma, S., & Zhang, X. (2021). Backdoor Scanning for Deep Neural Networks through K-Arm Optimization. *International Conference on Machine Learning.* IEEE.

Sheu, B. J., & Choi, J. (1995). *Neural Information Processing and VLSI.* Kluwer Academic Publishers. doi:10.1007/978-1-4615-2247-8

Shi, L. (2015). Development of a neuromorphic computing system. *2015 IEEE International Electron Devices Meeting (IEDM).* IEEE. 10.1109/IEDM.2015.7409624

Silvestrini, S., & Lavagna, M. (2022). Deep Learning and Artificial Neural Networks for Spacecraft Dynamics, Navigation and Control. *Drones, 6*(10), 270. doi:10.3390/drones6100270

Song, J. M., Kim, W., & Park, K. R. (2019). Finger-vein recognition based on deep DenseNet using composite image. *IEEE Access : Practical Innovations, Open Solutions, 7,* 66845–66863. doi:10.1109/ACCESS.2019.2918503

Soyer, H. P. (2004). Three-point checklist of dermoscopy. Dermatology, 208(1), 27-31. doi:10.1159/000075042

Srinivasan, D., & Gopalakrishnan, M. (2019). Breast Cancer Detection Using Adaptable Textile Antenna Design. *Journal of Medical Systems, 43*(6), 177. doi:10.100710916-019-1314-5 PMID:31073787

ST Microelectronics (2016). *28nm FD-SOI Technology Catalog.* ST Microelectronics.

ST Microelectronics (2017). *Efficiency At All Levels.* ST Microelectronics.

Stagsted, R. K., Vitale, A., Renner, A., Larsen, L. B., Christensen, A. L., & Sandamirskaya, Y. (2020, October). Event-based PID controller fully realized in neuromorphic hardware: a one DoF study. In *2020 IEEE/RSJ International Conference on Intelligent Robots and Systems (IROS)* (pp. 10939-10944). IEEE. 10.1109/IROS45743.2020.9340861

Stančić, A., Vyroubal, V., & Slijepčević, V. (2022). Classification Efficiency of Pre-Trained Deep CNN Models on Camera Trap Images. *Journal of Imaging, 8*(2), 20. doi:10.3390/jimaging8020020 PMID:35200723

Stasenko, S., & Kazantsev, V. (2023). Astrocytes Enhance Image Representation Encoded in Spiking Neural Network. In *International Conference on Neuroinformatics* (pp. 200-206). Springer. 10.1007/978-3-031-19032-2_20

Strickholm, A. (1981). Ionic permeability of K, Na, and Cl in potassium-depolarized nerve. Dependency on pH, cooperative effects, and action of tetrodotoxin. *Biophysical Journal*, *35*(3), 677–697. doi:10.1016/S0006-3495(81)84820-5 PMID:7272457

Strohmer, B., Manoonpong, P., & Larsen, L. B. (2020). Flexible spiking cpgs for online manipulation during hexapod walking. *Frontiers in Neurorobotics*, *14*, 41. doi:10.3389/fnbot.2020.00041 PMID:32676022

Strukov, D. B., Snider, G. S., Stewart, D. R., & Williams, R. S. (2008). The missing memristor found. *Nature*, *453*(7191), 80–83. doi:10.1038/nature06932 PMID:18451858

Subramaniyam, D., & Jayabalan, R. (2017). FPGA implementation of variable bit rate OFDM transceiver system for wireless applications. *2017 International Conference on Innovations in Electrical, Electronics, Instrumentation and Media Technology (ICEEIMT)*. IEEE. 10.1109/ICIEEIMT.2017.8116863

Subramaniyam, D., & Sagayam, M. (2019). An Improved Area Efficient 16-QAM Transceiver Design using Vedic Multiplier for Wireless Applications. *International Journal of Recent Technology and Engineering.*, *8*(3), 4419–4425. doi:10.35940/ijrte.C5535.098319

Sun, B., Li, W., Wang, Z., Zhu, Y., He, Q., Guan, X., Dai, G., Yuan, D., Li, A., Cui, W., & Fan, D. (2022). Recent Progress in Modeling and Control of Bio-Inspired Fish Robots. *Journal of Marine Science and Engineering*, *10*(6), 773. doi:10.3390/jmse10060773

Sun, J., Han, J., Wang, Y., & Liu, P. (2021). Memristor-Based Neural Network Circuit of Emotion Congruent Memory With Mental Fatigue and Emotion Inhibition. *IEEE Transactions on Biomedical Circuits and Systems*, *15*(3), 606–616. doi:10.1109/TBCAS.2021.3090786 PMID:34156947

Syril Keena, T. (n.d.). Cutaneous squamous cell carcinoma. *Journal of The American Academy of Dermatology, 78*(2), 237-432.

Tang, G. (2022). *Biologically Inspired Spiking Neural Networks for Energy-Efficient Robot Learning and Control* [Doctoral dissertation, School of Graduate Studies Rutgers, The State University of New Jersey]. ProQuest Dissertations Publishing. (15295701)

Tang, G., Kumar, N., & Michmizos, K. P. (2020, October). Reinforcement co-learning of deep and spiking neural networks for energy-efficient mapless navigation with neuromorphic hardware. In *2020 IEEE/RSJ International Conference on Intelligent Robots and Systems (IROS)* (pp. 6090-6097). IEEE. 10.1109/IROS45743.2020.9340948

Tang, G., & Michmizos, K. P. (2018, July). Gridbot: An autonomous robot controlled by a spiking neural network mimicking the brain's navigational system. In *Proceedings of the International Conference on Neuromorphic Systems* (pp. 1-8). IEEE. 10.1145/3229884.3229888

Tang, G., Shah, A., & Michmizos, K. P. (2019, November). Spiking neural network on neuromorphic hardware for energy-efficient unidimensional slam. In *2019 IEEE/RSJ International Conference on Intelligent Robots and Systems (IROS)* (pp. 4176-4181). IEEE. 10.1109/IROS40897.2019.8967864

Teka, W., Marinov, T. M., & Santamaria, F. (2014). Neuronal spike timing adaptation described with a fractional leaky integrate-and-fire model. *PLoS Computational Biology, 10*(3), e1003526. doi:10.1371/journal.pcbi.1003526 PMID:24675903

Temam, O., Luo, Lao., Chen, Y. (2014). DaDianNao: A Machine-Learning Supercomputer. *Proceedings of the 47th Annual IEEE/ACM International Symposium on Microarchitecture (MICRO-47).* (pp. 609–622). IEEE.

Thirumal, R., Rahul, B. R., Rahulpriyesh, B., Konguvel, E., & Sumathi, G. (2022). EVMFFR: Electronic Voting Machine with Fingerprint and Facial Recognition. *Proc. of 2022 IEEE Second International Conference on Next Generation Intelligent Systems (ICNGIS – 2022),* 1–6. 10.1109/ICNGIS54955.2022.10079752

Thoa Pham Thi, T., Timoney, J., Ravichandran, S., Mooney, P., & Winstanley, A. (2017). *Bike Renting Data Analysis: The Case of Dublin City.* arXiv e-prints, arXiv-1704.

Tran, B., Li, J., & Madry, A. (2018). Spectral Signatures in Backdoor Attacks. *Neural Information Processing Systems.*

Tsai, T. H., Ho, Y. C., & Sheu, M. H. (2019), Implementation of FPGA-based Accelerator for Deep Neural Networks. *International Symposium on Design and Diagnostics of Electronic Circuits & Systems (DDECS).* IEEE. 10.1109/DDECS.2019.8724665

Tsaniyah, D., Aspitriani, A., & Fatmawati, F. (2013). Prevalensi dan Gambaran Histopatologi Nevus Pigmentosus di Bagian Patologi Anatomi Rumah Sakit Dr. Mohammad Hoesin Palembang Periode 1 Januari 2009-31 Desember 2013. *Majalah Kedokteran Sriwijaya, 47*(2).

UK Gov Department for Business. (2019). *Regulation for the Fourth Industrial Revolution.* UK.gov. https://www.gov.uk/government/publications/regulation-for-the-fourth-industrial-revolution/regulation-for-the-fourth-industrial-revolution

V, G., Chenguttuvan, E., & Subramaniyam, D. (2022). Design of Power and Area Efficient Carry Skip Adder and FIR filter Implementation. El-Cezeri Fen ve Mühendislik Dergisi. https://doi.org/ doi:10.31202/ecjse.1162711

V., S., V., J., Srinivasan, D., & M., P. (2023). *A Concept-based Ontology Mapping Method for Effective Retrieval of Bio-Medical Documents.* 2023 9th International Conference on Advanced Computing and Communication Systems (ICACCS), Coimbatore, India. 10.1109/ICACCS57279.2023.10113073

van Wezel, M. (2020). A robust modular spiking neural networks training methodology for time-series datasets: With a focus on gesture control. https://doi.org/ doi:10.31234/osf.io/x7v3q

Venkatesh, S., Sivapirakasam, S. P., Sakthivel, M., Ganeshkumar, S., Prabhu, M. M., & Naveenkumar, M. (2021). Experimental and numerical investigation in the series arrangement square cyclone separator. *Powder Technology, 383,* 93–103. doi:10.1016/j.powtec.2021.01.031

Vicol, A. D., Yin, B., & Bohté, S. M. (2022, July). Real-time classification of LIDAR data using discrete-time Recurrent Spiking Neural Networks. In *2022 International Joint Conference on Neural Networks (IJCNN)* (pp. 1-9). IEEE. 10.1109/IJCNN55064.2022.9892006

Vineeth Reddy, C., Lohitt Venkata Saai, N., Konguvel, E., Sumathi, G., & Sujatha, R. (2022). Emergency Alert System for Women Safety using Raspberry Pi. *Proc. of 2022 IEEE Second International Conference on Next Generation Intelligent Systems (ICNGIS – 2022),* 1–4. doi:10.1109/ICNGIS54955.2022.10079823

Volinski, A., Zaidel, Y., Shalumov, A., DeWolf, T., Supic, L., & Tsur, E. E. (2022). Data-driven artificial and spiking neural networks for inverse kinematics in neurorobotics. *Patterns, 3*(1), 100391. doi:10.1016/j.patter.2021.100391 PMID:35079712

Wan, Z., Lele, A. S., & Raychowdhury, A. (2022, January). Circuit and system technologies for energy-efficient edge robotics. In *2022 27th Asia and South Pacific Design Automation Conference (ASP-DAC)* (pp. 275-280). IEEE.

Wang, M., Zhang, Y., & Yu, J. (2022). An SNN-CPG Hybrid Locomotion Control for Biomimetic Robotic Fish. *Journal of Intelligent & Robotic Systems, 105*(2), 1–25. doi:10.100710846-022-01664-7

Wang, N., Shu, L., & Jiang, L. (2019). Threshold Switching Memristive Devices for Neuromorphic Computing. *Advanced Intelligent Systems, 1*(5).

Wang, Z. (2017). Memristors for energy-efficient, neuromorphic computing. *Nature Materials, 16*(9), 101–110. doi:10.1038/nmat4756 PMID:27669052

Wang, Z. (2019). Regression Model for Bike-Sharing Service by Using Machine Learning. *Asian Journal of Social Science Studies, 4*(4), 16. doi:10.20849/ajsss.v4i4.666

Wayne, C. (2016). *Feeling sad, angry? Your future car will know*. CNET.

Weber, M., Xu, X., Karlas, B., Zhang, C., & Li, B. (2020). *RAB: Provable Robustness Against Backdoor Attacks*. ArXiv, abs/2003.08904.

Wei, J., Zhang, Y., Zhou, Z., Li, Z., & Faruque, M. A. (2020). Leaky DNN: Stealing Deep-Learning Model Secret with GPU Context-Switching Side-Channel. *2020 50th Annual IEEE/IFIP International Conference on Dependable Systems and Networks (DSN),* (pp. 125-137). IEEE.

WHO. (n.d.). *Statistics on skin cancer*. WHO. http//www.who.int/uv/faq/skincancer/en/ /index1. html

William, G. (2019). Future versions of Apple's Siri may interpret your emotions. *Apple Insider.* https://appleinsider.com/articles/19/11/14/future-versions-of-apples-siri-may-read-interpret-your-facial-expressions.

Wua, C., Fressea, V., Suffranb, B., & Konika, H. (2021). Accelerating DNNs from local to virtualized FPGA in the Cloud: A survey of trends [102257]. *Journal of Systems Architecture, 119*, 119. doi:10.1016/j.sysarc.2021.102257

Xia, Q., (2019). Memristor-CMOS hybrid integrated circuits for reconfigurable logic. *Advanced Materials 31*(4).

Xiang, K., Peng, L., Yang, H., Li, M., Cao, Z., Jiang, S., & Qu, G. (2021). A Novel Weight Pruning Strategy for Light Weight Neural Networks With Application to the Diagnosis of Skin Disease. *Applied Soft Computing*, *111*, 107707. doi:10.1016/j.asoc.2021.107707

Xiang, Y., Chen, Z., Chen, Z., Fang, Z., Hao, H., Chen, J., Liu, Y., Wu, Z., Xuan, Q., & Yang, X. (2019). Open DNN Box by Power Side-Channel Attack. *IEEE Transactions on Circuits and Wystems. II, Express Briefs*, *67*(11), 2717–2721. doi:10.1109/TCSII.2020.2973007

Xiao, T., Bennett, C., Ben, F., Sapan, A., & Matthew, M. (2020). Analog architectures for neural network acceleration based on non-volatile memory. *Applied Physics Reviews*, *7*(3), 031301. doi:10.1063/1.5143815

Xie, K., Zhang, Z., Li, B., Kang, J., Niyato, D., Xie, S., & Wu, Y. (2022). Efficient federated learning with spike neural networks for traffic sign recognition. *IEEE Transactions on Vehicular Technology*, *71*(9), 9980–9992. doi:10.1109/TVT.2022.3178808

Xu, X., Ye, Z., Li, J., & Xu, M. (2018). Understanding the usage patterns of bicycle-sharing systems to predict users' demand: A case study in Wenzhou, China. *Computational Intelligence and Neuroscience*, *2018*, 2018. doi:10.1155/2018/9892134 PMID:30254667

Yamazaki, K., Vo-Ho, V. K., Bulsara, D., & Le, N. (2022). Spiking neural networks and their applications: A Review. *Brain Sciences*, *12*(7), 863. doi:10.3390/brainsci12070863 PMID:35884670

Yan, M., Gopireddy, B., Shull, T., & Torrellas, J. (2017). Secure hierarchy-aware cache replacement policy (SHARP): Defending against cache-based side channel attacks. *2017 ACM/IEEE 44th Annual International Symposium on Computer Architecture (ISCA)*, (pp. 347-360). IEEE.

Yang, J., & Li, X. (2010, August). Efficient finger vein localization and recognition. In *2010 20th International Conference on Pattern Recognition* (pp. 1148-1151). IEEE. 10.1109/ICPR.2010.287

Yang, J., Wang, R., Ren, Y., Mao, J., Wang, Z., Zhou, Y., & Han, S. (2020). Neuromorphic Engineering: Neuromorphic Engineering: From Biological to Spike-Based Hardware Nervous Systems (Adv. Mater. 52/2020). *Advanced Materials*, *32*(52), 2070392. Portico. https://doi.org/ doi:10.1002/adma.202070392

Yang, H., Xie, K., Ozbay, K., Ma, Y., & Wang, Z. (2018). Use of deep learning to predict daily usage of bike sharing systems. *Transportation Research Record: Journal of the Transportation Research Board*, *2672*(36), 92–102. doi:10.1177/0361198118801354

Yang, J. J., Strukov, D. B., & Stewart, D. R. (2013). Memristive devices for computing. *Nature Nanotechnology*, *8*(1), 13–24. doi:10.1038/nnano.2012.240 PMID:23269430

Yan, Z., Klochkov, Y., & Xi, L. (2022). Improving the Accuracy of a Robot by Using Neural Networks (Neural Compensators and Nonlinear Dynamics). *Robotics (Basel, Switzerland)*, *11*(4), 83. doi:10.3390/robotics11040083

Yoon, J. W., Pinelli, F., & Calabrese, F. (2012, July). Cityride: A predictive bike sharing journey advisor. In *2012 IEEE 13th International Conference on Mobile Data Management* (pp. 306-311). IEEE. 10.1109/MDM.2012.16

Yu, C. B., Qin, H. F., Cui, Y. Z., & Hu, X. Q. (2009). Finger-vein image recognition combining modified hausdorff distance with minutiae feature matching. *Interdisciplinary Sciences, Computational Life Sciences*, *1*(4), 280–289. doi:10.100712539-009-0046-5 PMID:20640806

Yunlong, Y., & Fuxian, L. (2019). Effective Neural Network Training with a New Weighting Mechanism-Based Optimition Algorithm. *IEEE Access: Practical Innovations, Open Solutions*.

Zahra, O., Tolu, S., Zhou, P., Duan, A., & Navarro-Alarcon, D. (2022). A Bio-Inspired Mechanism for Learning Robot Motion from Mirrored Human Demonstrations. *Frontiers in Neurorobotics*, *16*, 16. doi:10.3389/fnbot.2022.826410 PMID:35360830

Zelgen, M. A. (2022). *Amygdala Modeling with Context and Motivation Using Spiking Neural Networks for Robotics Applications*. Wright State University.

Zeng, X., Ouyang, W., & Wang, X. (2013). Multi-stage contextual deep learning for pedestrian detection. Proc. IEEE Int. Conf. Comput. Vis. (ICCV), (pp. 121–128). IEEE. 10.1109/ICCV.2013.22

Zhang, D., Zhang, T., Jia, S., Wang, Q., & Xu, B. (2022). *Recent Advances and New Frontiers in Spiking Neural Networks*. arXiv preprint arXiv:2204.07050.

Zhang, Z., & Kouzani, A.Z., (2021). Resource-constrained FPGA/DNN co-design. *Neural Comput & Applic, 33*. doi:10.1007/s00521-021-06113-4

Zhang, R., Li, J., Zheng, P., Lu, Y., Bao, J., & Sun, X. (2022). A fusion-based spiking neural network approach for predicting collaboration request in human-robot collaboration. *Robotics and Computer-integrated Manufacturing*, *78*, 102383. doi:10.1016/j.rcim.2022.102383

Zhang, S., Zhou, Z., Hao, H., & Zhou, J. (2018). Prediction model of demand for public bicycle rental based on land use. *Advances in Mechanical Engineering*, *10*(12). doi:10.1177/1687814018818977

Zhao, P., Chen, P., Das, P., Ramamurthy, K.N., & Lin, X. (2020). *Bridging Mode Connectivity in Loss Landscapes and Adversarial Robustness*. ArXiv, abs/2005.00060.

Zheng, S., Qian, L., Li, P., He, C., Qin, X., & Li, X. (2022). *An Introductory Review of Spiking Neural Network and Artificial Neural Network: From Biological Intelligence to Artificial Intelligence*. arXiv preprint arXiv:2204.07519.

Zhong, S., Zhang, Y., Zheng, H., Yu, F., & Zhao, R. (2022). *Spike-Based Spatiotemporal Processing Enabled by Oscillation Neuron for Energy-Efficient Artificial Sensory Systems*. Advanced Intelligent Systems. doi:10.1002/aisy.202200076

Zhong, X., & Pan, H. (2022). A spike neural network model for lateral suppression of spike-timing-dependent plasticity with adaptive threshold. *Applied Sciences (Basel, Switzerland)*, *12*(12), 5980. doi:10.3390/app12125980

Ziegler, M. (2020). Novel hardware and concepts for unconventional computing. *Scientific Reports*, *10*(1), 11843. doi:10.103841598-020-68834-1 PMID:32678249

About the Contributors

S. Dhanasekar received his Bachelor of Engineering degree in Electrical and Electronics Engineering from K.S.Rangasamy College of Technology, Erode, Tamilnadu, India in 2004 and received his M.S Degree in VLSI CAD from Manipal Centre for Information Sciences, MAHE, Manipal, Karnataka, India in 2006. He worked as R & D Engineer (VLSI and DSP Division) in Scientech Technologies Pvt. Ltd, Indore, Madhya Pradesh, India. He has completed his Ph.D. degree in Information and Communication Engineering from Anna University, Chennai, India in 2019. He is currently working as Associate Professor in Electronics and Communication Engineering, Sri Eshwar College of Engineering, Coimbatore, Tamilnadu. He has 14 years of Teaching Experience and 2 years of Industry Experience. He had published more 30 articles in the reputed SCI, Scopus and Web of Science Journals. He is reviewer of Scopus and Web of Science Journals. He is an active member in IEEE and various professional bodies. His teaching & research interests includes low power VLSI design, signal processing communication systems and Artificial Neural Networks.

K. Martin Sagayam received his PhD in Electronics and Communication Engineering (Signal image processing using machine learning algorithms) from Karunya University, Coimbatore, India. He received his both ME in Communication Systems and BE in Electronics and Communication Engineering from Anna University, Chennai. Currently, he is working as Assistant Professor in the Department of ECE, Karunya Institute Technology and Sciences, Coimbatore, India. He has authored/ co-authored more number of referred International Journals. He has also presented more number of papers in reputed international and national conferences. He has authored 2 edited book, 2 authored book, book series and more than 15 book chapters with reputed international publishers. He has three Indian patents and two Australian patents for his innovations and intellectual property right. He is an active IEEE member. His area of interest includes Communication systems, signal and image processing, machine learning and virtual reality.

Mayank Singh is currently working as a Professor and Head in Computer Science and Engineering Department at JSS Academy of Technical Education, Noida, UP, India. Prior, he worked as Professor and Associate Dean (Research) at KIET Group of Institutions, Ghaziabad, Sr. Scientist at Consilio Research Lab, Tallinn, Estonia from Sep 2019 to Aug 2021 and worked as Post-Doctoral Fellow, Department of Electrical, Electronic and Computer Engineering, at University of KwaZulu-Natal, Durban, South Africa from Sep 2017 to Aug 2019. He also worked as Professor & Head, Department of Computer Science and Engineering at Krishna Engineering College, Ghaziabad from January 2013 to September 2017. He has 18+ years of extensive experience in IT industry, Academics and Research in India and abroad. He completed his Ph.D. in Computer Science and Engineering from Uttarakhand Technical University in 2011. He obtained his M.E. (2007) in Software Engineering from Thapar University, Patiala and B.Tech. (2004) in Information Technology from Uttar Pradesh Technical University, Lucknow.

***

Sriharipriya Chandrasekaran has an expertise in 5G communication, as I have been a part of Indigenous 5G Testbed Project at IIT, Madras, while doing Post-doctoral fellowship. Chandrasekaran's PhD is in the area of wireless communication engineering relating to Cognitive Radio and have publications in SCI/ Thomson Reuters indexed journals and book series.

Shivakumar Hunagund is an experienced Semiconductor technology development engineer with Intel corporation, currently working on next gen product development in Microprocessor and Graphics with a focus on failure analysis. His 8 years in research and development work in Quantum computing, Materials/Nuclear Engineering, Photonics and Nanotechnology has taken him across the Europe and US.

Ashok Nagarajan received B.E drgree in Electronics AND CommunicationEngineering from Anna University, Chennai, in 2007, M.E.degree in Applied Electronics from, Anna University Trichy in 2010 and Ph.D.degree from Anna University, Chennai in 2017. Currently, he is working as an Associate Professor in the department of Electronics and Communication Engineering at Mohan Babu University(MBU) erstwhile of Sree Vidyanikethan Engineering College,Tirupati,AndraPradesh, India. His Research Interests include Network-On-Chip(NoC), System-on-Chip(SoC) Low- Power VLSI systems and Parellel processing and Computing.

Prabhakaran Paulraj holds PhD in Robitics and published 17 papers in the international journals. He is having 17 years of teaching experience. Dr PRAB-

HAKARAN PAULRAJ is currently the Professor and Head of the Department for Electrical, Electronics and Communication Engineering, St Joseph University in Tanzania, Dar es Salaam, Tanzania.

Deepa Nivethika S. is working as Assistant Professor in the School of Computer Science and Engineering, Vellore Institute of Technology, Chennai. She has more than 8 years of experience in teaching and research. Her area of research is Antenna Design and VLSI.

Ganeshkumar S. obtained PhD in Tool condition monitoring from Anna University, Chennai. He received a Master degree in Engineering Design and has 12 years of Experience in teaching and two years of Experience in Pressure vessel and heat exchanger design. Currently, he is working as an Assistant Professor at Sri Eshwar College of Engineering, Coimbatore, Tamil Nadu. His research interests include Artificial intelligence in Mechanical Engineering, Machine learning, Digital twin and intelligent manufacturing. He authored four books and more than 20 research journals in Machine tool monitoring.

Swapnadeep Sarkar - Contributing Author| **Ganeshkumar S.** is a graduate in Electronics and Communication Engineering and a keen learner with proven management and technical skills. S. is punctual, confident, enthusiastic, and always tries to put knowledge to the best use.

Sathish Kumar Selvaperumal received his B.Eng. Degree in Electronics and Communication Engineering in 2001, and M.Eng. Degree in Applied Electronics in 2005 from Arulmigu Meenakashi Amman College of Engineering, affiliated to University of Madras and Anna University respectively. He received his Ph.D in 2014 from Sri Chandrasekharendra Saraswathi Viswa Mahavidyalaya in Electronics & Communication Engineering and C.Eng in 2016 from U.K. Currently he is working as Associate Professor & serving as Academic Leader, in the School of Engineering, Asia Pacific University of Innovation and Technology, Kuala Lumpur, Malaysia. He has an experience of 20 years in teaching. His research and teaching interests includes Wireless Sensor Network (WSN), MANET, Cognitive Radio Networks, Image Processing (Segmentation, Compression, Image Fusion, and Image Restoration), Speech Processing, Artificial Intelligence, Biomedical applications, Antenna design, Wireless communication, and Wireless power transfer, Internet of Things, Robotics and Sustainability. He has published more than 50 articles in international journals and conferences.

Kavitha Thandapani received her Bachelor of Engineering degree in ECE from Madurai Kamaraj University, Madurai, Tamilnadu, India in 1999. She obtained her Master Degree in Applied Electronics from Anna University, Chennai, Tamilnadu, India in 2004 and completed, Ph.D in Information Technology from Anna University, Chennai in 2014. Currently She is working as Professor in Veltech Rangarajan Dr.Sagunthala R & D Institute of Science and Technology, Chennai, Tamilnadu, India. Her research interests are Modeling of Multigate MOSFETs, Optical Networking, Wireless communication, VLSI.

Index

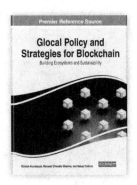

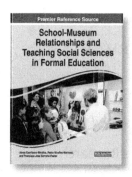
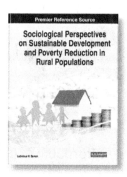